This book belongs

to Malcolm Baxter

PENGUIN BOOKS

THE PENGUIN BOOK OF CLASSICAL MYTHS

Dr Jenny March has taught at London, Reading and Southampton universities, was a British Academy Postdoctoral Research Fellow at University College London and is attached to Corpus Christi College, Oxford. Her several books include the acclaimed *Cassell Dictionary of Classical Mythology*, winner of the 1999 Runciman Award. She lives in Devon, on the edge of Dartmoor.

JENNY MARCH

The Penguin Book of Classical Myths

PENGUIN BOOKS

PENGUIN BOOKS

Published by the Penguin Group
Penguin Books Ltd, 80 Strand, London WC2R ORL, England
Penguin Group (USA) Inc., 375 Hudson Street, New York, New York 10014, USA
Penguin Group (Canada), 90 Eglinton Avenue East, Suite 700, Toronto, Ontario,
Canada M4P 2Y3 (a division of Pearson Penguin Canada Inc.)
Penguin Ireland, 25 St Stephen's Green, Dublin 2, Ireland (a division of Penguin Books Ltd)
Penguin Group (Australia), 250 Camberwell Road, Camberwell, Victoria 3124, Australia
(a division of Pearson Australia Group Pty Ltd)
Penguin Books India Pvt Ltd, 11 Community Centre, Panchsheel Park,
New Delhi – 110 017, India
Penguin Group (NZ), 67 Apollo Drive, Rosedale, North Shore 0632, New Zealand
(a division of Pearson New Zealand Ltd)
Penguin Books (South Africa) (Pty) Ltd, 24 Sturdee Avenue, Rosebank, Johannesburg 2196, South Africa

Penguin Books Ltd, Registered Offices: 80 Strand, London WC2R ORL, England

www.penguin.com

First published by Allen Lane 2008
This special edition for Sandpiper Books / Postscript published 2011

2

Copyright © Dr Jennifer March, 2008

Printed in Great Britain by Clays Ltd, St Ives plc
Typeset by TexTech International

A CIP catalogue record for this book is available from the British Library

ISBN: 978-0-241-95358-7

To Len
with love
for all the years

CONTENTS

LIST OF PLATES

LIST OF ILLUSTRATIONS

MAPS

THE GREEK WORLD

EDONIANS

R Strymon

MACEDONIA

Pella •

ADRIATIC
SEA

ILLYRIA

CHALKIDIKE

Phlegrai

PIERIA

Mt Olympos ▲

EPEIROS

Dodona •

THESSALY

Mt Ossa ▲

Kerkyra
(Corfu)

Trikka •

R Peneios

Ephyra •

R Acheron

R Enipeus

Pherai • Iolkos •

Mt Pelion ▲

THESPROTIA

R Acheloos

Phylake •   Pagasai •

PHTHIA
MALIS

AITOLIA

Argos •

Mt Oita • Trachis

C Kenaion

EUBOIA

Leukas

AKARNANIA

R Evenos

Mt Parnassos ▲

Orchomenos •

Chalkis •

DORIS • PHOKIS

Daulis •

Aulis •

Eretria •

Ithaca

Kalydon •

Delphi •

LOKRIS

Mt Helikon ▲

BOIOTIA

Mt Kithairon ▲

• Hyria

Kephallenia

Patrai •

Olenos •

ACHAIA

Sikyon •

Thebes •

Aphidnai ▲

Eleusis •

Marathon •

Mt Erymanthos ▲

Mt Kyllene ▲

Megara •

ATTICA

R Peneios

Psophis •

Nemea •

Corinth •

Athens •

ELIS

Stymphalos •

Mycenae • Salamis

Zakynthos

Mt Pholoe ▲

Mantineia •

Midea •

Epidauros •

Brauron •
Aigina

Olympia •

Pisa •

ARCADIA

Argos •

Tiryns •

C Sounion

Tegea •

Lerna • Nauplia •

Troizen •

IONIAN
SEA

Bassai •

PELOPONNESE

ARGOLID

Strophades °

Mt Ithome ▲

R Alpheios

Mt Taygetos ▲

C Maleia

Messene •

R Eurotas

• Sparta

MESSENIA

• Amyklai

Pylos •

Gerenia •

LAKONIA

Kythera

C Tainaron

250 km

150 miles

THRACE

R Hebros

Bosporos

Salmydessos

BEBRYKIANS

KIKONIANS

Abdera

Thasos

SEA OF
MARMARA

Samothrace

Kyzikos

Sestos

Perkote

Kolonai

Imbros

Elaios

Abydos

Troy DARDANIA

PHRYGIA

Hellespont

R Skamandros

Tenedos

Mt Ida

Lyrnessos

Lemnos

Pergamon

AEGEAN
SEA

R Kaikos

MYSIA

Lesbos

Skyros

R Hermos

LYDIA

R Paktolos

Mt Sipylos

Sardis

Chios

Smyrna

Mt Tmolos

Klaros

C Kaphareus

IKARIAN
SEA

R Maeander

Kolophon

IONIA

Andros

Ephesos

Kelainai

Tenos

Keos

Mt Latmos

R Marsyas

Ikaria

Miletos

Delos

CARIA

Seriphos CYCLADES

Halikarnassos

Paros

Naxos

Kos

LYCIA

Melos

Nisyros

Thera
(Santorini)

Rhodes

CRETAN
SEA

Karpathos

CRETE

Mt Ida   Knossos

Gortyn   Mt Dikte

Phaistos

THE MEDITERRANEAN WORLD

ATLANTIC
OCEAN

ALPS

ILLYRIA

R Rhine

R Rhone

R Eridanos (Po)

LIGURIA

ETRURIA

Adriatic Sea

R Tiber

*Tyrrhenian
Sea*

Tarquinii
Caere
Alba Longa
Rome
LATIUM
Argyripa

Cumae
Mt Vesuvius
Naples

CORSICA

C Palinurus

SARDINIA

*Str of
Messina*

Mt Etna

Eryx
SICILY
Syracuse

Tartessos

PILLARS OF
HERAKLES

Carthage

ATLAS MTS

L Tritonis

LIBYA

750km

450mls

SAUROMATIANS SCYTHIANS

TAURIANS

KOLCHIS

CAUCASIAN MTS

Aia

R Tanais

R Phasis

BLACK SEA

R Thermodon

Sinope

MARIANDYNI

R Danube (Istros)

HAIMOS MTS

RHODOPE MTS

BITHYNIA

Salmydessos

Sea of
Marmara

R Sangarios

Mt Dindymos

PAEONIA

THRACE

MACEDONIA

PHRYGIA

Troy

Mt Ida

CILICIA

SYRIA

Metapontium

Aegean
Sea

Mt Sipylos

LYDIA

R Maeander

EPEIROS

Sardis

Ephesos

Croton

Thebes

CARIA

LYCIA

Salamis

Athens

CYPRUS

Byblos

PHOENICIA

Sparta

Paphos

Sidon

Tyre

CRETE

Joppa

ARABIA

Kyrene

Cairo

Memphis

EGYPT

Chemmis

Thebes

ETHIOPIA

Milky Way

DELPHINUS

AQUILA

OPHIUCHUS

PEGASUS

CYGNUS

HERCULES
LYRA

SERPENS

ANDROMEDA

PISCES

CEPHEUS

LIBRA

CASSIOPEIA

CORONA
BOREALIS

DRACO

URSA MINOR

Arcturus

↑ Polaris
North Pole

ARIES

BOÖTES

URSA
MAJOR

PERSEUS

Capella

VIRGO

AURIGA

Pleiades
Hyades

CANCER

GEMINI

TAURUS

LEO

ORION

STAR CHART 1.
NORTHERN
HEMISPHERE

CANIS
MINOR

HYDRA

Milky Way

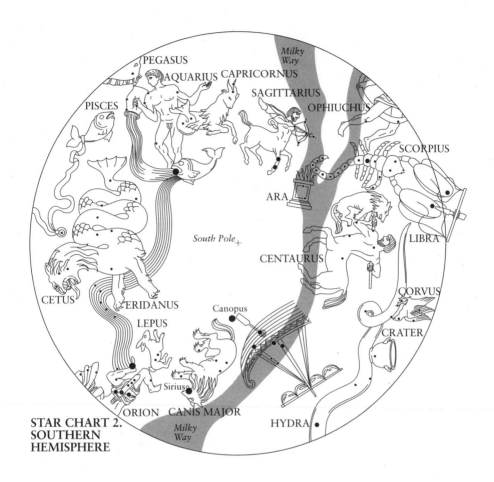

PEGASUS
AQUARIUS CAPRICORNUS
PISCES
SAGITTARIUS
OPHIUCHUS
SCORPIUS
Milky
Way
ARA
LIBRA
South Pole
CENTAURUS
CORVUS
CETUS
ERIDANUS
CRATER
LEPUS
Canopus
Sirius
ORION CANIS MAJOR
HYDRA
Milky
Way

**STAR CHART 2.
SOUTHERN
HEMISPHERE**

ACKNOWLEDGEMENTS

My warm thanks go to many people. To everyone at Penguin who saw this book through the press, and especially to my editor Georgina Laycock for her never-failing enthusiasm and support, and to Isabelle de Cat for her invaluable work on the illustrations. To Nigel Wilcockson, now at Random House, for originally commissioning the book. To Sue Willetts at the Joint Library of Hellenic and Roman Studies for her help with the constellation maps. To Patrick Hunt for permission to quote his poem 'Kithairon'.

Thanks also to all who have given permission to quote from copyrighted material, including the following:

To A. P. Watt Ltd, on behalf of Gráinne Yeats, for 'An Irish Airman Foresees His Death' and 'Leda and the Swan' by W. B. Yeats.

To Faber & Faber for 'Mythology', from *Private Property* by Andrew Motion.

To Gerald Duckworth and Co. Ltd for 'Children of Zeus', from *Legends and Pastorals* by Graham Hough.

For Edna St Vincent Millay's 'Sonnet 27', copyright 1931, 1958 by Edna St Vincent Millay and Norma Millay Ellis, reprinted by permission of Elizabeth Barnett, Literary Executor, the Millay Society.

While I have made every attempt to trace and acknowledge the copyright holders of all quoted material, any emendations will be gratefully received.

Finally, my thanks always to my dear family, just for being there: to my daughters, Alex, Robbie and Felicity, my grand-daughters, Jess, Rosanna, Jenny and Rachel, and my grandsons,

Tom, Joseph, Will, Sam and Harry. And of course to my husband Len, not only for his steadfast work on the index, but for being my mainstay from beginning to end, and down all the years – to him I dedicate this book.

INTRODUCTION

GREEK AND ROMAN MYTHS

The classical myths of our title are the myths of ancient Greece and Rome, though it will soon become clear to the reader that it is the Greek myths which hold the dominant place in this book. One reason for this is simply quantity: there are more Greek myths than Roman in existence, which is largely a result of their early prevalence and power.

The first recorded myths are found in the poems of Homer and Hesiod (eighth to the seventh century BC), and soon after this they appear widely in Greek art. It is clear from this point on that they were at the heart of ancient Greek life and culture. They held a central place at public and private gatherings. They were told and retold by the poets, and from the later sixth century BC onwards were the subjects of gripping dramas played out on the tragic stage. A major part of all education was the memorizing and reciting of epic poems on mythical subjects.

The myths were also depicted all around in the visual arts, again both publicly and privately, such as on temple sculptures, and on the pottery vessels of everyday domestic use which still exist in their thousands. Even the physical world – rivers, springs, woods, mountains, the very earth itself – was seen as alive with divine presences, many of them linked with particular mythological incidents.

Moreover these myths were more than mere stories. To the Greeks they were history, telling of real events in their heroic past. Certain of their details might be questioned. The historian Herodotus, for instance, writing in the later fifth century BC, may doubt some of the details of the myths about the great hero Herakles (p. 207), but he has no doubt at all that Herakles actually existed. And we have only to read Pausanias, who travelled widely through the Greek world in the second century AD and wrote *Description of Greece* in ten books, to realize that to him, and to the rest of the Greeks, our mythical characters were real people, living in real places, in the real past.

So the myths were central to Greek culture – which meant that they were known far and wide, since Greek culture itself was spread over a much more extensive area than the Greece we know today. During the Archaic (700–500 BC) and Classical (500–323 BC) periods, Greeks – that is, Greek-speaking peoples – occupied not only mainland Greece to the north through Macedonia, and to the east through Thrace to the Hellespont, but also the islands of the Aegean and the western coast of Asia Minor (present-day Turkey). Moreover many Greek colonies were founded in further-flung areas, both to the east, especially around the Black Sea, and to the west in southern Italy and Sicily, the colonies here being known by the Latin name Magna Graecia.

It was these latter settlements that were the most significant for the future of the classical world, since they would have a powerful influence on the developing city of Rome. The settlers of course brought their story-telling with them, and there is archaeological evidence in abundance, particularly from painted pottery, to show that the Greek myths were widely known in Italy, even as far north as Etruria, from the seventh century BC onwards.

Rome itself, expanding in power and prestige, came early on into contact with Greek culture, so that by the time the Romans won a final military victory over Greece in 146 BC, their own culture had for centuries been deeply permeated by Greek literature, Greek thought and Greek myths. 'Captured Greece took captive her crude conqueror', as Horace famously pronounced (*Epistles* 2.1.156). And just as the Romans took Greek literary and artistic works as models for their own, so they adopted the Greek gods, identifying them with their own native Italian divinities. They had certainly done so by the second century BC (and quite possibly much earlier), when the poet Quintus Ennius (239–169 BC) explicitly equated the twelve principal Roman gods with the twelve Greek Olympians.

And along with the Greek gods, the Romans adopted the Greek myths, endlessly reproducing them in their literature and art. Often they made their own eloquent literary adaptations of the Greek originals. Virgil's Dido (p. 485) comes at once to mind, or some of the moving metamorphoses in Ovid (Chapter 16). In art they gave their inheritance of Greek myths a particularly rich new life in the media of mosaic flooring, wall-painting, and relief sculptures on sarcophagi. But relatively speaking they added few new myths that were purely Roman.

So this is one reason for the preponderance of Greek myths in this book. A second reason is that, when it comes to a choice between versions of stories that were told and retold down the ages, it seems (to me at least) that the myths are often more powerful in their earlier incarnations – and for the most part this means Greek. This is not to deny the quality of the Roman versions, or the Romans' crucial role in transmitting the myths to the post-classical world by capturing the medieval imagination. The debt we owe to them, and especially to Ovid, who was the most widely read classical author in medieval times and the Renaissance, is immense. It is just that in Roman hands the myths become more literary, more sophisticated, more self-conscious – and somehow less immediate, less real. In the time of Homer, the gods still believably walk among men.

THE SCOPE OF THIS BOOK

A book such as this often begins by attempting to define just what a myth is, and by discussing the many and various theories about the origin and meaning of the myths. None of that is my concern here – nor even, I have to say, my interest. The word 'myth' comes from the Greek word *muthos*, which means 'word' or 'speech' or 'story', and I am content to accept the definition recently given (by Richard Buxton) that a myth is 'a socially powerful traditional story': a story, because it puts a set of events into a narrative sequence; traditional, because it is transmitted from generation to generation; and with social power, because myths explore the values of social groups and communities. Though I would add that another crucial charac- teristic of *classical* myths is their perennial power to inspire great art and great poetry, both in ancient times and down the ages, right up to the present day. More on this in a moment.

As for the various theories of myth, none is all-exclusive, since no single theory can cover all myths, be it aetiological, allegorical, ritualistic, structuralist, psychological, or whatever. All of these theories may shed light to a greater or lesser extent on, say, the origin of myths in general, but they are not in the least helpful for a book such as this, which sets out both to retell the whole corpus of classical myths from the creation of the universe onwards, and to give some idea of how these myths were treated in ancient literature.

For what has always fascinated me is the way that poets have presented the myths, retelling and reinterpreting them by adapting them for their own artistic purposes. (For this reason I called my first book on myths in ancient literature *The Creative Poet*.) They could do this because the myths were very diverse, there being no single canonical version of 'classical mythology' – though it was often the case that one particular ancient treatment might establish itself as more 'standard' than others, like Hesiod's account of the origin of the cosmos in his *Theogony* (p. 21), or the *Homeric Hymn to Demeter*'s story of Demeter's long search for her lost daughter Persephone (p. 62), or Sophocles' dramatic rendering of the myth of Oedipus in his *Oedipus the King* (p. 274).

So the poets were great innovators, and at best they would clothe their artistic vision in the kind of great poetry that grants immortality. Small wonder that ever since then the myths have stirred and shaped and enriched the western imagination, becoming inextricably woven into the fabric of our culture.

This book, then, is something of a celebration of myth in ancient literature, and wherever it seems appropriate I quote from the original texts to bring the narrative to life. (The translations are all my own.) Not only that, I bring in occasional pieces of post-classical poetry, to give some slight indication of the ongoing influence of the ancient myths. Obviously such a subject could fill many volumes just by itself, and there was no space here for any structured survey. So what we have is a purely personal selection of more modern poetry, inserted on a sporadic basis whenever a piece of verbal music became too much for me to resist.

The plan of the book is largely chronological. We begin in Chapter 1 with the creation of the universe and the birth of the gods, then Chapter 2 is devoted to the gods themselves: to the twelve great Olympians and a few of the minor gods who will play a part in the stories of mythology that follow.

In Chapter 3 we meet the first humans and look at the origins of one important Greek dynasty, the Deukalionids. Chapter 4 follows the fortunes of an early member of that family, Jason, whose quest for the Golden Fleece was one of the most famous expeditions in the ancient world.

Chapter 5 introduces a second great dynasty, stemming from

the river-god Inachos, one branch of which ruled for generations in Argos. One of the early Inachids was the great hero
Perseus, and his exploits are described in Chapter 6, together
with the heroic deeds of two other monster-slayers, Bellerophon and Meleagros. Then Chapter 7 deals with the deeds of
Herakles, the mightiest hero of them all, whose life was filled
with so many feats of courage that he was rewarded with
immortality at the end of it.

In Chapter 8 we turn to the myths of Athens and Crete, two
places linked by the great hero Theseus, Athens' most famous
king, and killer of the Cretan Minotaur. Chapter 9 tells the
story of another important city, Thebes, from its foundation
by the Inachid Kadmos to its destruction at the hands of the
Epigonoi.

Chapter 10 describes the Trojan War, the greatest war in
classical mythology and immortalized in the *Iliad* of Homer,
while Chapter 11 focuses on Homer's *Odyssey* and tells of the
return home at the end of the war of one of the Greek leaders,
Odysseus.

In Chapter 12 we look at the family of Agamemnon, the
main leader of the Greek expedition to Troy, and at the events
surrounding his murder when he returned home triumphant
once Troy was taken. The following chapter deals in greater
detail with his murder by his wife Klytaimnestra, and tells of
other 'dangerous women' who famously brought men to death.

In Chapter 14 we move to the myths of Rome, beginning
with the story of Aeneas, the legendary founder of the Roman
race, whose long journey from Troy to Italy and the bitter war
he and his followers fought on their arrival are described in
Virgil's *Aeneid*. Chapter 15 looks at the foundation of Rome
by Romulus and Remus and at the history of Rome's early
kings.

The last two chapters are collections of shorter myths, with

Chapter 16 containing twenty-four powerful stories of meta-morphosis, and Chapter 17 eight inspirational tales of love, and what so often goes with love, as in grand opera – death.

I should add a note on the spellings of ancient names, which is always a thorny problem. In this book the names of mytho-logical characters and places are usually given their Greek rather than their (perhaps more familiar) Latinized forms. Thus we find a *k* rather than a *c*, and *-os* at the end of a man's name rather than the Latinized *-us* (so Kronos not Cronus, Kadmos not Cadmus). The diphthongs *ai*, *oi*, *ei* and *ou* are not transliter-ated into the Latinized *ae*, *oe*, *i* and *u* (so we have Daidalos not Daedalus, Oinomaos not Oenamaus, Teiresias not Tiresias, Ouranos not Uranus).

There are exceptions to this policy. Sometimes a name is so well known in a non-Greek form that I keep the familiar usage, so we have Oedipus rather than Oidipous, Narcissus rather than Narkissos, Athens rather than Athenai, and Mycenae rather than Mukenai. And the names of ancient Greek authors retain their Latinized forms, since this is how they are referred to in non-academic literature, bookshops and library indexes (Homer not Homeros, Aeschylus not Aischylos).

As for the names of the gods, I use their Greek forms through-out for the sake of consistency, except in narratives that are purely Roman: in Chapters 14, 'Aeneas and the Destiny of Rome', and 15, 'The Foundation of Rome', and in the tale of Cupid and Psyche (p. 546).

THE ANCIENT SOURCES

Our two principal types of evidence for classical myths are first and foremost literary texts, which we possess in great abundance, and, secondly, visual images, of which by far the most plentiful and informative are the many thousands of Greek vase-paintings that survive. Let us first of all deal with the literary sources, though not with a full overview of all the ancient writers, but rather a summary of the main authors who will be mentioned in this book in connection with our myths.

Literary Sources

Our earliest literary sources for the myths are, as mentioned above, the epic poetry of Homer and Hesiod. Their works date from around 700 BC, give or take a few decades, though it is clear from their use of repeated 'formulaic' phrases (such as 'great Hektor of the shining helmet', or 'Zeus who thunders on high') that a long tradition of orally composed verse lies behind their poetry, possibly stretching back many centuries.

The two monumental epics ascribed to **Homer** are the *Iliad*, telling of the wrath of Achilles during the tenth year of the Trojan War (p. 325), and the *Odyssey*, describing the return home to Ithaca of Odysseus at the end of the war and his despatch of the suitors who were harassing his wife Penelope (p. 390). Both epics give a much broader view of early mythology than these brief summaries might suggest, since both incorporate many other myths about the gods and heroes. The identity of 'Homer' is controversial, there being disagreement as to whether the two epics were composed by one and the same poet or by two (or even by many). But to the Greeks there was only one Homer, and so supreme was he that they often called him simply 'the Poet', much as we refer to Shakespeare as 'the Bard'.

The two principal works of **Hesiod** are the *Theogony*, telling of the creation of the universe and the battles of the gods for supremacy (p. 21), and the *Works and Days*, a didactic poem giving instruction to the peasant farmer, but interwoven with tales from mythology. A number of other works were ascribed to Hesiod in antiquity, probably wrongly, of which two are the most relevant here: the *Shield of Herakles*, relating Herakles' fight with the brigand Kyknos, and the *Catalogue of Women*, a long epic detailing the unions of the gods with mortal women and the births of the heroes.

The **Epic Cycle** was a collection of epic poems, written by poets other than Homer and Hesiod in the seventh and sixth centuries BC and now lost but for meagre fragments, though in some cases there survive summaries by **Proclus** (perhaps a grammarian of the second century AD). They included a Trojan Cycle (*Kypria*, *Aithiopis*, *Little Iliad*, *Sack of Troy*, *Returns* and *Telegony*: see p. 294), a Theban Cycle (*Oidipodeia*, *Thebais* and *Epigonoi*), and a *Titanomachy*. Of a similar age are the thirty-three **Homeric Hymns** in honour of various gods, composed in epic metre (though not by Homer, despite their title). Four in particular are a valuable source of early myth, being several hundred lines long (those to Demeter, Apollo, Hermes and Aphrodite).

Another group of Greek poets, important between the seventh and fifth centuries BC, were the lyric poets: **Sappho** and **Alcaeus** from the island of Lesbos, born in the second half of the seventh century; **Stesichorus**, **Anacreon** and **Ibycus**, all active in the sixth century; **Simonides** from the island of Keos, perhaps 566 to 466; **Bacchylides**, also from Keos and nephew of Simonides, perhaps 520 to 450; and the Theban poet **Pindar**, of about 518 to 438. Huge amounts of their work have been lost. We possess only two complete, or nearly complete, poems of Sappho, for instance, the rest being either fragmentary or lost, and all the more to be mourned since she was hailed in antiquity as the Tenth Muse. Stesichorus's long lyric poems were collected into twenty-six books, but only a few fragments remain. Of all these poets, fate has dealt most kindly with Pindar, whose praise-poetry in honour of victors at the four great Games – at Olympia, Delphi, Nemea and Isthmia – has fortunately survived intact.

A new poetic art form came into existence in Athens towards the end of the sixth century BC: tragic drama (comedy came some time later). The traditional date of its origin is 530 BC, and it was supposedly invented by the otherwise unknown Thespis (though he has given us our word 'thespian'). During the fifth century, many hundreds of tragedies were staged at the Athenian Theatre of Dionysos, on the southern slope of the Acropolis, though almost all have been lost. But thirty-three still survive intact, or as close to intact as makes little difference. In performance, a few (as a rule, three) male masked actors took the individual roles, with each actor usually playing more than one part. A chorus, also all men, also masked, sang and danced a commentary on the action.

The three great tragedians whose plays survive were **Aeschylus** (who died in 456), **Sophocles** and **Euripides** (both of whom died in 406). We have seven extant plays of Aeschylus: *Persians*, *Suppliant Women*, *Seven Against Thebes*, the *Oresteia* trilogy, made up of *Agamemnon*, *Libation Bearers* and *Eumenides*, and (of disputed authorship) *Prometheus Bound*. We also have seven plays extant from Sophocles: *Women of Trachis*, *Ajax*, *Antigone*, *Oedipus the King*, *Elektra*, *Philoktetes* and *Oedipus at Kolonos*. We are luckier in the case of Euripides, with eighteen plays surviving: *Alkestis*, *Medea*, *Hippolytos*, *Children of Herakles*, *Hecuba*, *Elektra*, *Andromache*, *Suppliant Women*, *Trojan Women*, *Helen*, *Ion*, *Phoenician Women*, *Orestes*, *Madness of Herakles*, *Iphigeneia among the Taurians*, *Iphigeneia at Aulis*, *Bakchai*, and *Cyclops* (a satyr play, which was a mythological farce). The *Rhesos* was traditionally said to be by Euripides, although the attribution is doubtful.

The tragedies of these great playwrights dramatized events from the mythical past, exploring in great poetry the basic and timeless questions of the human condition: how human life is, how death is, the way in which mortals relate to other mortals and to the everlasting gods. These plays remain relevant today, and still they induce in their audiences the 'pity and fear' spoken of by the philosopher Aristotle, when discussing Tragedy in his *Poetics*, and still they bring about the kind of emotional release that he called 'catharsis'.

These tragedies are a vital source for many of the myths in this book. Comedy should be mentioned too. We have eleven plays extant from the comic playwright **Aristophanes** (born *c.*460–450 BC, died *c.*386), all of them imaginative fantasies based on contemporary Athenian life, but in which he was always happy to exploit the myths to comic effect and to poke fun at mythological characters. Also to be mentioned are the fifth-century historians, **Herodotus** and **Thucydides**, both of them writing prose and on a comprehensive scale never attempted before, Herodotus about the Greco-Persian Wars of the early fifth century, Thucydides about the protracted and bitter Peloponnesian War (431–404 BC) between Athens and Sparta. They both refer to the myths (that is, 'ancient history') as the background to their more contemporary inquiries, and both examine mythical events as to their plausibility. (And we note that the careful Thucydides accepts without question the historicity of the Trojan War.)

Next we move to the Hellenistic period (323–31 BC). In the wake of the wide conquests of Alexander the Great (356–323 BC), many new cities were founded on the Greek model, and new centres of culture arose. The most famous of these was the Egyptian city of Alexandria, where the Museum and Library, founded about 280 BC, became a centre of literary criticism and production, and scholars preserved the legacy of the past by collecting, copying and annotating older works of Greek literature. Two noteworthy poets of this era were the pastoral poet **Theocritus** and the scholar-poet **Callimachus**, but most relevant to our myths is **Apollonius of Rhodes**, head librarian at Alexandria at around 260 BC, who with his epic poem *Argonautica* ('Expedition of the Argonauts') is our main source for the story of Jason's quest for the Golden Fleece (p. 136).

From the first century BC onwards, there exist several long Greek treatises providing us with mythological information in prose. By far the most valuable in this respect is the *Library* of **Apollodorus**, once attributed to the Athenian scholar Apollodorus of the second century BC, though more probably written in the first or second centuries AD. The *Library* is a complete mythological history of Greece with no pretension to literary style, but it is the best surviving account of many stories, and since it is largely based on early sources such as the Hesiodic *Catalogue of Women*, it is an extremely useful guide to the early mythical tradition.

The *Description of Greece* by the traveller **Pausanias**, mentioned above, and written in the second century AD, is also very valuable for its rich repository of local myths. Occasionally useful too are **Diodorus Siculus**, a Sicilian Greek historian, who in the first century BC compiled a world history in forty books (not all surviving), centred on Rome; the geographer **Strabo** (*c.*64 BC to AD 20), who wrote a *Geography* in seventeen books of the chief countries in the Roman world; and **Plutarch** (*c.*AD 46 to 120), who is especially helpful for his life of the Athenian hero and king, Theseus (p. 229), in his collection of *Parallel Lives*. Probably of a similar period is **Antoninus Liberalis**, a mythographer and author of *Metamorphoses*, an anthology of forty-nine stories of transformation, written in prose (unlike the far more famous *Metamorphoses* of Ovid), and mostly based on Hellenistic sources.

Before we leave the Greek authors, there is one later Greek epic poet to note: **Quintus of Smyrna**, who probably lived in the fourth century AD and wrote the *Posthomerica* in fourteen books, which filled the gap in events between Homer's *Iliad* and *Odyssey*.

To turn now to the Roman poets, **Catullus** (*c*.84 to 54 BC), **Horace** (65–8 BC) and **Propertius** (born *c*.50 BC, died before 2 BC) should be mentioned. All of them, writing under the influence of earlier Greek poetry, used myths as a way of exploring their own ideas and feelings. But the two towering Roman poets to whom we owe most are Virgil and Ovid.

First of all, **Virgil** (70–19 BC), the poet who understood that *sunt lacrimae rerum*, 'there are tears at the heart of things' (*Aeneid* 1.462). He wrote the *Eclogues*, a book of pastoral poems, the *Georgics*, a didactic poem on agriculture, and the *Aeneid*, an epic poem in twelve books, describing how the Trojan prince Aeneas journeyed to Italy after the fall of Troy and established himself in Latium (p. 478). Virgil had not finished work on the *Aeneid* at the time of his death, and it was said that he had extracted a promise to have it burnt. Luckily his wishes were disregarded.

Ovid (43 BC to AD 17) – witty, sophisticated, playful – incorporated myths into every aspect of his many works. These include the *Heroides* ('Heroines'), letters from famous women of mythology to their lovers or husbands, though sometimes Ovid gives a pair of letters, one from each partner. But without doubt his crowning achievement was his epic poem the *Metamorphoses*, a collection of some 250 stories of transformations in fifteen books (p. 507). Completed about AD 8, it is probably the single most influential source of inspiration for the reworking of classical myths in later literature and art.

Soon after this, the politician, philosopher and writer **Seneca** (*c*.4 BC to AD 65) produced nine melodramatic – and often very gory – tragedies adapted from Greek originals of the fifth century BC: *Madness of Hercules, Hercules on Oeta, Trojan Women, Phoenician Women, Medea, Phaedra, Oedipus,*

Agamemnon, and *Thyestes* – this last (a particularly gruesome play) having no extant source.

Finally, three Roman prose-writers should be briefly mentioned: **Livy** (59 BC to AD 17), the author of a history of Rome (*Ab urbe condita libri*) from its foundation to his own times in 142 books, of which thirty-five survive; '**Hyginus**', the name given to an otherwise unknown author of the *Fabulae* ('Stories'), a handbook of mythology, and a *Poetic Astronomy*, both compiled from Greek sources, probably in the second century AD; and **Apuleius** (also second century AD), whose works include the *Metamorphoses*, more commonly known as *The Golden Ass*, the only Latin novel to survive complete, which gives us the story of Cupid and Psyche (p. 546).

Visual sources

Classical myths have been richly illustrated in many different ancient media, our first certain depictions occurring at around 700 BC. We find myths on sculptures, both free-standing and relief; on wall-paintings, with most of our extant examples being Roman; on mosaics, again mostly Roman; on coins, seals and gemstones; and on decorated bronze mirrors, many fine examples of which were made by the Etruscans. But of all our visual sources, the richest and most informative by far are the tens of thousands of surviving Greek vase-paintings (the term 'vase' denoting a wide range of pottery vessels, from wine cups to mixing bowls, from oil flasks to water jars).

There is no space here to do more than touch on the various ways in which we can learn more about the myths from ancient art – always remembering, when making any generalization, that we possess only a tiny fraction of the works that were actually created.

First, and most obviously, artistic images show how the ancients visualized the characters of myth, and also how their con-

ceptions could change over time. One example of this is the god
Dionysos, who begins as a bearded, ivy-wreathed, mature man,
wearing long robes and often a deerskin or a panther-skin, and
who by the end of the fifth century BC has become more usually
youthful, beardless, and naked or half naked. Another example
is the Gorgon Medusa, who is beheaded by Perseus (p. 172).
Gorgons in early art are extremely ugly, with snaky hair, staring
eyes, frightful grins, lolling tongues and fearsome tusks, but
again by the later fifth century they have become humanized,
and Medusa's face is that of a beautiful woman.

Second, these works of ancient art can show us, broadly
speaking, which myths were popular, and also (since they can
be dated by stylistic means) when, and (so long as we have an
artifact's provenance) where. Easily the most popular hero, for
instance, is Herakles, recognizable by his lion-skin, club and
bow, and usually bearded, though towards the end of the fifth
century BC and into the fourth he too is often beardless. His
fight with the Nemean Lion is by far the favourite of his exploits,
followed by the battle with the Amazons, while depictions of
the Stymphalian Birds are infrequent, and of the Augeian
Stables and the mares of Diomedes very rare. Of the divinities,
Dionysos is depicted most frequently of the gods, and Athene
of the goddesses, usually in her role as patron of heroes.

Third, these visual images can fill out the details of our literary
sources in several ways. Sometimes we have little or no explicit
description of an event in our texts, and we can piece together
the details from art. A good example here is the death of the
young Trojan Troilos at the hands of the mighty Achilles. References to his murder in extant literature are few, but on vase-
paintings we see all its stages, from Achilles lying in wait to
ambush the boy, to his death, and sometimes even decapitation,
and the battle over his mutilated body (p. 322).

Another way that art enhances literature is by filling out a literary characterization, such as that of Peleus, the father of Achilles. We know that he must have been a great hero, since he was chosen by the gods as a suitable husband for the sea-goddess Thetis (p. 307). Yet the general picture that we get of him from extant literature, from Homer and from Euripides' tragedy *Andromache*, is of an old and sorrowful man who shows little trace of his earlier heroic stature. But on the vase-paintings we meet the younger Peleus in action. We see him while out hunting, crouched in a tree with wild animals at its foot, and at the Kalydonian Boarhunt together with other great heroes. We see him wrestling at the funeral games of old king Pelias, most often with Atalanta, and grappling with Thetis to win her as his bride, then marrying his goddess-wife, and later giving his young son Achilles to be educated by the wise Centaur Cheiron. All of these images fill out our very partial literary portrayal.

Sometimes, and most frustratingly, we have a depiction of a mythical event, but no literary references at all to help us to understand it. One such is from the story of Jason's quest for the Golden Fleece. A cup by Douris (of about 480 BC) shows a huge dragon apparently regurgitating a naked Jason, who hangs down, weak and motionless, from the great serpent's mouth, while nearby is a vigilant Athene and the tree with the Fleece hanging in it. None of our literary sources describes this kind of confrontation, and we simply do not know exactly what has been happening.

So these are some ways in which visual images can enrich our appreciation of the ancient myths – although these brief comments are necessarily mere pointers towards a complex and engrossing subject. The reader who would like to follow it further will find a number of relevant books listed in the bibliography.

Jason and the dragon that guards the Golden Fleece.

The morality of the myths

In reading and imagining these classical myths, we step into another world, and, if we wish to appreciate it to the full, we should try not to import our own values and beliefs, or view the actions of the mythical characters in a modern light. Take, for instance, the question of rape. The myths are full of stories of divine copulation with humans. Often when a god looks down from Olympos, his eye is caught by a particularly beautiful mortal woman, so he comes down to earth to have his way with her. Whether we should call these sexual unions love affairs, or seduction, or rapes is not always clear – though they do often seem to have been rapes in our commonly accepted sense of the word, that of sexual congress without the woman's consent.

It is easy to condemn. But, on the other hand, you do not

refuse a god, and it could be seen as a great honour to be chosen by one. Moreover, as a Hesiodic fragment puts it, 'the beds of the gods are not unfruitful', and the chosen woman would bear to the god a strong son or sons. (Only one mortal woman, for instance, bore a daughter to Zeus: Leda, the mother by Zeus of Helen, who naturally enough grew up to be the most beautiful woman in the world.) These sons would confer honour on their mother and on their wider families, and their descendants would glory in having a god in their genealogy.

So we must not categorize these sexual encounters of gods with mortals as necessarily negative experiences, particularly in the early literature. It is the tragic playwright Euripides, when he dramatizes these myths for the stage in the later fifth century BC, who begins to explore fully what they really meant in human terms and human suffering. A good example is his portrayal in his *Ion* of Kreousa's pain and awe at the memory of the beautiful Apollo who raped her, and her abiding grief at the loss of the child she bore him (p. 234).

On the male side of things, Homer's Odysseus is all too often seen in modern eyes as a philanderer, whose vaunted love for his wife Penelope, waiting faithfully at home for him for twenty years, must be a sham. But no: his fidelity to Penelope was true in all but a superficial sense, as was his longing to be back at home with her in Ithaca. He did indeed have sex with the divinities Circe and Kalypso on his long journey home from Troy; again, you do not refuse a god. But his love for Penelope was such that he even refused the chance of being made immortal so that he might return home to her (p. 425).

Another Homeric hero is often judged harshly: Achilles, the mightiest fighter at Troy, is despised for 'sulking in his tent' when he retired from battle, after Agamemnon took his slave-girl Briseis away from him (p. 327). There he stayed, while his Greek comrades carried on fighting, and dying, in his absence.

But Briseis, as well as being a woman whom he loved, was also part of the war-booty that he had won with his spear, and the Homeric warrior's standing rested on his outward and visible spoils. Thus Agamemnon had dishonoured him, had publicly shamed him, by taking Briseis from him. Achilles believed himself fully in the right by refusing to carry on fighting, and so, crucially, did the other Greeks. It was only when he later refused Agamemnon's offer of more than full reparation for the offence that he put himself in the wrong. And by doing so he left himself open to the personal tragedy of losing his dearest friend, Patroklos.

It is also easy to misjudge revenge, which is another, often very bloody, theme that frequently crops up in the myths. But this raw world of myth is a more savage world than ours, where revenge is viewed in a quite different light. We might believe that hatred and revenge damage and debase the revenger, and that punishment is better left to the impersonal judicial system. But from the ancient point of view of, say, the fifth century BC, repaying evil for evil as well as good for good was accepted (if not always unquestioned) Greek morality. Euripides' Medea says: 'Let no one think me contemptible, or weak, or easy-going. No, quite the opposite, harsh to enemies and kindly to friends. Such people live a life of greatest glory' (*Medea*, 431 BC, 807–10). So revenge can be seen not only as the honourable course of action, but even as a heroic response to wrongs inflicted. The actions of our 'dangerous women', for instance (Chapter 13), who take revenge on the men who have harmed them, must be viewed in this light.

All this is to say that, when we enter the world of myth, we must come, as best we can, with a mind open to what may at first seem alien. The myths are another country. They do things differently here.

I

CREATION

In the beginning was the Void. The Void was called Chaos – a name with no suggestion of confusion or disorder, but meaning a dark, gaping space. After Chaos came three other entities: wide-bosomed **Gaia** (Earth), **Tartaros**, a dark and terrifying underworld far below the Earth, and **Eros** (Sexual Love), the fundamental cosmic force behind all the acts of procreation that would follow. From these four primal entities was made everything that was made.

This is how Hesiod recounts the ultimate beginning of all things in his *Theogony*, one of the earliest surviving Greek literary works (about 700 BC), which became the standard mythical account of the origin and development of the universe. As a poet, Hesiod took his inspiration from the Muses, and he leads into his great work by entreating them to reveal to him the truth of creation. 'Tell me,' he urges, 'how first gods and earth came to be, and the rivers and the boundless sea . . . the shining stars and the wide heaven above . . .' Then, beginning with primal Chaos, his account proceeds through the creation of the physical cosmos and the births of all kinds of divinities, through strife and battles and bloodshed, to the final supremacy of the Olympian gods under the sovereignty of **Zeus**.

So let us follow Hesiod's narrative with its intricate genealogical scheme, supplementing it where necessary from other sources, since this is the universe, and these the characters that form the background to all the myths that will fill these pages. For the sake of clarity and ease of reference, bold type will be used for what may seem a rather bewildering multitude of names.

NIGHT AND DAY

Out of **Chaos** were born **Erebos**, the darkness of the Under-world, and Nyx (**Night**), the darkness that covers the Earth. Then Erebos mated with Night – the very first sexual union – to produce **Aither** (the clear and bright upper air far away from the earth) and Hemera (**Day**). Night went to live in the depths of Tartaros, which was situated as far below the earth as heaven was above it, so that a bronze anvil dropped from heaven to earth, or from earth to Tartaros, would fall for nine days and arrive on the tenth. From here Night emerged each evening to bring her darkness to the cosmos, just as her daughter Day was returning (744–57):

There stands the dreadful house of shadowy Night, shrouded in clouds of blackness ... where Night and Day draw near and greet each other as they cross the great bronze threshold. One goes into the house and one comes out of the door, and the house never holds them both within, but always one is outside and passing over the earth, while the other waits at home until it is time for her to go. One carries far-seeing light for the people on earth, but the other, baleful Night, shrouded in misty clouds, carries in her arms Sleep, the brother of Death.

Without a mate Night brought forth a whole series of power-ful abstract forces, many of them dark and destructive: Moros (Fate), Thanatos (Death), Hypnos (Sleep), Oneiroi (Dreams), Momos (Blame), Oizus (Misery), the Hesperides (Daughters of Evening), the Moirai (Fates), the Keres (Dooms), Nemesis (Retribution), Apate (Deceit), Philotes (Tenderness), Geras (Old Age), and Eris (Strife).

Some of these are nothing more than abstractions and their names say all there is to be said about them. **Misery** speaks for itself, as does **Deceit**; **Tenderness** too (perhaps seeming a strange companion to all these other gloomier offspring, but here because of her connection to love, and love to night-time). **Blame** is the spirit of disapproval and faultfinding, and **Old Age** is here because he leads us towards Death.

Others are fleshed out with more detail and come to play a part in many later myths. Hesiod describes how **Death** and his brother **Sleep** live together in the depths of Tartaros (758–66):

There the sons of gloomy Night have their home, Sleep and Death, those terrible gods. The shining sun never looks upon them with his rays when he goes up to heaven, nor coming down again from heaven. Sleep roams the earth and the broad back of the sea, gentle and kind to men, but Death has a heart of iron, and in his breast is a spirit pitiless as bronze. Death holds fast to any man he catches, and is hated even by the immortal gods.

So kindly Sleep is seen as travelling and scattering slumber, something like the modern 'sand-man', while pitiless Death comes to mortals when their allotted time-span has run out, carrying them off irresistibly to the Underworld.

To Hesiod, **Dreams** are the brothers of Sleep, but they were later thought to be his thousand sons. Sent by the gods, they are the visions that visit dreamers in sleep, usually taking the form of a person familiar to them, and giving advice or comfort as a waking companion might. Ovid (*Metamorphoses* 11.592–649) envisages the Dreams living with their father in a dark and misty cavern in the land of the Cimmerians. Lethe, the river of forgetfulness, flows with a gentle murmuring through the cave, inviting slumber, and at its entrance poppies bloom, and countless herbs, all shedding drowsiness. All around is stillness, and here Sleep and his thousand sons repose. When a Dream is needed, he wakes and flies on his swift wings in seconds to anywhere on earth.

The **Hesperides** were singing nymphs who lived in a western garden beyond the sunset, at the far ends of the earth. In their garden grew a tree with golden apples, which it was their task to guard (and which, in due course, Herakles would steal as one of his twelve Labours). There were usually thought to be three Hesperides, though their number can vary from two to seven.

There were certainly three **Fates** (*Moirai* in Greek, *Parcae* in Latin), the goddesses who assigned individual destinies to mortals at birth. (Hesiod lists them here among the dark offspring of Night, though later in the poem he gives them different parents and has them fathered by Zeus on the Titan Themis.) They were called Klotho ('the Spinner'), Lachesis ('the Apportioner') and Atropos ('the Inflexible'), with their names revealing their particular tasks: Klotho spun the thread of a man's life, Lachesis measured it out to its allotted length, and Atropos, the smallest and most terrible of the three, cut it off with her pitiless shears when the time for death was come.

Even the gods were subject to the decrees of the Fates. In Homer's *Iliad* (16.433–61), Zeus knows to his sorrow that his dear son Sarpedon is destined to die at the hands of Patroklos, but he does nothing to save him: even Zeus, the greatest of the gods, must bow to the inevitable. If a death was destined by the Fates, then it had to be, as the goddess Athene explains in the *Odyssey* (3.236–8): 'Death comes to everyone alike, and not even the gods can fend it away from a man they love, when the destructive doom of death lays a man low and overpowers him.'

Nemesis was the goddess of Retribution and the righteous indignation felt (by gods and men) at anyone who violates the natural order of things, either by breaking a moral law, or by having an excess of some quality, such as riches or happiness or pride. Only once does she play an active part in the myths, when she is sometimes said to be the mother of Helen of Troy. Today Nemesis still gives her name to acts of just retribution.

The **Dooms** (Keres) were death-spirits who throve on the deaths of mortals. The Hesiodic *Shield of Herakles* describes them in bloody action on the battlefield (248–57):

The black Dooms, gnashing their white teeth, grim-eyed, fierce, bloody, terrifying, fought over the men who were dying, for they were all longing to drink dark blood. As soon as they caught a man who had fallen, or one newly wounded, one of them clasped her great claws around him and his soul went down to Hades, to chilly Tartaros. And when they had satisfied their hearts with human blood, they would throw that one behind them, and rush back again into the battle and the tumult.

Eris too, the goddess of Strife, was at home on the battlefield, as we see from battle scenes in the *Iliad*. Homer describes her as:

Strife incessantly raging, sister and comrade of the murderous War-god, who at first holds her head low, but thereafter strides the earth with head rearing to heaven. And now she moves through the throng of battle, casting evil strife in their midst and ever increasing men's sorrow. (4.440–45)

It would be Eris who set in motion the greatest war in ancient myth, the Trojan War, by bringing about the Judgement of Paris.

Eris was the only child of Night to produce children of her own. Hesiod makes her the mother of many personified abstractions as disagreeable as herself: she bore Toil, Neglect, Famine, Pain, Battles, Conflicts, Bloodshed, Slaughter, Quarrels, Lies, Pretences, Disputes, Lawlessness, Oath and Delusion (Ate).

Of these, only **Ate** had any distinct mythological identity. She was the personification of Delusion, the clouding of the mind that leads people to commit acts of blind folly. She would make much trouble among men, but Zeus later sent his daughters the *Litai* – 'Prayers' for forgiveness, and thus 'Apologies' – whose task was to follow in Ate's wake, and help to heal the harm she caused among deluded humanity.

So all these make up a dark brood of children indeed: suitable offspring, one feels, to emerge from the darkness of Night. Yet significant as these members of Chaos's family may be, it was the descendants of another of the primal entities, **Gaia**/Earth, who would play the most important part in the history of the universe. Gaia founded two great families, uniting with two partners, Sky and Sea, whom she generated from herself. The *Homeric Hymn* (30) in her honour praises her accordingly as the mother of all (*pammeter*), the oldest being who nourishes every living thing in the world from her bounty.

EARTH AND SKY

From out of herself, **Gaia**/Earth brought forth **Ouranos** (Sky), **Mountains** and **Pontos** (Sea). Then Ouranos mated with Gaia, and she bore the race of primordial gods known as the **Titans:** Okeanos (Ocean), Koios, Kreios, Hyperion, Iapetos, Theia, Rheia, Themis, Mnemosyne, Phoibe, Tethys, and, last of all, 'Kronos the wily, the youngest and most terrible of her sons, who hated his lusty father' (137–8).

Next Gaia bore two sets of monsters, the three **Hundred-handers**, grotesque giants with fifty heads and a hundred arms springing from their shoulders, and the mighty one-eyed **Cyclopes**, who would become forgers of the thunderbolt and had names to match: Brontes ('Thunderer'), Steropes ('Lightner') and Arges ('Vivid').

Ouranos hated his children so much that he would not allow them into the light of day, where they might threaten his sovereignty. He pushed them all back into the womb of their mother the Earth, until Gaia was overwhelmed by the pain of it and by the endless intercourse that Ouranos imposed on her. She begged her other sons to help her, but they were all afraid –

except for **Kronos**, who took from her a great sickle of adamant and lay in wait for his father.

Ouranos came with the night and, as he spread himself over Gaia, Kronos reached out and sheared off his genitals, flinging them far away into the sea. Drops of blood and semen were scattered over Gaia, all still capable of generating life, and from these were born the Erinyes (Furies), the Gigantes (Giants), and the Meliads (Tree-nymphs).

The **Furies**, appropriate offspring from such an act of violence, were goddesses of retribution who exacted punishment for murder and other serious crimes, particularly within families, and who guarded the established order of the world. They were later said to be three in number, and to be named Alekto ('the Relentless'), Megaira ('She who Holds a Grudge') and Tisiphone ('Avenger of Bloodshed').

An aura of dread surrounded them, later famously displayed in Aeschylus's *Eumenides*, the third play in his tragic trilogy the *Oresteia*, where the Furies were pursuing the mother-murderer Orestes. They appeared on stage as disgusting, loathsome creatures, repulsively dressed in black, wreathed in snakes, crawling on all fours to scent their prey, whining and howling like dogs. So terrifying were they, that at the first performance of the play (458 BC) women in the audience reputedly fainted and suffered miscarriages. At the end of the trilogy, Orestes was acquitted and the Furies were granted honourable worship at Athens (p. 442), with the new and euphemistic name *Eumenides*, 'Kindly Ones', to help neutralize their dark powers.

The **Giants** too were alarming: monstrous beings of invincible strength, with huge bodies terminating in snaky coils instead of legs. Hesiod has them born in full armour, carrying long spears – perhaps in readiness for their great battle with the gods that would soon follow. But the third group, the **Meliads**, unlike their siblings were unthreatening creatures:

female nature spirits, often of an amorous disposition, who dwelt in trees, each one having her life bound up with her own particular tree. There would be many other kinds of nymphs apart from the Meliads, all of them named according to where they dwelt, including **Dryads** and **Hamadryads** (other kinds of tree-nymphs), **Oreads** (mountain-nymphs), **Alseids** (nymphs of groves), **Naiads** (water-nymphs) and **Nereids** (sea-nymphs).

The *Homeric Hymn to Aphrodite* (5) vividly depicts the lives of nymphs living on Mount Ida (259–72):

They rank neither with mortals nor immortals. Long indeed do they live, eating the food of heaven and dancing among the gods, and the silens [p. 101] and watchful Hermes lie with them in the depths of lovely caves. But at their time of birth, pines or high-crowned oaks spring up on the fruitful earth, trees beautiful and flourishing, towering high on the high mountains, and men call them precincts of the gods, and never cut them down. But when the nymphs' allotted time of death is near at hand, first these lovely trees wither upon the earth, and their bark shrivels up, and their branches fall away, and then with the trees the souls of the nymphs leave the light of the sun.

These, then, were the births from the liquid drops shed over Gaia from Kronos's savage act. Meanwhile, says Hesiod, Ouranos's severed genitals were carried over the waves, and from the foam that gathered around them was born **Aphrodite**, the goddess of love (190–210):

They were carried a long time on the waves, and around the immortal flesh a white foam rose, and in it grew a girl. First she approached holy Kythera, and from there she came to sea-girt Cyprus. She emerged a dread and beautiful goddess (Plate 8), and grass grew up beneath her slender feet. Gods and men call her Aphrodite, because she grew in the foam (*aphros*), and Kythereia because she came to Kythera, and Cyprus-born because she was born in wave-washed Cyprus, and laughter-loving (*philommedes*) because she appeared from the genitals (*medea*). Eros and fair Desire attended her birth and followed her when she joined the company of the gods. This honour she has from the beginning, and among men and the immortal gods she wins as her due the whisperings of girls, and smiles, and tricks, and sweet delight, and the gentleness of love.

THE TITANS

Now that Ouranos's power was overthrown, Kronos was the new lord of the universe. The Titans could emerge from their imprisonment within their mother Gaia and produce progeny of their own, many of them the features of the natural world.

Okeanos (**Ocean**), the eldest of the Titans, was god of the great river that the Greeks imagined as completely surrounding the flat earth, marking for mortals its furthest bounds. On the far side of Ocean were only the strange and awesome places beyond mortal ken. ('Ocean' in its usual sense was a much later concept.) Ocean mated with his sister-Titan **Tethys** to produce the 3,000 **Rivers**, great and small, that flow upon the earth, and the 3,000 beneficent nymphs of land and water, the **Oceanids**. 'They are scattered far and wide,' says Hesiod (365–6), 'and everywhere alike they haunt the earth and the depths of the waters, shining goddess-children.' In particular they watch over the young.

Theia mated with her brother-Titan **Hyperion** and bore three children who would bring light to the heavens: Helios (Sun), Selene (Moon) and Eos (Dawn). **Helios** (Sol to the Romans), the Sun-god, brought daylight to the world by driving his four-horse sun-chariot across the sky from east to west, as his *Homeric Hymn* (31) describes:

> Driving his horses, he shines upon men and immortal gods.
> His eyes gaze piercingly out of his golden helmet,

bright rays beam brilliantly from his temples,
and the shining hair of his head graciously frames
his far-away face. A rich, fine-spun garment
gleams on his body and flutters in the winds,
and stallions carry him.

By night he sailed with his horses and chariot in a great golden bowl back to his palace in the east, floating along the river of Ocean that encircled the earth.

Helios had many children of his own who would play their part in mortal legends, the most notable of these being **Aietes**, the ruthless king of Kolchis who owned the Golden Fleece, the enchantress **Circe**, **Pasiphae**, the mother of the Minotaur, and **Phaithon**, who would come to a tragic end when he insisted on borrowing his father's sun-chariot for a day and driving it on its fiery journey.

Helios's sister **Selene** (Luna to the Romans) lit the darkness by driving through the night sky on her moon-chariot, drawn by two milk-white horses. The *Homeric Hymn* (32) in her honour draws a radiant picture of her journey:

From her immortal head a radiance from heaven
embraces the earth, and great is the beauty that comes
from her shining light. The dark air grows bright
from her golden crown, and her rays fill the sky,
when her fair skin is fresh from the waters of Ocean,
and divine Selene dons her far-shining raiment,
and yokes her lustrous horses, with their arching necks
and glorious manes, and drives forward her team
full speed, at even-time in the middle of the month,
when her great orb is full and her light is brightest.

One of Selene's lovers was the goat-god **Pan**, who lured her into the woods as she was riding by in her silver chariot, then won her favours with the gift of a fine fleece. But her most famous love affair was with a handsome mortal, **Endymion**. One night on her journey through the sky, Selene saw him lying asleep in a cave on Mount Latmos, in Caria, and at once she fell in love with him. Because of her divine favour, Zeus allowed Endymion to choose whatever fate he wished, and he chose to sleep for ever, remaining always young. Every night Selene would visit him in his cave and gaze upon his beauty, or else awaken him to fulfil her desires. According to Pausanias (5.1.4) she bore him fifty daughters.

Edna St Vincent Millay eloquently adapts the myth for a twentieth-century audience (Sonnet XXVII of *Fatal Interview*):

> Moon, that against the lintel of the west
> Your forehead lean until the gate be swung,
> Longing to leave the world and be at rest,
> Being worn with faring and no longer young,
> Do you recall at all the Carian hill
> Where worn with loving, loving late you lay,
> Halting the sun because you lingered still,
> While wondering candles lit the Carian day?
> Ah, if indeed this memory to your mind
> Recall some sweet employment, pity me,
> That with the dawn must leave my love behind,
> That even now the dawn's dim herald see!
> I charge you, goddess, in the name of one
> You loved as well; endure, hold off the sun.

The third light-bearing child, **Eos** (Aurora to the Romans), was the goddess of Dawn. 'She shines upon all who live on earth, and upon the immortal gods living in the wide heaven,' says Hesiod (372–3). Homer calls her 'rosy-fingered' (*rhododaktulos*) and 'saffron-robed' (*krokopeplos*). She brought not just the early light of dawn, but helped to bring the light of day as well, since she accompanied her brother Helios on his journey through the sky, driving her own two-horse chariot.

Both Helios and Eos could see and hear everything that happened on earth during their daily journey, a circumstance that Eos sometimes used to her advantage, since she was of an amorous disposition and was quite ready to seize any particularly handsome young man she noticed and carry him off for her own delight. Her divine mate was Astraios (see below),

Eos pursuing a youth who has caught her fancy.

but her greatest mortal love would be **Tithonos**, son of King Laomedon of Troy, whom she carried off to her home in Ethiopia in the farthest east. She loved him so much that she had Zeus grant him immortality, but she forgot to ask that he might remain forever young. As time went by he grew older and older, slowly withering away to a dry husk, which yet could never die. While he still had his vigour he had two sons by Eos, **Memnon** and **Emathion**, who became kings, respectively, of Ethiopia and Arabia.

The Titan **Kreios** coupled with **Eurybia,** a daughter of Pontos/ Sea, and she bore him three sons, Astraios, Pallas and Perses. **Astraios** ('Starry') and his cousin **Eos,** goddess of Dawn, produced the three main **Winds** of the world: **Boreas,** the violent and icy North Wind, **Notos,** the soft and moist South Wind, and **Zephyros,** the West Wind, who is sometimes stormy, sometimes zephyr-like, warm and gentle.

Eos also bore to Astraios all the **Stars** of the heavens. Most notable of these are the morning and evening stars, Phosphoros and Hesperos (in fact one and the same 'star', the planet Venus). **Phosphoros** ('Light-bringer', also called Eosphoros, 'Dawnbringer') announces the approach of his mother Dawn, while **Hesperos** is the kindly evening star that brings the quiet night. Homer names them both (*Iliad* 23.226–7; 22.317–18):

> The morning star passes over the earth,
> harbinger of light, and after him
> gold-robed Dawn is spread across the sea.
>
> A star moves among stars in the darkening night,
> Hesperos, the loveliest star in the sky.

Hesperos was later associated with wedding songs and marriage. A few lines of Sappho, addressing Hesperos, survive, and these may have been part of a marriage hymn (fr. 104a):

> Hesperos, bringing all that the bright dawn scattered,
> you bring home the sheep, you bring home the goat,
> you bring home the child to its mother.

Kreios's second son, **Pallas,** mated with **Styx,** a daughter of Ocean and the chief river of the Underworld, and she bore him a daughter, Nike (**Victory**), and three sons, Zelos (**Aspiration**), Kratos (**Power**) and Bia (**Might**). All four of these children would later become the constant companions of Zeus, an honour accorded them after they and their mother supported him in his war against the Titans. Styx herself was honoured by Zeus's decree that the most solemn oath the gods might swear would be by her waters. Whenever one of the gods wished to swear an oath, Iris, the divine messenger, was sent with a golden jug to fetch some of Styx's icy water, and the god would swear while making a libation. If anyone swore falsely, he would lie insensible for a year, then be banished from the company of the gods for another nine years. So severe were these penalties that we never hear of any broken oath.

Koios united with his sister-Titan **Phoibe** and fathered two daughters, Asteria and Leto. **Asteria** bore the goddess Hekate to **Perses**, the third son of Kreios and Eurybia. Hesiod praises **Hekate** as a powerful goddess with dominion over earth, sea and sky, who – if she wishes – can bring countless blessings to men, and wealth and success in all their endeavours. To Hesiod she seems to have none of the sinister associations that she acquired later, when she became a menacing figure, an Underworld goddess associated with magic and witchcraft, ghosts and creatures of the night. This later Hekate made her fearful appearances on earth in the dark of night, accompanied by packs of barking hell-hounds, and just as Selene (and later Artemis/Diana) represents the calm and moonlit splendour of night, so Hekate represents its darkness and terrors.

Asteria was also loved by Zeus, and to escape his attentions she turned herself into a quail (*ortyx*) and jumped into the sea. Here an island appeared, named Ortygia, though it was later renamed Delos. It would offer a haven to Asteria's sister **Leto,** when she was about to bear the important gods **Apollo** and **Artemis** to Zeus. 'Leto was always gentle,' says Hesiod (406–8), 'mild to men and to the immortal gods, gentle from the beginning, the kindest in all Olympos.'

The Titan **Iapetos** fathered four sons on his Oceanid niece,

Klymene, all of whom will enter this narrative somewhat later: **Atlas** and **Menoitios,** who would be punished for their part in the battle of the Titans with the gods, **Prometheus,** the benefactor of mankind, and **Epimetheus.**

Two female Titans, Themis and Mnemosyne, would in due course bear children to Zeus. **Themis** was seen as the personification of order in the universe, and she bore the three **Fates** (or perhaps they were born to Night: see p. 24), and also the **Horai,** the three goddesses of the seasons. Hesiod gives the Horai names with ethical connotations, Eunomia ('Good Order'), Dike ('Justice') and Eirene ('Peace'), and thus reflects their function as goddesses of order who maintained the stability of society. The systematic procession of the seasons was seen as proof of the divine order of the world.

Mnemosyne (Memory) lay with Zeus for nine nights and gave birth to nine daughters, the **Muses,** in Pieria at the foot of Mount Olympos; thus they were often known also as the Pierides. They were goddesses on whom poets (like Hesiod himself, as we have seen) and other creative artists, thinkers and philosophers depended for their inspiration – so the goddesses of the arts were the daughters of Memory, an apt metaphor in a time before the widespread use of writing. The Muses were the finest of all singers and, like all divinities, resentful of any challenge to their supreme powers. When the bard Thamyris later boasted that he could surpass them in singing, they blinded him and took away his musical and poetical skills. The daughters of Pieros, for a similar challenge, were turned into magpies (p. 514).

Hesiod gives each of the Muses a name, but makes no further distinction between them. Later their functions were differentiated, with each Muse thought to preside over a specific area of intellectual or creative endeavour. Usually they were: Kalliope ('Lovely Voice'), epic poetry (Hesiod says that Kalliope was the most important Muse because she had the tutelage of kings); Kleio ('Renown'), history; Euterpe ('Gladness'), the playing of the *aulos* (double pipe); Thaleia ('Good Cheer'), comedy; Melpomene ('Singer'), tragedy; Terpsichore ('Delighting in the Dance'), choral lyric and dancing; Erato ('Loveliness'), lyric poetry; Poly(hy)mnia ('Many Songs'), hymns and (later, Roman) pantomime; and Ourania ('Heavenly One'), astronomy.

Mount Helikon in Boiotia was sacred to the Muses, and it was here that they came to Hesiod and gave him the gift of song. They liked to dance around Hippokrene, the 'Horse's Spring', created when the winged horse Pegasos kicked the ground with his hoof. Its water was said to bring poetic inspiration to all who drank from it: thus Keats in his *Ode to a Nightingale*:

> O for a beaker full of the warm South,
> Full of the true, the blushful Hippocrene,
> With beaded bubbles winking at the brim,
> And purple-stained mouth;
> That I might drink, and leave the world unseen,
> And with thee fade away into the forest dim.

Finally, the most significant union of Titan with Titan was that of **Kronos** and **Rheia**, from whom were born many of the Olympian gods. This will bring us to the next violent stage in the cosmic struggle for ultimate power, so first we should fill in more of Hesiod's genealogical framework by detailing the second great family founded by Gaia. From her union with her son Pontos came many wondrous creatures of land, sea and air, some of them beautiful, some monstrous.

EARTH AND SEA

The eldest child of **Gaia**/Earth and **Pontos**/Sea was the sea-god **Nereus,** often called the Old Man of the Sea. Hesiod describes him as 'truthful and honest . . . trusty and gentle, never forgetting what is right in the sight of the gods, and ever thinking just and kindly thoughts' (233–6). Like other sea-deities he had both the gift of prophecy and the ability to change his shape. His fifty daughters, born to the Oceanid **Doris**, were the **Nereids**, sea-nymphs renowned for their beauty. Usually they appear in art and literature as a group, sporting with sea-beasts in the waves or dancing together on the shore, and only a few of them, such as Amphitrite, the wife of the sea-god Poseidon, or Thetis, the mother of the great warrior Achilles, play any individual part in myth.

Then Pontos fathered four more children in union with Gaia, two sons, Thaumas and Phorkys, and two daughters, Keto and Eurybia (who, as we have seen, was the wife of Kreios and the mother of Astraios, Pallas and Perses).

Thaumas is a rather obscure figure, presumably another sea-god, though his children by the Oceanid **Elektra** were very much creatures of the air. These were **Iris**, goddess of the rainbow and messenger of the gods, fleet as the winds, and the **Harpies** ('Snatchers'), winged female monsters, goddesses of the storm-winds who swept people away so that they were never seen again. In ancient art the Harpies appear as birds with women's faces. Hesiod's two Harpies are called Aello ('Storm') and Okypete ('Swift-flying'). 'On their swift wings,' he says (268–9), 'they keep pace with the blasts of the winds and the birds, hurling themselves through the high air.' Later writers add a third, Kelaino ('Dark', like the storm-clouds), and Homer knew of a Harpy called Podarge ('Fleetfoot'), who mated in the form of a mare with the West Wind, Zephyros, and brought forth

Xanthos and Balios, the immortal horses of Achilles who ran like the winds.

Phorkys, like his brother Nereus, was often called the Old Man of the Sea. His partner was his sister **Keto,** whose name suggests any large inhabitant of the sea, and together they bred a group of monstrous children: the Graiai, the Gorgons, Echidna and the snake who helped the Hesperides to guard their golden apples (as Hesiod puts it, 'the fearful serpent who guards the golden apples in a secret region of the dark earth, at the far edge of the world'). He was later given the name of **Ladon.**

The names of the **Graiai** were Enyo, Pemphredo and Deino, though Hesiod mentions only the first two, 'fine-robed Enyo and saffron-robed Pemphredo' (270–3). He calls them 'fair of cheek', which suggests that they were young and lovely, and says that they were called Graiai, 'Old Women', simply because they were white-haired from birth. In later legend, how-ever, they live up to their name rather better, for here they are blind and toothless, apart from a single eye and a single tooth which they share among themselves, passing them around as necessary.

The **Gorgons** were fearsome monsters who lived in the far west beyond the river of Ocean. Two of them, Stheno and Euryale, were immortal, while the third sister, Medusa, was mortal. Their heads were entwined with writhing snakes, they had great tusks like a boar, hands of bronze and wings of gold, and they turned to stone anyone who beheld them. (So Apollodorus describes them, 2.4.2.) Depictions in ancient art often add staring eyes, frightful grins and lolling tongues, and give the Gorgons an odd, striding gait. **Medusa** would be killed by Perseus, and from her severed neck would be born her two children by the sea-god Poseidon, the winged horse **Pegasos** and **Chrysaor,** 'of the Golden Sword'.

Even more terrible than the Gorgons was **Echidna**. Hesiod describes her as half beautiful woman and half monstrous, speckled snake, deathless and ageless, dwelling in a lair beneath the earth and devouring raw flesh. She mated with **Typhon** (a monster even more frightful than herself: see below) to produce a troop of monstrous creatures: **Kerberos**, the multi-headed dog who guarded the entrance to the Underworld, **Orthos**, the two-headed watchdog of Geryon, **Phaia**, the ferocious wild sow of Krommyon, the many-headed **Hydra of Lerna** with her snaky coils, and probably (the text is uncertain) the fire-breathing **Chimaira** with her three heads (lion at the front, goat in the middle, and snake at the rear). Probably also (again the text is ambiguous) Echidna mated with her son Orthos to produce two more fearsome beasts, the **Sphinx** who plagued Thebes with her famous riddle, and the **Nemean Lion** with his hide impervious to weapons.

Phorkys's monstrous children, and the monsters which they in turn generated, would later test the mettle of the heroes Bellerophon, Perseus, Theseus and especially Herakles, all of whom would win undying fame and honour by ridding the world of such dangerous creatures. Edmund Spenser, in the *Faerie Queene*, appositely calls Phorkys 'the father of that fatal brood / By whome those old Heroes wonne such fame'.

KRONOS AND RHEIA

From his parents Ouranos and Gaia, Kronos had learnt that he was destined to be overthrown by his own son but, like his father before him, he was determined that his children should never have the power to threaten his rule. Ouranos's tactic had been to keep his family imprisoned within their mother Gaia, though eventually this proved futile. Kronos tried a different ploy. Rheia bore him five children (Hestia, Demeter, Hera, Hades and Poseidon), none of whom could be killed because they were immortal, so as each of them was born, Kronos devoured them whole (Plate 3).

When Rheia was pregnant for the sixth time, and still suffering endless grief for all her lost children, she turned to her parents for help. On their advice she went to Crete, and there at Lyktos she gave birth to a son, **Zeus** (other sources speak of Mount Dikte or Mount Ida as his birthplace). Gaia hid him safely, then handed over to Kronos a stone wrapped in swaddling clothes in place of the baby. Kronos noticed nothing amiss and swallowed it down.

Zeus was reared in secret, by the local nymphs say later sources, including Amaltheia, who fed him with milk from her she-goat. Some minor Cretan divinities, the Kouretes, guarded the cave in which he was hidden, dancing around the entrance and clashing their shields and spears so as to drown his infant cries. He soon grew to maturity. Then he confronted his father Kronos and forced him to disgorge the children he had swallowed. First to be vomited up was the stone that had been substituted for the last-born infant, and this Zeus set in the earth at Delphi as a wonder for mortals. It was still exhibited there in the second century AD, when the traveller Pausanias saw it (10.24.6). Then came Zeus's brothers and sisters, in the reverse order to that in which they had first been born: **Poseidon, Hades, Hera, Demeter** and **Hestia**.

THE BATTLE OF THE GODS AND THE TITANS

This younger generation of gods, under the leadership of Zeus, now set about seizing power for themselves. They fought against Kronos and those of the Titans (by no means all) who supported him, in a great war known as the *Titanomachia*, that lasted for ten years, with the Titans fighting from Mount Othrys and the gods from Mount Olympos. The outcome was indecisive until Zeus brought in some valuable allies: on the advice of Gaia he set free the Cyclopes and the Hundred-handers from the depths of the earth where their father Ouranos had imprisoned them, and he fed them nectar and ambrosia to give them strength. The Cyclopes forged for Zeus the mighty thunder and lightning, and the Hundred-handers hurled great rocks, three hundred at a go. Now the battle reached truly cosmic proportions (678–711):

The boundless sea roared terribly around, the earth crashed loudly, and the broad sky groaned and trembled. High Olympos was shaken to its foundations by the onslaught of the immortals, and heavy tremors reached down to gloomy Tartaros from the terrible din of their pounding feet and their hard missiles. So it was when they hurled their grievous weapons against one another. The shouts of both sides reached up to starry heaven, and they came together with great battle-cries.

Now Zeus held back his strength no longer. At once his heart was filled with fury and he showed forth all his might. Direct from heaven and Olympos he came, hurling continuous lightning, and the bolts with flashes and thunder flew thick and fast from his sturdy hand, with a whirling of wondrous flames. The life-giving earth roared all around as it burned, and the vast forests crackled loud with fire on every side. All the land seethed, and the streams of Ocean, and the barren sea. The hot blast engulfed the earth-born Titans, flame unspeakable reached the divine sky, and the flashing glare of thunder-bolts and lightning blinded the strongest eyes ... The fearful din of a terrible strife arose, and the power of great deeds was displayed.

The scales of battle turned ...

Kronos and the Titans who supported him were at last defeated, and Zeus, now reigning in his father's place, imprisoned them in the depths of Tartaros and appointed the Hundred-handers to guard them.

We hear of the individual fates of a few of the Titans. **Menoitios**, the son of Iapetos, was hurled directly to Tartaros by one of Zeus's thunderbolts, 'because of his wickedness and his overbearing strength' (516). **Iapetos** himself, so Homer tells us (*Iliad* 8.478–81), sits with **Kronos** for ever in the gloomy dark, far from the delights of sun and winds. Elsewhere Kronos is sometimes viewed more sympathetically and given a different and happier fate, ruling over the Islands of the Blest (p. 111). In Roman myth too, Kronos's counterpart, **Saturn**, was seen as a benefactor. He became an early king of Latium after he was banished from his rule of Olympos, and he taught his people the arts of agriculture and the blessings of civilization. His reign was a blissful Golden Age, when all lived in peace and prosperity. His annual festival, the Saturnalia, was celebrated at the winter solstice and was the merriest time of the year (and taken over in large part by our Christmas). Saturn's wife was the Goddess of Plenty, **Ops**, who was identified with Kronos's wife Rheia.

Keats, writing about the Titans' defeat by the gods in his unfinished *Hyperion*, merges both strands of the myth: he too portrays Kronos/Saturn as sympathetic and benign, but still has him end his existence in a gloomy Tartaros:

> Deep in the shady sadness of a vale
> Far sunken from the healthy breath of morn,
> Far from the fiery noon, and eve's one star,
> Sat gray-hair'd Saturn, quiet as a stone,
> Still as the silence round about his lair;
> Forest on forest hung about his head
> Like cloud on cloud. No stir of air was there,
> Not so much life as on a summer's day
> Robs not one light seed from the feather'd grass,
> But where the dead leaf fell, there did it rest.

Atlas ('Very Enduring'), another son of Iapetos, had a special punishment: he was condemned to hold up the sky for all

Atlas and Prometheus (p. 130) suffering their punishments.

eternity, standing at the far ends of the earth, near the garden of the Hesperides. 'He stands immovably,' says Hesiod (746–8), 'upholding the broad heaven on his head and hands that never find rest.' Only once would Atlas be relieved of his burden, when Herakles came to steal the golden apples of the Hesperides as one of his Labours for Eurystheus, and then only for a short time (p. 208).

Luckily Atlas had had children before he was condemned to his eternal travail. By the Oceanid **Pleione** he was the father of **Kalypso,** the goddess-nymph who would keep Odysseus with her for seven years, and of the seven sisters known as the

Pleiades: Maia, Elektra, Taygete, Alkyone, Kelaino, Sterope and Merope. Six of the Pleiades bore children to gods, most notably **Maia**, who was the mother by Zeus of the god **Hermes**, and **Elektra**, who was the mother by Zeus of **Dardanos**, the ancestor of the Trojan kings. The seventh sister Merope married the mortal Sisyphos.

By the Oceanid **Aithra**, Atlas was the father of **Hyas** and the sisters known as the **Hyades**, whose number ranges in different accounts from two to seven. When Hyas was killed while out hunting, either by a lion or a boar or a snake, the Hyades died of grief for him, and the Pleiades died in turn from mourning their half-sisters. Zeus out of pity immortalized them all in the night sky, and now the star cluster Hyades lies in the constellation Taurus, close to that of the Pleiades, a cluster of seven stars also known as the Seven Sisters. One of the seven stars shines more faintly than the rest, and this is said to be either Merope, hiding her head in shame for marrying a mere mortal, or Elektra, veiling her face in mourning for the death of her son Dardanos and for the destruction of Troy.

Another version of the Pleiades' transference to the stars involves the mighty hunter **Orion**, who was either born from the earth, or was the son of Poseidon and Euryale, a daughter of Minos, king of Crete. Orion pursued the Pleiades and their mother for five (or seven) years, intent on rape, and in the end Zeus intervened to save them by transferring them to the sky. But even now they could not entirely escape their pursuer, for Orion too was placed in the stars. In Crete he had spent his time hunting wild animals in the company of Artemis and Leto, and so great was his prowess that he boasted he would kill every animal on earth. Gaia in anger sent a giant scorpion that stung him to death and, at the request of Artemis and Leto, Zeus immortalized Orion in the stars, where he has become one of the best-known constellations in the night sky. The scorpion was made a constellation too because of his great service to the beasts of the earth.

Orion lies immediately south of the constellation Taurus in which the Pleiades' star cluster lies, so he still pursues his old loves for ever through the night sky. As a great hunter he is naturally accompanied by a dog, the constellation Canis Major, which includes the brilliant Dog Star, Sirius, 'the Scorcher', so called because its appearance marked the season of greatest heat in Greece. 'When the thistle is in flower,' says Hesiod in his *Works and Days* (582–8), 'and the singing cicada sits in a tree, pouring down his shrill music thick and fast from under his wings, in the season of wearying heat, then goats are plumpest and wine is sweetest; women are most lustful, but men are weakest, because Sirius parches their head and knees, and their skin is dried out from the heat.'

Orion also has in his sights a Hare (Lepus) and a Bull (Taurus), while a Bear (Ursa Major) keeps a watchful eye on him from a distance, and the Scorpion (Scorpio) is still in relentless pursuit of his old enemy. When the Scorpion rises, Orion sets.

THE BRIDES OF ZEUS

After the defeat of Kronos and the Titans, Zeus was the new lord of the universe, and he now took a succession of wives and procreated more gods, some major, some minor. Hesiod lists the wives all in their due order. First was the Oceanid **Metis**. When she became pregnant, Zeus learnt from his grandparents Ouranos and Gaia that once Metis had given birth to the daughter now in her womb (a daughter who would be almost as wise and strong as her father), she was destined to bear a son who would displace him as king of gods and men.

Naturally Zeus was unwilling to lose his hard-won power, so he followed the example of his father Kronos: deceiving his wife with wily words, he swallowed her. He thus forestalled the birth of the son who would have overthrown him, and at the same time assimilated into himself Metis's powers of practical wisdom (her name means 'intelligence' or 'cunning'). When the time came for their daughter to be born, Hephaistos split Zeus's head with an axe and out leapt **Athene**, fully armed.

Next Zeus married the Titan **Themis**, who, as we have seen, bore the **Fates** and the **Horai** (Seasons). Then **Eurynome**, a daughter of Ocean, bore him the **Graces** (Charites). These minor goddesses were the personifications of beauty, charm and grace, and also of favour and gratitude for favour. Hesiod makes them three in number and names them Aglaia ('Splendour'), Euphrosyne ('Gaiety') and Thalia ('Festivity'). They play little individual part in myths, though as a group they appear frequently in literature and art in contexts of joy or festivity. They are often the companions of the Muses or they attend upon some god. They are often associated with Aphrodite and Eros as creators of the love bond between men and women: 'From their glancing eyes,' says Hesiod (910–11), 'flows love that melts the limbs' strength, and beautiful is their gaze from beneath their brows.'

Zeus's fourth wife was his sister **Demeter**. She bore him a daughter, **Persephone**, who would be abducted by Hades and become queen of the Underworld. The Titan **Mnemosyne** was Zeus's next wife, and she, as we have seen, bore him the nine **Muses**. Next came another Titan, **Leto**, who bore the great gods **Apollo** and **Artemis**. And seventh, and last of all, Zeus married his sister **Hera**.

Hera bore Zeus three children: **Ares**, the god of war, **Eileithyia**, the goddess of childbirth, and **Hebe**, the goddess of youth. The crippled smith-god **Hephaistos** was said by some to be their fourth child, and by others (including Hesiod) to have been born of Hera alone.

Hera from now on would be Zeus's permanent consort and

the queen of Olympos. This did not, of course, stop him from pursuing liaisons with a whole variety of other women. They all bore him children, including two of the great gods: the Pleiad **Maia** was the mother of **Hermes**, and the mortal **Semele**, daughter of Kadmos, king of Thebes, was the mother of **Dionysos**. We shall look in detail at all the most important gods in our next chapter.

ZEUS AND TYPHON

The Titans had been thoroughly overthrown, but soon Zeus's supreme power was once again under threat from a huge and terrifying monster named Typhon (also known as Typhaon or Typhoeus). According to the *Homeric Hymn to Apollo*, he was the child of Hera alone, who was angry with Zeus for bringing forth Athene from his own head, and particularly so because her own son Hephaistos was such a poor physical specimen. So she prayed for a son stronger than Zeus, and Typhon was born to her.

In Hesiod's more usual version, Typhon was the offspring of Gaia and Tartaros. He had on his shoulders a hundred fearsome snake-heads, all with black tongues flickering and eyes flashing fire, and these heads were able to imitate every conceivable sound – the bellow of a great bull, the roar of a lion, the baying of a pack of hounds, the hissing of serpents. Apollodorus (1.6.3) adds that he was taller than any mountain and his head brushed the stars. If he stretched out his arms, his one hand touched East and the other West, and instead of fingers he had a hundred snakes' heads. His mouth shot forth flames, his body was winged, and from the thighs down he was a mass of huge, coiling serpents.

This monster challenged Zeus, and he would have become the ruler of the universe on that very day, says Hesiod, if Zeus had not at once responded to his threat (839–56):

Zeus thundered hard and mightily, and the earth and the wide heaven above resounded with fearsome noise, as did the sea, and the streams of Ocean, and the nethermost parts of the earth. Great Olympos shook under the immortal feet of the king as he went forth, and the earth groaned in reply. A conflagration gripped the purple sea, from the god's thunder and lightning and the monster's fire, from the flaming bolt and tornado winds. The whole earth seethed, and the sea and the sky . . . and Zeus leapt from Olympos and struck, scorching on all sides the awesome heads of the dreadful monster.

Typhon collapsed, crippled, and Zeus flung him into Tartaros. There Typhon became the father of all the irregular storm-winds that bring harm to people and cause shipwrecks, thus giving his name to our word typhoon.

Apollodorus makes the encounter a more threatening one for Zeus, and in his version the other gods are affected by the conflict as well. When they saw Typhon making for heaven with jets of flame spouting from his mouth, they all fled in terror to Egypt and changed themselves into various animals. (From other sources we know that Apollo became a hawk or a crow, Artemis a cat, Ares and Aphrodite fishes, Hermes an ibis, Hera and Hephaistos oxen, Dionysos a goat, and Leto a mouse. This story was probably invented to explain the animal forms of Egyptian gods whom the Greeks identified with their own deities. Typhon himself was identified with Seth, the enemy of Osiris, and Zeus was said to accompany the flight to Egypt disguised as a ram with curling horns, to account for the cult of Zeus Ammon in ram-shape.)

In this version, Zeus attacked Typhon from a distance, flinging thunderbolts, and then fought him at close quarters, striking him with a sickle made of adamant. But Typhon enveloped Zeus in his coils and wrested the sickle from him, then cut the sinews from his hands and feet. He carried the now helpless god off to his cave in Cilicia (southern Asia Minor) and hid the sinews in a bearskin, setting a fellow-monster to guard them, the she-dragon Delphyne, who was half-serpent, half-woman.

Luckily for Zeus, Hermes and Aigipan ('Goat-Pan') managed to steal back the sinews unobserved, then refitted them to Zeus's hands and feet. The god, his vigour restored, pursued Typhon once again, hurling his thunderbolts. Now the Fates came to help their father. They fed Typhon weakening fruit, while pretending that it would give him greater power; but even though the monster lost strength, he was still able to heave whole mountains back at Zeus as he fled from him. In Thrace one of these rebounded and wounded Typhon, and ever afterwards it has been called Mount Haimos from his blood (*haima*) that spurted over it. Finally, when they came near Sicily, Zeus hurled Mount Etna on top of Typhon and crushed him beneath it for all eternity. This has become his legacy, for here his anger pours forth in volcanic streams of fire as he struggles to free himself. Apollodorus, less dramatically, says that the flames are the remains of Zeus's thunderbolts.

THE BATTLE OF THE GODS AND THE GIANTS

With Typhon vanquished, there was still one more challenge for Zeus and the rest of the gods to face before their supremacy could be counted secure. Gaia was angry because Zeus had flung her children, the Titans, into Tartaros, so she stirred up their brothers, the Giants, into rebellion against the new divine regime, and there took place another huge battle, known as the *Gigantomachia*.

Hesiod makes only a brief reference to the story (954), but we know that it was popular during the sixth and fifth centuries BC because of its many depictions in art. Apollodorus is the first author to give a full surviving account of the battle (1.6.1–2).

The Giants opened the hostilities by hurling huge rocks and

flaming trees at the heavens. Faced with this threat, the gods prepared for battle, and discovered from an oracle that they alone would never kill the Giants, but if they had the help of a mortal, then the Giants would die. Gaia learnt of this and produced a magic herb that would protect her sons from all comers, mortal or divine. Zeus responded by forbidding the Sun and the Moon and the Dawn to bring light to the earth, then plucked the herb himself before anyone else could find it. Having destroyed it, he sent Athene to summon the aid of the greatest of mortal heroes, Herakles.

The strongest of all the Giants were Alkyoneus and Porphyrion, so these were dealt with first. Herakles shot Alkyoneus with an arrow, but the Giant was destined to remain immortal as long as he remained within the land of his birth, Phlegrai in Macedonia, later called Pallene, so when he fell on his native ground he began to revive. On Athene's advice, Herakles dragged him beyond the bounds of Pallene and he died.

Zeus inspired Porphyrion with lust for Hera, then when he tried to rape her, felled him with a thunderbolt. Herakles finished him off with one of his arrows. Ephialtes was slain by two arrows, one from Apollo in his left eye and one from Herakles in his right. Dionysos killed Eurytos with his thyrsos, the magical wand made from a fennel rod with a bunch of ivy leaves attached to the tip. Klytios and Mimas were burnt to death, Klytios by Hekate's infernal torches and Mimas by missiles of red-hot iron hurled by Hephaistos. Enkelados fled westward, but Athene flung the island of Sicily on top of him, since when his fiery breath has blazed forth from Mount Etna (so he shares with Typhon the credit for causing the volcano). Athene also killed and flayed Pallas and used his tough skin as a shield.

Poseidon pursued Polybotes through the sea to Kos, then broke off a piece of the island and flung it on top of him, crushing him beneath what then became the island of Nisyros. Hermes, wearing the cap of invisibility that belonged to Hades, slew Hippolytos. Artemis killed Gration. The Fates, fighting with cudgels of bronze, killed Agrios and Thoas. The rest of the Giants were felled by Zeus's thunderbolts and finished off by Herakles' arrows as they lay dying.

Thus the gods, with a mortal's help, were victorious over the Giants, and they could now reign, secure in their power, for all time.

THE GODS

THE GREAT GODS

Zeus now reigned supreme as king of the gods, though his brothers too were allotted lordship over their own particular domain: while Zeus retained the heavens, Poseidon took the seas and Hades the misty darkness of the Underworld. The other gods too had their own powers and functions, as we shall see. There were now fourteen major Greek deities, all of whom the Romans adopted in due course, identifying them with their own native Italian divinities. And since their own gods had very few stories of their own attached to them, they also adopted all the myths that were associated with their Greek counterparts.

The gods' names, Greek (and Roman), were Zeus (Jupiter), Hera (Juno), Poseidon (Neptune), Hades (Pluto), Demeter (Ceres), Hestia (Vesta), Aphrodite (Venus), Apollo (he had no Italian equivalent, so for the Romans his name remained the same), Artemis (Diana), Athene (Minerva), Ares (Mars), Hephaistos (Vulcan), Hermes (Mercury) and Dionysos (Bacchus). These fourteen were more usually reduced to a canon of twelve principal gods (the Twelve Olympians) by omitting Hades, whose realm was beneath the earth, and Hestia. She was one of the older order of gods, and her place was taken by Dionysos, a great deity but a latecomer to the pantheon, being born of Zeus and a mortal woman, Semele.

The gods are imagined as glorious beings, human in form and character – and with human failings too, for they can be lustful, vengeful and petty – and having family and social lives similar to those of mortals. Yet they are far more beautiful than humans, more powerful, more knowledgeable; and, most important of all, they are very different from mortals in being ageless and deathless. Some are imagined as being mature and majestic (Zeus, Poseidon, Demeter), others forever young (Apollo, Artemis, Aphrodite); but having reached whatever is their ideal maturity, there they remain. (Which is not to say that the image of a god was necessarily fixed for ever, since Dionysos, for instance, became younger as the centuries passed, while Eros, first conceived by Hesiod as a cosmic force and later seen as a beautiful youth, the son of Aphrodite and Ares, even became a young and mischievous child.)

They feast and drink, but their food is ambrosia and their drink nectar, and the divine fluid that runs through their veins is ichor, not blood. From early times they were believed to live on Mount Olympos, the highest mountain in Greece at almost 10,000 feet (3,000 metres) high, situated near the borders of Macedonia and Thessaly, and this gave them their familiar name of the Olympian gods. Gradually the concept of 'Olympos' became distinct from the mountain itself, and the gods were rather nebulously imagined as living a blissful life in the heaven above Mount Olympos, dwelling in divinely beautiful houses. Homer describes their blessed abode (*Odyssey* 6.42–6):

> Here, they say, the dwelling of the gods
> stands firm forever. No winds disturb it,
> rains drench, nor does snow come near,
> but the clear air stretches away, cloudless,
> a bright radiance playing over it. Here
> the blessed gods live all their days in bliss.

A gate of clouds kept by the Horai, the goddesses of the seasons, opened to allow passage out of Olympos, so at any time the gods might leave their homes and come down to earth to interfere in human lives, helping or harming the mortals of their choice – and thus playing a very real part in the myths.

Zeus

Zeus (Jupiter) reigns over the heavens and is, therefore, a weather-god, the sender of rain, hail, snow and thunderstorms. His weapon is the thunderbolt, the symbol of his invincible

Zeus hurling a thunderbolt, accompanied by his eagle.

power over gods and men. In Homer he is called 'cloud-gatherer', 'thunderer on high', 'lord of the lightning', Zeus who 'delights in the thunder', the 'father of gods and men'.

The overall impression of the Homeric Zeus, especially in the *Iliad*, is of one who dominates by tremendous physical power. He once punished Hera for persecuting his mortal son Herakles by suspending her from Olympos, her hands bound with a

golden chain, and with anvils tied to her feet (15.18–20). When
her son Hephaistos tried to help her, Zeus picked him up by his
leg and flung him out of Olympos and down to earth. He is
very ready to threaten any misbehaviour by the other gods
with physical violence, and he himself boasts of his awesome
supremacy (8.19–27):

> 'If you hang down from heaven a chain of gold,
> and lay hold of it, all you gods and goddesses,
> you could never drag me down from heaven to earth,
> not Zeus the counsellor most high, not if you try
> full hard. Yet if I set my mind to drag you up,
> then I'd hoist you up together with earth and sea,
> and tie the chain around the peak of Olympos,
> leaving the whole world hanging in mid-air.
> By so much am I stronger than gods and men.'

In the *Odyssey*, Homer depicts Zeus as rather more diplo-
matic; and as time went by he was seen more and more as a
god who dominates by wisdom and justice, rather than by force
and threats.

Certainly he was seen as the protector of law and justice on
earth, with his epithets indicating the spheres over which he
had jurisdiction. He was the defender of the household
(*Herkeios*), the hearth (*Ephestios*), property (*Ktesios*), friend-
ships (*Philios*), oaths (*Horkios*), hospitality (*Xenios*), suppliants (*Hikesios*), and mankind in general (*Soter*, Saviour). In
contrast to this, he himself was a serial adulterer and his children
by his many lovers were legion – though perhaps this is no
surprise, since it would have been seen as the greatest glory to
have Zeus as the divine progenitor of a human genealogy. He
was such an incorrigible philanderer, and told so many of his
own lies to Hera, that he was said to pardon all false oaths
made by mortals in the name of love. (Shakespeare's Juliet

would echo this: 'at lovers' perjuries, they say, Jove laughs.')
He often came to mortal women in disguise, both to trick his
unwitting quarry and to evade his jealous wife, who was always
(and justifiably) ready to suspect him of misbehaviour. As the
poet and critic Graham Hough would put it (*Children of
Zeus*):

> Ageless, lusty, he twists into bull, ram, serpent,
> Swan, gold rain; a hundred wily disguises
> To catch girl, nymph, or goddess; begets tall heroes
> . . . All that scribe or sculptor
> Chronicle is no more than fruit of his hot embraces
> With how many surprised recumbent breasts and haunches.

In ancient art Zeus is depicted as a stately, bearded figure,
often holding his invincible weapon, the thunderbolt, and a
long sceptre, which was also the symbol of authority among
human rulers. He is often accompanied by his emblematic bird,
the majestic eagle, lord of all other birds. His most famous
representation in antiquity was the colossal statue in gold and
ivory, created by the artist and sculptor Pheidias for the god's
great temple at Olympia. Although it has long been lost, we
know a great deal about it from written descriptions, such as
that of the traveller Pausanias (5.11). It was judged to be one
of the Seven Wonders of the World.

Hera

Hera (Juno) is the sister and wife of Zeus and the queen of
heaven. As we have seen, she bore Zeus three (or four) children:
the war-god Ares, Eileithyia, the goddess of childbirth, and
Hebe, the goddess of youth. Their fourth child, the crippled
smith-god Hephaistos, was sometimes said to have been born
of Hera alone.

As the goddess of marriage, married women and childbirth,

she was worshipped at sanctuaries throughout the Greek world. Her two most renowned centres of cult were on the island of Samos, where her temple was one of the largest in Greece, and her Argive temple between Argos and Mycenae. Her connection with Argos was particularly close. In the *Iliad* (4.51–2) Hera names it as one of her three favourite cities, the other two being Mycenae and Sparta; and both Homer and Hesiod refer to her as Argive Hera.

In ancient art Hera is depicted as a regal and matronly woman, often carrying a sceptre or wearing a crown. Her royal bird is the peacock, its tail decorated with the many eyes of All-seeing Argos after his death at the hands of Hermes (p. 161). In the Argive Heraion there was a colossal ivory and gold statue of Hera on her throne, fashioned by the great sculptor Polykleitos and famous for its beauty, but now familiar only from its depictions on Argive coins. Pausanias (2.17.3–4) says that on her crown were depicted the Graces and the Horai, and in one hand she held a pomegranate, in the other a sceptre. On the sceptre was seated a cuckoo, the bird whose form Zeus took to seduce Hera before their marriage. He was always a master of successful disguise, and Hera caught the enchanting bird to be her pet – at which point, of course, Zeus returned to his real form and made love to her. ('This story and suchlike tales about the gods I relate without believing them,' says the rational Pausanias, 'but I relate them nonetheless.')

Despite her great importance as a goddess of cult, Hera is most often presented in literature and myth as a wronged wife with a vindictive nature, continually jealous of Zeus's many infidelities, who persecutes both his mistresses and the children that result from his liaisons. For instance, she tried to deny Leto a place to give birth to Apollo and Artemis; she turned Kallisto into a bear and Io into a cow; she caused Semele's death; she plagued Herakles, Zeus's son by Alkmene, throughout his whole life. Yet perhaps her most memorable portrayal is a more kindly one: it occurs in the *Iliad*, where Homer describes how Hera seduces Zeus so as to draw his attention away from the battlefield at Troy (14.153–353). She makes careful preparations, and bribes Hypnos (Sleep) to lull Zeus into slumber as soon as her plan succeeds and their lovemaking is over. Then she borrows Aphrodite's alluring girdle, worn next to the breasts, and this makes her so overpoweringly attractive that Zeus cannot restrain his desire to make love to her. 'Never before have I wanted anyone so much,' he says, 'not when I loved Ixion's wife, not when I loved Danae, not when I loved Europa, not when I loved . . .', and so he goes on, tactlessly chronicling his many infidelities. Hera is tolerant, for she is achieving her aims. Then:

> the son of Kronos clasped his wife in his arms,
> and beneath them the holy earth sprouted fresh-grown grass,
> and dewy clover, and crocuses, and hyacinths
> so thick and soft it held the hard ground from them.
> On this they lay together, and a beautiful golden cloud
> covered them, from which fell glistening drops of dew.

Poseidon

Poseidon (Neptune) is the god of the sea, and like the sea itself he can at times be serene and kindly, and at others violent and tempestuous, when his fearsome rage brings terrifying storms on the world. Homer vividly depicts both sides of the mighty god. Here he journeys peacefully across his territory (*Iliad* 13.23–30):

> He harnessed to his chariot his two bronze-shod horses,
> swift of foot, with long, streaming manes of gold.
> Himself clothed in gold, he seized his well-wrought
> golden whip, then climbing into his chariot he drove

across the waves. On every side, from the deeps of the sea,
came dolphins, playing in his path, acknowledging their lord,
and the sea parted in joy, cleaving a path before him.
So swiftly sped the horses that never once
was the axle of bronze beneath made wet with foam.

And we see the god in violent action when he wields his
trident to send storms against Odysseus, in revenge for his
blinding of the Cyclops Polyphemos, Poseidon's son (*Odyssey*
5.291–7):

He drew the clouds together and grasping his trident
he stirred up the sea. He roused the stormblasts
of all the winds together, and covered with clouds
both earth and sea alike. Night rushed down from heaven.
East wind and south wind struck, and stormy west wind,
and heaven-born north wind, rolling up great waves.

On land, too, Poseidon wields his tempestuous power, for he
is *Enosichthon* and *Ennosigaios*, the Earth-shaker, and with his
trident he can stir up earthquakes at will. He is also god of
horses, in which guise he is known as Poseidon *Hippios*, 'Horse
Poseidon'. Some say that he created the very first horse, either
by fertilizing the rocky ground with his semen, or by striking it
with his trident. Certainly he fathered the winged horse Pegasos
on the Gorgon Medusa, and he often provided wondrous horses
for his mortal favourites. When the goddess Demeter turned
herself into a mare to avoid his amorous attentions, he himself
became a stallion and mounted her, and she bore the divine
horse Areion. In a modern poem, Roy Campbell epitomizes
Poseidon's dual nature as sea-god and god of horses in his
Horses on the Camargue:

I heard a sudden harmony of hooves,
And, turning, saw afar

A hundred snowy horses unconfined,
The silver runaways of Neptune's car
Racing, spray-curled, like waves before the wind.
Sons of the Mistral, fleet
As him with whose strong gusts they love to flee,
Who shod the flying thunders on their feet
And plumed them with the snorting of the sea . . .
But when the great gusts rise
And lash their anger on these arid coasts,
When the scared gulls career with mournful cries
And whirl across the waste like driven ghosts:
When hail and fire converge,
The only souls to which they strike no pain
Are the white-crested fillies of the surge
And the white horses of the windy plain.
Then in their strength and pride
The stallions of the wilderness rejoice;
They feel their Master's trident in their side
And high and shrill they answer to his voice.
With white tails smoking free,
Long streaming manes and arching necks, they show
Their kinship to their sisters of the sea –
And forward hurl their thunderbolts of snow.

In ancient art Poseidon is a majestic bearded figure, not unlike Zeus, but wilder in appearance and easily recognized by his emblem, the three-pronged trident, which served as both sceptre and weapon. He sometimes holds a fish and is often accompanied by some of his sea creatures; occasionally he rides a hippocamp (a hybrid with the foreparts of a horse and the tail of a fish).

Like Zeus, Poseidon had a host of mortal sons, many of them as rough and unpredictable as their father. His divine wife was the Nereid Amphitrite. At first she was a reluctant bride, for when he began to woo her, she fled from him into the sea, so he sent all the sea-creatures, his servants, to seek for her. A dolphin was the first to find her, and pleaded so persuasively for his master that she gave in and married him. Out of gratitude, the sea-god immortalized the dolphin in the stars as the constellation Delphinus.

Poseidon and Amphitrite lived together in a splendid golden palace in the depths of the sea. They had a son, Triton, a merman with a human head and torso and a coiling, fishy tail, who is often depicted blowing on his conch-shell horn. Originally only one, he later becomes pluralized into a whole range of Tritons who make up Poseidon's retinue, or sport with Nereids in the waves. A Triton blowing his horn, raising the great shell to his bearded lips, has been a popular choice for fountain-figures, as on Bernini's Triton Fountain in the Piazza Barbarini in Rome, and with his father Poseidon on Rome's famous Trevi Fountain. In Wordsworth's passionate sonnet *The World is Too Much with Us*, Triton, together with the sea-god Proteus, becomes a symbol of a lost and less materialistic world:

> Great God! I'd rather be
> A Pagan suckled in a creed outworn;
> So might I, standing on this pleasant lea,
> Have glimpses that would make me less forlorn;
> Have sight of Proteus rising from the sea,
> Or hear old Triton blow his wreathed horn.

Demeter

Demeter (Ceres) is the goddess of corn, the giver of grain and thus of bread, man's staple food, and so the great sustainer of life on earth. To her brother Zeus she bore a daughter, Persephone (Proserpina), also known as Kore ('the Girl'), with whom she was closely associated in Greek cult, the two of them often being called simply 'the Two Goddesses', or even 'the Demeters'. Mother and daughter frequently appear together in ancient art, often holding torches and wearing crowns, sometimes holding sceptres and stalks of grain.

Demeter's principal myth concerns Persephone's abduction by Hades, the god of the Underworld, and her own long search for her beloved daughter, movingly recounted in the early *Homeric Hymn* (2) in her honour. Zeus supports Hades' desire to have Persephone for his wife, but he is well aware that Demeter would not agree, so he secretly abets his brother. One day, when Persephone is gathering flowers in a meadow with her friends, she wanders apart from the others and sees a glorious narcissus, covered with a hundred fragrant blooms, which Zeus has created to ensnare her. As she reaches out with both hands to pick the radiant flower, the earth gapes open and out from the chasm speeds Hades in his golden chariot. He snatches up the girl, caring nothing for her screams, and carries her down into his gloomy realm below. While she can still see the light of the sun, she cries out for her mother, and Demeter, hearing her, darts towards the sound as swift as a bird. But she is too late, for Persephone has disappeared.

For nine days and nights Demeter does not eat or drink, but wanders the earth with flaming torches in her hand, seeking her daughter. On the tenth day she meets the goddess Hekate, who also heard Persephone's cries, and together they go to consult the Sun-god Helios, who sees all things on his daily journey across the sky. He tells them that Hades has carried the girl off to be his bride and that Zeus approves of the match, and he tries to reassure Demeter that Hades is a worthy husband for her daughter. But Demeter is so angry that she deserts Olympos and the dwellings of the gods, and goes to live among mortals disguised as an old woman.

In her wanderings she comes to Eleusis in Attica. Here, sad at heart, she rests in the shade of an olive tree, near the Maiden Well from which the women draw their water. The four daughters of the local king, Keleos, come to the well and greet her kindly, pitying her great age and her loneliness, and she tells them that she is seeking domestic work of some kind. They take her home to their mother Metaneira, who welcomes her warmly and makes her the nurse of her late-born baby son, Demophon. In this friendly home the goddess's spirits are cheered by the jokes of the old serving woman, Iambe, and she laughs for the first time since the loss of her daughter.

Demophon flourishes under her care and, in gratitude for the kindness shown her, Demeter begins to make her infant charge immortal, secretly burning away his mortal part in the fire each night and anointing him with ambrosia each day. But one night Metaneira interrupts her and cries out in alarm, horrified at seeing her little son in the fire. At once Demeter rebukes her soundly and reassumes her divine splendour. Revealing her true identity, she tells Metaneira that if the Eleusinians wish to win back her favour, they must build her a great temple.

Keleos and his people duly do so, and here Demeter lives for a whole year, longing for her daughter and still resolutely keeping away from Olympos. Now in her grief she makes the whole earth barren. No corn will grow and a great famine afflicts mankind, so that Zeus is afraid there will soon be no men left to offer sacrifices to the gods. He sends Iris with a message to Demeter, ordering her to Olympos, but she refuses to come. He sends all the gods, one by one, to offer her gifts and plead with her, but still she refuses, saying that she will never again set foot on Olympos, nor allow the earth to yield, until she sees her dear daughter once again. So Zeus gives in and sends Hermes to fetch Persephone home. But before she leaves the Underworld, Hades secretly gives her a pomegranate seed to eat.

Hermes drives her in Hades' golden chariot to the temple at Eleusis, and when Demeter sees him bringing her daughter, she rushes out in joy. Persephone leaps down and runs to her, and the two of them embrace, rejoicing. But because Persephone has eaten while in the Underworld, she cannot leave it completely and is obliged to spend four months of every year as the wife of Hades. These are the months when winter grips the land and the seed lies dormant within the earth. For the rest of the year, the spring and summer months of life and growth and harvest, Persephone lives joyously with her mother. Demeter, accepting this compromise, now makes the earth bring forth rich harvests once again, and she returns to Eleusis, where she teaches the Eleusinians the new and secret rites, known as the Eleusinian Mysteries, that will be performed for many centuries in her honour.

Although Demeter was widely worshipped throughout the ancient world, Eleusis was always her best-known place of cult and her rites became the greatest of all mystery religions. There is evidence at Eleusis of at least eighteen centuries of continuous worship, from Mycenaean times until the sanctuary was destroyed in AD 395. Although the details of the rites were successfully kept secret, it seems that they centred on Demeter's search for her lost daughter and Persephone's return and reunion with her mother, symbolizing both the rebirth of the crops in spring and the mystic rebirth of the initiates after death.

Demeter's *Homeric Hymn* names the leading citizens of Eleusis to whom she taught her rites: Keleos, Diokles, Eumolpos, Polyxeinos – and Triptolemos. In later literature Triptolemos became a more significant figure: not just a citizen of Eleusis, but the eldest son of Keleos and Metaneira, and more importantly the mortal whom Demeter chose to transmit her gift of grain and agriculture to the world. She gave Triptolemus a supply of corn and a chariot drawn by winged dragons, and in this he flew over all the earth, scattering the corn and teaching the people how to cultivate crops.

Another significant figure was the son borne by Demeter to Iasion, son of Zeus and the Pleiad Elektra, after lying with him in a thrice-ploughed field in Crete. This son was the divine Ploutos, 'Wealth', who represented the wealth and good fortune yielded by the earth. Hesiod (*Theogony* 972–4) describes him as 'a kindly god, who goes everywhere over the earth and the broad back of the sea, and whoever finds him, and into whose hands he comes, that man he makes rich and bestows much fortune on him'. Ploutos had an important part to play in the Mysteries of Eleusis, and he is depicted in art in the company of Demeter and Persephone, usually as a naked boy holding a cornucopia or a bunch of grain stalks. As for Iasion, Homer records (*Odyssey* 5.125–8) that Zeus struck him down with a thunderbolt for his presumption in lying with a goddess.

Later tradition added further incidents to Demeter's myth. During her long search for her daughter, according to Pausanias (1.37.2), an Athenian called Phytalos gave the weary mother hospitality and in return she rewarded him with the gift of the first fig tree. Pausanias saw Phytalos's grave, with its inscription recording the honour in which he and his race were held because he had won such a rich gift for mankind.

Ovid gives us several tales of metamorphosis. One of these concerns a Sicilian water-nymph named Kyane ('Blue') who saw Hades making off with Persephone in his chariot (Ovid, *Metamorphoses* 5.409–77). Kyane rose from her pool and tried to block his path, but Hades drove straight into her waters, hurling his royal sceptre into their depths and opening up a pathway down into the Underworld. The chariot hurtled through the yawning crater, and Kyane was left alone to grieve for the fate of Persephone, and for the contempt that Hades had shown for her own dear pool. She grieved so much that she wasted entirely away with weeping, dissolving into her own waters until nothing remained of her. When Demeter came by during her search, Kyane could no longer speak to tell her what she knew, so instead she showed Persephone's belt floating on the surface of her pool as a silent token of the girl's fate.

A second story (5.446–61) relates how Demeter, hot and thirsty from her long travels, stopped at the door of a cottage to ask for a drink. The old woman who lived there gave her some barley water, which she gulped down so thirstily that the woman's cheeky son, Askalabos, laughed at her and taunted her for being greedy. The offended goddess threw the remains of the drink into his face and he was changed into a spotted lizard. His mother wept, putting out her hand to touch the little creature, but it fled away in fear and she never saw it again.

A similar fate was suffered by another boy, Askalaphos, the son of the Underworld river-god Acheron (5.533–50). When Persephone ate seven pomegranate seeds on her visit to Hades, Askalaphos was the only witness, and unfortunately he told of what he had seen. Because this meant that Persephone could not now return permanently to her mother, but would have to spend part of each year in the Underworld, she punished him by flinging water from the river Phlegethon into his face and transforming him into an ill-omened bird of the dark, the screech-owl. In Apollodorus' version (1.5.3, 2.5.12) it was Demeter who punished him. She imprisoned him under a heavy rock, and there he stayed until Herakles came down to fetch Kerberos and rolled the rock away. But Demeter was still angry with the boy, and she turned him once again into an owl.

Finally, an even less happy fate was suffered by the impious Erysichthon (8.738–878). When he needed some timber to build a banqueting-hall, he had no hesitation in cutting down the trees in Demeter's sacred grove. He even attacked one huge, old oak, towering high above all the other trees and, as his axe blade cut into the wood, blood began to flow out of it from the nymph who lived inside the tree. Despite this he carried on, and when a bystander objected, Erysichthon lopped off his head.

The tree fell, and all the nymphs who had often danced beneath it begged Demeter to punish its destroyer, so she laid an insatiable hunger on Erysichthon while he was asleep. When he woke up he could think of nothing but food: he ate continually, and the more he ate, the more he longed to eat. He used up all his worldly wealth buying food, and still he was afflicted with a raging greed. At last, to raise more money, he sold his daughter Mestra into slavery. She had once been the lover of Poseidon, so now she prayed for help to the sea-god and he granted her the power of metamorphosis. She escaped by turning into a fisherman, and then became herself once again. After this her father often sold her as a slave to raise money for food, and each time she changed her shape and went free, ready to be sold again. Yet even this was not enough, and in the end Erysichthon began to gnaw at his own flesh, feeding his body by eating it away, and so died.

Yet the most memorable of Demeter's mythical stories remains her long, anguished search for her lost daughter, hauntingly alluded to by Milton in *Paradise Lost* (4.268–72, where he gives mother and daughter their Roman names, and places Persephone's abduction at Enna, in central Sicily):

> . . . that faire field
> Of Enna, where Proserpin gathring flours
> Her self a fairer Floure by gloomie Dis
> Was gatherd, which cost Ceres all that pain
> To seek her through the world.

Hestia

Hestia (Vesta) is the goddess of the hearth, the sacred fire at the centre of every home and every community. She was wooed by her brother Poseidon and her nephew Apollo, but instead of marrying she renounced sexual love and swore an oath of eternal chastity. While other gods travelled the world, Hestia remained quietly on Olympos and so played no part in the stories of mythology. In compensation Zeus granted her special honours, for as goddess of the hearth she was worshipped in every household and in all the temples of the gods, and thus she had a very real power. As her *Homeric Hymn* (29) puts it:

Hestia, you have won an eternal home and the greatest of honours in the high dwellings of all, both immortal gods and men who walk the earth. Glorious is your privilege and your praise. For without you men can have no feasts, and to you the sweet wine is poured both first and last.

Hestia's Roman counterpart, Vesta, was not only goddess of the hearth, but guardian of the community. The priestesses who oversaw her cult at Rome were known as the Vestal Virgins, and they kept an eternal fire burning on her altar, tending it night and day. Attached to Vesta's temple was the cult of the state Penates (*Penates Publici*, protectors of Rome), which were said to have been saved from the flames of Troy and brought to Italy by Aeneas. These were the public equivalent of the domestic Penates, the household gods who protected the home.

At Vesta's festival, the *Vestalia*, asses were adorned with necklaces of loaves and did no work, because Vesta was once saved by an ass from the amorous designs of the ithyphallic god Priapos. After a feast of Kybele, where all the gods and nymphs and satyrs ate and drank their fill, Vesta fell asleep. Priapos saw her and desired her, and he would have had her too, if a bray from Silenos's ass had not woken her in time to see him advancing on her with his gigantic phallus erect. So the goddess escaped a painful fate, and ever afterwards asses were honoured in her name.

Aphrodite and Eros

Aphrodite (Venus) is the goddess of erotic love and the giver of beauty and sexual attraction. Literature from Homer onwards celebrates the power of love and the dominion of Aphrodite. Her longest *Homeric Hymn* (5) begins: 'Tell me, Muse, the deeds of golden Aphrodite, the Cyprian, who stirs up sweet desire in the gods, and overcomes the tribes of mortal men, and the birds that fly in the air, and all the creatures that live on dry land and in the sea.' The only living beings immune to her influence were the three virgin goddesses Athene, Artemis and Hestia. Everyone else, mortal and immortal alike, was open to the power and pain of love. Sappho begins her famous *Hymn to Aphrodite* with the words, 'Richly enthroned, immortal Aphrodite, daughter of Zeus, weaver of wiles, I pray you, Lady, break not my spirit with heartache or grief.'

As we have seen, Aphrodite was born, according to Hesiod, from the sea-foam that gathered around the severed genitals of Ouranos. There was also a more conventional version of her birth, for to Homer she was simply the daughter of Zeus and Dione, who is a rather obscure figure and may have been a Titan, an Oceanid or a Nereid. Whatever Dione's origin, she was once most likely an important goddess, especially as her name seems to be the feminine form of Zeus (Greek stem *Di-*).

Aphrodite herself was married to the crippled smith-god, Hephaistos, but she bore him no children and was an unfaithful wife. Her regular lover was the war-god, Ares. The *Odyssey* (8.266–366) recounts a famous episode during their liaison, in which the Sun-god Helios, travelling across the sky, spotted the

The Venus de Milo.

lovers lying together and reported the affair to Hephaistos. The crafty god planned a clever revenge on his errant wife and her lover: he fashioned a magical, invisible net over his marriage-bed, then pretended to go away on a journey to Lemnos (an island always particularly associated with him).

Naturally the lovers took this opportunity to go to bed together, but in the midst of their passion the net descended, catching them immovably in its snare. Hephaistos at once came in, calling all the other gods to witness the humiliation of the naked and helpless pair. The goddesses stayed away out of modesty, but all the gods came and laughed their fill, with Hermes confessing to Apollo that to be in bed with golden Aphrodite would be worth a far greater penalty. Poseidon at last persuaded the angry Hephaistos to release the lovers, on the understanding that Ares would pay a fine. Ares went off to Thrace and Aphrodite to her sacred precinct on Cyprus, where the Graces bathed and adorned her, soothing her wounded dignity.

Aphrodite bore several children to Ares: a daughter, Harmonia, who married the mortal Kadmos, and two sons, the warrior-twins Phobos and Deimos. Their names mean 'Terror' and 'Fear', suitable children for the war-god, whom they often accompanied on the battlefield: 'They are terrible gods,' says Hesiod (*Theogony* 935–6), 'who, along with Ares, sacker of cities, put to rout the close-packed ranks of men in chilling war.'

According to later tradition (first in the lyric poet Simonides, 575) Aphrodite's most famous son by Ares was Eros, the god of love. This was not so in early myth, for in Hesiod's *Theogony* Eros was one of the primal entities, born at the beginning of time (p. 21). To Hesiod he was a fundamental cosmic force, like Aphrodite herself inspiring love, and omnipotent over mortals and gods alike: 'the most beautiful of the immortal gods, he melts the limbs, and overpowers the reason and the careful plans in the breasts of all gods and all men' (120–22). He was present at Aphrodite's birth to welcome her to the world, and thereafter became her constant companion (192–202), inflicting love on whomever she chose.

Eros kindling love.

Perhaps the archaic lyric poets give us the most memorable images of Eros's violent impact on body and mind. From Sappho: 'Eros shook my heart, like a wind falling on mountain oaks' (47); and 'Once again Eros melts my limbs and spins me round, bitter-sweet creature, irresistible' (130). From Anacreon (413): 'Once again Eros, like a blacksmith, has struck me with his great axe, and has plunged me into an icy mountain torrent.' From Ibycus (287): 'Once again Eros looks at me meltingly from under his dark eyelids, and with all his enchantments flings me into the inescapable nets of Aphrodite. How I tremble at his onset, like a prize-winning horse, now old, who is put once again in the chariot-yoke and goes all unwilling to the race.' Euripides (*Medea* 530–31) is the first to mention the bow and arrows with which Eros pierces his victims and takes them captive.

In ancient art Eros (or even a plurality of Erotes) naturally often accompanies Aphrodite. He appears first as a beautiful winged youth, but he grows younger as time passes, and in Hellenistic times and later he is depicted by both poets and artists as a mischievous infant, with a torch that could inflame love, and a bow and quiver full of inescapable arrows.

Aphrodite herself was a favourite subject of sculpture. Early statues from the archaic and classical periods usually show her decorously draped in long robes; but from the fourth century she is regularly portrayed nude (or nearly so), as the ideal of female beauty. Her two most famous statues are the Aphrodite of Melos (Venus de Milo) of the second century BC (p. 70), now in the Louvre, Paris (probably the most famous female nude of all time), and the Aphrodite of Knidos by Praxiteles, of about 350 BC, showing a modest Aphrodite about to enter her bath, now lost, but well known to us from coins and many Roman copies.

Aphrodite so often inflicted helpless love on the other gods, including of course Zeus, that Zeus in retaliation made her suffer the humiliation of falling in love with a cowherd, Anchises, so that she might know what it was like to be tormented with desire for a mortal. Her *Homeric Hymn* (5) describes her passion. She saw Anchises tending his cattle on Mount Ida and was seized with desire for him. Bathed and bedecked by the Graces, she went down to earth in the guise of a Phrygian princess (68–74):

> So she came to Ida of the many springs,
> the home of wild beasts, and went straight

> to his dwelling across the mountain. After her
> came grey wolves and bright-eyed lions,
> bears and swift leopards, eager for deer,
> all of them fawning on her. And seeing them
> she was glad in her heart, and put desire
> in their breasts, so that two and two they mated,
> all through the shadowy groves.

She came to Anchises 'clad in a robe outshining the brightness of fire, a beautiful golden robe of rich and varied work, which shimmered like the moon over her tender breasts, a wonder to behold. And she wore twisted bracelets and shining earrings like flowers, and around her soft throat were lovely necklaces. Love seized Anchises . . .' (86–91).

He thought her a goddess, but she assured him that she was merely a mortal girl, the daughter of the Phrygian king Otreus, and had been carried to Ida by Hermes to be a bride for Anchises himself. Let them, she said, consummate their union here and now. Joyfully Anchises agreed (155–67):

> He caught her by the hand, and laughter-loving Aphrodite
> turned, and with her lovely eyes cast down, she crept
> to his well-strewn bed, already laid with soft covers,
> the skins of bears and loud-roaring lions
> which he himself had slain in the high mountains.
> And when they had come to the well-made bed,
> Anchises first took off the gleaming ornaments,
> the pins and twisted brooches, earrings, necklaces,
> and loosed her girdle and took off her bright robes
> and laid them down on a silver-studded chair.
> Then, by the will of the gods and destiny, he lay with her,
> a mortal man lying with an immortal goddess,
> without knowing clearly what he did.

After their union she drifted sweet sleep over him, and only when he awoke did she reveal her true identity. At once Anchises was afraid, certain that now he would be punished, and he turned away his face and begged the goddess to have mercy on him. She reassured him, saying that she would bear him a son, Aineias (better known as Aeneas), who would be reared by the mountain-nymphs until his fifth year, and then she would bring the boy to his father. All would be well so long as Anchises never named his son's real mother, but said that he was a nymph's child.

It happened as Aphrodite predicted, except that years later, while Anchises was drunk, he told his great secret and was punished for diminishing Aphrodite's honour: Zeus struck him with a thunderbolt and either blinded or crippled him.

Apollo

Apollo (so called by both Greeks and Romans) is the patron of music and the arts, and the leader of the Muses. He is the god of prophecy and divination, presiding at Delphi over the most famous oracle in Greece. He is the god of purification and healing, often called Paion; but just as Zeus wields the thunderbolt and Poseidon the trident, Apollo's weapon is the bow, and his arrows can bring plague and death. Homer calls him 'Lord of the silver bow' and Apollo the 'Far-shooter'. Also known, from Homer onwards, as Phoibos Apollo, the Shining One, he came to be seen during the fifth century BC as a sun-god and was sometimes identified with the Sun-god Helios, an identification that later became standard.

Apollo embodies the values of order and harmony, reason and moderation, exemplifying the proverbial Greek maxims 'Know thyself' and 'Nothing too much'. In ancient art he is young, almost always beardless and often naked, the epitome of youthful male beauty. His attributes are the lyre and the bow, and sometimes a wreath of laurel. Perhaps the finest depiction of this austere and rational god is the sculpture on the west pediment of the temple of Zeus at Olympia, where he oversees the violent battle between the Lapiths and the Centaurs, a guarantor of final order and serenity.

Apollo was the son of Zeus and the Titan Leto, and the twin brother of Artemis. As the time approached for her babies to be born, Leto wandered through many lands, seeking a place for her labour, but no country dared let her rest because they feared the wrath of Hera, who was always vindictive to Zeus's loves. Finally Leto came to the little island of Delos in the Cyclades, which alone was brave enough to receive her, but even now she was still beset by Hera's fury. The jealous goddess kept Eileithyia, who presided over childbirth, close by her on Olympos so that she would not hear of Leto's distant sufferings and deliver her of her child.

Leto was racked with labour pains for nine days and nights, all fruitless, until at last the other goddesses, pitying her, sent Iris to fetch Eileithyia, offering her a splendid necklace strung with golden threads if she would come and end Leto's long labour. The *Homeric Hymn to Apollo* (3) relates how the first child, Apollo, was born (115–19): 'As soon as Eileithyia, goddess of childbirth, set foot on Delos, Leto's time was come and she strove to bring forth her child. She clasped her arms around a palm tree, kneeling on the soft meadow while the earth laughed for joy beneath, and the child leapt forth to the light.'

The *Hymn* does not dwell on the birth of Artemis that followed (and indeed it was sometimes said that Artemis was born first, then acted as midwife for the birth of Apollo). Instead it goes on to recount the early days of the young god. As soon as he was born, Themis fed him with nectar and ambrosia, then at once he sprang up to stride forth into the world. His first words declared his three major concerns (131–2): 'The lyre and the curved bow shall ever be my special care, and I shall prophesy to men the infallible will of Zeus.'

The young Apollo travelled over the earth, seeking a place to found his oracular shrine. His first choice was Haliartos in western Boiotia, but the nymph of the local spring, Telphousa, had no wish to share her pleasant spot. She persuaded the god to move on to the area of Krisa, on the southern slopes of Mount Parnassos, claiming that it would be far more peaceful there than at her spring, often frequented by horses and mules.

So Apollo chose the ideal spot, at Delphi, but found that it was the lair of a monstrous she-dragon, later called Python, who was plaguing the surrounding countryside, killing the inhabitants and ravaging their flocks. He shot the great serpent dead, after which the locality was also named Pytho because her carcase rotted away (*pyth-*) in the sun beside the sacred spring. He himself was called Pythian Apollo, and now the place was his. But he returned to Haliartos to punish Telphousa for sending him into Python's lair: he covered the nymph's spring with a great mound of rocks, and he subordinated her cult to his own by creating an altar to Telphousian Apollo in a nearby grove. In later times the famous blind seer Teiresias, whose prophecy was inspired by Apollo, died after drinking Telphousa's waters, so perhaps this was the nymph's revenge.

At Delphi, Apollo established his oracular shrine. In the form of a dolphin, he diverted a shipload of Cretans sailing to Pylos and brought them to Delphi to be his priests. Later it was said that he founded the Pythian Games – celebrated every four years and second only to the games at Olympia – to commemorate the dead Python, and that his prophetess at Delphi was known as the Pythia in her memory. His victory over the serpent symbolizes the triumph of the Olympian god of light over the chthonian forces of darkness, and his Oracle became the most important in Greece. Near to Delphi was the famous Kastalian

Spring, whose waters have always been said to have the power of inspiration. Mount Parnassos itself came to be seen not only as the home of Apollo, but as the haunt of the Muses and the seat of poetry and music.

In Apollo's temple at Delphi stood the omphalos, a stone conical in form and shaped like an old-fashioned bee-skep, marking the centre (the 'navel') of the earth. Zeus had once determined this exact centre by releasing two eagles, one from the eastern bounds of the earth and one from the west, then marking the place where they met. Delphi was also in many ways the spiritual centre of the ancient world. The Pythia's seat of prophecy was a tripod, a metal bowl supported by three legs, and from this she gave out Apollo's oracles in a state of trance. Interpreted for the inquirer by priests, these oracles were re-nowned for their ambiguity; and indeed one of Apollo's epithets was Loxias, 'he who talks obliquely'. (Although the most famous of all mythical oracles, telling Oedipus that he would kill his father and marry his mother, was entirely clear – simply misleading.)

Apollo had a number of children by mortal women, many of whom were graced with their father's special accomplishments. Three in particular will be mentioned at this point, all of whom were skilled in healing and/or prophecy. The first of these was the god of healing and medicine, Asklepios (Aesculapius to the Romans). In the usual version of the myth, Asklepios's mother was the Thessalian Koronis, daughter of Phlegyas. It was said that Apollo fell in love with her when he saw her washing her feet in Lake Boibias; but even after she was made pregnant by the god, she still preferred the mortal Ischys, son of Elatos. She knew that Apollo would tire of her when her beauty faded, whereas Ischys would, in the nature of things, grow old along with her, so she planned to marry her mortal lover, even against her father's wishes. Unfortunately, Apollo left a crow to keep watch on Koronis, and when it spotted her making love with Ischys, it flew excitedly to the god to report her infidelity. The angry god cursed the crow, turning it black when it had previously been white – since when all crows have been black.

He sent his sister Artemis to kill Koronis, but as her corpse lay burning on the funeral pyre, he saved her baby, snatching him from her body even as it burned. He gave this son of his, Asklepios, to be reared by the wise Centaur Cheiron, who educated the boy and taught him the arts of medicine. Eventually Asklepios had two sons of his own well skilled in the medicinal arts, Machaon and Podaleirios who fought at Troy, and also several daughters who were the personifications of one aspect or another of healing, including Hygeia, the personification of health.

Asklepios himself became a superb healer who finally encroached on the gods' preserve by bringing a corpse back to life. Zeus struck doctor and patient dead with a thunderbolt, making Apollo so angry that he in turn killed the Cyclopes, who had forged the lethal bolt for Zeus. As punishment, Apollo was forced to serve a mortal, Admetos, for a year (p. 554).

Asklepios's principal sanctuary in Greece was at Epidauros in the Peloponnese. Here people seeking cures slept in the temple overnight to await visitation from the god. Snakes were sacred to Asklepios and were present at his many shrines, regularly assisting in the cures. Following a plague in 293 BC, his worship was taken to Rome. In art, he is shown carrying a staff with a snake coiled around it, and his eternal symbol in the heavens is the constellation Ophiuchus, the Serpent-holder.

Another son of Apollo who was skilled in both healing and prophecy was Aristaios, son of the nymph and huntress Kyrene. Pindar describes her encounter with the god in his *Pythian Ode* 9 (1–70). Apollo fell in love with Kyrene one day when he saw her on Mount Pelion, wrestling single-handedly with a huge lion, and asked the Centaur Cheiron who she was. Cheiron, realizing that Apollo was dissembling, could not resist teasing him a little:

'Do you ask, lord, the girl's birth? You who know the appointed end of all things, and all the ways that lead there. You know how many leaves the earth puts forth in spring, you know how many grains of sand in the sea and the rivers are driven before the waves and the rushing winds. You know what will be, and why it will be – all this you see clearly.'

The Centaur then predicted that Apollo would carry Kyrene off to Libya and make her queen of a city named after her – and this the god did, bearing her away in his golden chariot.

Kyrene's son by the god, Aristaios, not only inherited his father's gifts of prophecy and healing, but was the inventor of many country crafts, such as bee-keeping, olive-growing, cheese-making, shepherding and the preparation of wool. He married Autonoe, a daughter of Kadmos, and as such came to play a part in the saga of Thebes. After his death he was worshipped as a rustic god.

A third son of Apollo was the seer Iamos, whose mother was Euadne, the daughter of Poseidon and a Spartan nymph, Pitane. Euadne had been brought up by Aipytos, a king of Arcadia, and when she became pregnant by Apollo she tried to conceal it from her guardian. In due course he discovered the painful truth and hurried off to the Delphic Oracle for advice. There he was told that Apollo was the father of the child, who was destined to become a great prophet and to found an unfailing line of seers. Easy in his mind at last, Aipytos returned home, only to find that in his absence Euadne had given birth to her son out in the countryside. With a heavy heart, not daring to take him home, she had left him there. Now, five days later, she and her guardian went to look for the infant, not expecting to find him still living. But Apollo had sent two snakes to feed his son with honey, and Euadne found her baby alive and well, lying in a bed of violets, so she named him Iamos, 'child of the violets'.

Despite fathering these and other mortal children, Apollo was often unlucky in love. He pursued the nymph Daphne, for instance, only to have her turned into a laurel tree as he reached out to grasp her (p. 520). He gave Kassandra prophetic powers in return for her favours, but she changed her mind and rejected him; so he left her with the power to foretell the future truly, but condemned her to the fate of never being believed. He loved the beautiful Marpessa, daughter of Euenos, a son of Ares, but she reacted much as had Koronis. At first the god bided his time while many other suitors wooed the girl, all of whom Euenos challenged to a chariot race, promising to bestow his daughter on anyone who could beat him. He always won, then cut off the heads of his vanquished opponents and nailed them to the walls of his house – until one final suitor came: Idas, who was known as the son of Aphareus, king of Messenia, but was really a son of Poseidon. His chariot was drawn by winged horses given him by his divine father, and in it he carried off Marpessa. Euenos pursued them, but he had no chance of catching them with his merely mortal horses, and when at last he came to the river Lykormas in Aitolia, he gave up in despair. He killed his horses and drowned himself in the river, which was renamed the Euenos after him.

Idas took his new wife back to Messenia, and it was now that Apollo made his move. He too came to Messenia and seized Marpessa by force. At once Idas drew his bow against the god, ready to fight for his bride, but Zeus came between them and told Marpessa to choose which suitor she preferred. She chose Idas, preferring the mortal to the god, for the same reason as had Koronis. Apollo had to withdraw, and in due course Marpessa bore Idas a daughter whom they named Alkyone after the kingfisher (a bird believed to have a plaintive cry), in memory of Marpessa's sorrowful weeping when Apollo seized her. Alkyone would marry Meleagros, the great hero who killed the Kalydonian Boar.

Apollo also loved two youths, Hyakinthos and Kyparissos, both of whom returned his love; but both died tragically. Hyakinthos was loved not only by Apollo, but also by the bard Thamyris (the first instance of homosexual love among mortals, according to Apollodorus) and by the god of the West Wind, Zephyros. The lad himself loved only Apollo, and one day, when boy and god were throwing a discus to one another, Zephyros, out of jealous spite, deflected the discus with a gust of his wind just as Apollo made his throw. The discus swerved, hitting Hyakinthos on the head and killing him at once. Apollo tried to revive him, but failed, so in his grief he gave his lover a kind of immortality: he transformed the blood shed from his mortal wound into a dark blue flower, the 'hyacinth', a form of iris. The flower was born again every spring, and on its petals were marks that read 'AI AI' ('Alas! Alas!'), forever recalling Apollo's cry of grief at his lover's death.

Kyparissos was another young favourite of Apollo, and like Hyakinthos he returned the god's love. He also dearly loved a tame stag, a beautiful beast that was sacred to the nymphs. He would lead it to water or to fresh grass, and hang wreaths of flowers on its antlers, and even ride upon its back, guiding it with scarlet reins. But one summer's day, as the stag was sleeping, stretched out in the shade of some trees, he threw his hunting-spear and accidentally killed it. Filled with grief, he longed only to join it in death, and Apollo could not comfort him, try as he might. As Kyparissos wasted away in sorrow, he begged as a last gift from the gods that he might go on mourning forever, so Apollo transformed him into a cypress tree, the eternal symbol of grief.

Let us end as we began with Apollo as god of music. Naturally he resented any slur on his supreme musical abilities and was quick to exact vengeance if these were challenged. Ancient myth tells of two famous contests in which Apollo's musicianship was tested. One was between Apollo and the goat-god Pan, where Apollo was judged the winner by all but Midas, on whom the god took a memorable revenge (p. 534). The other contest took place between Apollo and the Phrygian satyr Marsyas.

Originally the *aulos*, or double pipe, had been invented by Athene, in imitation of the wild lamentations voiced by the two surviving Gorgons after the death of their sister Medusa. But the goddess threw her new instrument away in disgust when she found that it distorted her face unbecomingly as she played. The satyr Marsyas found the pipes and was enchanted by their music, becoming in time so proficient a performer that he challenged Apollo to a musical contest. God and satyr agreed that the Muses should be the judges and that the victor might do whatever he liked with the loser.

The contest began, with Marsyas playing his pipes and Apollo his lyre, and both performing equally well. Finally Apollo turned his lyre upside down and played on it with great skill, then challenged the satyr to do the same with his pipes – which of course was impossible – so Apollo was adjudged the winner. The price that he exacted from Marsyas was an agonizing death: he suspended him from a tall pine tree and flayed him alive. The tears of all the woodland creatures who loved the satyr became the river Marsyas, a tributary of the Maeander and the clearest river in Phrygia.

Herodotus (7.26) tells us that the shaggy hide of Marsyas could still be seen in his day exhibited at Kelainai, near the source of the river Marsyas. According to Pausanias (2.7.9), the satyr's discarded pipes reputedly floated away down the river and eventually reappeared far away in the river Asopos, where a shepherd found them and dedicated them to Apollo in a temple at Sikyon, though by Pausanias's time they had been burnt in a temple fire.

The shorter *Homeric Hymn* (21) to Apollo pays tribute to Apollo the musician:

Phoibos, about you even the swan sings high and clear, as he wings his way to alight on the banks of the swirling river Peneios; and about you the sweet-tongued minstrel with his clear-voiced lyre always sings both first and last.

So hail to you, lord! I seek your favour with my song.

Artemis

I sing about Artemis of the golden shafts, chaste virgin of the clamorous hunt, who with her arrows strikes down the stag, own sister to Apollo of the golden sword. Over the shadowy hills and windy heights she draws her golden bow, delighting in the chase as she sends forth her grievous shafts. The peaks of the high mountains tremble, the dark wood echoes terribly with the outcry of beasts, and the earth and fish-filled sea shudder . . .

Thus begins one of the two *Homeric Hymns* (27) to Artemis (Diana), twin sister of Apollo. Brother and sister are together the two great archer deities and both embody a contradiction: just as Apollo is the god of healing, and yet his unerring arrows can bring plague and death, so Artemis is mistress of all wild animals (*Potnia Theron*), and yet is also the goddess of hunting, who kills the very creatures she has nurtured. Although a virgin herself, as Artemis *Locheia* (she of the childbed) she presides over childbirth along with Eileithyia; and as Artemis *Kourotrophos* (nurse of the young) she is the protector of all young living things, human and animal alike. One of her most famous places of cult was at Brauron, in Attica, where little girls in yellow dresses served her as *arktoi*, bears, and performed a bear dance at her annual festival, the *Brauronia*.

She was sometimes identified with Eileithyia because of their mutual concern with childbirth; and just as Apollo was known as Phoibos, the Shining One, and came to be identified with the Sun-god Helios, so Artemis was conflated with Selene, the Moon-goddess, and both were known as Phoibe. Artemis was also sometimes identified with that other goddess of the night, her cousin Hekate, who was associated with crossroads (great centres of ghostly and magical activities), and who ranged the night with a retinue of ghosts, the shades of the restless dead, and with a pack of terrifying hell-hounds. Indeed, Hekate was sometimes known as Artemis of the crossroads.

The dominant conception of Artemis in both literature and art is as virgin huntress. Ancient art typically portrays her as a young and beautiful woman, carrying bow and arrows, sometimes dressed in long robes and sometimes in a short tunic reaching to her knees. Often she wears animal skins or is accompanied by animals, especially by deer. The great temple of Artemis at Ephesos, one of the Seven Wonders of the World, contained a rather different image: a celebrated statue covered with what are assumed to be multiple breasts, perhaps to mark the goddess's connection with childbirth.

Artemis was believed to roam the mountains and forests with a band of attendant nymphs, all of them delighting in the hunt and sworn to a determined chastity like their leader. If this were violated, Artemis was merciless. When Kallisto was raped by Zeus, for instance (p. 517), one of the versions of her tragic fate, quite apart from being transformed into a bear, was death at Artemis' hands. But the archer-goddess was also seen as an agent of death in a more general sense, with or without the need for punishment. Any unexpected death of a woman could be attributed to the sudden and unerring arrows of Artemis. In

Homer's *Odyssey*, when Odysseus meets his mother's shade in Hades and thus learns for the first time of her death, he asks her how she died. 'Was it a long illness?' he inquires. 'Or did Artemis the archer-goddess visit you and bring you down with her gentle shafts?' (11.172–3).

There was always a close and mutually protective relationship between Artemis and Apollo and their mother. When the giant Tityos tried to rape Leto, brother and sister together killed him, and because of his crime he was punished in Hades with eternal torment from vultures tearing at his liver. They also shot the sons and daughters of Niobe, the wife of King Amphion of Thebes, when she boasted that she had far more children than Leto, with Apollo killing the boys and Artemis the girls.

Leto would often go hunting with her daughter and, as we have seen (p. 44), their companion was at one time the giant hunter Orion. It was they who asked for him to be immortalized in the stars after he was stung to death by a massive scorpion. But there are many intricate variations of Orion's story, and in one of these Artemis herself killed him accidentally. It was said that she enjoyed Orion's company so much that she was thinking of marrying him (the only hint in myth of Artemis, the eternal virgin, being moved by sexual passion). This made Apollo deeply jealous. He pointed to an object far out to sea and challenged her to hit it with an arrow, which she did – and realized that the object had been Orion's head only when his corpse floated to shore.

Two other famous giants, challengers to the gods, were killed by either Artemis or Apollo. Otos and Ephialtes were twins, and were called the Aloadai after their nominal father Aloeus, but were really the sons of Poseidon. Their mother was Iphimedeia, who had been so much in love with the sea-god that she would often go down to the sea and cup the seawater in her hands, pouring it over her body. One day Poseidon came and made love to her, and in due course she bore twin sons.

The boys grew at an alarming rate. Iphimedeia herself tells their story in Homer's *Odyssey*, when Odysseus meets her shade in Hades (11.305–20). Her sons were the largest and handsomest of all mortals after the giant hunter Orion, and by the time they were nine years old they were over 50 feet (16 metres) tall. They threatened to do battle with the gods themselves, and to pile Mount Ossa on Mount Olympos, and Mount Pelion on Ossa, until they reached the very heavens. 'And they would have done it too,' says Homer, 'if they had grown to manhood.' But before then Apollo killed them: 'before the down bloomed below their temples, or covered their chins with the blossom of youth'.

In Apollodorus' version (1.7.4) it was Artemis who saved the gods. Here the giants actually succeeded in piling Ossa on Olympos and Pelion on Ossa. When they reached the home of the gods, they put the war-god Ares out of action by tying him up, then pursued two of the goddesses, Otos going after Artemis, and Ephialtes after Hera. But Artemis killed them by a trick. She turned herself into a deer and ran between them, and when they each flung a spear at the beast, they missed, but struck each other and died.

Perhaps the most famous myth associated with Artemis is that of her confrontation with the mortal Aktaion, son of Aristaios and Autonoe, and grandson of Kadmos, king of Thebes. Aktaion was a skilled huntsman whose tragic fate was to be turned into a deer by Artemis, and then to be torn to pieces by his own hounds.

Various motives are given for this agonizing death. The earliest, attested in a lost poem by Stesichorus, was that Zeus was angry with Aktaion for wooing his aunt Semele, the very woman whom the god himself desired. Others said that Aktaion had enraged Artemis by boasting that he was a better hunter than she was, or even by thinking himself good enough to marry her. But in the most familiar version of his fate, Artemis was angry because he came on her suddenly while he was out hunting on Mount Kithairon, and saw her bathing naked with her attendant nymphs in a shady spring.

The affronted goddess splashed him with water and transformed him into a stag, though his mind remained as it was and he was all too aware of the hideous fate in store for him. He fled into the forest, where his own hounds gave tongue and hunted him, while he ran before them in terror. At last they dragged him down. They tore at him while his hunting friends cheered them on, all the while calling for Aktaion himself to join in the sport. Only when the life was at last torn out of him was the anger of Artemis appeased. It was said that his hounds, finding that their beloved master had disappeared, sought for him everywhere, howling in grief, until the Centaur Cheiron took pity on them and made a statue of Aktaion, so lifelike that they were comforted.

This death of Aktaion is a popular subject in ancient art from the sixth century BC, with Artemis almost always shown in attendance. In earlier pictures Aktaion sometimes wears a deerskin, and the first vases on which he sprouts antlers are after the middle of the fifth century. Artemis surprised bathing appears first in Pompeian paintings.

The myth has inspired many poets too, right down to the present day. It was given an ironic twist by the Poet Laureate, Andrew Motion, writing on the death of Diana, Princess of Wales, in September 1997. Here it is not Aktaion but Artemis/ Diana herself who is the victim, with Diana hunted to death by the media hounds who in life had idolized her (*Mythology*):

Earth's axle creaks; the year jolts on; the trees
begin to slip their brittle leaves, their flakes of rust;
and darkness takes the edge of daylight, not
because it wants to – never that. Because it must.

And you? Your life was not your own to keep
or lose. Beside the river, swerving underground,
your future tracked you, snapping at your heels:
Diana, breathless, hunted by your own quick hounds.

Athene

Athene (Minerva) is the virgin goddess of war and of handi-crafts. As war-goddess, she presides over the disciplined and rational use of war to protect the community, in contrast to the war-god Ares, who delights in the bloodlust and slaughter and frenzy of battle. In ancient art Athene is regularly depicted fully armed, with crested helmet, spear and *aigis* (a goatskin cape, worn as a kind of breastplate and often fringed with snakes). A grim image of the Gorgon, instiller of fear, is often set on her *aigis* or on her shield, and her special bird, the owl, seated on her shoulder.

As the goddess of handicrafts, she not only presided over women's work of spinning and weaving, but was also the patroness of craftsmen such as carpenters, metalworkers and potters. In this capacity, she was often said to be involved in the skilled projects of mortals. She supervised the building of the famous ship *Argo*, for instance, and the construction of the Wooden Horse that enabled the Greeks to take Troy.

Suitably for a warrior goddess, she was born not in the usual fashion but from the male head of Zeus, after which she natur-ally became his favourite daughter. When Zeus's first wife, Metis, was pregnant with their first child, Zeus learnt that she was destined to bear, as second child, a son who would displace him as king of gods and men. He solved the matter by swallowing his pregnant wife (p. 45). When the time came for the first child to be born, Hephaistos split Zeus's head with an axe and out sprang Athene, fully armed and shouting her war cry that resounded throughout heaven and earth.

Thus Athene was in a sense a reincarnation of *metis*, intelligence, and she was always seen as the personification of wisdom. She was known as *glaukopis* Athene, the meaning of which is uncertain, but 'grey-eyed', or 'flashing-eyed', or 'owl-faced' are possibilities. There are likewise various explanations of her epithet 'Pallas' Athene, the most likely being that it means 'Girl' or 'Maiden', or was derived from *pallein*, to brandish, for Athene was often depicted brandishing a spear.

On the whole Athene had benevolent relationships with mortals. Like all the gods, she could punish wrongs if need be, though usually not too vindictively. She blinded Teiresias, for instance, when he saw her bathing naked, but she gave him various benefits in reparation, including the art of prophecy (p. 289). She punished Arachne for presuming to challenge her to a weaving contest, then took pity on her and changed her into a spider, who would go on weaving for ever (p. 516). But she is more usually seen as supporting and encouraging her mortal favourites. Throughout Homer's *Odyssey* she is the constant friend and adviser of Odysseus, who is intelligent, resourceful and valiant like herself; and in art she watches over the mighty Herakles in hundreds of depictions of his various dangerous exploits.

Athene was the protectress of many cities throughout the Greek world, but she had a very special and intimate relationship with Athens, which is reflected in her name (though the precise relationship between the names of place and goddess is much debated). She vied with Poseidon to be patron of the city during the reign of Kekrops, both demonstrating their divine powers – Poseidon by creating a well of seawater on the Acropolis, Athene by planting an olive tree. Athene's gift was judged the greater benefit and thereafter she was Athens' special patron. She was even, in a sense, the ancestor of the Athenians themselves through their fifth king, Erichthonios, who was born when Hephaistos tried to ravish her against her will. In the struggle, his semen fell on her thigh and she wiped it off with a scrap of wool, which she threw to the ground. Where it fell, the earth conceived and subsequently brought forth Erichthonius. Athene became his foster-mother.

Between 447 and 438 BC the Athenians built in her honour the crowning monument of Athens on their Acropolis: the Parthenon (*parthenos*, virgin). Inside was the huge and famous statue of Athene, in ivory and gold, created by the great artist and sculptor Pheidias – which of course has been lost, but we know a great deal about its appearance from Pausanias's description (1.24.5–7) and from small Roman copies. Pheidias also made a colossal bronze statue of Athene that stood on the Acropolis (also lost). We know also from Pausanias (1.28.2) that the crest of Athene's helmet and the tip of her spear could be seen by homecoming Athenians from the sea, the bronze catching the sunlight, as soon as Cape Sounion was passed.

Ares

Ares (Mars), son of Zeus and Hera, is the god of war. In contrast to Athene, who oversees the controlled use of war to safeguard the community, Ares stands for the brutal aspects of warfare – battle-frenzy, bloodlust, cruelty, slaughter – all relished for their own sakes. His warlike sons by Aphrodite, Phobos ('Terror') and Deimos ('Fear'), often accompany him on the battlefield, as sometimes does Eris, goddess of strife, and the war-goddess Enyo (Bellona to the Romans), who is little more than a personification of bloody war.

Not surprisingly, Ares is generally disliked, both on earth and on Olympos (except by Aphrodite). In the *Iliad*, when Ares is wounded by Diomedes on the battlefield at Troy, he flees bellowing up to Olympos to complain to Zeus (5.888–98):

And cloud-gathering Zeus glared at him and said: 'Do not sit beside me and whine, you two-faced liar. To me you are the most hateful of all the gods on Olympos, for always strife is dear to your heart, and wars, and battles . . . Yet I cannot long endure you to suffer pain, for you are my own child, and it was to me that your mother bore you. But were you sprung from any other god, you pestilence, I would long ago have thrown you out of heaven.'

Ares never married, though he had several children by his lover Aphrodite (p. 71), and was the father of many mortal children, who were often savage and belligerent like Ares himself. These include the brigand Kyknos, who cut off the heads of passing strangers and used the skulls to build a temple to his father; Diomedes, king of the Thracian Bistones, who fed his horses on human flesh; Oinomaos, king of Elis, who forced the suitors of his daughter Hippodameia to run a lethal chariot race with him, then nailed their heads to the walls of his palace; and the Thracian king Tereus, who raped and cut out the tongue of the Athenian princess Philomela – cruel acts savagely avenged by her sister Prokne.

Ares was relatively little worshipped by the Greeks. In ancient art he is depicted fully armed, but he is not a popular figure and is usually a mere bystander in scenes with the other gods. The only myth illustrated with any frequency in which he is a key figure is his son Kyknos's fight with Herakles.

Ares' Roman equivalent, Mars, was in contrast a very important god, second only to the sovereign deity Jupiter. There was also a uniquely Roman story of Mars' birth. Juno was annoyed with Jupiter for producing Minerva from his own head without the need of a female, so she appealed for help to Flora, the goddess of flowers and spring. Flora had originally been a nymph named Chloris, who was loved by the West Wind, Zephyros. At his kiss she was transformed into Flora, and breathed out flowers that spread over all the earth, just as in spring the gentle West Wind warms the cold earth into blossoming. Flora now gave Juno a herb at whose touch she at once became pregnant, and Mars was the result.

Another uniquely Roman myth, related by Ovid, is the comic tale of Mars' association with the aged goddess Anna Perenna. He persuaded her to act as his go-between in his pursuit of the virgin goddess Minerva, though Anna knew that Minerva would never succumb to him. Despite this, she gave Mars every encouragement to think the opposite, and one night she herself took Minerva's place, heavily veiled, in an assignation with the god. Mars came eagerly to claim her favours, only to discover beneath the veil the old crone Anna.

Mars was the father of twin sons, Romulus and Remus, by Rhea Silvia, a Vestal Virgin, one of whom, Romulus, would grow up to be the founder of Rome (p. 498).

Hephaistos

Hephaistos (Vulcan) is the god of fire and metalworking, the divine blacksmith. He is sometimes said to be the son of Zeus and Hera, sometimes of Hera alone because she was angry with Zeus for bringing Athene to birth from his own head; but all sources agree that the smith-god was lame. Hera was so ashamed of his deformity that she flung him out of Olympos. He fell into the great river of Ocean surrounding the earth and was saved by the Nereid Thetis and the Oceanid Eurynome. For nine years he lived in a cave by the ocean, practising his smith's craft and fashioning all manner of fine jewellery for his two benefactresses.

Year by year his skill grew, and at last he used his expertise to take revenge on his cruel mother. He sent her a beautiful golden throne, which she accepted with delight, but attached to it were invisible fetters, and these held her fast as soon as she sat down. The other gods begged Hephaistos to come back to Olympos and release her, but he stubbornly refused to do so. Eventually Dionysos solved the problem: he plied Hephaistos with wine, then brought the intoxicated god up to heaven on the back of a mule (a favourite scene in ancient art, with Hephaistos riding on an ithyphallic mule and followed by satyrs and nymphs). Only then did he give in and set his mother free.

Dionysos brings Hephaistos to Hera, bound fast to her throne.

He must have forgiven Hera, for he tried to defend her when Zeus hung her from Olympos, with anvils tied to her feet, to punish her for persecuting his beloved son Herakles. Zeus was so angry at this interference that he grabbed Hephaistos by the feet and flung him a second time from Olympos. This time he fell through the air for a whole day before landing at sunset,

half dead, on the island of Lemnos – a fall which Milton immor-
talizes in *Paradise Lost* (1.742–6):

> ... from Morn
> To Noon he fell, from Noon to dewy Eve,
> A Summer's day; and with the setting Sun
> Dropt from the Zenith like a falling Star,
> On Lemnos th' Aegaean Ile ...

Here the inhabitants tended him, and ever afterwards he had a
special affection for the island, which in historical times was his
chief cult-centre in the Greek world. In due course he rejoined
the immortals on Olympos, apparently bearing no resentment
against Zeus.

In Hesiod's *Theogony*, Hephaistos is married to Aglaia, the
youngest of the Graces, and in Homer's *Iliad* simply to Charis
(Grace personified), but he is more usually said to be married
(unlikely as it might seem) to Aphrodite, the goddess of love
herself. In the *Odyssey*, Homer recounts the famous episode
when he takes his revenge on his unfaithful wife and her lover
Ares by trapping them beneath a magical, invisible net and
calling the other gods to witness their humiliation (p. 71). He
had no children by any of these wives and very few by mortal
women. The most significant of these is probably Periphetes,
who was weak on his legs like his father, and was known as the
'Club-bearer' because he always beat travellers to death with a
club of bronze. Theseus killed him.

As the divine master-craftsman, Hephaistos created master-
pieces of unparalleled beauty and intricacy. He built the palaces
of the gods themselves in gold and bronze, and his many other
works of art on Olympos included golden robots that attended
him in his forge, and tripods with golden wheels that moved at
his command. He made splendid arms and armour, both for
the gods and for favourite mortals, and he fashioned the great

golden cup of the Sun, which carried Helios around the streams of Ocean from west to east every night. He also created beautiful, ornate jewellery and other artefacts, usually for the gods, but occasionally these came into the hands of mortals and played a significant part in their lives (like the robe and necklace of Harmonia in the Theban saga; see Chapter 9). In ancient art the smith-god often wields an axe or a pair of blacksmith's tongs, and sometimes wears a tunic and a brimless workman's hat.

As god of fire, Hephaistos was thought to have not only a workshop on Olympos, but forges elsewhere in the world, wherever the earth gave forth emissions of smoke and fire, and especially beneath the volcanic Mount Etna in Sicily. Here, it was said, the one-eyed giants, the Cyclopes, worked under his direction, and the mountain resounded with the noise of their hammering, and quaked and smoked from the ceaseless fiery activity. (Though the monster Typhon and the giant Enkelados are also, as we have seen, credited with causing Etna's volcanic tumult.)

Three episodes from the *Iliad* vividly illustrate the three main, and very different, aspects of Hephaistos. In Book 18, Homer depicts the master-craftsman, with his massive, hairy torso and spindly legs, at work in his forge. He sweats and puffs over his anvil as he makes marvellous armour for Achilles, most notably a famous, fantastically ornate shield, in gold and silver, bronze and tin, decorated with a multitude of intricate pictures. Lame and ugly Hephaistos may be, but he can still create objects of magical beauty. Yet his deformity also makes him something of a figure of fun, and in Book 1 the comical aspect of the crippled smith-god comes to the fore, as he tries to make peace after a quarrel between Zeus and Hera. He bustles clumsily about, pouring wine, so that all the gods laugh at him and harmony is restored.

Finally, Book 21 presents the powerful and fearsome god of

fire, when Hephaistos comes, on Hera's command, down to the plain of Troy to dry up the floods of the river Skamandros (also called Xanthos), which is angrily trying to drown Achilles (21.361–7):

> The river blazed with fire, his lovely streams seething.
> And as a cauldron boils, set on a fierce flame,
> melting the fat of a well-fed hog, bubbling up
> on every side as dry sticks burn beneath,
> so Xanthos' lovely streams were burned with fire,
> and the water boiled, and would not flow along,
> but was stopped by the mighty blast of Hephaistos.

Hermes

Hermes (Mercury) is the gods' herald and messenger. Being such a mobile divinity, he is naturally the god who protects all travellers. He is also the god of boundaries, and his statues, known as *hermai*, 'herms', were set up wherever boundaries needed to be marked: at the roadside, at crossroads, and in particular at the thresholds of houses. These herms were four-sided stone pillars, topped with a bearded head of the god and with an erect phallus projecting from the front, and were believed to bring good fortune.

As god of travellers, Hermes acts as guide and escort to both men and gods; and as god of boundaries, he helps men to travel over the most formidable boundary of all, that between the land of the living and the land of the dead. In this role, known as Hermes *psychopompos*, 'conductor of souls', he leads the souls of the dead down to the Underworld.

Crafty and full of trickery himself, Hermes is suitably the god of merchants and traders, tricksters and thieves. He is the god of flocks and herds, and is especially concerned with their fertility (in art he is often shown carrying a ram over his shoulders).

As the patron of athletic contests, his statues were often erected in gymnasia.

In general he was benevolent to mortals and brought them luck and prosperity: a lucky find, a windfall, was known as a *hermaion* or a *hermaia dosis*, a 'gift of Hermes'. Not surprisingly, he is a very popular figure in ancient art, where he is easily recognized by his trademark symbol, the herald's staff (*caduceus* or *kerykeion*), and by his wide-brimmed traveller's hat (a *petasos*, sometimes winged) and winged boots or sandals.

Hermes was the son of Zeus and the Pleiad Maia, daughter of the Titan Atlas. He was born at dawning in a deep and shadowy cave on Mount Kyllene in Arcadia. The delightful *Homeric Hymn* (4) in his honour recounts the first deeds of this god who is 'wily and charming, a thief, a cattle-rustler, a bringer of dreams, a spy by night, a watcher at the door . . .' (13–15). As soon as he is born, Hermes is ready for mischief. At noon he springs from his cradle, and finding a tortoise outside the cave he creates the first lyre, using the shell for a sounding board and sheep gut for the seven strings. For a time he is content to make marvellous music with his new instrument, but all the while trickery is brewing in his heart.

At evening he sets off to steal the cattle belonging to Apollo. He finds the god's herds pasturing in the mountains of Pieria and carries off fifty cows, driving them backwards so as to confuse the trail and masking his own footprints with sandals made of brushwood. An old man, tilling a nearby vineyard, sees what he is doing, but Hermes sternly forbids him ever to speak of it.

Near the river Alpheios the little god pauses to build a fire. Here he sacrifices two of the cows, dividing the meat into twelve portions for the gods but eating none himself, much as he would like to. Then leaving the rest of the cattle behind, he returns to his mother's cave and creeps back into his cradle, pulling his swaddling clothes over him and looking the very picture of baby innocence. Maia is not deceived. 'Where have you come from at this hour of the night, all covered in shamelessness?' she cries, '. . . Your father got you to be a great worry to mortal men and to the immortal gods' (155–61).

In the morning, Apollo sets off to hunt for his stolen cows. The old man who witnessed the theft tells the god that he has seen a child driving them off, and Apollo, with his powers of prophecy, now knows who the culprit is. He goes angrily to Maia's cave (235–42):

And when the little son of Zeus and Maia saw Apollo in a rage about his cattle, he snuggled down inside his fragrant baby-clothes; and just as the deep embers of tree-stumps are covered over with wood ash, so Hermes cuddled down when he saw the Far-shooter. He drew his head and hands and feet together into a little space, like a newborn baby seeking the sweetness of sleep, even though in fact he was wide awake.

After searching the cave and finding nothing, Apollo demands to know where his cattle are, even threatening to cast Hermes down to Hades and make him the ruler of all the babies there. Hermes innocently denies all knowledge of the theft. 'Do I look like a cattle-rustler, a strong man?' he asks. 'This is no task for me; rather I care about other things. I care about having my sleep, and my mother's milk, and shawls round my shoulders, and warm baths.' He even denies all knowledge of what cows are, claiming to know of them only by hearsay.

Apollo is amused, but not convinced. He takes the infant up to Olympos and tells the whole story to Zeus. Hermes resolutely carries on lying, but despite his protestations of innocence, Zeus orders him to show Apollo where he has hidden the cattle. So he does (this is, after all, Zeus speaking); then to avert Apollo's anger he takes up his lyre and plays so enchantingly that the god wants the instrument for himself. They make a bargain: Apollo will keep the lyre and Hermes will become divine keeper of herds. The two are ever afterwards firm friends.

The old man who saw Hermes stealing Apollo's cattle is called Battos in later accounts, which develop his part in the story. According to Ovid (*Metamorphoses* 2.679–707), Hermes bribes the old man with a cow to say nothing of what he has seen, and he replies that a stone will more readily tell of the theft than he. A little while later the god returns in disguise and tests Battos, offering him a cow and a bull if he can tell him anything about the stolen cattle. Tempted by the double reward, the old man tells all he knows, so Hermes transforms his betrayer, very appropriately, into a stone.

Dionysos

Dionysos (Liber, Bacchus) is the god of wine and intoxication, of ritual madness and ecstatic liberation from everyday identity. Homer calls him a 'joy for mortals' (*Iliad* 14.325) and Hesiod 'he of many delights' (*Theogony* 941). He introduced wine to men, says Euripides, 'which, when they drink their fill, banishes the sufferings of wretched mortals, and brings forgetfulness of each day's troubles in sleep. There is no other cure for sorrow . . .' (*Bakchai* 278–83). Dionysos is a nature god, representing the sap of life, the coursing of the blood through the veins, the throbbing excitement and mystery of sex and life and growth.

He is also the god of the theatre and impersonation, the theatrical mask being the symbol of this transformation of identity. At the dramatic festivals of Athens, the image of Dionysos, as god of the theatre, was carried in to watch the performances put on in his honour. And in two very different plays from the late fifth century BC, the god himself takes part, becoming a richly comic character in Aristophanes' *Frogs*, and in Euripides' *Bakchai* the sinister, smiling god who orchestrates Pentheus' destruction (p. 473).

Dionysos had a revelling train of ecstatic followers: maenads, satyrs and silens, all celebrating the god's rites with wine and music, song and dance, and sometimes, in their ecstasy, tearing animals to pieces (*sparagmos*) and eating the flesh raw (*omophagia*). These bacchanals are an ever-popular theme in ancient art. Maenads ('frenzied women') – also known as Bakchai (Bacchae) or Bacchants ('women of Bacchus') – wear fawnskins and wreaths of ivy, oak or bryony, and sometimes girdle themselves with snakes. They carry the thyrsos, the magical wand of the god, made from a fennel rod with a bunch of ivy leaves attached to the tip, and sometimes torches or branches of oak or fir.

From ancient literature we get a dramatic picture of maenads in miraculous action, both peaceful and violent, from Euripides' tragedy *Bakchai*. Up on Mount Kithaeron, they handle snakes and suckle wild animals. At a touch they draw springs of water and wine and milk from rocks and earth, while from their thyrsoi flow streams of sweet honey. But when enraged, they are inspired with tremendous physical strength: they uproot trees, and tear cattle and even humans to pieces. Their thyrsoi become dangerous weapons against an enemy, while their own bodies are impervious to iron and fire.

Satyrs and silens (their names were often used interchangeably) were also natural followers of Dionysos, for they were male creatures of the wild with a voracious appetite for sex and wine, and a love of music and revelry. The Romans identified them with their native woodland spirits, the fauns. They were primarily human in form but with some animal features. Three labelled silens appear on the famous (and early, *c*.570 BC) François Krater, each with horses' ears, tails and hind-legs. Their activities give a neat visual summary of their character: one carries a wineskin, one plays the double pipes, and one embraces a nymph.

In later art satyrs more commonly have human legs, and are usually depicted with rough hair, snub noses, horses' ears and tails, and perpetual proud erections; while later still, in Hellenistic art, they often have goatish features. They are shown in typical satyrs' pursuits – accompanying Dionysos, making music, dancing, helping with the vintage, chasing nymphs or maenads, copulating with animals, and masturbating.

The satyrs' leader was Silenos, old and wise and the most drunken of them all, who was said to have been the young Dionysos' tutor. 'A drunken old man,' says Ovid (*Metamorphoses* 4.26–7) 'who supports his tottering limbs with a staff, or clings unsteadily to his hump-backed donkey.' Yet intoxication inspired Silenos's wine-hazed mind with special knowledge and powers of prophecy. The Phrygian king Midas once sought to share his wisdom, so he caught the old man by lacing with wine the fountain at which he drank. When Silenos fell asleep after drinking, the king's servants seized him and took him to their master. The satyr's philosophy was pessimistic: he told Midas that the best thing for man is not to be born at all, and the second best thing is to die as soon as possible.

Dionysos himself is depicted most frequently of all the gods in ancient art. He is easily identified by his attributes of drinking vessel and ivy wreath, and by his special emblem, the thyrsos. He often appears as god of wine, accompanied by his ecstatic followers and sometimes by panthers or snakes. Until about 430 BC, he is shown as a bearded, ivy-wreathed, mature man, wearing long robes and often a deerskin or panther-skin. He grows younger with time, and after 430 he is usually youthful, beardless and naked or semi-naked. Sometimes he is accompanied by Ariadne, the mortal bride whom he carried to Olympos and made immortal after Theseus abandoned her (p. 251).

He was the son of Zeus and a mortal woman, Semele, daughter of Kadmos, king of Thebes. When Hera found out that Semele was pregnant, she came down to earth to destroy her rival. Disguised as Semele's old nurse, she sowed doubt in the girl's mind as to whether her lover really was Zeus, and suggested that she settle the question by asking him to appear to her in all his godlike glory, just as he had appeared to Hera herself when he wooed her.

So the credulous Semele did just this: she persuaded Zeus to promise her any favour she chose, then made her request. He had no choice but to carry out his promise. He came to her as the great storm-god, lord of the lightning, and she was burnt to ashes. Yet even as she died, he snatched the unborn child from her womb and stitched him into a gash cut in his own thigh. There Dionysos grew until he could be born full-term. It was said that Semele's tomb at Thebes continued to smoulder for years; but everything ended well for her after all, for she was later made immortal – fetched by Dionysos from Hades and taken to Olympos, where she was renamed Thyone.

When the infant was born, Zeus sent him to be brought up by Semele's sister Ino and her husband Athamas. They dressed him as a girl to hide him from the ever-jealous Hera, but eventually she learnt the truth. She punished Ino and Athamas by driving them mad, and in their madness they killed their own children.

Next Zeus evaded Hera by transforming Dionysos into a young goat, then took him to be brought up by the nymphs of Mount Nysa (variously located). Yet even when he had grown to manhood, Hera was still hostile to him. Driven mad by her, he wandered the world, through Egypt and Syria to Phrygia, and here at last he was cured by Rheia/Kybele. He still travelled on, even as far as India, before returning to Greece, spreading his worship on his journeys and dispensing to mortals knowledge of the vine and its pleasures.

One such mortal to receive a vine from the god was the Attic farmer Ikarios (p. 232). Another was said to be Oineus, the king of Kalydon, perhaps because of his name's similarity to that of wine (*oinos*). Some said that the boon came to him through his herdsman, Staphylos ('Bunch of Grapes'), when he noticed that one of his goats had taken to coming home from pasture later than the rest and in a very frisky mood. When Staphylos followed the goat, he found it enjoying grapes from a vine, so he carried some of this new fruit to his master, and Oineus squeezed the juice from the grapes and made the first wine.

At one stage Dionysos was kidnapped by pirates, a story recounted in one of the *Homeric Hymns* (7) to the god. The pirates saw him as their ship came in to land (2–6):

He appeared on a headland by the shore of the barren sea, looking like a young man in the first flower of his youth. Beautiful were the dark locks of hair that waved about him, and on his sturdy shoulders he wore a purple cloak.

The pirates took him for a person of royal birth who would fetch a large ransom, so they seized him and carried him off in their ship, even though the bonds with which they tied him fell away of their own accord. The helmsman alone recognized that this was no ordinary mortal and tried to warn his comrades, but they paid him no heed.

In mid-ocean, strange miracles began to occur: wine ran streaming through the ship, and vines and ivy grew from the mast and sail. A ravening bear appeared on the deck, and the god became a dreadful, roaring lion and sprang upon the pirate captain. The terrified sailors leapt overboard and were transformed into dolphins (which is why dolphins, having once been human themselves, have ever since been friendly to men). The only one to be spared was the helmsman who had spoken out on the god's behalf. He became an ardent follower of Dionysos.

Several of Dionysos' myths tell how mortals persecuted him, refusing to recognize his divinity or to accept his rites. Usually they came to a bad, and often bloody, end. A good example is the myth of Lykourgos, king of the Edonians in Thrace. His story first occurs in Homer (*Iliad* 6.130–40), who says that he pursued Dionysos and his nurses down from the sacred mountain of Nysa, striking at them with an ox-goad. He terrified them so much that the god had to dive into the sea and take refuge with the sea-goddess Thetis. Lykourgos was struck blind by Zeus in punishment and soon afterwards died, hated by all the gods.

His fate becomes bloodier as time goes by. According to Apollodorus (3.5.1), Dionysos punished Lykourgos by driving him mad, and in his madness he struck his son Dryas dead with an axe, believing that he was pruning a grapevine. After cutting off his son's extremities, he regained his sanity, but soon afterwards the land became barren, and his people learnt that it would bear fruit again only if they put him to death. He was torn to pieces by wild horses. Hyginus has yet another version (*Fabula* 132) in which Lykourgos became drunk and tried to rape his own mother, then killed his wife and son, and finally cut off his own foot, believing it to be a vine. Dionysos then had him devoured by panthers.

Women too were punished for refusing to worship the god. Minyas, the king of Orchomenos, had three daughters, Leukippe, Alkathoe (or Alkithoe) and Arsippe (or Arsinoe). All three of them ignored the festival of Dionysos: being industrious girls, they preferred to stay indoors all day, weaving at their looms, instead of going out and joining in the revels with the other women. In one version of the story (Antoninus Liberalis 10), Dionysos himself appeared to them in the form of a young girl and urged them not to neglect his rites. When they spurned his advice, he turned himself into a bull, a lion and a leopard, while milk and nectar flowed from their looms. The terrified sisters drew lots to see who should sacrifice to the god, and when Leukippe's lot came out, they seized her son Hippasos and tore him to pieces, then went outdoors to join the revelling maenads. Finally they were turned into a bat and two kinds of owl; or, in another version, a crow, a bat and an owl.

In Ovid's version (*Metamorphoses* 4.1–415), they worked at their looms all day, contentedly telling stories to one another. Then suddenly at dusk their looms sprouted grapevines and their threads vine-tendrils, the rooms glowed with fire, and the house was filled with smoke and the sound of wild beasts howling. The three girls fled in terror to remote corners of the house, and there all three were turned into bats.

The most famous of all these opposition myths is that of Pentheus, the young king of Thebes, who was torn to pieces by his own mother (his fate will be the subject of a later chapter, p. 473). Dionysos was indeed a god with a dual nature: as Euripides puts it (*Bakchai* 861), he was a god 'most terrible and most gentle to mortals'.

Hades and the Underworld

When the three sons of Kronos divided the universe among themselves, Zeus and Poseidon ruled in the upper world, while Hades took as his domain the misty darkness of the Underworld – which itself is often called simply Hades. Here he presided over the souls of the dead. He was certainly a grim and sinister god, but he was in no sense evil or Satanic, just as his kingdom was very different from the Christian Hell. His wife, and the queen of the Underworld, was his niece, Demeter's daughter Persephone (Proserpina), whom he had once abducted (p. 62).

Hades had other names: he was called euphemistically Plouton, 'Rich One', because of all the riches that come from the earth. The Romans too adopted this title, Latinizing it to Pluto, and also calling him Dis, a contraction of *dives* ('rich'), and Orcus. He was given a wide variety of epithets, such as *Stugeros*, 'Hateful', *Polydektes* and *Polydegmon*, 'Receiver of Many', *Polyxeinos*, 'Host to Many', *Klumenos*, 'Renowned', *Eubouleus*, 'Good Counsellor'; and he was known too as *Zeus Katachthonios*, 'Zeus of the Underworld', this last emphasizing his absolute power over his realm. He had almost no cult, since his jurisdiction was confined to the souls of the dead and he had no interest in the living. Unsurprisingly, he is seldom the subject of ancient art. When he is, he often carries a sceptre or a key as a symbol of his authority, or a cornucopia in his nature of Plouton.

His subterranean realm was a chill and sunless place, watered by five rivers: the Styx (Hateful River), the Acheron (River of Woe), the Kokytos (River of Lamentation), the Phlegethon (River of Flame), and the Lethe (River of Forgetfulness). In *Paradise Lost*, Milton neatly sums up the attributes of all five (2.577–86):

> Abhorred Styx, the flood of deadly hate,
> Sad Acheron of sorrow, black and deep;
> Cocytus, nam'd of lamentation loud
> Heard on the rueful stream; fierce Phlegethon
> Whose waves of torrent fire inflame with rage.
> Far off from these a slow and silent stream,
> Lethe, the River of Oblivion, rolls
> Her wat'ry labyrinth, whereof who drinks
> Forthwith his former state and being forgets,
> Forgets both joy and grief, pleasure and pain.

Of the five rivers, Lethe was seen as comparatively kindly, since the ability to forget the pains of human existence can be a blessing – as Byron emphasizes in his *Don Juan*. (The reference here to the sea-goddess Thetis concerns her attempt to make her son Achilles immortal by immersing him in the river Styx.)

> And if I laugh at any mortal thing,
>   'Tis that I may not weep; and if I weep
> 'Tis that our nature cannot always bring
>   Itself to apathy, for we must steep
> Our hearts first in the depths of Lethe's spring
>   Ere what we least wish to behold will sleep:
> Thetis baptized her mortal son in Styx;
> A mortal mother would on Lethe fix.

Homer puts the entrance to Hades in the far west, beyond the river of Ocean, but the ancients believed that there were also entrances within the known world: through a cave at Tainaron (still to be seen at the tip of the middle promontory of the southern Peloponnese), through a bottomless lake at Lerna in the Argolid, and through a cave by Lake Avernus, near Naples.

At the boundaries of the Underworld lay the rivers Styx and Acheron, and to their banks came the souls of the dead, escorted by Hermes. If they had received proper burial, the aged ferryman Charon carried them across the waters in his boat, charging a fee of one obol for his trouble. (It was customary to bury the dead with this coin left in their mouths as Charon's payment.)

Charon himself was naturally seen as something of a forbidding figure. He appears in Aristophanes' comedy *The Frogs* (180–270), where he is portrayed as brusque, churlish and abusive as he conveys Dionysos across Acheron to Hades. The god has to do his own rowing while Charon steers. Our first extant picture of Charon in ancient art is on a black-figure vase of about 500 BC, and after that he is frequently depicted on white-ground funerary lekythoi, dressed as a labourer and standing with a punt-pole at the stern of his boat. He becomes more squalid as time goes by. Virgil sees him as distinctly unsavoury (*Aeneid* 298–301): 'a dreaded ferryman, frightful and foul, his chin covered with unkempt hoary hair, his fierce eyes lit with fire, and a filthy cloak hanging from a knot on his shoulder'.

The Styx itself was thought to have its source within the mortal world, then to drop from a sheer, high cliff before flowing through the darkness beneath the earth. At Nonakris in Arcadia there is a real-life Styx, so named at least as early as the sixth century BC, with waters cold from the snows that feed it and just such a waterfall. Pausanias (8.17.6–18.6) records that its waters were instantly fatal, and that they broke or corroded all materials except the hooves of horses. There was a rumour that Alexander the Great met his death by water from the Styx, sent to him in a mule's hoof. Conversely, there is a modern superstition that anyone who drinks from the Arcadian Styx on the right day in the year will become immortal.

Once across the Styx, the dead soul entered Hades by its gates, which were guarded by a fearsome watchdog, Kerberos, offspring of the monsters Typhon and Echidna. His task was to ensure that those who entered the Underworld never left. 'Wagging his tail and drooping his ears he fawns on those who enter,' says Hesiod (*Theogony* 770–3), 'though he never lets them go back out again, but lies in wait and devours anyone he catches trying to pass out of the gates.' Hesiod describes him as 'unmanageable, unspeakable Kerberos who eats raw flesh, the hound of Hades with a voice of bronze, fifty-headed, bold and strong' (310–12), though he was more usually said to have only three heads. (In art, for practical reasons, he is usually shown with two or three heads, and occasionally just one.) His tail was a fierce serpent and hissing snakes sprouted from his body.

The myths tell of a few privileged mortals who visited Hades while still living, yet managed to escape safely back to earth again. Herakles did so, when as one of his twelve Labours he captured Kerberos himself and took him up into the world to show to Eurystheus – after which he returned the dog to his post. Odysseus travelled to the edge of the Underworld, to seek advice from the shade of the seer Teiresias about his journey home to Ithaca, and there met many souls of the dead. Aeneas travelled down to meet the shade of his father Anchises, who told him of the future greatness of Rome. Orpheus descended, hoping (and failing) to bring his dead wife Eurydice back to life. These all made the journey safely back again to the light of the sun. But when Theseus and Peirithoos went down to the Underworld with the intention of abducting Persephone, Hades trapped them in seats from which they had no power to move. Theseus was eventually rescued by Herakles, on his quest for Kerberos, but Peirithoos stayed fixed firmly in his seat for ever.

Within the Underworld the dead souls lived a shadowy existence on the Plain of Asphodel. Homer's Achilles best sums up the quality of this afterlife when his shade meets Odysseus at the edge of Hades. Odysseus tries to console Achilles for his death by speaking of the authority he must now hold among the dead. Achilles replies unforgettably (*Odyssey* 11.489–91): 'I would rather be alive and toiling as serf to another man, one with no land and nothing much to live on, than be a king over all the perished dead.'

According to later writers, Hades had a distinct area known as Elysion (or Elysium, or the Elysian Fields) which became the dwelling place for a few privileged mortals after death. Here through the favour of the gods they lived for ever in blissful ease. Certainly Homer mentions Elysion as the place where favoured souls went when dead, naming it as the future home of Menelaos, who, as the son-in-law of Zeus, would win a blessed eternal life there (*Odyssey* 4.561–8), though he locates Elysion, not in Hades, but near the stream of Ocean at the

western bounds of the earth. Ruled over by the wise Rhadamanthys, it never sees snow, or harsh winter, or rain.

Hesiod, in his *Works and Days* (167–73), calls this happy
land the Islands of the Blest, ruled over by Kronos (so here he
gives the Titan a happier end than he does in his *Theogony*,
where, as we have seen, Kronos and the other Titans were
thrown into Tartaros). Hesiod naturally emphasizes – hard-
working farmer that he was – a life of ease on these Islands,
where the earth gives forth harvest three times a year of its own
accord. Pindar too (*Olympian Ode* 2.56–83, fr. 129) speaks of
a world without labour and without tears, a land of eternal
sunlight, of golden fruit and flowers, of meadows red with
roses, where favoured mortals have unending leisure to enjoy
peaceful occupations of their choice. Pausanias (3.19.11–13)
even locates the abode of the blessed within the known world,
on Leuke, the White Island, near the mouth of the Danube.
Here a certain Leonymos saw the shades of heroes living in
eternal bliss, and among them Achilles – now no longer, we
assume, mourning his lost life on earth.

It was later commonly thought that this Elysion was a particular part of Hades, isolated from the area where the shades
of ordinary mortals lived their dreary life after death. This is
certainly the case in Virgil, where in the *Aeneid* (Book 6) Aeneas
meets his father Anchises in the Underworld. For Virgil, Elysion
is the place where the good soul rests before being reborn.

There was in Hades, as well as a special place for blessed
souls, an area where wrongdoers were punished for their sins
committed on earth. This in due course came to be known as
Tartaros (rather different from Hesiod's Tartaros, which was
one of the primal entities along with Gaia and Eros). Four
famous sinners in particular are said to have suffered eternal
punishment, three of whom were seen by Odysseus on his visit
to the Underworld described in the *Odyssey* (Book 11). The

giant Tityos was shot dead by Apollo and Artemis for trying to rape their mother Leto, and Odysseus saw him tied to the ground in Hades, sprawled over two acres, while two vultures squatted on either side of him, tearing at his liver. The tissues always re-grew, so his torment never ended.

Next Odysseus saw Tantalos, once a wealthy Lydian king and a favourite of the gods, even invited to dine at their divine tables; but he abused their trust, offending them so much that they punished him for eternity in Hades. Homer does not specify his crime, but various offences are ascribed to him in later sources. Either he invited the gods to a feast at which he served them the flesh of his own son Pelops, cut up and stewed, with the presumptuous intention of testing their omniscience (p. 427), or he divulged the gods' secrets to men, or he stole some of their nectar and ambrosia to share with his mortal friends. His punishment caused him eternal 'tantalizing' torment, as described by Odysseus (11.582–92):

'I saw Tantalos, suffering pains hard to bear,
standing in a lake with water up to his chin.
Thirsty he was, but unable to quench his thirst,
for every time the old man stooped, longing to drink,
the water drained away and vanished, and black earth
showed at his feet where the god dried it up.
Above his head, fruit cascaded from towering trees,
pears and pomegranates and shining apples,
and sweet figs and ripened olives, but whenever
the old man reached for them with his hands, a wind
tossed them away towards the shadowing clouds.'

Odysseus also witnessed the punishment of Sisyphos, once the king of Corinth and a great trickster, famous for his cunning and ingenuity (and sometimes said to have been the father of the wily Odysseus himself). Sisyphos was altogether a rather endearing rogue. His first crime was to tell tales on Zeus, who in his usual amorous fashion had carried off Aigina, the beautiful daughter of the river-god Asopos. Sisyphos had seen the abduction, and he promised to tell the girl's frantic father all he knew, in return for a spring of fresh water for his high citadel at Corinth. The river-god at once granted him the spring of Peirene, so Sisyphos told him exactly what had happened. Intent on saving his daughter, Asopos furiously pursued Zeus, but he was finally driven back to his own river by the great god's thunderbolts. (In historical times, coal could be found in the river Asopos and was thought to be the result of Zeus's attack.)

Zeus carried Aigina off to the island of Oinone, where in the fullness of time she bore him a son, Aiakos, who, when he grew up, renamed the island after his mother. In time he grew lonely, so Zeus gave his son companions by turning all the Aiginetan ants (*murmekes*) into humans, who were then known as Myrmidons.

Despite this happy outcome for Zeus, he still took revenge on his informer by sending Thanatos (Death) to take Sisyphos off to the Underworld – but the great trickster was a match even for Death. He outwitted Thanatos and tied him up, so that for a while no mortal at all could die. The gods were displeased by this state of affairs, so they sent the war-god Ares to deal with the situation. Ares released Thanatos and handed Sisyphos over to him to meet his death, but the rascal still had a trick up his sleeve, since before dying he had instructed his wife Merope on no account to perform the customary funeral rites. This so affronted Hades that he sent Sisyphos back to earth to reproach his wife and make the proper arrangements. Sisyphos, of course, did no such thing, but stayed happily on earth and lived to a ripe old age.

When he finally reached the Underworld at the end of his natural life, he was set an eternal punishment of perpetually rolling a great boulder up a hill, only to have it roll down again just as he neared the top (a 'sisyphean task' indeed, demanding endless and frustrating labour). Odysseus describes it (11.593–600):

'I saw Sisyphos, suffering pains hard to bear.
With both arms embracing a gigantic stone,
pushing with hands and feet, he would thrust
the stone to the top of a hill, but when it was about
to go over the top, a mighty force turned it round,
and the pitiless stone rolled back to the ground below.
He strained once more to push it, and the sweat
ran from his limbs, and dust rose from his head.'

From a mortal's point of view, a man who could cheat Death deserves an accolade rather than punishment, so perhaps it is happier to view Sisyphos' efforts as does Albert Camus, in his *Le mythe de Sisyphe: Essai sur l'absurde*. Camus takes Sisyphos' strivings as a symbol for the absurdity of this life and the futility of man's endeavours, but he asserts that happiness can still be found in the recognition of our condition and in the struggle to rise above it. He ends:

I leave Sisyphos at the foot of the mountain. One always finds one's burden again. But Sisyphos teaches the higher fidelity that negates the gods and raises rocks. He too concludes that all is well . . . The struggle towards the heights is enough to fill a man's heart. One must imagine Sisyphos happy.

A fourth great sinner was Ixion, a Thessalian king and ruler of the Lapiths. He was the Greek Cain, the first mortal to shed a kinsman's blood. He married Dia, the daughter of Deioneus (or Eioneus), promising his father-in-law bride-gifts and inviting him to collect them. When Deioneus arrived, he fell into a pit of fire prepared by Ixion and perished. Yet evil though this murder was, it was not the crime for which Ixion was eternally punished.

No mortal was willing to purify Ixion of so terrible a deed, but at last Zeus took pity on him and took him up to Olympos, where he not only purified him, but cured him of the madness that had beset him after the murder. Ixion repaid his benefactor by trying to rape Hera. When she told Zeus what had happened, he fashioned a cloud (*nephele*) in her likeness and put it in Ixion's bed to test the truth of her story. Ixion ravished the cloud, which in due course produced a child, Kentauros. He in turn copulated with wild Magnesian mares on the slopes of Mount Pelion, and from these were born the Centaurs, part man and part horse, a race of savage and brutal beasts.

Zeus punished Ixion by binding him to the four spokes of an ever-turning wheel of fire. In early times this wheel was thought to revolve around the world in the sight of men, to teach them the dangers of ingratitude to benefactors, but later Ixion and his wheel came to be located in Tartaros. Sometimes it was said that the wheel was covered with snakes.

Some dead souls were thought to suffer in Hades endless and futile tasks in the same way as Sisyphos. The daughters of Danaos, who in life had murdered their husbands, forever tried to draw water into leaking vessels that had always to be refilled. And Oknos endured an eternal task that reiterated his sufferings on earth. In life he had been an industrious man with an extravagant wife who, work as hard as Oknos might, at once spent everything that he earned. After death he was forced continually to plait a rope, while by him stood a she-ass, eating the rope as fast as he could plait it.

But this is all relatively mild, compared to the fearsome place that Tartaros was to become late on in the ancient world, where the wicked in general were subjected to eternal torment for their crimes committed on earth. Three adjudicators passed judgement on dead souls: Aiakos, who also kept the keys of the kingdom, and the brothers Rhadamanthys and Minos. In life Minos and Rhadamanthys had been members of the Cretan royal house, celebrated for their wisdom and justice as law-givers, while Aiakos (the son born to Aigina: see above) had always been a paragon of righteousness. Now they condemned all evildoers to Tartaros, and here the Furies punished sinners after death, torturing and terrifying the shades of the dead, as in Virgil's powerful account in *Aeneid* Book 6. This would greatly influence the Christian conception of the torments of Hell.

MINOR GODS

A few minor gods should be mentioned who, important though they are, still do not rank with the great Olympians.

Pan

Pan is a rural god, a god of shepherds and flocks, part man and part goat, and identified by the Romans with the rustic gods Faunus and Silvanus. In ancient art he is at first depicted as all goat, but later he becomes mainly human, but with a goat's horns, ears and legs. His *Homeric Hymn* (19) celebrates his birth in Arcadia, the wild and mountainous central region of the Peloponnese. His father was the god Hermes, who had fallen in love with the (unnamed) daughter of an Arcadian hero, Dryops, and for her sake spent his time tending her father's sheep. He won her love, and she bore him a most unusual son (35–47):

... who from his birth was a wonder to behold, with the feet of a goat and two horns – a noisy, laughing child. When the nurse saw his uncouth face and bearded chin she was afraid, and springing up she fled and left the boy. But Hermes the luck-bringer took him in his arms, and immeasurable joy filled his heart. He went quickly to the abodes of the immortal gods, carrying the child wrapped in the warm pelts of mountain hares, and setting him down beside Zeus and the rest of the gods, he showed them his son. Then all the immortals were filled with rejoicing, especially Dionysos, and they called the child Pan ('All') because he delighted all their hearts.

Pan is a god of the wild countryside, a lustful and sportive nature-spirit. He spends his days wandering the lonely reaches of mountain and forest, sleeping in the heat of the noontide (when it is thought very dangerous to disturb him), and playing soft and haunting melodies on the pipes of reed which he himself invented. This came about, according to Ovid (*Metamorphoses* 1.689–712), when he was pursuing a nymph who had taken his fancy – another favourite occupation of his. Syrinx was her name. But she rejected Pan's advances, preferring to live the life of a virgin huntress, and she fled from him until she reached the river Ladon. Here she could go no further. Desperately she prayed to the river-nymphs to save her, and they did so, for just as Pan thought he had at last caught hold of her, he found that instead of the nymph's body he was clutching a bunch of marsh reeds. He sighed with disappointment, and as the air blew through the reeds it produced a sad and haunting sound. Enchanted by so sweet a music, he cut the reeds into different lengths and joined them into the first set of Pan-pipes, giving them the Greek name of *syrinx* after his lost love.

Pan pursued other nymphs – indeed, no nymph was safe from him. (Nor, on occasion, were shepherd boys, nor even the animals from their flocks.) One such nymph was Pitys, who, like Syrinx, fled from his advances. She was turned into a pine tree (*pitys*), and this is why Pan often liked to decorate his brow with wreathes of pine leaves. In another version, Pitys looked with favour on Pan, but he had a rival for her love: Boreas, the wintry god of the North Wind. Boreas was so jealous when

Pitys chose Pan that he blew her to her death from the top of a cliff. The Earth where her body landed took pity on her and turned her into a pine tree, and she can be heard weeping whenever Boreas blows through her branches.

In the fifth century BC, Pan's worship spread from Arcadia into Attica and Boiotia, and from there to the rest of the Greek world. Having such a lustful nature, he was thought to be responsible for the fecundity of flocks and herds, and of the animal domain in general: when a need was felt to encourage reproduction, his statue was beaten with squills to stimulate his powers of fertility.

He showed particular favour to the Athenians, appearing to the runner Philippides (sometimes wrongly named Pheidippides) on a mountain track in Arcadia, while he was running from Athens to Sparta to ask for help against the Persians on the eve of the battle of Marathon (490 BC). Pan asked why the Athenians did not worship him, since he had often helped them in the past and would do so again in the future. As it turned out, the Spartans could give no aid, but nevertheless (clearly with Pan's help) the Athenians won a great victory at Marathon. They dedicated to Pan the cave-shrine still to be seen on the slopes of the Acropolis, and instituted sacrifices and torch races in his honour. Menander's comedy *The Bad-tempered Man* shows us a religious celebration in honour of Pan, held at the god's cave at Phyle in Attica. A sheep is sacrificed, a meal is enjoyed, and the happy and rowdy celebrations last all night, with drinking and dancing in the presence of the god.

A legend recorded by Plutarch (*Moralia* 419b–d) tells of the 'death of Pan'. During the reign of Tiberius (AD 14–37), the passengers of a ship sailing along the western coast of Greece heard a mysterious voice apparently calling to the pilot, an Egyptian named Thamuz, that 'Great Pan (*Pan megas*) is dead'. This was most likely a misinterpretation of a ritual cry, when the title *pammegas* ('all-great') was applied to the Syrian god Tammuz, identified with Adonis, during the annual celebration of his death and resurrection. But Christians took the statement to relate to the death and resurrection of Christ, and to signify the death of the pagan gods and the end of the pagan era. It was said that at this very same time the responses of the pagan oracles ceased forever.

Despite this, Pan lives on, for his unseen presence is the cause of 'panic' (*panikos*), the overwhelming and irrational terror that can strike violently and unexpectedly, particularly in the silence (or the inexplicable sounds) of the lonely, rocky places where he dwells.

The Dioskouroi

The Dioskouroi ('Boys of Zeus') were the 'Heavenly Twins' Kastor and Polydeukes (Latinized to the Dioscuri and Castor and Pollux). They were the sons of Leda by Zeus and her husband Tyndareos, the king of Sparta: Kastor was the mortal son of Tyndareos and Polydeukes the immortal son of Zeus.

The twins were inseparable from the time of their birth. Kastor was renowned for his skill at horsemanship (though both brothers rode swift white horses), while Polydeukes excelled at boxing. They lived the normal life of any great hero of their generation, together voyaging with the Argonauts to win the Golden Fleece and taking part with Meleagros in the Kalydonian Boarhunt. But they were killed before they could fight in the Trojan War, or succeed to the Spartan throne.

The trouble began when they quarrelled with their cousins Idas and Lynkeus, the sons of Aphareus, king of Messenia, a dispute that finally resulted in death for three out of the four. Sometimes the quarrel was said to be over their cousins Hilaeira and Phoibe, the daughters of Leukippos (brother to both Tyndareos and Aphareus), and often called simply the Leukippides. Idas and

Lynkeus were betrothed to these girls, but the Dioskouroi seized them, perhaps on their very wedding day, and carried them off to Sparta. Hilaeira married Kastor, and Phoibe married Polydeukes, and both girls gave birth to sons.

The other reason for the quarrel was a disagreement over cattle. This seems to have been the older version, for Proclus reports that the *Kypria* told of the Dioskouroi stealing their cousins' cattle. Pindar, who recounts the results of the final, fatal argument (*Nemean Ode* 10), simply says, 'Idas was in some way angered about his cattle', but in Apollodorus we find a delightfully detailed story (3.11.2). The four cousins together stole a great herd of cattle from Arcadia and it was given to Idas to divide the spoils. He cut a cow into four, and said that half the spoils would go to the one who ate his share of the meat first, and the rest to him who ate his share second. Before they knew where they were, Idas, who was a prodigious trencherman, had himself eaten both his own and his brother's share. He then drove the whole herd of cattle off to their home in Messenia. In revenge for what seemed to them very unfair dealing, the Dioskouroi marched against Messenia and recovered the stolen cattle, taking many more besides. They then lay in wait for Idas and Lynkeus.

For an account of the fatal battle we go back to Pindar. Lynkeus, who was gifted with superhuman vision so acute that he could see even through solid objects, ran to the top of Mount Taygetos and from there, scanning the countryside below, he saw Kastor and Polydeukes hiding in a hollow oak tree. So he and Idas were able to take the Dioskouroi by surprise, Idas mortally wounding Kastor by stabbing through the tree with his spear. Polydeukes, being immortal, was safe from injury, and now he leapt out and pursued the brothers to the tomb of their father Aphareus. Here they turned to fight, and in desperation uprooted the tombstone and flung it at their pursuer. Undeterred, Polydeukes killed Lynkeus with his spear while Zeus hurled a thunderbolt at Idas.

With both cousins dead, Polydeukes returned to Kastor, who was now on the point of death. Weeping, Polydeukes begged Zeus to allow him to die with his brother, so the god offered him a choice. Either Kastor went to Hades while he himself took his rightful place among the gods on Olympos, or Kastor could share his immortality, so long as the brothers spent alternate days in the Underworld with the shades, and the other days on Olympos with the gods. With no hesitation Polydeukes chose the latter fate, and Zeus immortalized the brothers in the stars as the constellation Gemini, the Twins, to commemorate their mutual devotion.

Kastor and Polydeukes were important gods, particularly in their native Sparta, and they were the special patrons of sailors, to whom they appeared as St Elmo's fire, the luminous phenomenon sometimes seen playing round the masts of ships in a storm. It was said that one ball of fire was a bad omen, while two balls of fire were a sure sign of the Dioskouroi's protective presence. The lyric poet Alcaeus of Lesbos hymns this aspect of the twin gods:

> You who journey the wide earth
> and all the sea on swift horses,
> easily delivering men
> from freezing death;
> you leap to the peaks of their sturdy ships
> and shine out brilliant from afar,
> bringing light to the black vessel
> in the grievous night . . .

They were important also at Rome. When in 499 (or 496) BC, the Romans were fighting a great battle against the Latins at Lake Regillus, near Tusculum, the twins appeared on their white horses and fought on the Roman side. As soon as the battle was over, they appeared again in the Forum at Rome, their horses bathed in sweat, and announced the resounding Roman victory. Having watered their horses at a spring sacred to the water-nymph Juturna, they vanished. The nearby temple of Castor, three columns of which still stand, was erected to commemorate this event.

Priapos

Priapos (Priapus) is a god of sexuality and fertility characterized by a gigantic, erect phallus. He was a latecomer to the Greek pantheon, originating in the Hellespont region and said to be the son of Aphrodite and Dionysos. His mother was so ashamed of his physical deformity that she abandoned him after his birth, leaving him in the mountains, where he was found and brought up by shepherds. Because of this he was always a rustic god, a guardian of vineyards, orchards, gardens, bees and herds. His cult spread rapidly during the third century BC and he was later well known through most of the Roman Empire.

His sacrificial animal was usually the donkey, though various reasons are given for this choice. Perhaps he had an argument with a donkey as to which of them had the biggest male appendage, and Priapos lost. Or a donkey had interfered in his amorous pursuits, at a time when he was creeping up to rape the sleeping nymph Lotis (or, in another version, Vesta: p. 68). He was all ready to have his way with her, when at the crucial moment she was woken by a bray from Silenos's ass. Seeing what fate was almost upon her, she fled in panic, and Priapos was exposed to general ridicule.

Or perhaps donkeys were sacrificed to Priapos because they were believed to be the most lustful of all animals, and so were deemed the most suitable offering for a god with such an exceptional sexual endowment.

Kybele

Kybele (Cybele) was the great mother-goddess from Phrygia, often called simply 'the Great Mother', with powers over fertility and the whole of wild nature, symbolized by her attendant lions. In art they flank the throne on which she sits, or they draw her chariot, and Kybele herself wears a turreted crown to show that she protects her people in war. She was thought to be accompanied by revelling maenads and male attendants, the Korybantes, who produced her celebratory music with the clash of cymbals and the sound of pipes and drums.

The Greeks often identified her with Rheia, the wife of Kronos and mother of the gods, or with Demeter. Kybele's chief sanctuary was in the mountains at Pessinus in Phrygia, where her sacred image in stone was believed to have fallen from heaven. From here her cult spread over the whole of the Greek world, and later into the Roman world as well when (traditionally in 204 BC) the Romans brought the goddess's sacred stone to Rome and built her a temple on the Palatine Hill.

Kybele was associated in myth and cult with a young male consort, Attis, whose story centred on his self-castration. It has a number of variants, such as this Phrygian version. While Zeus was asleep, his semen fell upon the ground, and from it was born Kybele (also known as Agdistis), with both male and female sex organs. The gods castrated this hermaphrodite creation, and from the severed male genitals there sprang an almond tree. One day an almond fell into the lap of the nymph Nana, daughter of the river-god Sangarios, and when it moved into her womb she conceived Attis. When her son was born she abandoned him, but a he-goat miraculously suckled the baby, who grew into a beautiful youth with whom Kybele, now all female, fell passionately in love. She was so possessive and jealous that to prevent him marrying another she drove him mad, and in his frenzy he castrated himself, and died.

In Kybele's orgiastic cult her priests too were eunuchs, who in a state of religious ecstasy castrated themselves in ritual commemoration of Attis's self-mutilation and death.

Adonis

Adonis was a god of vegetation and fertility, introduced into Greece from further east, and his festival, the *Adonia*, was widely celebrated every year, his cult being particularly popular with women. He was born of an incestuous union between Kinyras, the king of Cyprus, and his daughter Myrrha (p. 528), and he was so beautiful that he was loved by Aphrodite (p. 542). He died young, gored by a wild boar while out hunting.

His followers mourned his death by planting at midsummer 'gardens of Adonis', seeds set in shallow soil that sprang up quickly and as quickly withered, symbolizing the brief life of the god. This mourning for his death was followed by rejoicing at his resurrection as a god. Byblos in Phoenicia was especially sacred to him, and it was said that the nearby river of Adonis was stained with blood each year at the time of his death.

Janus

Let us end this catalogue of gods with the uniquely Roman god Janus. His temple stood in the Forum at Rome and had double gates, kept closed in rare times of peace and left open in war. He was the god of gateways and doorways (*ianuae*) and presided over all beginnings, which the Romans believed were crucial to the success of any undertaking. He (appropriately) gave his name to the first month of our year, January. Suitably too for such a god, he had two faces, one looking forwards and one backwards, just as every door looks two ways.

This useful attribute helped him in his pursuit of Cranae, a nymph who was dedicated to virginity. She would trick any amorous pursuer by sending him ahead of her into a shady cave, promising to follow him and enjoy the delights of love, but instead of doing so, she would run and hide in the forest. Janus managed to outwit her, for when she sent him off to a cave, he spotted her with the eyes in the back of his head, just as she was hiding behind a rock. He caught her before she could escape and had his way with her. She became the goddess Carna, and Janus appointed her the protector of door hinges, and gave her a branch of flowering hawthorn that would keep out all evil spirits. She especially protected infants in their cradles from vampires, thought to attack them by night and suck their blood.

There were many other Roman divinities, each with powers over specific aspects of life, but they seem merely personified functions, with no individual character. To list them all would be tedious, and also superfluous, for, important though they may have been to the Romans, they played no part in the stories of mythology that will fill these pages.

3

THE FIRST HUMANS

When we come to the creation of humanity, we find no one dominant account such as Hesiod provides for the creation of the cosmos. Instead there are a number of diverse, sometimes contradictory, explanations of how mankind came to be. Yet once again it is often Hesiod who enlightens us about these early ideas of humanity's origins.

The Five Races of Man

Hesiod is the first ancient author to speak of earlier races of men who lived in happier times than the present (*Works and Days* 109–201). He identifies five races altogether, four of which are named after metals decreasing in value, just as the races themselves deteriorate in happiness and peace. First of all, in the time of Kronos, the gods created a Golden Race who lived a life of blissful ease, the 'Golden Age' (112–20):

They lived like gods, with carefree hearts, remote from toil and grief. Nor did wretched old age beset them, but always with vigour in their hands and feet they took their joy in feasting, far from all ills, and they died as though overcome by sleep. All good things were theirs, for the fruitful earth of its own accord put forth its plentiful harvest without stint, while they enjoyed a life of peace and ease in abundance, rich in flocks and loved by the blessed gods.

In time this Golden Race passed away and became beneficent spirits (*daimones*) who wander the earth, protecting mortals from harm.

The gods then created the Silver Race of men, inferior both in mind and body to the Race of Gold. These men took a hundred years to grow up, and then were foolish and aggressive and neglectful of the gods. By this time Zeus had replaced Kronos as lord of the universe, so he put an end to the Silver Race and created the Race of Bronze out of ash trees. Their armour, their weapons, their tools, even their houses were made of bronze, and they themselves were so dedicated to warfare and slaughter that they exterminated themselves through their relentless violence.

Zeus then created a fourth and non-metallic race, the Race of Heroes. These were the mighty mortals who lived in the 'Heroic Age' and fought nobly at Thebes and Troy – and who are the subjects of our Greek myths. Some were so glorious that they were rewarded with a life after death in a paradise at the far ends of the earth, called by Hesiod the Islands of the Blest (p. 111).

Fifth and finally came the Race of Iron. This is Hesiod's world, and our own: 'And men never rest from toil and misery by day, nor from perishing by night; and the gods lay harsh trouble upon them' (176–8). And things are only ever going to get worse . . .

PROMETHEUS AND PANDORA

Another tradition credited the creation of mankind to the Titan Prometheus, son of Iapetos and Klymene (p. 34). 'Prometheus moulded men out of earth and water,' says Apollodorus (1.7.1); and although there is no reference to this story in our extant sources before the fourth century BC, it may well have been much older. When the traveller Pausanias visited Panopeus in Phokis, he saw two huge rocks, apparently smelling of human flesh, which were said to have been formed from the left-over clay after Prometheus had fashioned the human race (10.4.4).

What is certain, however, is that Prometheus was from early times seen as the champion and benefactor of mankind, as

Prometheus creates the first humans, supervised by Athene.

Hesiod once again bears witness (*Theogony* 521–616). When gods and men were once about to share a meal at Mekone (later Sikyon), it was Prometheus' task to divide up a great ox and set out two portions of food, one for the gods and one for mortals. He produced, on the one hand, a choice selection of succulent meats unappealingly covered with the ox's stomach, and, on the other, a pile of bones, dressed in a layer of appetizing fat. Zeus was to choose the gods' portion, and although Hesiod defends the great god's wisdom by saying that he was not deceived, nevertheless Zeus still chose the fat-covered bones. From that day forward, men always took the best meat from sacrifices for themselves and burned the bones for the gods.

Zeus was angry at this trick and he punished mankind by withholding from them the gift of fire. So Prometheus stole fire from heaven and carried it secretly down to earth in a hollow fennel stalk (the white pith of which burns slowly and so makes it possible to carry fire from one place to another).

Once again Zeus was full of wrath, so he decided to balance this blessing of fire by giving men a bane to plague their lives: woman, a beautiful evil (*kalon kakon*, 585). Before this time men had lived lives free from toil and sickness, but now the first woman would change this forever. Hesiod gives a more detailed description of her creation, and of all the troubles she caused, in his *Works and Days* (47–105). (We should, however, bear in mind when reading her story that Hesiod had no very high opinion of women: elsewhere in the work (373–5) he says, 'Don't be deceived by a wheedling, sweet-talking woman, flaunting her body, she's only after your barn. Anyone who trusts a woman is trusting a cheat.')

This first woman's name was Pandora ('Allgifts'), and she is the nearest thing the Greek tradition has to the biblical Eve. She was created out of earth and water by the smith-god Hephaistos. Athene dressed and adorned her, and taught her domestic crafts, Aphrodite showered beauty and grace over her, and Hermes put in her breast a nature of cunning and deceit. Then Zeus sent his beautiful but treacherous creation to Prometheus' brother, the gullible Titan Epimetheus, who forgot that Prometheus had warned him never to take any gift offered by Zeus.

Epimetheus, charmed by this vision of loveliness, welcomed Pandora with open arms and took her as his bride, and in so doing condemned mankind to a lifetime of suffering. For Pandora brought with her as dowry a *pithos*, a great jar in which were stored sorrows and diseases and hard labour. When she opened the lid of her jar (usually now referred to as 'Pandora's Box'), these poured out and spread over all the earth, and mortals have never since been free of them. Only hope remained in the jar, still in man's own control, to be some kind of consolation for all the troubles that Pandora had let loose on the world.

As for Prometheus, Zeus punished him too for his gift of fire to mankind: he had him chained to a cliff in the Caucasian Mountains and he sent an eagle, offspring of the monsters Typhon and Echidna, to prey on him. Every day the eagle tore out Prometheus' liver, which every night grew whole again so that his torment might continue. Long ages passed before this daily agony ended, when Zeus allowed his mightiest son, Herakles, to shoot the eagle and release the Titan (p. 208).

The chaining of Prometheus is dramatized in the tragedy *Prometheus Bound*, traditionally said to be by Aeschylus, which was the first (and only extant) play in a Prometheus trilogy. Here Zeus is depicted as a brutal tyrant, and Prometheus is represented as having done more for mankind than simply bring them fire: he has taught mortals many useful and civilizing skills, including architecture, agriculture, writing, medicine, the domestication of animals, the use of ships, mining for metals and divination.

Prometheus is chained to his crag by an unwilling Hephaistos, at the bidding of Kratos ('Power') and Bia ('Might'), yet despite all his sufferings he regrets none of his deeds, and continues to cry heroic defiance at Zeus, fearless of his thunderbolts (1041–53):

> 'Let the twisted fork of lightning fire be flung
> against me: let the high air be stirred
> with thunderclaps and the convulsive fury
> of the winds: let earth to the roots of her foundations
> shake before the blasting storm: let it confound
> the waves of the sea and the paths of the heavenly stars

in a wild turmoil, and let him raise
my body high and dash it whirling down
to murky Tartaros. He cannot make me die.'

At the end of the play Zeus hurls Prometheus down to Tartaros, rock and all.

We know something of the second play, *Prometheus Freed*, from fragments. Herakles killed the eagle, and Prometheus was reconciled with Zeus and set free in exchange for an important secret told him by Themis: that the Nereid Thetis was destined to bear a son greater than his father. At that time Zeus was pursuing Thetis, so this knowledge saved him from having by her a son who would overthrow him, the very fate that he had inflicted on his own father, Kronos. Zeus gave up his pursuit and Thetis was later married off to Peleus, and the fruit of their union was Achilles, a son who was indeed greater than his father.

THE GREAT FLOOD

Another tradition has Prometheus as the originator of mankind in another sense, when his son, Deukalion, and Pyrrha, the daughter of Epimetheus and Pandora, became the sole survivors of the Great Flood – a myth that in one form or another appears in a number of cultures across the world.

In the Greek version, Zeus decided to destroy the human race with the Flood because of mankind's wickedness. Sometimes his decision was put down to the specific iniquity of the family of Lykaon, one of the earliest kings of Arcadia. Some said that Lykaon tried to trick Zeus by setting before him the cooked flesh of a human child, and Zeus responded by blasting his family with thunderbolts and by transforming Lykaon himself into a wolf (*lykos*), so his story becomes one version of the werewolf tradition. Others said that it was Lykaon's sons who were wicked, and who set before Zeus the flesh of a murdered child, and it was this which inspired Zeus to send the Great Flood.

Prometheus knew of Zeus's intention, so he warned Deukalion, telling him to build a large chest and stock it with food. Endless rain brought the Flood, and Deukalion and Pyrrha floated in their chest for nine days and nine nights until at last the rain ceased and the chest came ashore on Mount Parnassos, above Delphi. They disembarked and made a thank-offering to Zeus for their preservation. Now, as the only mortals left alive, it was their task to repopulate an empty world, so on Zeus's instructions, brought to them by Hermes, they picked up stones from the earth and threw them over their shoulders. Deukalion's stones were transformed into men and Pyrrha's into women. The human race had begun afresh.

Deukalion and Pyrrha had several children of their own, most notably Hellen. He gave his name to the whole Greek race, for they called themselves Hellenes and their country Hellas. Hellen in turn was the father of three sons, Aiolos, Doros and Xouthos, from whom sprang the four main branches of the Greek people: Aiolos was the ancestor of the Aiolians, Doros of the Dorians, and the two sons of Xouthus, Ion and Achaios, of the Ionians and Achaians. It was traditionally said that Hellen divided the Greek lands among his three sons, and that Aiolos succeeded his father where he ruled in Thessaly, while Doros and Xouthos moved away and settled in different areas of Greece.

Of these descendants of Deukalion, it was Aiolos whose branch of the family was the most mythologically significant, for from him were descended many great heroes and heroines of legend. He himself had seven sons (Salmoneus, Kretheus, Athamas, Sisyphos, Deion, Magnes and Perieres) and five daughters (Kanake, Alkyone, Peisidike, Kalyke and Perimede).

Let us begin by tracing the story of a granddaughter of Aiolos,

Tyro. She was the daughter of Salmoneus and (as so often happened with early – and beautiful – women) she lay with a god and bore great sons. Her grandson was Jason, the hero who led one of the most famous expeditions of the ancient world: the quest for the Golden Fleece.

TYRO AND HER SONS

Salmoneus left his father Aiolos's house in Thessaly and founded a city in Elis called Salmone. He was a proud and arrogant man who thought himself the equal of Zeus. He ordered his people to make sacrifices to him and not to the god, and he even imitated Zeus's thunder and lightning by dragging dried hides and bronze pots behind his chariot and by flinging lighted torches into the sky. He was not a popular ruler, for his people objected to having burning torches hurled among them by their king. But worse was to come, for Zeus retaliated by striking Salmoneus and his city with a genuine thunderbolt, and king and people were utterly destroyed.

Salmoneus's daughter Tyro, however, had opposed her father's presumptuous attempts to claim divine honours, so Zeus spared her and took her to her uncle, Kretheus, who was king of the Thessalian city of Iolkos. Kretheus welcomed her with pleasure and brought her up. Homer tells of her divine encounter in the *Odyssey*, where Tyro is one of the great heroines of legend whose shade Odysseus meets in Hades (11.238–55):

> She fell in love with the river, divine Enipeus,
> most beautiful of rivers that flow upon the earth,
> and she would haunt Enipeus' lovely waters.
> So the god who holds the earth, the Earth-shaker,
> took his likeness, and lay with her at the mouth
> of the swirling river, and a great dark wave,

a mountain of water, curved up and around them
and hid the god and the mortal women. He loosed
her virgin belt and drifted sleep upon her,
then when he had ended his act of love, the god
took her hand in his and said to her:
'Be happy, lady, in this love of ours, and when
the year goes by you will bear splendid sons,
for love with a god is never without issue.
Take care of them and raise them. Now go home
and hold your peace. Tell nobody my name.
But I tell you, I am Poseidon, the Earth-shaker.'
He spoke, and plunged back into the swelling sea.
And she conceived, and bore Pelias and Neleus.

Homer tells us no more of Tyro's story, so we turn to Apollodorus (1.9.7–11) for the continuation. Despite Poseidon's injunction, Tyro did not bring up her twin sons: she bore them in secret and left them out in the countryside to die, then went back to Kretheus' house. The babies were found and brought up by a horse-breeder. He gave them their names: Pelias, because of the livid (*pelios*) mark made on the infant's face by a kick from a horse, and Neleus.

When they grew up they found their mother again, and discovered that for many years she had been treated with great cruelty by her foster-mother, Sidero. They went to punish Sidero, but she ran away into a sanctuary of Hera, and Pelias killed her on the very altar of the goddess (one of many acts of disrespect that would earn him Hera's undying hatred). This recognition and revenge most likely formed the plot of one at least of Sophocles' two lost tragedies named *Tyro*, where according to Aristotle in the *Poetics* (16) the recognition of mother and sons occurred by means of the box in which the infants had been abandoned.

Later the two brothers quarrelled and Pelias drove Neleus out of Iolkos. He took refuge with Aphareus, the king of Messenia, who gave him many of his coastal lands. Neleus settled in Pylos and made it one of the most flourishing cities in the Greek world.

Tyro's sad story ends happily, for she married Kretheus and had by him three more sons, Aison, Pheres and Amythaon. Aison would become the father of Jason.

4

THE QUEST FOR THE GOLDEN FLEECE

The story of the quest for the Golden Fleece by Jason and the Argonauts has been famous since very early times. The enchantress Circe in Homer's *Odyssey* speaks briefly of the *Argo*'s voyage as a tale 'on all men's tongues', when she is describing to Odysseus some particularly dangerous rocks that he must avoid on his journey home (12.61–72):

The blessed gods call them the Wandering Rocks. No bird passes them safely, not even the trembling doves that carry ambrosia to Father Zeus, but the sheer rocks always seize one of them, and the Father sends another to make up their number. No ship of men that came there has ever yet escaped, but the waves of the sea and blasts of deadly fire carry away together the ship's timbers and the dead bodies of the crew. One sea-going ship alone has ever sailed clear, on her way home from the land of Aietes: the *Argo*, whose name is on all men's tongues. Yet even she would have been quickly dashed against the great rocks, if Hera, for love of Jason, had not sped her past.

Unfortunately no epic version of the whole story survives from the archaic period. Pindar's *Fourth Pythian Ode*, written for the chariot victory in 462 BC of Arkesilas of Kyrene, gives a first, relatively brief, account of the expedition. Our fullest and best-known version comes from the late epic *Argonautica* (third century BC) of Apollonius of Rhodes, and this, for the most part, will be the main source of our narrative in this chapter. First, however, we must recount the origin of the Golden Fleece itself, and also the early history of Jason, the heroic leader of the expedition. Perhaps he does not appear so very heroic in the late epic of Apollonius, where he often seems timid and confused, and is quickly prone to doubts and despair. But we should bear in mind that the archaic Jason would no doubt have been conceived rather differently: he would have been seen primarily as a great achiever of apparently impossible tasks, like Perseus, or Bellerophon, or Herakles, and would have had a heroic nature to match. Like all the early heroes, he would have been handsome, athletic and brave, a man who rose eagerly to every challenge set before him.

THE GOLDEN FLEECE

Athamas, son of the powerful Thessalian king Aiolos (p. 132), was himself king of Orchomenos in Boiotia. By his first wife, Nephele, he had a son and a daughter, Phrixos and Helle. When Nephele died, he married again, but his second wife Ino, daughter of Kadmos, king of Thebes, was jealous of her stepchildren and plotted against them. She began by persuading the Boiotian women to roast the grain set aside for the next sowing, which of course made it sterile and resulted in complete crop failure. Then when Athamas sent messengers to ask the Delphic Oracle how the land might be saved from famine, Ino bribed them to report that Phrixos must be sacrificed to Zeus.

Naturally Athamas was unwilling to perform such a sacrifice, but eventually, for his people's sake, he agreed to do so. Just as he was about to cut Phrixos's throat, a wondrous ram appeared, sent by Nephele to save her son. Given to her by Hermes, it could talk and fly, and its fleece was of spun gold. At the ram's command, Phrixos and Helle leapt on to its back and it flew off, carrying them far away to safety.

Unfortunately, while the ram was flying over the straits dividing Europe from Asia, Helle fell off its back and drowned in the sea below, which was later named the Hellespont ('Helle's

Sea') after her. The ram flew onwards with Phrixos, and at last it set him down at Aia, the capital of Kolchis at the eastern end of the Black Sea, a land near the edge of the known world. Here Aietes, son of the Sun-god Helios, was king. He welcomed Phrixos and gave him the hand of one of his daughters, Chalkiope, in marriage. In gratitude for his salvation, Phrixos sacrificed the ram to Zeus, who immortalized it in the stars as the constellation Aries.

Phrixos gave the ram's beautiful golden fleece to Aietes. The king hung it in an oak tree, in a grove sacred to the war-god Ares, and set a sleepless dragon to keep it safe. Here it hung untouched for many years, while its fame spread throughout the Greek world.

JASON

Jason was the son of Aison, who as the eldest son of Kretheus and Tyro should have become king of Iolkos when his father died. Instead, the throne was usurped by Aison's older half-brother Pelias, the son of Tyro and the sea-god Poseidon. When Jason was born his parents hid him, afraid that Pelias would have him killed. They told Pelias that their baby had been born dead, then secretly sent him to be brought up on Mount Pelion by the wise Centaur Cheiron, the educator of so many great heroes. Pelias, meanwhile, ruled on, though he learnt from an oracle that he must beware of a man, coming from the country and wearing a single sandal, for it was this man who would bring about his death.

When he grew to manhood, Jason returned to Iolkos. He arrived wearing only one sandal, for he had lost the other while he was carrying the goddess Hera, disguised as an old woman, across the flooded river Anauros. Hera hated Pelias because he had so often ignored the honours due to her divinity, and in this way she marked Jason as the instrument of her enemy's destruction, from then onwards aiding him in all his tribulations until the day of Pelias' death.

Now, as soon as Pelias saw Jason and the single sandal, he remembered the oracle and realized his danger. He asked Jason what he would do if he learnt from an oracle that a certain man would kill him, and Jason, perhaps inspired by Hera, replied that he would send such a man to fetch the Golden Fleece. Thus he sealed his own fate. Pelias at once ordered him to set off on this surely impossible mission, convinced that he could never return.

In Pindar's *Pythian* 4 we have our earliest description of Jason: he strides into Iolkos, an awesome figure clad in a leopard-skin and brandishing two spears, his long hair flowing down his back. In Pindar's version he claims the throne from Pelias, while offering to let him keep the land and flocks that he has seized. Pelias gives a smooth reply, pretending that the spirit of the dead Phrixos keeps haunting his dreams and ordering him to fetch the Fleece from Kolchis. Since he himself is too old, says Pelias, Jason must go on his behalf, and he promises that on the successful completion of this quest, he will give up the throne to him. Here too, of course, Pelias is quite sure that Jason will never survive to claim it.

In whatever way the expedition came about, Jason, eager for glory, swiftly prepared for the adventure. A sailing ship with fifty oars was built with the help of Athene. Constructed of timber from Mount Pelion, it was named *Argo* after its builder, Argos, and into its prow was fitted a miraculous speaking plank from Zeus's sacred oak tree at Dodona.

Jason invited the bravest heroes in Greece to accompany him. Lists of the crew differ, but the most important names from the various sources include the mighty Herakles and his squire Hylas; the great Athenian hero, Theseus; Meleagros, who later killed the Kalydonian Boar; the two sons of Aiakos, Peleus and Telamon; Orpheus, the world's finest musician; Zetes and Kalais, the swift-flying sons of Boreas, the North Wind; the Dioskouroi, Kastor and Polydeukes; the two sons of Aphareus, Idas and Lynkeus; the seers Idmon and Mopsos; a son of Poseidon, Euphemos, who was so swift-footed that he could run over the sea without getting his feet wet; the helmsman Tiphys; the Lapith Polyphemos; Neleus' son Periklymenos, who had the power to change his shape into anything he might wish; Augeias, later famous for his 'Augeian Stables'; Poias, the king of Malis; Admetos, Pheres' son from Pherai; Argos, who built the ship; Pelias' son Akastos; and Ankaios, the son of Lykourgos, dressed in a bearskin and armed with a two-headed axe, who because of his great strength was chosen to row next to Herakles.

Herakles' own part in the expedition is rather anomalous, for he was by far the greatest of the heroes on board, and yet the expedition was traditionally captained by Jason. Apollonius gets over this difficulty by having Herakles unanimously elected as captain, but stepping down in favour of Jason, then getting left behind at an early stage in the voyage when they put in at Mysia.

When all was prepared, they joyfully set off, with Tiphys at the helm and the oarsmen keeping time to the sound of Orpheus' lyre (*Argonautica* 1.541–6):

The waves broke over the oar-blades, and on both sides the dark ocean seethed with foam, whipped up by the might of these powerful men. As the ship sped onwards, their armour flashed in the sun like flame and their wake gleamed white far behind, like a road showing clear over a green plain.

THE VOYAGE TO KOLCHIS

The long and dangerous voyage began well, and on the fifth day they put in at the island of Lemnos, where Hypsipyle was queen. She had divine blood in her veins, for her father was Thoas, a son of Dionysos and Ariadne. At this point in time the island was inhabited only by women, who the previous year had massacred all their menfolk. It all began when Aphrodite punished the women for failing to honour her, by afflicting them all with a repulsive smell. Their husbands then brought slave girls from the neighbouring mainland of Thrace and had sex only with them. The neglected women retaliated by murdering not only their husbands and the slave girls, but the entire male population of the island. Alone of all the women, Hypsipyle was merciful and spared her aged father Thoas. She set him adrift on the sea in a chest, and he eventually came safely to shore. She herself took his place as ruler of Lemnos.

Although the women had found such masculine labours as cattle-rearing and ploughing a welcome change from their usual indoor occupation of weaving, nevertheless they realized too well the disadvantages of an all-female society. Now when they found that the Argonauts had landed, they welcomed them to their homes and beds, hoping to have many sons by them. (Luckily they had by now lost their offensive smell.) Naturally Jason fell to Hypsipyle's lot.

Day after day the sailing was deferred while the time was spent in pleasures. At last Herakles, impatient for action, reminded the men of their mission and urged them back to their rowing benches. They all travelled onwards once again, but the women's purpose was achieved and Lemnos was in due course repopulated with males. Hypsipyle herself had two sons by Jason, Euneos, who would be ruling Lemnos at the time of the Trojan War, and Thoas.

The Argonauts put in briefly at the island of Samothrace, where they celebrated the mysteries of the Kabeiroi, minor divinities who would help to ensure the safety of their voyage. Next, passing through the Hellespont, they stayed overnight with the Doliones, a Mysian tribe living on the southern shores of the Propontis. Their king, Kyzikos, was still a very young man, recently married to Kleite, the daughter of Merops, king of Perkote. Kyzikos welcomed the Argonauts warmly and entertained them hospitably.

Nearby, however, there lived a savage and violent race of giants called the *Gegeneis* ('Earthborn'), each with six huge arms, and the next day these attacked the ship. Herakles led out the crew, and after a mighty battle all the giants were slaughtered. The *Argo* now set sail once again, but during the following night a storm came up and the Argonauts were blown all the way back to the land they had just left. In the darkness they failed to recognize the place, and the Doliones, in their turn, failing to recognize them, attacked them, believing them to be enemy invaders. In the ensuing battle, Jason unwittingly killed Kyzikos.

At first light both sides realized their tragic error. For three days they all mourned the young king, then buried him with full funeral honours and named his city Kyzikos in his memory. Kleite hanged herself from grief, and the woodland nymphs mourned for her, shedding so many tears that these were turned into a spring, named Kleite in honour of the unhappy bride.

In due course the voyage was resumed, but off the coast of Mysia Herakles broke his oar, so when they put ashore in the evening he went off into the forest to find wood for a new one. Meanwhile his young squire and lover Hylas went to draw water from a local spring. The nymph of the spring saw his beauty in the light of the full moon, and when he leant over to dip his pitcher into the stream, she reached up and drew him down to kiss him. He fell into the water, and the only Argonaut to hear his cry of fear was Polyphemos, who rushed at once to his aid. Finding no trace of the boy, he ran to tell Herakles that Hylas must have been dragged off by bandits or wild beasts. Herakles was wild with grief at his loss and went raging through the woods all night, bellowing for his dear companion (1.1265–72):

As when a bull is stung by a gadfly and rushes off, leaving the meadows and marshlands, and has no thought for the herd or the herdsmen, but runs on, now without resting, now again standing still and lifting his broad neck to bellow in torment at the sting of the cruel fly; so Herakles in his frenzy would now move his legs swiftly and without respite, now again he would pause from his labour and shout aloud into the distance with a great resounding cry.

When dawn was approaching, the rest of the Argonauts set sail without noticing in the dimness that Herakles and Polyphemos were missing, so they were both left behind. Polyphemos would later found the city of Kios among the Mysians; but always he longed to rejoin his comrades, so eventually he left Mysia and travelled far in search of them. Finally he died in the land of the Chalybes, on the Black Sea's southern coast, and there a tomb was built for him under a tall, white poplar, close to the edge of the sea.

As for Herakles, when at last he gave up hope of finding Hylas, he left for home, but not before threatening to lay waste the land if the local Mysians did not promise to continue the search once he was gone. To make sure that they obeyed him, he took boys from noble families as hostages and settled them at Trachis. So the Mysians carried on searching, but of course to no avail, and for centuries they sacrificed annually to Hylas at the spring where he had disappeared.

This, however, was in the future. Now the Argonauts continued on their way, lacking two of their crew, and only in the light of dawn realizing their mistake. They very nearly turned back again, but Zetes and Kalais persuaded them to carry on. (This was a rash act, for which Herakles later punished them with death when he encountered them on the island of Tenos. After killing them he piled earth over their bodies, then set up two pillars on their grave, one of which swayed whenever their father the North Wind blew.)

The sea-god Glaukos appeared out of the ocean depths, and he too urged the Argonauts to sail on regardless. Glaukos had once been a mortal, living in the Boiotian city of Anthedon, but even as a mortal he passionately loved the sea and spent all his days near it, fishing with nets or with rod and line. One day he laid out his catch on some particularly verdant grass, only to see each fish come to life again and wriggle back into the sea. He realized that the grass must possess magic powers, so he ate some of it, and at once he was seized with an overwhelming desire to leave the land and live in the sea forever. He plunged beneath the waves, where he soon found that he had taken on a new, sea-going form with sea-green hair and the tail and fins of a fish. The sea-gods received him as one of themselves, cleansing him of any last traces of mortality, and, like other sea-gods, he became renowned for his prophetic powers. Thus, when the Argonauts heard his instructions to continue on their journey, they obeyed him, much reassured.

They arrived next in the land of the Bebrykians, which was ruled over by Amykos, a son of Poseidon. He was a savage man, in the habit of challenging all visitors to his land to a boxing contest. He always won, then killed the unfortunate loser. When the Argonauts landed he issued his usual challenge, and this was eagerly taken up by one of the Dioskouroi, the expert boxer Polydeukes. Amykos gazed at what he thought would be his next victim (2.25–9):

He [Amykos] turned and glared at him, like a lion struck by a spear and surrounded by hunters on the mountain; and although hemmed in by a crowd of men, it pays no heed to them, but keeps its eyes fixed only on that man alone who struck it first, though did not kill it.

They prepared for the fight, each man having his hands bound with hard leather thongs. They were two men very different in size and stature: Amykos, says Apollonius, looked like a monstrous son of terrible Typhon, that last great challenger of Olympian Zeus, while Polydeukes was as beautiful as Hesperos, the evening star. When all was ready, they came fiercely to meet each other. Boxing in the ancient world was a more violent, bloody and deadly affair than its modern equivalent, so the fight was a brutal one, in which Polydeukes' skill and suppleness were set against Amykos's huge size and brute strength. At last, in the final onslaught, 'they rushed at one another like a pair of bulls angrily fighting over a grazing heifer'; Amykos stretched up to crash his great fist down on his opponent's head, but Polydeukes evaded the blow and struck back, hitting Amykos above the ear and shattering the bones of his head.

With their king dead, the Bebrykians advanced to attack the Argonauts, but were soon routed (2.130–36):

As shepherds or beekeepers smoke out a huge swarm of bees from a rock, and the bees for a while buzz furiously in a throng within their home, then, demented by the murky smoke, they dart far away from the rock, just so the Bebrykians did not stand their ground for long, but scattered through all their land, passing on the news of Amykos's death.

The Argonauts' next port of call was Salmydessos in Thrace, whose king was the blind seer Phineus, the son of Agenor, king of Tyre, and thus the brother of Europa, who was carried off to Crete by Zeus in the form of a bull, and of Kadmos, the founder of Thebes. Phineus had been given the gift of prophecy by Apollo, but because he had revealed too much of the future to men, Zeus had blinded him in punishment. This was not his only suffering: he had also been afflicted with the Harpies (p. 37), swift winged monsters who would swoop down whenever he had food and snatch it from his mouth and hands, then make what little they had left him inedible by fouling it with their excrement. When the Argonauts arrived, Phineus was almost dead of starvation, but now at last he was hopeful, for with his seer's vision he knew that two of the company, Zetes and Kalais, were destined to save him from his persecutors.

Filled with pity for his plight, the men laid out a feast to lure down the Harpies once again, while Zetes and Kalais stood nearby at the ready (2.266–72):

As soon as the old man touched his meal, the Harpies without warning darted from the clouds like sudden storms or flashes of lightning, swooping down and screaming in their lust for food. The heroes cried out when they saw them, but the Harpies devoured everything, and with a cry flew off far across the sea, leaving behind an unbearable stench.

Zetes and Kalais, being the winged sons of Boreas, the North Wind, were the swiftest men on earth, and now they sped off in pursuit, their swords drawn. They caught up with the Harpies at the Floating Islands (*Plotai*), traditionally identified as the Echinades in the Ionian Sea, and this would have been the end of the monsters, if their sister Iris, goddess of the rainbow, had not flown down to intervene. She promised that the Harpies would never trouble Phineus again, so Zetes and Kalais turned and went back to their comrades, after which the islands were renamed the Strophades, the 'Islands of Turning'. The Harpies went off to Crete, where they settled in a deep cave on Mount Dikte.

In gratitude for his deliverance, Phineus advised the Argonauts about the hazards that lay ahead in their voyage, particularly the dangers of the Symplegades, the dreaded Clashing Rocks at the northern end of the Bosporos, guarding the entrance to the Black Sea. These rocks were not rooted in the seabed, but were constantly on the move, clashing together with tremendous force and crushing all ships that tried to pass between them. No ship had ever survived the attempt.

When the Argonauts approached these terrifying rocks, they did exactly as Phineus had advised. First they launched a dove, whose fate would be a sign as to whether or not the *Argo* could succeed in passing through. She flew between the huge cliffs and came safely out on the other side, with just the tips of her tail-feathers caught in their rocky jaws as they crashed together. So now it was the turn of the *Argo* herself.

The rocks opened up again and the helmsman Tiphys screamed to the men to row with all their might. They rowed desperately through the narrow channel, but a great surge held them back, while on each side of them the massive cliffs shook and thundered. At the last moment, just as the rocks were about to clash together, the goddess Athene intervened, giving the ship a heave that sent her safely through them into the open sea, with just the tip of her stern-ornament sheared off as the rocks met. After this the Symplegades posed no further danger to men, for they were now immovably locked together and rooted in one spot for ever.

Now the worst of the Argonauts' journey was behind them as they sailed over the open water of the Black Sea. They were welcomed by Lykos, king of the Mariandyni in Mysia, a people who had long been at war with the Bebrykians. Lykos entertained them royally, for their fame as the destroyers of Amykos had preceded them.

However they suffered two losses in Lykos's land: the helmsman Tiphys died of a sickness, and the seer Idmon by violence.

Idmon had known full well that he was fated to die if he joined the expedition, but still he did so, wishing to win a glorious reputation. Now he met his fate in the shape of a white-tusked boar, so huge and deadly that even the nymphs of the swamp where it lived were afraid of it. It leapt out at Idmon as he was walking alongside a muddy river and gored him in the thigh, cutting through bone and sinews. His comrades hurried to his aid. Peleus threw his javelin at the boar, which turned and rushed at its attacker, but then Idas struck out at it, and with a hideous snarl it impaled itself on his spear. They left it dead and carried Idmon back to the ship, but he died in his companions' arms. They all mourned his passing for three days, then on the fourth day they buried him with lavish honours and crowned his burial mound with wild olive.

When they put to sea again, Lykos's son Daskylos had joined the crew and Ankaios had taken Tiphys' place at the helm. Passing by the land of the Amazons, they came to the island of Ares, where an enormous flock of hostile birds attacked them by dropping their feathers, sharp as arrows. The Argonauts defended themselves by locking their shields over their heads, and scared away the birds by screaming and shouting ferociously.

Following Phineus's instructions they put in at the island, and there they encountered the four sons of Phrixos, the very man who had originally flown into Kolchis on the ram with the golden fleece. Phrixos had recently died, and his sons (Argos, Melas, Phrontis and Kytorissos) had been shipwrecked on the island while trying to sail back to Greece, hoping to claim an inheritance from their grandfather, Athamas. Now they were happy to join the Argonauts, and they guided them on the last lap of their journey up the River Phasis and to Aia, the capital city of Kolchis. There the crew thankfully dropped anchor.

WINNING THE GOLDEN FLEECE

Jason hoped to persuade Aietes to hand over the Fleece peaceably, so, with the sons of Phrixos to guide him, he went with Telamon and Augeias to the king's splendid palace. Now the goddess Hera took a part in the action. Because of her desire to avenge herself on her old enemy Pelias, she needed Jason to succeed in his quest and to return to Iolkos with Aietes' young and beautiful daughter Medea – who was also a priestess of Hekate, the Underworld goddess associated with sorcery and witchcraft. Medea, with her magical skills, would be the agent of Pelias' destruction. So Hera enlisted the help of Aphrodite, who bribed her son Eros to shoot one of his inescapable arrows into Medea and make her fall in love with Jason. As soon as Medea set eyes on the handsome stranger, she burned with desire for him.

Aietes was sure that the Greeks had come to kill him and seize his throne, and even when Jason assured him of their true purpose, he refused to believe him. The king wondered whether to attack and slay them all on the spot, or to make trial of Jason's strength and courage, but he soon decided on the latter course. Pretending compliance, he said that he would willingly hand over the Fleece if Jason would perform certain (apparently impossible) tasks. In the course of a single day he must yoke two bronze-hooved, fire-breathing bulls and plough a field end to end, then sow the ground with some of the teeth from Kadmos's dragon (p. 265), provided by Athene, and kill the host of armed warriors who would spring up from the earth.

Jason was dismayed at the thought of the deadly tasks ahead of him, but Medea, fired up by love, was on hand to help. Urged on by her sister Chalkiope, she overcame her natural modesty and went at dawn to meet Jason at the shrine of Hekate. There Medea gave him a magic salve that for one day would make him completely invulnerable, and in return he promised to marry her if she came to Greece.

On the following night, obedient to Medea's instructions, he made sacrifices to enlist the aid of Hekate. At dawn he anointed his body and armour with the magic salve, and at once he felt invincible in power and strength. 'As when a war-horse, eager for the fray, neighs and beats the ground with his hoof, arching his neck and pricking up his ears for joy, so did the son of Aison exult in the strength of his limbs' (3.1259–62). He was now ready to face Aietes' challenge. Meanwhile Aietes himself and the people of Kolchis had assembled on the plain of Ares to be entertained by Jason's struggles.

Jason strode out to meet the great bulls naked and armed only with a shield. At once they charged at him, but for all their ferocity and fire he forcibly yoked them to the plough. Then using his irresistible spear to goad them on, he tilled the soil and sowed the dragon's teeth. Now he had only the armed warriors to contend with. Pausing to quench his thirst from the nearby river, 'he bent his knees to make them supple and filled his great heart with courage, raging like a wild boar that sharpens its tusks against the hunters, while foam streams to the ground from its angry mouth' (3.1350–53).

The warriors were now springing up all over the ploughed furrows, and the field bristled with shields and spears and helmets (3.1357–63):

The brilliance flashed through the air all the way from earth to Olympos; and as when heavy snow has fallen, and storm winds suddenly scatter the wintry clouds in the dark of night, and all the stars of heaven shine out from the darkness, just so did the warriors shine as they rose from the earth.

Jason remembered Medea's advice and flung a massive boulder into their midst. Like fierce dogs they turned on each other and fought among themselves, while Jason hacked away at them with his sword. The furrows filled with blood as more and more warriors fell. As the sun sank below the horizon, the field was strewn with dead and Jason stood alone and triumphant.

Aietes, of course, had no intention of giving up the Fleece, so during the night he and the leading men of Kolchis plotted how to kill the Argonauts. Meanwhile Medea, terrified of her father's anger, fled to Jason's camp for safety. She led Jason to the dense grove of Ares where the Fleece hung on its sacred oak tree, guarded by the huge unsleeping dragon. It saw them approaching and at once stretched out its great neck, hissing, and began to uncurl its scaly coils. As it slithered towards them, Medea fixed it in the eye and put it straight to sleep with incantations and powerful drugs. It had raised its head to strike, but now its jaw dropped to the earth and its vast coils stretched out far behind it, back through the dense wood.

Jason lifted down from the sacred oak the object of his long quest and carried it, shimmering with a golden radiance, back to the *Argo*. There was no time to waste. Taking Medea with them, the Argonauts set off on their long journey back to Iolkos, and the ship raced forwards as they rowed with all speed down the river Phasis. Soon Aietes' ships would be streaming in hot pursuit.

THE RETURN TO IOLKOS

Rather than return the way they had come, the Argonauts took a quite different route homeward. This gave Apollonius the opportunity of having them encounter some of the most famous adversaries of the Homeric Odysseus, even though in mythological time the *Argo*'s voyage was a generation earlier than the Trojan War. They began by sailing up the Istros (Danube) and down the branch that was thought to flow into the northern

Adriatic. The Kolchian fleet, meanwhile, had divided up in an attempt to block all escape routes, and one section, led by Aietes' son Apsyrtos, had taken the quicker of the two entrances to the Istros and was sailing along the river ahead of them. (In other versions of the myth, Apsyrtos was only a child at the time of Medea's flight. She took him with her, then murdered him and strewed the fragments of his dismembered body over the sea to delay Aietes' pursuit: see p. 453).

When the Argonauts emerged from the river mouth into the Adriatic they found the Kolchians waiting in ambush, but there was no battle, for Apsyrtos was a reasonable man and was willing to let Jason carry off the Fleece. After all, Aietes had promised it to him and he had won it fairly. But unfortunately Apsyrtos insisted that Medea be taken back to Kolchis, and rather than face this fate, she was quite prepared to resort to murder. She sent a message luring her brother to a meeting on a nearby island, pretending that she had been taken on the *Argo* by force and now wished to trick Jason out of the Fleece and return to her home.

In the dead of night they met, and Apsyrtos questioned her to find out whether she truly intended to betray the Argonauts – 'as a little child tries out a wintry torrent that not even a grown man will cross,' says Apollonius pathetically (4.460–61). Jason had been waiting in ambush, and now he leapt out, sword in hand. While Medea turned away her eyes, he murdered Apsyrtos, then ritually cut off his hands, feet, nose and ears (the so-called rite of *maschalismos*) to prevent his ghost from taking vengeance. Three times he licked and spat out his victim's blood in an attempt to remove blood-guilt. He buried the body, then the rest of the Argonauts attacked Apsyrtos's ship and killed the entire crew.

As the *Argo* sailed onwards, the speaking plank from Zeus's sanctuary at Dodona announced that the great god was angry because of this pitiless murder and demanded that Jason and Medea be purified by the enchantress Circe, Aietes' sister. Circe lived on the island of Aiaia on the west coast of Italy, so they now travelled up the Eridanos (Po) and down the Rhone (rivers thought by Apollonius to be linked), sailing on until they reached the Tyrrhenian Sea.

Circe welcomed them when they arrived on Aiaia and duly purified Jason and Medea, making propitiatory offerings and prayers. Only afterwards did she realize the full gravity of their crime. She drove them from her home, so the Argonauts set off on their journey once again, sailing down the coast of Italy.

The voyaging was easy, since Hera had arranged for gentle breezes to blow them onwards. They passed the island of the Sirens, the singing enchantresses who lured men to their doom (p. 404), and the Sirens sang as always their irresistible songs. The crew would have put in to shore, and that would have been the end of them, but Orpheus played his lyre to drown out the fatal music and the *Argo* was carried safely past by the winds. Only Boutes succumbed to the magic of the Sirens' song and leapt overboard to swim to them, but before he reached the island and certain death, Aphrodite snatched him from the water and carried him safely to Sicily.

They avoided the horrors of Skylla and Charybdis (p. 405), who haunted the Straits of Messina separating Italy from Sicily, but to do so they had to pass through the Planktai, the 'Wandering Rocks', beset with terrible waves and storms of blazing fire. Hera had asked the sea-goddess Thetis and her sister-Nereids to help, so these sped the *Argo* swiftly through the passage between the frightful rocks, while all around the ship the waters seethed and boiled.

Sailing eastwards across the Ionian Sea, the *Argo* landed on Scheria (Drepane/Corfu), the island of the Phaiakians. King Alkinoos welcomed them warmly, but soon afterwards a fleet of Kolchian ships sailed in and demanded Medea's return. It was for Alkinoos to arbitrate on the matter. Medea pleaded with the queen, Arete, to save her from being sent home to her father, and Arete, deeply moved by her plight, did so. Since Alkinoos had decided that if Medea was still a virgin, she should be returned to her father but, if not, she should stay with her husband, Arete arranged at once that the couple should consummate their love that very night. A sacred cave became their nuptial chamber and the Golden Fleece their marriage-bed.

Setting sail once again, the Argonauts were blown off course across the sea to Libya. For nine days and nights the North Wind drove them on until they were stranded deep within the gulf of Syrtis, surrounded by stagnant shallows and desert wastes. At first they were all despairing, ready now to die, but then they received a wondrous sign from the sea: a giant horse with a golden mane sprang from the waters and galloped inland. It was Poseidon's horse, they reasoned, and would be heading for some navigable gulf of the sea, so they lifted up the *Argo* and carried it on their shoulders in the same direction.

For twelve days and nights they travelled wearily through the sandy desert, burdened by their ship, until at last they came with great relief to Lake Tritonis. Before they could leave this land, however, they lost two more of their comrades: the seer Mopsos died, bitten by a snake, and Kanthos was killed by a Libyan shepherd named Kaphauros, a grandson of Apollo, when he tried to steal some sheep to feed the hungry crew. The other Argonauts killed Kaphauros in revenge and took all his sheep.

They buried their two comrades and launched the *Argo* on the lake. Now the sea-god Triton, son of Poseidon and Amphitrite, came to help them, disguised as a local king, Eurypylos. He presented Euphemos with a clod of earth as a gift of friendship, then he reverted to his true form of a merman, with a human head and torso and a coiling, fishy tail, and swam beside the ship, guiding it safely back to the Mediterranean.

When they reached Crete they tried to put in to harbour, but were pelted with rocks by the bronze man, Talos, who guarded the island. Some said that Talos had been made by the smith-god Hephaistos and given to King Minos, though Apollonius has him as the last survivor of the Race of Bronze and presented to Europa by Zeus when he won her love. Talos's task was to walk three times a day around the island on his untiring feet and get rid of strangers. His body was invulnerable except for one weak spot near his foot: a single vein containing ichor, the blood of the gods, ran all the way down from his neck to his ankle and was sealed at the bottom with a thin membrane of skin (some said with a bronze nail). Now, when he attacked the Argonauts, Medea put a spell on him from a distance by staring into his eyes and he stumbled, grazing his ankle on a sharp rock. The vital fluid that filled his single vein gushed out and he dropped lifeless to the ground.

North of Crete, Euphemos dropped the clod of earth that Triton had given him into the sea, where it became the island of Kalliste ('Most Beautiful'), later to be known as Thera (Santorini) and colonized by Euphemos's descendants. Then, after a final stop on the island of Aigina, the *Argo* sped on the final lap of her long journey and arrived safely back in Iolkos. Joyfully the Argonauts stepped ashore.

Thus ends Apollonius' *Argonautica*, but this is not quite the end of the story. Pelias had taken advantage of Jason's absence by killing his father Aison and other members of his family. Now it was the time for Pelias himself to die.

Jason, with Medea, delivers the Golden Fleece to Pelias.

THE DEATH OF PELIAS

Jason gave the Fleece to Pelias, but he did not enjoy his prize for long, since Medea, sent to Iolkos by Hera for just this purpose, cleverly brought about his death by persuading his own daughters to kill him. She applied her magic arts to an old ram with dramatic results, vividly described by Ovid (*Metamorphoses* 7.312–21):

A woolly ram, worn out with untold years, was dragged in, his horns curling around his hollow temples. Medea cut his scraggy throat with her Thessalian knife, barely staining the blade with his scanty blood.

She plunged his carcass into a bronze pot, throwing in with it magic herbs of great potency. These made his body shrink and burnt away his horns, and with his horns, his years, until a thin bleating was heard from within the pot. While they were all marvelling at the sound, out jumped a lamb and ran frisking away, in search of some udder to give him milk.

Pelias's daughters were so impressed that they readily agreed to have their ageing father rejuvenated as well. They killed him and cut him up, then boiled his mangled body in the bronze pot, fully believing that he would now have his youth renewed. Medea, of course, had left out the appropriate herbs, and that was the end of Pelias.

His son Akastos buried him with all due honour and held funeral games that became famous throughout the ancient world, with great heroes coming from all over Greece to compete. Jason and Medea fled from Iolkos and found refuge with Kreon, the king of Corinth. Jason dedicated the *Argo* to Poseidon and lived in Corinth for the rest of his life. Many years later he was killed when a beam, falling from the rotting carcase of his once glorious ship, fell on him and crushed him to death.

As for Medea, she would go on to commit several more murders – but this will be the subject of a later chapter (p. 453).

IO AND ARGOS

We have looked at the beginnings of one great family of Greek heroic mythology, the Deukalionids (p. 131), who originated in central Greece and then spread over wider areas. Another important family line had its origins in the Peloponnese and sprang from Inachos, god of the greatest river in the Argolid, through his daughter, Io.

Io and exile from Argos

Io's story is one that tells, as so often, of the great god Zeus's desire for a beautiful mortal woman and its consequences. Very often his amorous pursuits involve a transformation of some kind: Zeus turns himself into a swan, or a bull, or a shower of golden rain, so as to deceive his unwitting quarry and evade his jealous wife Hera. In Io's story, it is Io herself who is transformed – and into a cow.

Io was virgin priestess in the temple of Hera at Argos when her beauty caught the attention of Zeus. For a while he did nothing but send her seductive dreams, night after night urging her to come and lie with him in the grassy meadows of Lerna. Io always awoke bewildered and afraid, and at last she dared to confess her dreams to her father. Inachos too was perplexed as to their meaning, so he consulted the oracles at Delphi and Dodona, only to be told that he must drive his daughter out of home and country, or else his whole race would be blotted out by Zeus's thunderbolts. Father and daughter parted in great sadness. As soon as Io left her home she was transformed into a cow by the vindictive Hera, then was driven far through the world by a stinging gadfly, sent by Hera to stop her resting long enough for Zeus to make love to her.

This is the story told by Io herself, when she appears on stage, cow-horned, in Aeschylus's tragedy *Prometheus Bound*. Stung by the gadfly, she has roamed far to come to the rocky crag where Prometheus is chained, but he tells her that she still has far to travel. She will cross the channel that divides Europe from Asia, and it will ever afterwards be called the Bosporos ('Cow's-ford') after her. She will journey to the far ends of the earth, visiting the lands of the Scythians, the Amazons, the Graiai and the Gorgons, the Griffins and the one-eyed Arimaspians, the dark-skinned Ethiopians; and she will come at last to Egypt. Here her wanderings will finally be over. She will recover her human form and will give birth to a son, Epaphos, beside the Nile, naming him for the gentle touch (*epaphe*) of Zeus by which she conceived him.

Ovid is our most detailed source for the tale of Io's pathetic transformation (*Metamorphoses* 1.583–750). Here Zeus tried to entice Io to come with him into the woods, and when she ran away from him in fear, he covered the earth with a dark cloud and had his way with her. Hera, looking down from Olympos and seeing the unnatural clouds over Argos, at once suspected some mischief on the part of her husband and came to investigate. Dispersing the clouds, she found Zeus in the company of a beautiful white cow, for he had sensed his jealous wife's approach and had quickly transformed the unfortunate girl. Hera asked to have the cow as a gift – a request that Zeus could not reasonably refuse – but she was still suspicious of her philandering husband's intentions, so she set All-seeing Argos to guard her new possession. And none better to do so, for Argos was a monster with a hundred eyes, of which only two slept at any one time while the rest remained alert, so he could watch Io night and day.

Hermes attacks Argos as he guards Io (shown as a bull).

When Io in her new guise tried to speak, she was terrified by the lowing sound that came from her lips, and terrified too by the sight of her horns and gaping jaws reflected in her father's river. She followed Inachos continually, longing to tell him what terrible thing had happened, but of course he did not recognize her, and simply plucked some grass and held it out for her to eat. She licked her father's hand and tried to kiss it, and at last she managed to tell him her sad story by writing it in the dust with her hoof. When Argos drove her away to more distant pastures, Inachos, overcome with grief, hid himself in a cave at the source of his river, weeping for his beloved daughter and swelling his streams with his tears.

Now Zeus took pity on Io, and he set Hermes the difficult task of killing her unsleeping guardian. Never at a loss, Hermes cleverly disguised himself as a goatherd and soothed Argos with music from his panpipes, telling him the story of Syrinx, the nymph whose transformation led to the creation of his instrument (p. 117). At last all those watchful eyes slept, and Hermes struck off Argos's head with a sickle – 'and now one night filled his hundred eyes' (1.721). To mark this deed, Hermes was ever afterwards called *Argeiphontes*, 'Slayer of Argos', and Hera set Argos's many eyes into the tail of her royal bird, the peacock.

But Io's sufferings were far from over. Hera now had her driven in terror through all the world until she came to Egypt, and only then was the goddess's hostility appeased. Io regained her human form and bore Zeus's son, Epaphos. At last in Egypt she found peace. She married the Egyptian king, Telegonos, and was worshipped there as the goddess Isis, while Epaphos was worshipped as the bull-god Apis.

The return to Argos

There are a few more events in Egypt to record before the narrative returns to Argos. Epaphos married Memphis, a daughter of the river-god Nile, and in her name founded the great city of Memphis in Lower Egypt. She bore him a daughter, Libya, who gave her name to the lands west of Egypt (a much wider area than modern Libya). Libya had twin sons by Poseidon: Belos, who stayed in Egypt and succeeded Epaphos as king, and Agenor, who migrated to Phoenicia and established a kingdom of his own. (Two of his children, Europa and Kadmos, later founded royal lines in Crete and Thebes: see pp. 243 and 264). Belos's descendants returned to Argos and reclaimed their ancestral homeland.

Belos's name is simply the Hellenized form of the Levantine *Baal* and the Babylonian *Bel*, both of which mean 'lord', and his only importance lies in his children. He too married a daughter of the river-god Nile, Anchinoe, who bore him twin sons, Aigyptos and Danaos. Both brothers had children by many wives, Danaos fifty daughters, known as the Danaids, and

Aigyptos fifty sons. Belos, who ruled a huge empire centred on the kingdom around the Nile, settled Danaos in Libya and Aigyptos in Arabia; but Aigyptos was not content with his share and set his sights on future conquests.

First he overcame the tribe of the Melampodes ('Black-feet') and named the land Egypt and the people Egyptians (*Aiguptioi* in Greek) after himself. Next he offered his fifty sons in marriage to Danaos's fifty daughters. Such alliances would mean that Danaos's family would be absorbed into that of his brother and his own position greatly weakened, so he could see that Aigyptos was now intending to steal Libya. The brothers quarrelled and, on the advice of Athene, Danaos built a large ship and with his fifty daughters sailed away to Argos, since it was the birthplace of his ancestress Io.

There they found the land under the rule of Gelanor, who was also a descendant of Inachos, though from another branch of the family. Danaos claimed the kingdom on the basis of his descent from Io. According to a local Argive legend, recorded by Pausanias (2.19.3–4), Gelanor disputed the claim and the two of them debated the matter in the Argive assembly. The citizens decided in favour of Danaos because of what they saw as a portent from the gods. On the morning of the judgement, a wolf came from nowhere and attacked a herd of Argive cattle, killing the leading bull, and this seemed to be a sign that the newcomer should prevail. So Danaos won the kingdom, and because he believed that Apollo, god of prophecy, had sent the wolf, he showed his gratitude by founding a sanctuary of Apollo *Lykeios* (meaning 'Wolf-god' in this interpretation of the word).

He gave his name to his people, who were known as *Danaoi*, Danaans, and this became a general name for the Greek nation in Homer and later poets. He also brought water to Argos, which had been a dry land as a result of Poseidon's anger, ever since the time when the sea-god and Hera had both claimed overlordship of the country. Inachos and other river-gods had judged the dispute in favour of Hera, so in revenge Poseidon had caused them to run dry for much of the year.

Danaos now showed his people how to dig wells, and he sent his daughters out into the arid land to search for water. One of the Danaids, Amymone, was exploring the district of Lerna, a few miles south of the city of Argos, when she saw a deer and threw her javelin at it. She missed, but hit a sleeping satyr. The satyr leapt to his feet, and in the lecherous way of his kind he tried to rape the girl. She was saved by the sudden appearance of Poseidon, who flung his trident and drove the satyr away (satyrs were as cowardly as they were lustful), then took the girl for himself. Later, when the god tore his trident from the rock, out gushed springs of water, and ever afterwards Lerna was a well-watered region, with permanent springs, streams and even swamps. (It would later house the monstrous Hydra that Herakles had to kill.) Amymone was pregnant by Poseidon, and she bore the sea-god a son, Nauplios, who would become a famous seafarer.

According to Aeschylus's tragedy *Suppliants*, the first play in his Danaid trilogy, when Danaos came to Argos the kingdom was ruled, not by Gelanor, but by Pelasgos. Danaos arrived with his fifty daughters, hotly pursued by the fifty sons of Aigyptos, all eager for marriage. But the Danaids wanted none of it and begged Pelasgos for protection from their pursuers. At first he was unwilling to risk the violence that might ensue, but when all the girls threatened to hang themselves from the city altars, he agreed to help them.

Sadly the two following plays, *Egyptians* and *Danaids*, are lost, but the general outcome is well known from many other accounts. Danaos was eventually forced to agree to the marriages, so he allotted each of his daughters to one of their cousins. He gave a great feast in celebration, but he secretly presented each girl with a dagger and instructed them all to murder their new husbands during the wedding-night. Forty-nine of them obeyed. The eldest Danaid, Hypermestra, spared her husband Lynkeus, either because she had fallen in love with him or because she was grateful to him for respecting her virginity. He escaped to nearby Lyrkeia and there lit a fire-signal to let her know that he was safe.

Danaos punished Hypermestra with imprisonment and even put her on trial for her disobedience, but the Argive court acquitted her. Perhaps in Aeschylus this was through the inter-vention of Aphrodite, for we know that the goddess had a role in the third play, *Danaids*, and made a speech in favour of love and sexual union, through which all life is nurtured and renewed.

The other forty-nine Danaids hacked off their husbands' heads and took them to their father as proof of their obedience. The bodies were given proper funeral rites near the walls of the city and the heads were buried at Lerna. Zeus commanded Athene and Hermes to purify the girls of their murders, then Danaos had the task of finding new husbands for them. The young men of Argos were understandably disinclined to choose such doubtful brides, so Danaos promised to give them away, without asking for the customary bride-gifts in exchange, as prizes for whoever would run for them in foot-races. The winner would take his pick, and so on, until all the girls were chosen. Eventually they all remarried.

Lynkeus was later reunited with Hypermestra and reconciled with his father-in-law. He took the throne of Argos on Danaos's death, and he and Hypermestra had a son, Abas, through whom they were the generators of a splendid royal line that included the great heroes Perseus and Herakles. The fate of the other Danaids was not so happy, for after their deaths they were punished for their crime in the Underworld. They were forced to spend all eternity drawing water into leaking vessels, that had to be forever refilled.

The feuding brothers Akrisios and Proitos

By his wife Aglaia, Abas had twin sons, Akrisios and Proitos. The boys fought each other even in their mother's womb and grew up still implacably hostile to one another. When their father died, they fought over the rule of Argos – Apollodorus (2.2.1) tells us that it was during this war that shields were invented. Finally Akrisios drove Proitos out and seized the throne. Proitos fled for refuge to the court of Iobates, king of Lycia, and there married his daughter, who is usually called Stheneboia, though Homer calls her Anteia. Iobates provided Proitos with an army of Lycians to attack Argos, but now the twins at last came to an agreement: they divided the Argolid between them, with Akrisios ruling at Argos and Proitos at Tiryns. The great walls of Tiryns, built with stones so huge that it seemed impossible for human hands to have lifted them, were traditionally said to have been erected for Proitos by the one-eyed giants, the Cyclopes.

Stheneboia bore Proitos three daughters, Lysippe, Iphinoe and Iphianassa. They were famously afflicted with madness, either by the god Dionysos because they would not accept his rites, or by the goddess Hera because they showed disrespect to her. In their frenzy they roamed over the whole country in a wild and unseemly fashion, divesting themselves of their clothes. Some say that they imagined they were cows, or even that the angry Hera turned them into cows outright. After months, or even years, of madness they eventually recovered. In one version by the lyric poet Bacchylides (*Ode* 11.40–112), Proitos prayed to Artemis, promising her twenty red-haired oxen, never yoked, if only she would cure the girls. Artemis interceded with Hera, who at last took the madness from them.

In the more usual version, they were said to have been cured by Melampous, one of the greatest of Greek seers, who was at that time living at Pylos in Messenia. He had once saved the young of some snakes killed by his servants, then looked after them until they were fully grown. They repaid him by licking his ears one night as he slept, and after this he could understand the language of birds and animals and learn the future from them.

His skill at divination was first proven when his brother Bias fell in love with Pero, the beautiful daughter of Neleus, king of Pylos. She had many suitors, so her father said that he would give her to the man who brought him the splendid cattle belonging to Phylakos, king of Phylake in Thessaly. This would be a formidable task, for a ferocious dog guarded them night and day. Melampous undertook it on his brother's behalf, prophesying that he would be caught while trying to steal the cattle and would be imprisoned for a year, but at the end of that time the cattle would be his.

It fell out just as he said. Phylakos caught Melampous and imprisoned him, and when the year was nearly up, he heard woodworms talking in the roof of his cell, saying that the wood of the main beam had been almost eaten through. He demanded to be moved to another cell, and shortly afterwards the roof of the first cell collapsed. Phylakos was so impressed by his prophetic powers that he consulted him about the impotence of his son, Iphiklos, and Melampous promised to cure Iphiklos in return for the famous cattle.

Having sacrificed two bulls and summoned the birds, he learnt from an old vulture that once, when Phylakos was castrating rams, Iphiklos had been terrified by the bloody knife, so his father had stuck the knife in a sacred oak tree. Bark had since grown around the knife, but if it was now retrieved, and the rust scraped off and given to Iphiklos in a drink for ten days, he would have a son. Melampous did exactly as the vulture advised, and in due course Iphiklos had two sons, Podarkes and Protesilaos.

Melampous drove the cattle to Neleus at Pylos and won the hand of Pero for Bias. Many years later, when he heard of the madness of Proitos's daughters, he came to Tiryns and offered to cure them in return for a third of the kingdom. Proitos thought this too high a price and refused his offer, but then the girls became madder than ever, and the madness spread to the rest of the Argive women. They all abandoned their homes, even killing their own children, and went roaming through mountains and forests.

At this, Proitos accepted Melampous's offer – but too late, for now the seer had raised his price and was demanding two-thirds of the kingdom, a third for himself and a third for his brother Bias. Proitos gave in, fearing that the price would become even higher, and Melampous effected his promised cure by taking a band of strong young men with him and chasing the girls down from the mountains with shouts and frenzied dancing. During the pursuit Iphinoe died, but her two sisters and the rest of the women were purified and restored to sanity. Proitos in gratitude gave his two surviving daughters in marriage to the seer and his brother: Melampous married Iphianassa, and Bias (Pero having by this time died) Lysippe. After this Stheneboia bore Proitos a son, and Proitos called him Megapenthes ('Great Sorrow') to commemorate the grief he had suffered because of his daughters' madness.

Proitos suffered another misfortune when Stheneboia fell in love with the hero Bellerophon (see p. 176). But his twin Akrisios too had his share of adversity, which all began when his beautiful daughter Danae caught the eye of Zeus.

DANAE AND THE BIRTH OF PERSEUS

Akrisios wished for sons, but he and his wife Eurydike (daughter of Lakedaimon, the king of Sparta) had only one child, and that a daughter, Danae. He consulted an oracle about his lack of a male heir, and – as so often – the oracle gave no helpful answer, but instead responded with an alarming prophecy. He was told that Danae would give birth to a son, and this son would kill him. Hoping to outwit this fate by keeping his daughter away from all contact with men, he imprisoned her in a bronze, underground chamber along with her nurse. (The earliest source of the popular later notion that the prison was a bronze tower seems to be Horace, *Odes* 3.16.) But this solution reckoned without Zeus's desire for Danae. The chamber had a small aperture for light and air, and Zeus came to her in a shower of golden rain, pouring down into her lap (Plate 1). In due course she gave birth to a son, Perseus. Akrisios refused to believe that the father was Zeus, so he shut mother and child in a wooden chest and threw it out to sea, where it drifted far away.

A few poignant fragments remain from a poem by the lyric poet Simonides, in which Danae laments to her baby within the wooden chest (fr. 543):

> . . . When, in the finely wrought chest,
> the blowing wind and the swelling sea
> struck her with fear, her cheeks wet
> she put her loving arms round Perseus
> and said, 'My child, what trouble is mine.
> But you sleep sound, your little heart
> at peace as you lie on comfortless
> bronze-nailed wood, drowsing in the unlit night,
> the black dark. You care nothing
> for the deep spray of the swelling sea

above your head, nor the roaring wind,
as you lie there, your pretty face
bright in the crimson shawl.
If this danger were danger to you,
your tiny ear would hear my words.
But as it is, I tell you, sleep,
my baby, and let the sea sleep,
and let our endless suffering sleep . . .'

Zeus protected mother and baby, and had the chest drift safely to the island of Seriphos in the Cyclades. Here it was caught in the fishing nets of Diktys, brother of the local king, Polydektes, and he took Danae and her baby into his home. There Perseus grew uneventfully to manhood, but this quiet state of affairs could not last, for he was a son of Zeus and destined for great achievements. He was also, of course, destined to kill his grandfather, Akrisios.

6

HEROES AND MONSTERS

The measure of a great hero, apart from his strength and courage, was often his extraordinary ability to confront and defeat some terrifying and frequently monstrous opponent. Jason, as we have seen, had to yoke the fire-breathing bulls (though not without the help of Medea's magic potions). Herakles is the supreme example of this kind of hero, for time and time again he outfaced the worst that the world, and even the gods, could send against him. His many triumphs, almost always achieved by his own unaided endeavours, deserve a chapter to themselves. Here in this chapter we shall consider three other outstanding heroes, who had a more limited range of achievement than Herakles, but nevertheless accomplished great feats of courage and endurance. We begin by continuing the story of Perseus.

Perseus and the Gorgon Medusa

Perseus's heroic career began when Polydektes, the king of Seriphos, fell in love with Danae and resolved to have her, by fair means or foul. He realized that the presence of a grown son, well able to protect his mother, would be an obstacle to his courtship, so he planned to get rid of Perseus once and for all. He pretended that he wanted to marry Hippodameia, the daughter of Oinomaos, king of Pisa, and was collecting horses as contributions to the bride-gift. Perseus, when asked for his donation, boasted that if necessary he would even fetch the head of the Gorgon Medusa, so Polydektes took him up on his offer, quite sure that he could never return alive, since a glance at the Gorgon turned a man to stone.

Perseus naturally felt daunted at having to fulfil his rash

promise, until Athene and Hermes marked him out as a favourite of the gods by offering him divine help in his mission. On
their advice he went first of all to visit the three Graiai, daughters
of the ancient sea-god Phorkys and the sea-monster Keto, and
sisters of the three Gorgons. These white-haired old crones were
blind and toothless, apart from a single eye and a single tooth
which they shared among themselves, passing them around as
necessary.

Perseus needed to find out from them the whereabouts of
certain nymphs who could help him in his perilous quest. The
Graiai were naturally loath to give him any assistance that
might endanger their sisters, so Perseus stole their eye and tooth,
and refused to return them until the old women told him what
he wanted. Eventually, out of helplessness, they did so.

The nymphs provided Perseus with winged sandals to carry
him to the lair of the Gorgons at the ends of the earth, a cap of
darkness belonging to Hades that would make him invisible,
and a special bag in which to carry the Gorgon's severed head.
Added to these, Hermes gave him a sickle of adamant with
which to behead her, and he carried his own shield of polished
bronze. He was now fully armed for his task.

Using his winged sandals and wearing his cap of darkness,
he flew beyond the river of Ocean in the far west to the land of
the three Gorgons, the immortal Stheno and Euryale and the
mortal Medusa. He found them all asleep. They were fearsome
creatures, with heads covered by writhing snakes, great tusks
like a boar, hands of bronze and wings of gold. Medusa was
his target because of her mortality, and he was careful not to
look directly at her, or he would be turned to stone. He gazed
only at her reflection in his shining shield, while Athene helped
him by guiding the hand that held the sickle. He struck off
Medusa's head and thrust it into his bag – later he would use it
against his enemies – then flew swiftly away.

Perseus, followed by Athene, escapes after slaying Medusa.

Medusa had been pregnant by the god Poseidon, and now from her severed neck leapt two offspring: the winged horse Pegasos, who would play a part in the legend of Bellerophon, and Chrysaor ('Golden Sword'), about whom we know very little, except that he fathered triple-bodied Geryon, one of Herakles' monstrous victims. Stheno and Euryale did their best to pursue their sister's killer, but with Perseus wearing the cap of darkness they were bound to fail. They returned to mourn their dead sister, and Pindar (*Pythian Ode* 12.6–27) tells us that Athene invented the mournful music of the *aulos*, the double pipe, to imitate the sound of their sad lament.

No early account of the expedition against the Gorgons exists, but the Hesiodic *Shield of Herakles* (sixth century BC) captures the moments just after Perseus has succeeded in beheading Medusa. The poem includes a description of the wondrous shield made by Hephaistos for Herakles before his battle with Kyknos, a bloodthirsty son of the war-god Ares.

Many marvels were depicted on it, and one of these was a figure of Perseus, fashioned in gold (220–37):

On his feet he wore winged sandals, and across his shoulders on a belt of bronze was slung a sword in a black scabbard. He was flying as swift as thought. On his back was the head of a terrible monster, the Gorgon, carried in a bag of silver, a wonder to behold, and from the bag hung tassels of shining gold. Upon the hero's head lay the fearful cap of Hades with its awful darkness of night. Perseus himself, the son of Danae, was travelling at full stretch, as though he were rushing onwards and shuddering with horror. After him darted the Gorgons, unspeakably dreadful, longing to catch hold of him, and as they trod upon the pale adamant, the shield rang sharp and clear with a great clanging. Two snakes hung down from their belts, their heads arching forwards. Their tongues were flickering, they were gnashing their teeth with fury, and their eyes were glaring fiercely. And on the dreadful heads of the Gorgons, great Terror was menacing.

Fearsome as the Gorgons were, Perseus escaped safely with his prize and began to make his way home to Seriphos. One story had him come to the land of the Hesperides (here imagined to be in north-west Africa), where he asked the Titan Atlas for hospitality. Atlas turned him away, so Perseus showed him the head of Medusa, and the Titan was transformed into massive Mount Atlas, huge enough to support heaven and all its stars on his shoulders. Soon afterwards, as Perseus was flying over the sandy deserts of Libya, drops of blood fell to the ground from Medusa's severed head and became deadly snakes, with which Libya now abounds.

Finally he came to the land of the Ethiopians, where Kepheus was king, and saw below him a beautiful girl chained to a rock on the sea-shore – Andromeda, the daughter of Kepheus and Kassiepeia. The vain Kassiepeia had boasted that she was more beautiful than the Nereids, and when they complained to Poseidon, the god sent a flood and a sea-monster to destroy the land. An oracle predicted that deliverance would come only if Andromeda was given over to the monster, so Kepheus was forced by his people to chain his daughter up and leave her to be devoured. It was at this critical point, while she waited for the monster to come for her, that Perseus flew by on his winged sandals.

He fell in love with Andromeda at first sight, and promised her father that he would save her, so long as he might have her hand in marriage. When the monster appeared, cleaving its way through the ocean, he flew up and attacked it from above, killing it with his sickle. Then he claimed Andromeda as his bride. Unfortunately she had been betrothed to Kepheus' brother, Phineus, who now stirred up opposition to the match – but this was short-lived, for Perseus simply uncovered Medusa's head and turned Phineus and all his supporters to stone. The wedding could now take place.

Within the year, Andromeda had given birth to their first son, Perses. Perseus then returned to Seriphos, taking his new wife with him but leaving their little son to be brought up by Kepheus, who had no male heir to succeed him. Perses would give his name to the Persians and become the ancestor of the Persian kings.

Back in Seriphos, Perseus found his mother and Diktys being cruelly persecuted by Polydektes. Once again Medusa's head came into play. Perseus caught Polydektes and his retinue feasting within the palace and turned them all into stone. He made Diktys king in Polydektes' place. Then, with his mission finally over, he gave the winged sandals and his other aids back to Hermes and the Gorgon's head to Athene. She put it in the centre of her breastplate as a threat to her enemies.

Perseus returned to Argos with Andromeda and Danae,

intending to settle in his homeland and make himself known to his grandfather – but Akrisios had heard of his impending arrival and had fled, still in fear for his life because of the sinister oracle. Perseus went on to Larissa in Thessaly to compete in some funeral games, but unfortunately Akrisios happened to be there too, and, while throwing the discus, Perseus accidentally struck and killed his grandfather. The oracle was fulfilled (as oracles always were).

After causing his grandfather's death, Perseus was ashamed to succeed to his rightful inheritance of the throne of Argos, so he exchanged Argos for Tiryns, the kingdom of Megapenthes, son of Proitos. Perseus also founded Mycenae, and had the Cyclopes build the massive ('Cyclopean') walls for him, just as they had built those of Tiryns for Proitos. Andromeda bore him more children: a daughter, Gorgophone (meaning 'Killing of the Gorgon', to celebrate Perseus' greatest deed), and five more sons, Alkaios, Sthenelos, Elektryon, Mestor and Heleios. Their great-grandson would be the mighty hero Herakles.

After their deaths, Perseus and Andromeda were immortalized in the stars as the constellations named after them, as were Kepheus and Kassiepeia (more commonly Cepheus and Cassiopeia) and even the sea-monster (Cetus). Cassiopeia with its 'W' shape is one of the most easily recognized constellations in the night sky. The queen is imagined as sitting on a chair, and she spends half her time upside down, to give her a lesson in humility.

BELLEROPHON AND THE CHIMAIRA

The story of Bellerophon (or Bellerophontes), the greatest of Corinthian heroes, is one of virtue and courage rewarded, and finally of presumption punished. He was grandson of the arch-trickster Sisyphos and his wife Merope (one of the seven Pleiades), and son of Glaukos, king of Corinth, though he was also sometimes said to be a son of Poseidon. Glaukos is most notable for the hideous manner of his death. He was in the habit of feeding his horses on human flesh so as to make them race more aggressively, but when he took them to Iolkos, to take part in the funeral games of King Pelias, they were deprived of their usual fare, so they tore Glaukos himself to pieces and devoured him. For generations after this, Glaukos's ghost, known as Taraxippos ('Horse-frightener'), haunted the stadium at Corinth where the Isthmian Games were held, and terrified the horses as they raced.

Bellerophon, however, did not become king of Corinth in his father's place, having been forced to leave his native city for accidentally killing a man (his name means 'Belleros-slayer'). His story first occurs in Homer's *Iliad* (6.144–211), when the Lycian leader Glaukos (great-grandson of the first Glaukos) relates his ancestry to the Greek hero Diomedes on the battle-field at Troy, beginning with a famous simile:

'Like the generations of leaves are those also of men.
The wind scatters the leaves on the earth, but the live trees
burgeon anew when the season of spring is come.
So one generation of men is born as another dies away.'

Glaukos goes on to relate how Bellerophon went to stay with Proitos, the king of Tiryns, whose wife unfortunately fell in love with their young guest. Homer calls her Anteia, though she is better known as Stheneboia, the name found in all later accounts. She tried to seduce Bellerophon, but he was a virtuous young man and rejected all her advances. Angry and vengeful, she accused him to her husband of trying to rape her, hoping that Proitos would now kill him. And he would have liked to do so, but he was afraid of angering the gods by killing a guest. So instead he sent Bellerophon away to stay with his father-in-law Iobates, the king of Lycia, sending with him a sealed letter containing instructions to kill the bearer. 'Dire, life-destroying symbols' is how Homer describes the message, in his only certain reference to the art of writing.

For nine days Iobates feasted Bellerophon, and it was only on the tenth day that he opened the fateful letter from his son-in-law. Now he too hesitated to kill a guest directly, so he set Bellerophon what he hoped would be a fatal task: to kill the deadly Chimaira, offspring of two other huge and terrifying monsters, Echidna and Typhon. It is Hesiod (*Theogony* 319–25) who gives our best description of her:

She breathed invincible fire, a great and terrible creature, swift of foot and strong. She had three heads, one of a fierce-eyed lion, the second of a goat (*chimaira*, 'she-goat'), and the third of a snake, a mighty serpent. The lion was at the front, the snake at the rear, and the goat in the middle breathing out a great blast of blazing fire.

Bellerophon, mighty hero that he was, succeeded in killing the Chimaira, only to be set two further tasks by Iobates: to fight single-handed against the Solymoi, enemies of Lycia, and next against the Amazons, that powerful tribe of fierce warrior-women. From both these battles he returned victorious. Iobates then made one final attempt to have him killed: he sent the bravest men in Lycia to ambush him, but Bellerophon slaughtered them all. At last Iobates recognized that his guest must have divine blood in his veins, so he capitulated, giving him half his kingdom and the hand of his daughter, Philonoe, in marriage. This younger sister of Anteia/Stheneboia bore Bellerophon two sons, Hippolochos (Glaukos's father) and Isandros, who was killed fighting the Solymoi, and a daughter, Laodameia. She was loved by Zeus and bore him Sarpedon (Glaukos's commander at Troy, soon to be killed by Patroklos), and herself died 'killed by Artemis in anger'.

Homer does not explain how Bellerophon managed to complete his tasks successfully, but in all later accounts he does so by flying high on the winged, immortal horse Pegasos and attacking his opponents from above. Pegasos, as we have seen, was the offspring of Poseidon and the Gorgon Medusa, born from his mother's neck when Perseus struck off her head. Pindar (*Olympian Ode* 13.60–92) describes how Pegasos was caught and tamed by Bellerophon, who first saw the wondrous horse grazing by the spring of Peirene at Corinth and longed to have him for his own. On the advice of the seer Polyeidos, he slept for a night in the shrine of Athene. There he dreamed that the goddess gave him a golden bridle and told him to sacrifice a white bull to Poseidon, Tamer of Horses. He awoke to find the bridle beside him, so he duly made the appropriate sacrifice and dedicated an altar in thanks to Athene. Now he 'tamed the winged horse by stretching the gentle charm around his mouth' and mounted easily on his back.

From this vantage point he was able to accomplish the deadly tasks set him by Iobates. The battle with the Chimaira was a favourite scene in ancient art, and from the early decades of the seventh century BC onwards we see Bellerophon mounted on

Pegasos.   *The Chimaira.*

Pegasos and attacking the monster, at first confronting her head-on, later flying above her to bring her to her death. But in a sense the Chimaira lives on, for she was a popular subject in post-classical art too, appearing in such fantastic guises, often winged, that she has given her name to our own word 'chimera', meaning a wild fancy.

Bellerophon's later fortunes were dramatized by Euripides in two tragedies, now lost but for fragments. In *Stheneboia* Bellerophon returned to Tiryns, to take vengeance on the woman who had tried to have him killed. He persuaded her to mount Pegasos with him, then flew out high over the sea and threw her down to her death. His own tragic end was dramatized in *Bellerophon*, when he tried to ride Pegasos up to the gods' home on Olympos – a scene famously parodied to great comic effect in Aristophanes' comedy *Peace*, when Trygaios tries to do the same, though mounted on a dung-beetle. Zeus, furious at Bellerophon's presumption, sent a gadfly to sting his winged steed. Pegasos threw his rider back to earth again and left the mortal world forever, living thereafter with the gods on Olympos, where he drew the chariot that brought Zeus his thunder and lightning. Zeus honoured Pegasos by placing in the stars the constellation named after him.

Bellerophon survived his fall and appeared on stage in Euripides' play, crippled and in rags. (Aristophanes again parodied this in his comedy *The Acharnians*.) Possibly he died at the play's end. Homer, as we have seen, makes no mention of Pegasos, nor, therefore, of the attempt on Olympos. Of Bellerophon's sorry end, he says simply: 'Hated by all the gods, he wandered alone over the Aleian plain, eating his heart out and keeping far away from the trodden paths of men.'

MELEAGROS AND THE KALYDONIAN BOAR

The Kalydonian Boarhunt, like the quest for the Golden Fleece, was one of the great exploits of the ancient world, with many famous heroes of the generation before the Trojan War taking part in it. It all began when Oineus, king of the Aitolians of Kalydon, was offering the first fruits of his harvest to all the gods but happened to forget Artemis. Because of this slight, the vengeful goddess sent into Kalydon a gigantic wild boar that ravaged the countryside, destroying crops and killing cattle and men.

In ancient accounts of the Boarhunt, the boar seems to become more terrible over time. The story first occurs in Homer (*Iliad* 9.529–99), and here the boar sounds not too dreadful: '. . . a fierce wild boar, with white tusks, who in the way of his kind did much harm in the orchards of Oineus, uprooting many tall trees and casting them to the ground, roots and apple blossom and all'. He becomes rather more fearsome when the story is told by Bacchylides (*Ode* 5.93–154): '. . . a mighty wild boar, a remorseless fighter, who in the floodtide of his strength cut down fruit trees with his tusks, and slaughtered sheep and any mortal who stood against him'. And by the time we get to Ovid, the boar has become quite monstrous (*Metamorphoses* 8.284–9):

His eyes glared with a bloody fire, his neck was stiff and hairy, his hide was covered with bristles that stuck straight out like spears. He squealed harshly, hot foam streaming over his broad shoulders, and his tusks were as long as an elephant's. Flames came out of his mouth, and the leaves were burnt up by his breath.

The son of Oineus and his wife Althaia was Meleagros, though he was sometimes said to be a son of the war-god Ares. Meleagros had sailed with Jason and the Argonauts, and had won the javelin competition at the funeral games of Pelias. Now he gathered a large band of the best men from all over Greece to hunt the enormous boar. According to the list in Apollodorus (1.8.2), these heroes included the Dioskouroi, Kastor and Polydeukes; Idas and Lynkeus, the sons of Aphareus; the great Athenian hero Theseus and his friend Peirithoos; Jason, the leader of the Argonauts; Admetos from Pherai; Ankaios and

Kepheus, the sons of Lykourgos from Arcadia; Iphikles, the half-brother of Herakles; the two sons of Aiakos, Peleus and Telamon; Eurytion, the king of Phthia; Pelias' son Akastos; the seer Amphiaraos; and the huntress Atalanta. Once they were all assembled, along with their hounds, the Boarhunt began.

It was Meleagros himself who killed the boar. Homer gives no details of the hunt itself, because his attention is on the hunt's aftermath, when Artemis, still angry, stirred up strife over the head and hide of the boar. This led to a violent battle between the Aitolians of Kalydon and the Kouretes of Pleuron, the clan to which Meleagros's mother Althaia belonged. All went well for the Aitolians while Meleagros was fighting, for under his leadership they easily had the upper hand, but this changed when, in the heat of battle, he killed his mother's brothers. Althaia cursed him, calling on Hades and Persephone to bring about his death (and, ominously, 'the Fury who walks in darkness, she of the pitiless heart, heard her from Erebos'). Because of this, Meleagros retired from battle in anger and refused to fight any more.

With Meleagros out of action, the Kouretes attacked Kalydon more and more violently. The city elders offered Meleagros gifts if only he would return to battle, and his father, his mother, his sisters and his dearest comrades all in turn begged him to do so. He refused again and again, and only when his wife Kleopatra entreated him did he give in. (Kleopatra was the daughter of Idas and Marpessa, and was elsewhere called Alkyone.)

Meleagros fought, and brought victory to his people – but this, says Homer, was too late for him to receive the promised gifts. He does not mention how Meleagros died, but in other early versions of the myth, the lost epic *Minyas* and the fragmentary Hesiodic *Catalogue of Women*, he died a typical epic death, killed by the god Apollo who was fighting in support of the Kouretes.

Later accounts give us a few more details of the Boarhunt. Many hounds were attacked and killed by the boar. Many men were wounded and some lost their lives. One of these was Eurytion, accidentally killed by a javelin shot from Peleus. Another was Ankaios, who had come to the hunt dressed in a bearskin and armed with a two-headed axe, the same equipment that he had taken on the voyage of the Argonauts. He survived that dangerous expedition, but here he was not so fortunate. As he rushed at the huge boar, swinging his great axe, the beast gored him in the groin and he died.

Archaic art is a helpful source here, since the Boarhunt was a popular subject for vase-painters. It appears first on the François Krater (c.570 BC), where most of the participants, including dogs, are named. Meleagros and Peleus, side by side, face the enormous boar, with Atalanta and her lover Melanion behind them, while beneath the boar Ankaios (though here spelt Antaios) and a disembowelled dog lie dead. After this Ankaios becomes a standard figure in such scenes, and Atalanta too is often prominent.

Meleagros had fallen in love with the beautiful huntress, so he was delighted when she drew first blood by shooting an arrow into the boar's back. He himself finally killed the huge beast with a stab in the flank, though he refused the trophies of the hunt that were due him, the head and hide of the boar, and presented them instead to Atalanta as an acknowledgement of her skill. This caused resentment among the other hunters. Once again a fight broke out, during which Meleagros killed his mother's brothers, either accidentally, or in anger because they had taken the spoils away from Atalanta. In this version too he lost his life – but here in a far more pathetic way than in earlier epic.

Just after his birth, his mother Althaia had been told by the Fates that he would live until a log, then burning on the hearth, was completely burnt away. Althaia immediately quenched the flames and put the log in a chest, keeping it safe for many years. Then came the Boarhunt. When Meleagros killed her brothers during the fight over the spoils, she took the log from its safe hiding place and threw it into the fire. As soon as it was burnt up, Meleagros died.

In the aftermath of the Boarhunt, Althaia and Meleagros's wife Kleopatra both killed themselves, Althaia in remorse and Kleopatra in grief. His sisters mourned for him so inconsolably that Artemis pitied them and transformed them into guinea-hens (*Meleagrides*) – though not Deianeira, who would marry Herakles. Bacchylides describes how Herakles met the shade of Meleagros in the Underworld when he went down to capture the monstrous guard-dog Kerberos. Meleagros told him the story of the hunt and of his own sad fate, dead at the hands of his mother, which moved Herakles to ask if he had any sisters like himself whom he could make his wife. Meleagros named Deianeira, thus setting in motion the events that would lead to Herakles' own death (p. 221).

The traveller Pausanias (8.46.1,5) records in the second century AD that the boar's tusks had originally been preserved in Athene's temple at Tegea in Arcadia, but that Augustus had taken them to Rome, where one was still to be seen, and was about three feet long. Pausanias himself (8.47.2) saw the hide of the boar at Tegea, though by then it was rotted by age and had lost all its bristles.

7

HERAKLES

The greatest hero of them all was Herakles (known to the Romans as Hercules). He was an immensely popular mythological character, a man of superhuman strength, courage and endurance; a man also of violent passions and of hearty and unashamed appetites, with a tremendous voracity for food, wine and sex. He lived an arduous life of toil and hardship, and was given the title of *Alexikakos*, 'Averter of Evil', because he purged the world of so many monsters and evildoers. Because of his great feats, he was rewarded at the end of his life with immortality among the gods, though in Homer's *Odyssey*, Odysseus sees Herakles' shade still in the Underworld – token no doubt of a time before his apotheosis became an established part of his legend. Herakles is a lonely and awesome figure, fearsome even in death (11.605–12):

> Around him the dead cried out like frightened birds,
> fleeing in every direction. Like dark night he came,
> holding his bow uncovered, an arrow on the bowstring,
> glaring round him fiercely, forever about to shoot.
> A fearsome sword-belt lay across his chest,
> a golden baldric emblazoned with wondrous works,
> bears and wild boars, and lions with flashing eyes,
> conflicts, and battles, and deaths, and slayings of men.

Sadly, no great epic of Herakles' deeds survives, but consecutive narratives of his life have been given us in prose by Apollodorus (2.4.8–2.7.8) and Diodorus Siculus (4.9–4.39), and his mighty achievements are depicted on many thousands of ancient vase-paintings. His exploits are traditionally divided into three main categories. First and most important were the twelve Labours performed for Eurystheus; *athloi* in the Greek, meaning contests – usually for a prize – and hence arduous struggles or ordeals. The canonical list of these Labours seems to have been established by the fifth century BC, when all twelve were depicted on the metopes of the temple of Zeus at Olympia, dated at around 460. Then there were the *parerga*, the incidental achievements of Herakles while he was performing his Labours; and finally the *praxeis*, the deeds which he undertook of his own accord. The chronology of these various exploits varies somewhat, and what follows here is the sequence of events recorded by Apollodorus, with slight adaptations.

Prelude to Herakles' birth

Herakles was the greatest son borne to Zeus by a mortal woman. His mother was Alkmene, the daughter of Elektryon, king of Mycenae, who had succeeded to the throne on the death of his father Perseus, slayer of the Gorgon Medusa. Alkmene was married to her cousin Amphitryon, the son of Alkaios, another son of Perseus. For a long while, however, she remained a virgin, because Elektryon had decreed that the marriage must not be consummated until vengeance had been taken on the Taphians (also called the Teleboans), who in a violent raid had stolen his cattle and killed Alkmene's nine brothers.

First Amphitryon recovered the cattle and brought them safely back to Mycenae, but, as he was returning them to the king, one of the cows charged and he hurled a club at her, which rebounded from her horns and killed Elektryon. Elektryon's brother Sthenelos at once banished Amphitryon from the whole of the Argolid and seized the throne for himself. Amphitryon went with Alkmene to Thebes, where he was purified of his unintentional manslaughter by Kreon, the ruler of the city.

The deaths of Alkmene's brothers had still to be avenged,

and Kreon agreed to help if Amphitryon first got rid of the Teumessian Vixen – a huge and ferocious fox, fated never to be caught, which had been sent by the gods to torment the people of Thebes. Every month, to appease the beast, a son of one of the Theban citizens was put out as its prey. Amphitryon called for the aid of a famous hunting dog called Lailaps ('Hurricane'), belonging to Kephalos, the son of Deion, king of Phokis. Lailaps was fated never to miss his quarry, so the inescapable hound chased on and on after the uncatchable fox – until Zeus intervened and put an end to the everlasting pursuit by turning both animals to stone.

After this success, Kreon helped Amphitryon in his vengeance on the Taphians, who lived on a group of islands just outside the entrance to the Corinthian Gulf. Together with a few other allies, he and Amphitryon made a triumphant raid on most of the islands, but they failed to take Taphos itself because of the Taphians' king, Pterelaos. He seemed invincible, for at his birth his grandfather Poseidon had put in his hair a single strand of gold that would keep him immortal as long as it remained there. Now Amphitryon was helped by the king's daughter, Komaitho, who had fallen in love with the invader: she pulled out the golden hair of immortality from her father's head and he died. Amphitryon could now subjugate all the islands, but if Komaitho expected gratitude, she received none. Amphitryon killed her for her treachery.

With Elektryon's sons thus fully avenged, Amphitryon could return home with the right to consummate his marriage at last – but Zeus had pre-empted him. The great god had been waiting for the right opportunity to sleep with the beautiful Alkmene, and when Amphitryon was on the point of arriving home, triumphant and laden with booty, Zeus saw his moment. He came to Alkmene disguised as Amphitryon and told her all about the victory over the Taphians. Delighted to hear that her brothers had been avenged, and completely taken in, she welcomed the god to her bed. Zeus even prolonged the night to three times its usual length so that he could enjoy Alkmene to the full.

As soon as Zeus left, Amphitryon himself arrived and was amazed to find, when he went to his wife's bed, that she knew all about his victory and thought she had already slept with him. Bewildered, he consulted the blind Theban seer Teiresias, who told him the truth of what had happened, explaining Zeus's trick and Alkmene's innocence.

In the course of time Alkmene gave birth to twins, Zeus's son Herakles and Amphitryon's son Iphikles. Zeus was well aware that Herakles would be his mightiest son and he intended him to become king of all the Argolid, which included Mycenae and Tiryns. However, he himself inadvertently destroyed this prestigious future on the day that his child was born. Homer tells the story (*Iliad* 19.95–133). When Alkmene was about to give birth, Zeus rashly boasted that on that very day would be born a child of his own lineage who would grow up to rule over all those around him. His wife Hera, bitterly resentful of this son by a mortal woman, craftily made Zeus swear that this would indeed be so. She then came down to earth from Olympos, and with the help of the birth-goddess, Eileithyia, she held back the birth of Herakles. At the same time she brought forward the birth of the child due to be born to Sthenelos, now king of Mycenae, and his son Eurystheus was born prematurely at seven months. Zeus would now be obliged to grant the rule of the Argolid to this child instead of to Herakles.

Triumphantly she returned to Olympos:

> And she said to Zeus, son of Kronos: 'Father Zeus,
> lord of the lightning, I have news to warm your heart.
> Today is born an illustrious man who will rule

over all the Argives: Eurystheus, son of Sthenelos,
descended from Perseus, so born of your own stock.
He is not unfit to rule over all the Argives.'
So she spoke, and a bitter sorrow struck Zeus
deep in his heart . . . and ever afterwards
he would grieve when he saw his own dear son
toiling at one of his shameful tasks for Eurystheus.

These tasks would be the twelve great Labours, performed while Herakles served Eurystheus for twelve years. He would, moreover, endure persecution throughout his life because of Hera's continuing jealousy and resentment.

Ovid describes Herakles' birth in some detail (*Metamorphoses* 9.280–323): for seven days and seven nights Alkmene was in painful and fruitless labour, while Eileithyia held back the birth by sitting outside the bedroom door, with legs crossed and fingers intertwined, murmuring spells. Luckily for Alkmene, a faithful slave girl called Galanthis thought of a way to help her mistress. She tricked Eileithyia by suddenly announcing that the baby had been born, at which the goddess leapt to her feet in astonishment, loosening her clasped hands. In that moment of inattention, Herakles was at last born, soon to be followed by Iphikles. Eileithyia punished Galanthis by turning her into a weasel (*gale* in Greek).

THE EARLY YEARS

So despite Hera's intervention, Alkmene finally gave birth to her twin boys. When they were only eight months old, it became clear which of the pair was the son of Zeus when two huge snakes crawled into the boys' bed. Iphikles screamed in terror, while Herakles seized the snakes by their necks and choked them to death with his baby hands. Some say that Hera sent the snakes because of her enduring hostility to Herakles, others that Amphitryon did so to find out which of the children was his own son.

As Herakles grew up, he was instructed by experts in all the usual skills of a young man. He was taught to drive a chariot by Amphitryon, to wrestle by the great trickster Autolykos, and to shoot with the bow by Eurytos of Oichalia, who was a grandson of the archer-god Apollo. Kastor, one of the Dioskouroi, taught Herakles the arts of war; and the fine musician Linos, brother of the even finer musician Orpheus, taught him to play the lyre – though not very successfully. One day the master struck out in irritation at his inexpert pupil, and Herakles retaliated by killing Linos with his own lyre.

By his eighteenth year Herakles had become a magnificent specimen of manhood and was ready to begin on his adult life of toil and glory. He was well equipped for it, for he possessed a bow and arrows given him by Apollo, a sword by Hermes, a golden breastplate by Hephaistos, horses by Poseidon, and a robe by Athene; he himself had cut a great club at Nemea.

The first of his many dangerous exploits was the slaying of the ferocious lion that was preying on the flocks of Mount Kithairon. It took Herakles fifty days to hunt it down, during which time he stayed each night with Thespios, the king of nearby Thespiai. Thespios was anxious to have as many grandchildren as possible by such a hero, so he sent his fifty daughters to Herakles' bed, either over fifty nights, or seven nights, or even just one night. Herakles fathered sons on them all, and twins on the eldest and youngest.

On the way back to Thebes, he encountered the heralds of Erginos, king of the Minyans of Boiotian Orchomenos, who were travelling to Thebes to demand payment of an annual tribute. Some years previously, Erginos's father Klymenos had been mortally wounded by a stone thrown by a Theban and with his dying breath had called on his son to avenge him.

Erginos had marched on Thebes, killed a good many Thebans, and imposed a tribute on them of a hundred head of cattle every year for twenty years. Now Herakles resolved to rid Thebes of this burden, so he lopped off the ears and noses and hands of the heralds, hung them around their necks, and told them to take these back to their master by way of tribute. The furious Erginos once again marched on Thebes, but this time against an army led by Herakles. Erginos was killed and his men put to flight. Herakles then imposed on the people of Orchomenos a tribute of 200 head of cattle every year.

The grateful Kreon rewarded him with marriage to his daughter Megara. The marriage was a happy one and the couple had several children, but it ended in tragedy when Hera afflicted Herakles with a fit of homicidal madness, during which he murdered his children and, in most accounts, Megara as well. (There are, as ever, variants, and according to Euripides' powerful tragedy *The Madness of Herakles*, the madness came at the end of the twelve Labours, so that Hera crushed Herakles at the very height of his success.)

Returning to sanity, and overcome with grief and remorse, Herakles condemned himself to exile. He went back to Thespios for the necessary ritual purification, then travelled to the Delphic Oracle for advice. The Pythian priestess instructed him to go and live in Tiryns, and to serve the king of the Argolid, Eurystheus, for twelve years as expiation for his crime. He must carry out all the tasks imposed on him by the king, however seemingly impossible, and their completion – if he survived them – would earn him immortality. These tasks became his famous twelve Labours.

THE TWELVE LABOURS

Herakles' first six Labours were set in the northern Peloponnese, not too far from Mycenae, while his second six, becoming more daunting as time went on, took him much further afield: first to Crete, Thrace and Asia Minor, and finally to the far ends of the earth, and even down to the land of the dead in the Underworld. 'I was a son of Zeus,' says the shade of Herakles to Odysseus in Homer, 'but infinite was my suffering; for I was slave to a far inferior man, and heavy were the labours he laid upon me' (*Odyssey* 11.620–23).

1 THE NEMEAN LION

Herakles' first Labour was to kill the Nemean Lion and take its skin to Eurystheus. This was no ordinary lion: it had a skin impervious to weapons and was the monstrous offspring of monstrous parents. Hesiod names its mother as either the snaky Echidna or the fire-breathing Chimaira (*Theogony* 326–32, with the text being ambiguous) and its father as Orthos, the two-headed hound of Geryon; while Apollodorus (2.5.1) names its father as the horrific monster Typhon. It was Hera who nurtured the lion, in the hope of causing Herakles harm. She settled it in the foothills of Nemea in the north-western corner of the Argolid, and there it terrorized the neighbourhood, preying on men and beasts alike.

On his way to Nemea, Herakles lodged at Kleonai with a poor labourer called Molorchos, whose son had been killed by the lion. Molorchos wanted to offer a sacrifice in honour of his courageous guest, but Herakles told him to wait for thirty days, and then to sacrifice either to Zeus the Saviour if he had returned safely from the hunt, or to Herakles himself as a hero if he had been killed.

When Herakles finally tracked down the lion, he soon realized that it was invulnerable when his arrows bounced off its hide. The beast took refuge in its lair, a cave with two mouths, so Herakles blocked up one entrance and went in by the other. He seized the lion by the neck and strangled it with his bare hands, then carried its body back to Eurystheus at Mycenae. On his journey he once again passed through Kleonai. This being the last of the thirty days, he was just in time to stop Molorchos sacrificing to him as a dead hero. Molorchos now sacrificed instead to Zeus the Saviour.

Eurystheus was a cowardly man, and when he saw the lion's body he was so alarmed by its immense size, and by the thought of Herakles' tremendous prowess, that he ordered him never to enter Mycenae again, but to display his trophies outside the city gates. He even had a great bronze jar set in the earth so that he could hide in it if Herakles came near, and from this point on he gave him no direct commissions, but sent his commands through a herald, Kopreus, a son of Pelops. This man, like his master, was viewed in antiquity as a generally despicable character.

Herakles skinned the lion's body by using its own claws to cut its otherwise impenetrable hide, and ever afterwards he wore its pelt as a trophy, with its front paws knotted around his neck and its scalp serving as a helmet. (This becomes his standard costume in ancient art from the sixth century BC onwards.) The lion was immortalized in the stars by Zeus as the constellation Leo, an everlasting memorial of his son's first great task.

2 THE HYDRA OF LERNA

The second Labour was to kill the Hydra of Lerna, another monster nurtured by Hera in her anger against Herakles and once again the offspring of monstrous parents, this time of Echidna and Typhon. It was a poisonous, many-headed water-snake, with the number of its heads varying in art and literature from just a few to as many as fifty or a hundred. It lurked in the swamps of Lerna to the south of Argos and preyed on the flocks of the neighbouring countryside.

Herakles, in the skin of the Nemean Lion, attacks the Hydra.

Herakles found it in its lair near the spring of Amymone and forced it to come out by shooting at it with burning arrows. He could then come to grips with the monster, but he found that whenever he destroyed one head with his great club, two sprouted in its place. A giant crab added further difficulties by coming to the aid of the Hydra and nipping Herakles' foot, so he killed it. Hera was so pleased with the crab's efforts that she immortalized it in the stars as the constellation Cancer.

Herakles finally killed the Hydra with the help of his nephew Iolaos, the son of his half-brother Iphikles. Iolaos had become Herakles' charioteer and would be his faithful companion through all his Labours and his many expeditions. Now, as soon as Herakles had cut off one of the Hydra's heads, Iolaos seared the neck-stump with a burning brand to prevent more heads growing, and bit by bit the creature died. Apollodorus (2.5.2) adds that one of the (here, nine) heads was immortal, and this one Herakles chopped off and buried beside the road from Lerna to Elaios, putting a heavy rock on top of it.

When the Hydra had at last been despatched, Herakles slit open the body of his victim and took its poisonous blood, which ever afterwards he used as a deadly venom on his arrow-tips. This would in future years kill many of his enemies, but it would also eventually bring about his own death when his wife Deianeira gave him a robe mistakenly impregnated with the poisoned blood of the Centaur Nessos, slain by one of these arrows.

3 THE KERYNITIAN (OR KERYNEIAN) HIND

Herakles' third Labour, unlike his first two, was neither dangerous nor violent, but became instead a feat of endurance. He was to catch the hind with the golden horns, sacred to the goddess Artemis, that lived by the river Kerynites (or on Mount Keryneia) in north-eastern Arcadia, and bring her alive to Eurystheus. He hunted her for a whole year and eventually captured the weary deer near the river Ladon in Arcadia, bringing her down with a careful arrow-shot just as she was about to cross the stream. He put her across his shoulders and carried her alive to Mycenae, on his way meeting Artemis and Apollo. Artemis was angry and would have taken the hind from him, but he explained his subservience to Eurystheus and she allowed him to pass on his way. After he had shown the deer to the king, he set her free once again.

In Pindar's unique version of the myth (*Olympian Ode* 3.28–32), the hind had been dedicated to Artemis out of gratitude by Taygete, one of the seven Pleiades, after the goddess had transformed her for a time into a deer to save her from being raped by Zeus. In this account Herakles had to pursue the hind to the far north and the land of the Hyperboreans, the men who lived beyond the North Wind.

Callimachus gives the animal a different origin (*Hymn to Artemis* 98–109), saying that Artemis found five golden-horned hinds, larger than bulls, at Parrhasia in Arcadia, four of which she captured and harnessed to her chariot. But the fifth one escaped with Hera's help and took refuge on Mount Keryneia. Once again Hera had provided a difficult task for her enemy, Herakles.

4 THE ERYMANTHIAN BOAR

Herakles' fourth Labour was to bring back another beast alive to Eurystheus, but this time a rather more dangerous one: the Erymanthian Boar, a ferocious wild boar that lived on Mount Erymanthos in north-western Arcadia and was ravaging the neighbouring countryside.

On his journey to search out the boar, Herakles had a violent encounter with the Centaurs on Mount Pholoe. The Centaurs were a race of wild creatures, part horse and part man, who had been born when Ixion's son Kentauros copulated with wild Magnesian mares on the slopes of Mount Pelion in Thessaly. Driven from their home by the Lapiths, after the famous battle of Lapiths and Centaurs at the wedding of Peirithoos and Hippodameia (p. 255), they had travelled to the Peloponnese and had settled on Mount Pholoe.

The Centaurs had the body and legs of a horse, and growing from their shoulders the torso, head and arms of a man. Their natures matched their monstrous forms, for they were wild, brutal and lascivious – with the exception of two Centaurs with different parentage. These were the civilized and hospitable Pholos – the son of a Melian nymph and the satyr Silenos, chief companion of the god Dionysos – and the wise and humane Cheiron – the immortal son of Kronos, who had taken on the form of a horse to mate with Cheiron's mother, the Oceanid Philyra. Cheiron was skilled in archery, medicine, hunting and the arts, especially music, and was the educator of many renowned heroes, including Jason and Achilles.

It was Pholos who first met Herakles when he came to Mount Pholoe. The Centaur welcomed him and set roast meat before his guest, though Herakles, with his usual voracious appetites, asked for wine as well. Pholos hesitated to open the great jar of wine that belonged to all the Centaurs in common, but Herakles had no such misgivings and opened it for himself. The smell from the open jar soon attracted the other Centaurs, who galloped up armed with rocks and fir-branches and tried to share the wine. A fight broke out, during which Herakles shot some of the beasts dead with his unerring arrows, tipped with the Hydra's fatal venom. The rest fled far away to Maleia in the southern Peloponnese, with Herakles in hot pursuit.

In Maleia they took refuge with the kindly Centaur Cheiron. Herakles approached, still firing his arrows, and to his sorrow one of them accidentally struck Cheiron on the knee. Because of the Hydra's deadly poison, the wound was quite incurable, but neither could it kill the immortal Cheiron, even though his agony was so great that he longed to die. His sufferings were finally eased when Zeus allowed him to give up his immortality, and Cheiron, relieved to be spared eternal suffering, could at last succumb thankfully to death. He still achieved an immortality, however, for Zeus set him in the stars as the constellation Sagittarius.

The surviving Centaurs dispersed to various places. Some went to Mount Maleia; some went to Eleusis where Poseidon, god of horses, gave them secret refuge on a mountain. Two of them would again become adversaries of Herakles in the future: Eurytion, who returned to Pholoe, and Nessos, who went to the river Euenos in Aitolia, where he acted as ferryman to travellers wishing to cross the water. Both when the time came would be Herakles' victims, although Nessos would eventually have his revenge by being instrumental in causing Herakles' own death.

After the sad accident to Cheiron, Herakles returned to Mount Pholoe only to find the result of another. In his absence Pholos had pulled an arrow from one of the Centaurs' corpses, wondering that so small an object could bring death to so large a creature, and had accidentally let it fall on his foot. So he too had died from the Hydra's venom, and Herakles was left to bury his friend before going on his way to complete his task for Eurystheus.

He found the boar in its lair on Mount Erymanthos and chased it far through the mountains. Finally he seized it after driving the exhausted beast into deep snow, then carried it across his shoulders back to Mycenae. At his approach, the terrified Eurystheus once again hid in his great jar – as we see frequently depicted in ancient vase-paintings, where Herakles looms above the cowering king and lifts the boar high, threatening to ram it down on top of him.

5 THE AUGEIAN STABLES

The fifth Labour was entirely different from the previous four: Herakles had to clean up the 'Augeian Stables'. Augeias was a son of Helios, the Sun-god, and king of Elis in the Peloponnese. He had many herds of cattle which he kept in stables that had never been cleaned, and Herakles' task was to clear up the dung of years in a single day. He asked Augeias to reward him, if he succeeded, with a tenth part of his herds, and the king agreed, thinking the task impossible. But he had underrated his man, for Herakles broke openings through the walls of the stables and diverted the two main rivers of the area, the Alpheios and Peneios, to flow through the yards and buildings, sweeping away all the filth. Augeias, however, refused to pay the agreed reward. His son Phyleus, who had witnessed the agreement, supported Herakles' claim, and the king, in a rage, banished both Herakles and his own son – though Herakles would in due course exact his revenge.

Phyleus went to live in Doulichion and Herakles was given hospitality by Dexamenos, the king of Olenos in Achaia. He arrived at just the right time to do a great service to his host. The Centaur Eurytion was plaguing the family, trying to force the king's daughter, Mnesimache, into marriage. Dexamenos asked for help, so Herakles, in his second encounter with the Centaur, killed the would-be bridegroom.

6 THE STYMPHALIAN BIRDS

Herakles' sixth Labour was to drive away the vast flocks of birds that were infesting the deeply wooded shores around Lake Stymphalos in north-eastern Arcadia. Pausanias reflects a late tradition when he says (8.22.4) that the birds were bronze-beaked and man-eating, and as big as cranes, but in the usual story the birds were not at all dangerous: they simply created a nuisance by their very numbers. According to Apollodorus (2.5.6), they had taken refuge in the trees to avoid wolves. Herakles dealt with them fairly easily: he flushed them out from the trees by creating a fearsome din with a bronze rattle, made by Hephaistos and given him by Athene, and when the birds flew up in fright he shot them.

7 THE CRETAN BULL

For his seventh Labour, Herakles had to leave mainland Greece and travel to Crete, where he was to bring back alive the magnificent white bull that Poseidon had once sent out of the sea to Minos, the Cretan king. Minos had promised to sacrifice the sea-god's gift, but the bull was so beautiful that he could not bear to kill it, so he sacrificed another in its place. Poseidon, angry at this broken vow, inflicted on Minos's wife Pasiphae a passion for the bull, and from the union of bull and woman the Minotaur was born.

The god also made the huge bull savage, so Herakles' task was both difficult and dangerous. He had to wrestle long and hard with the beast to subdue it, but he succeeded so well that he was able to ride on its back all the way across the sea to the Peloponnese. He drove it up to Mycenae and showed it to Eurystheus, then set it free. The bull made its way to the plain of Marathon in Attica, where it ran wild and became a plague to the inhabitants of the area. There, from being the 'Cretan Bull', it became known as the 'Marathonian Bull', and its final despatch would provide a task for the Athenian hero Theseus.

8 THE HORSES OF DIOMEDES

The eighth Labour took Herakles to the land of Thrace, lying to the east of Macedonia between the Aegean and the Black Sea. Thrace was a country always regarded by the Greeks as cruel and barbaric, and the myths connected with it are often violent and bloody – this Labour being a case in point. Diomedes, a son of the war-god Ares, was king of the Bistones, one of the warlike Thracian tribes, and he owned four mares which he kept tethered to bronze mangers with iron chains. He fed them with human flesh. Herakles' task was to capture these savage mares and bring them to Eurystheus.

On his journey he stayed with Admetos, king of Pherai in Thessaly, where he saved his host's wife Alkestis from death (p. 556). Arriving in Thrace, he tamed the vicious mares by feeding them with their own master Diomedes: they tore him to pieces and gorged on his flesh, and after this were cured of their man-eating tastes. Herakles drove them as a chariot team back to Eurystheus, who dedicated them to Hera and bred from them. Their descendants were said to have lived on to the time of Alexander the Great.

Apollodorus (2.5.8) gives a rather different version of the story. Herakles overpowered the grooms, then drove the mares down to the sea, where he left them in the charge of his young lover Abderos, a son of Hermes. While he himself fought off the pursuing Bistones and killed Diomedes, the fierce mares dragged Abderos to his death. Herakles buried the boy, and by his grave founded the city of Abdera in his memory, before returning with the captive animals to Eurystheus. In this version the king let the mares go, and they wandered to Mount Olympos where they were torn apart by wild beasts.

9 THE BELT OF HIPPOLYTE

For his ninth Labour Herakles had to travel to the southern shores of the Black Sea. Here by the river Thermoden lived a tribe of Amazon warriors, whose queen, Hippolyte, owned a belt (sometimes called a 'girdle') that was a symbol of her royal authority. Herakles was to fetch this belt, at the request of Eurystheus' daughter, Admete.

Herakles set sail, taking with him a band of allies including Telamon, king of Salamis, and (some say) the Athenian hero Theseus. When he arrived among the Amazons, Hippolyte received him kindly and promised to give him her belt, but his old enemy Hera thought this far too easy a victory. Disguising herself as an Amazon, she inflamed the other women by claiming that their queen had been abducted. The Amazons charged on horseback down to Herakles' ship, and he, assuming treachery, killed Hippolyte and took her belt, then with his comrades fought and overcame the entire Amazon army.

On his way home Herakles called in at Troy, where he saved King Laomedon's daughter, Hesione, from a sea-monster (p. 300). Laomedon had promised to reward him with the divine horses once given by Zeus in exchange for Ganymede, but he went back on his word and refused to hand them over – to his later cost, for Herakles now left Troy empty-handed, but vowing revenge.

10 THE CATTLE OF GERYON

The tenth Labour was to bring to Eurystheus the cattle of Geryon, the monstrous son of the Oceanid Kallirhoe and Chrysaor (the son of Poseidon born from the Gorgon Medusa's severed neck when Perseus cut off her head). To achieve this Herakles had to travel to the land of Erytheia, 'the Red Land', located as its name suggests in the far west, the place of the setting sun, beyond the river of Ocean. Here Geryon kept great herds of red cattle, guarded by his ferocious herdsman Eurytion and his two-headed hound Orthos, offspring of the monsters Echidna and Typhon and thus the brother of two other monstrous opponents of Herakles, Kerberos and the Hydra of Lerna. Geryon himself, according to Hesiod (*Theogony* 981), was the strongest of all men – not surprisingly, since although Hesiod calls him merely three-headed, elsewhere in literature and art he is triple-bodied, with his three forms joined at the waist. Usually in art he has three torsos and three pairs of legs, but just occasionally the tripling is from the waist up and he has only two legs.

Clearly Geryon would be a formidable opponent, since Herakles would have to overcome each of his three bodies individually before he could defeat the whole. To make his way to Erytheia would also be a problem, for he would need to find some way of crossing the great river of Ocean which encircled the earth. He achieved this through a lucky confrontation with the Sun-god Helios. He had travelled through North Africa, clearing the country of wild beasts as he went, and at the western boundaries of the land had erected the Pillars of Herakles, the promontories on the northern and southern sides of the Straits of Gibraltar, Calpe (the Rock of Gibraltar) and Abyla (Ceuta). Either he had broken apart the continents and opened up the straits, or he had narrowed the existing straits to keep the monsters of the Atlantic from bursting into the Mediterranean. These Pillars marked the western limits of the known world, beyond which only a hero as outstanding as Herakles might travel. (As Pindar says, *Olympian Ode* 3.44– 5: 'All places beyond are impassable by both the wise man and the fool.')

It was after this mighty feat that Herakles, wearied by the relentless heat of the African sun, dared to draw his bow and threaten the Sun-god – who was so impressed by his audacity that he offered to lend him his wondrous cup in which to travel to Erytheia. This was the great golden bowl in which Helios sailed with his horses and sun-chariot every night, floating along the river of Ocean, away from his place of setting in the west and towards the east, from which he would bring his morning light to the world. So Herakles happily borrowed the cup and sailed to Erytheia. Ocean sent huge waves to rock the vessel, but Herakles threatened him too with his bow and frightened him into calm.

As Herakles was approaching the pasturing herds of cattle, Geryon's monstrous hound, Orthos, rushed to attack him. He clubbed the dog to death, and then the herdsman Eurytion too, who ran up close behind. Another herdsman, Menoites, who was tending the cattle of Hades nearby, saw what had happened and ran to tell Geryon, so just as Herakles was driving away the herds, Geryon arrived, determined to stop this theft of his stock. After a fierce fight, Herakles killed him.

Their encounter was described by Stesichorus in a long lyric poem called the *Geryoneis*, now mostly lost. Fortunately a number of papyrus fragments still survive, and these tell us something about this early version of the myth. Geryon here is not only triple-bodied, with three torsos and six hands and feet, but he also has wings. The situation is seen from his point of view, and he seems to be shown (with some justification, all things considered) as a sympathetic and apparently innocent defender of his own property in face of attack. His mother Kallirhoe pleads with him not to risk his life, but Geryon is heroically determined to withstand Herakles. He argues that either he himself is immortal and ageless, in which case he cannot be harmed, or he is mortal, and in this case it is better, as the son of Chrysaor, to die a noble death now than to wait for hateful old age.

A few lines describing the fatal combat survive. It seems that Herakles attacked one of Geryon's heads with a club, and tackled another by knocking off the helmet, perhaps with a stone, then by shooting Geryon with one of his arrows poisoned with the blood of the Hydra. 'By a god's dispensation it cut through the flesh and bone and held on straight to the crown of his head, and stained his breastplate and bloody limbs with crimson gore. And Geryon drooped his neck to one side, like a poppy that suddenly sheds its petals, spoiling its tender beauty . . .'

With their owner dead, Herakles loaded the cattle into the golden cup and sailed back across the river of Ocean. He landed in southern Spain, then returned the cup to Helios and drove the herds overland on the long journey home, across the Pyrenees and through southern Europe to Greece. He had various adventures on the way, usually because people were tempted to steal his splendid cattle. While he was passing through Liguria in southern France, for instance, he was attacked by a large force of warlike natives with just that intention. He shot at them until he ran out of arrows, then, forced to his knees, he called in desperation to his father Zeus, who rained down stones from the sky. Still on his knees, Herakles pelted his enemies until they retreated. The stones still lie thickly there on the plain west of Marseilles (Strabo 4.1.7).

A Roman myth, first narrated by Virgil in the *Aeneid* (8.193–272), makes Cacus, a hideous, fire-breathing monster and son of Vulcan (the Roman Hephaistos), the cattle-thief. The aged Evander tells the story. Cacus lived in a cave in the Aventine Hill on the future site of Rome – to the terror of all who dwelt nearby, for he lived on human flesh and nailed the heads of his victims around the entrance to his cave. On his journey home, having made a detour into Italy, Herakles paused to pasture his cattle near Cacus's lair. The monster spotted the splendid beasts, and while Herakles slept he slyly stole eight of them, four bulls and four cows, dragging them back to his cave by their tails so as to leave no hoof prints pointing towards their place of concealment. He almost got away with his theft, but when Herakles at last made to move on, his cattle began to low plaintively at leaving their lush pastures, and a single cow, from deep in the cave, lowed in reply. Blazing with anger, Herakles dashed up the mountain in pursuit.

'Never before,' says Evander, 'had anyone seen Cacus afraid, never before had there been terror in his eyes. But now he fled back to his cave swifter than the wind, with fear lending wings to his feet.'

Once in his refuge, he jammed a vast boulder into the doorway, quite immovable, so Herakles had to tear up by its roots the great rock that formed the roof of the cave. With his den open to the sky, the monster vomited fire and smoke up at his pursuer, while Herakles bombarded him from above with branches of trees and rocks the size of millstones. At last, losing all patience, Herakles leapt down into the cave, aiming for the spot where the smoke boiled thickest. Gripping hold of Cacus, he strangled him until his eyes started from their sockets. For ridding the district of its scourge, the Ara Maxima (Greatest Altar) was raised to him and he was honoured at the site ever after.

With his herds of cattle complete once again, Herakles continued on his way, but at Rhegium in southern Italy a bull broke away and swam to western Sicily, where it joined the herds of the local king, Eryx, a son of Poseidon. Herakles set off to reclaim it, leaving the rest of his cattle in the care of Hephaistos. He located his bull with no trouble, but Eryx refused to surrender the magnificent beast unless Herakles beat him in a wrestling match. Herakles accepted the challenge and brought Eryx down in three consecutive falls, then killed him.

Reclaiming his bull, he resumed his journey home, but he had to cope with one final disaster before he could reach Mycenae and complete this tenth Labour. Hera afflicted the cattle with a gadfly and they scattered as far as the mountains of Thrace, so Herakles had the weary task of collecting them all over again. Some he was unable to find, and these became the ancestors of the wild cattle of Thrace. The rest he drove at last to Mycenae, where Eurystheus sacrificed them to Hera.

11 THE APPLES OF THE HESPERIDES

The eleventh Labour also took Herakles to the far ends of the earth, to fetch the golden apples from the garden of the Hesperides. These were a group of singing nymphs, the daughters of Night, and in their garden grew the beautiful golden apples which Gaia (Earth) had once put forth as a wedding-gift for Zeus and Hera. The tree that bore these apples was guarded by a giant serpent called Ladon, 'the fearful snake who guards the golden apples in a secret region of the dark earth, at the far edge of the world', says Hesiod (*Theogony* 333–6), making Ladon, like the Gorgons, the offspring of Phorkys and Keto. Apollodorus (2.5.11) says that, like the monsters Kerberos and the Hydra and Geryon's hound Orthos, he was born to Typhon and Echidna, and he adds that the serpent had a hundred heads and many different voices. Ladon, together with the Hesperides, kept the apples safe.

Herakles' first task was to discover the way to this remote and mysterious land, and he knew that he could force this crucial information from Nereus, an ancient sea-god often known as the Old Man of the Sea. So he leapt on Nereus while he slept, then wrestled with him while the sea-god – who, like other sea-divinities, had the power of metamorphosis – turned himself into many different shapes. Herakles held on through all these transformations, refusing to release him until the Old Man told him what he needed to know.

The location of the Hesperides' land was uncertain even in antiquity. The nymphs were most commonly thought to live on a western island beyond the sunset, as their name suggests (*hespera*, 'evening'); while Apollodorus locates them in the far north among the Hyperboreans, the men who lived beyond the North Wind; and Apollonius in north-west Africa, near the Atlas Mountains. What is certain is that Herakles had a long and arduous journey to reach them, and on his way (whichever way that may have been) he had a number of adventures that tested his strength and courage.

In Libya he came across Antaios, a son of Poseidon and Gaia (Earth). Antaios was a giant who forced all passing strangers to wrestle with him, and because his strength was constantly renewed while he stayed in contact with the earth, his mother, he always defeated and killed his opponents. He used the skulls of his victims to roof the temple of his father Poseidon. But he made the mistake of challenging Herakles, who soon discovered the giant's secret source of strength and lifted him high in the air, then crushed him in his arms until he was dead.

In Egypt Herakles came up against another son of Poseidon, Bousiris, who had been king of the land for many years. Once, after nine years of famine, Bousiris had in desperation consulted Phrasios, a learned seer from Cyprus, who assured him that the earth would be fruitful again if every year he sacrificed a foreigner to Zeus. The ungrateful Bousiris began by sacrificing Phrasios himself, then carried on killing any foreigner who came to the country. When Herakles arrived, he too was caught and dragged to the sacrificial altar, but he burst his bonds and killed Bousiris, together with his son and many attendants.

The historian Herodotus tells the story, adding his own rationalistic comments (2.45):

The Greeks tell many unbelievable tales. One silly one is the story which they tell about Herakles, of how, when he came to Egypt, the Egyptians crowned him with a wreath and took him in solemn procession to be sacrificed to Zeus. He submitted quietly until they began the ritual of the sacrifice at the altar, but then he at last resisted and killed them all. Now the Greeks in saying this seem to me to be completely ignorant of Egyptian character and customs. For it is against their religion to kill animals for sacrifice, except geese and sheep and such bulls and bull-calves as are deemed suitably clean. So would they be likely to sacrifice humans? Besides, if Herakles was, as they say, one man on his own, how would he kill tens of thousands of people? And now may the gods and the heroes forgive me for saying these things!

In the Caucasian Mountains, Herakles passed the place where the Titan Prometheus had been chained long ages ago by Zeus, as punishment for bringing the gift of fire to mankind. Every day, year in, year out, an eagle tore out the Titan's liver, which every night grew whole again so that his torture might continue. Herakles shot the eagle and released Prometheus – and Zeus allowed it, pleased that this feat would increase the fame and honour of his son. When he learnt of Herakles' quest, the grateful Titan advised him that he would easily acquire the golden apples if he sent Atlas to fetch them from the Hesperides' garden.

Atlas was another Titan who was being punished by Zeus. His offence had been to take part in the Titans' ten-year battle against Zeus and the other Olympians (p. 42), and his punishment was to stand at the ends of the earth and hold up the sky for all eternity. Herakles found Atlas and followed Prometheus' advice, offering to support the sky for the giant if he would go and fetch the apples. Atlas happily relinquished his weary load and went off to pick the golden fruit.

He planned never to take up his burden again and he told Herakles that he himself would deliver the apples to Eurystheus, but Herakles easily tricked the gullible Titan. He asked Atlas to take hold of the sky just for a moment, while he made himself more comfortable with a padded cushion for his head, and the dull-witted giant took back his load, never to set it down again. Herakles seized the fruit and made good his escape. After Eurystheus had seen the apples, the goddess Athene returned them to the Hesperides' garden, for they were too sacred to remain in mortal hands.

In some accounts Herakles himself confronted and killed the serpent Ladon before picking the apples himself. Apollonius (*Argonautica* 4.1383–449) describes how the Argonauts found the snake killed and the Hesperides mourning its death at the brutal hands of Herakles:

The snake lay fallen by the trunk of the apple tree. Only the tip of his tail was still twitching, but from his head to the end of his dark spine he lay lifeless. Where the arrows had left in his blood the sharp venom of the Lernaian Hydra, flies wilted and died on the festering wounds. Nearby, the Hesperides made shrill lament, their silvery arms flung over their golden heads . . . 'That most heartless man took away the life of our guardian snake and carried off the golden apples of the goddesses. Bitter is the grief he has left to us.'

After his death, Ladon was immortalized in the sky as the constellation Draco, curling between the Great and Little Bears and with Herakles, club raised, right next to him.

12 KERBEROS

Herakles' twelfth and final Labour was to go down to the land of the dead and fetch Kerberos, the monstrous, multi-headed dog, offspring of Typhon and Echidna, who guarded the entrance to the Underworld and ensured that those who entered never left (p. 109). If they tried to do so, Kerberos devoured them.

This was certainly the most difficult and daunting of all the Labours. Accompanied by Hermes, the god who escorts the souls of the dead down to Hades, Herakles set off on his frightful quest through the deep and gloomy cave at Tainaron in the Peloponnese. Descending to the Underworld, he passed through the gates that were ferociously guarded by his intended quarry.

Herakles delivers Kerberos to a terrified Eurystheus.

As he travelled through Hades, the shades of the dead all fled in terror when they saw this formidable mortal in their midst – all except the fearsome Gorgon Medusa, slain by Perseus, and the hero Meleagros, killer of the Kalydonian Boar. Herakles drew his sword against Medusa, until Hermes explained that she was merely a harmless phantom. Meleagros related the story of his sad death (p. 183) to Herakles, who was so moved by admiration and compassion that he offered to marry his sister, if Meleagros had one still living. He named Deianeira, who would indeed become Herakles' wife, but would also unwittingly bring about his death.

Herakles next came across the heroes Theseus and Peirithoos, held fast in their seats as punishment for trying to carry off Persephone, the queen of Hades, as Peirithoos' bride. He took Theseus' hand and pulled him to his feet, free to return to the land of the living, but when he tried to raise Peirithoos, the ground shook and he had to let him go.

He also had a second encounter with the herdsman Menoites,

the man who had warned Geryon of the theft of his cattle. When Herakles sacrificed one of Hades' cows as blood for the ghosts, Menoites challenged him to a wrestling match – and had his ribs broken for his pains. He would have suffered worse than this, if Persephone had not intervened to save him.

Finally Herakles came face to face with Hades himself, Lord of the Underworld, who gave him permission to take Kerberos back to earth for a short time, so long as he mastered him without using weapons. So Herakles overcame the hound by brute strength alone, even though he was savagely bitten by the serpent that formed the monster's tail. He dragged his captive, mad with rage and fighting every inch of the way, growling and barking from his three huge mouths, up into the bright daylight. The flecks of foam that spattered from the hound's jaws took root and grew into the aconite plant with its deadly poison. (It was this poison that Medea later used when she tried to kill Theseus.) In Mycenae Eurystheus once again hid in terror inside his great jar. Then Herakles returned Kerberos to his lawful abode in Hades, and at long last his servitude to the ignoble king was at an end.

LATER EXPLOITS

Now that his time was once more his own, Herakles decided to marry again and father more children. Eurytos, king of Oichalia and the very man who had taught Herakles archery, was offering his beautiful daughter Iole as bride for anyone who could defeat him and his sons at an archery contest. All contenders had failed until Herakles took up the challenge, and he of course was victorious. Even so, Eurytos refused to give him Iole, afraid that he might one day go mad again and kill any children he had by her, just as he had killed his children by Megara. The king stubbornly held to this decision throughout the inevitable quarrel, and Herakles left Oichalia, vowing revenge.

Soon afterwards twelve mares owned by Eurytos (or cattle, according to Apollodorus) went missing, either taken by Herakles out of vindictiveness, or stolen by the arch-thief Auto-lykos and sold to him. Eurytos's eldest son, Iphitos, was well disposed to Herakles and had taken his side in the squabble over Iole; now he was confident that his friend was innocent of theft. He visited Herakles at Tiryns to show his good will, but Herakles was suddenly overtaken by another fit of manic rage. He took Iphitos up to the top of his palace walls and hurled him down to his death.

Because of this shameful murder, Herakles became afflicted with a dire disease, so he set off to seek purification from Neleus, the king of Pylos in Messenia. Neleus refused to help because of his old friendship with Eurytos, and once again Herakles left a city in anger, swearing that he would have his revenge.

He went to the Delphic Oracle for advice, but the Pythian priestess refused to answer him because of his pollution, so Herakles, in a great rage, seized her sacred tripod, declaring that he would set up an oracle of his own. Apollo intervened and tried to wrest the tripod from him. Before the violence could escalate, Zeus hurled a thunderbolt between his two sons and separated them. Peace was restored, and the Pythia now told Herakles that he would be cured if he were sold as a slave for three years. He was bought by Omphale, queen of Lydia.

SERVITUDE TO OMPHALE

Omphale had ruled Lydia since the death of her husband Tmolos. Now, with Herakles as her slave, it was said that she wore his lion-skin and brandished his club, while he wore women's clothing and helped her and her ladies with their spinning. Perhaps he did this under compulsion, but it may be that he submitted willingly to this treatment because he had

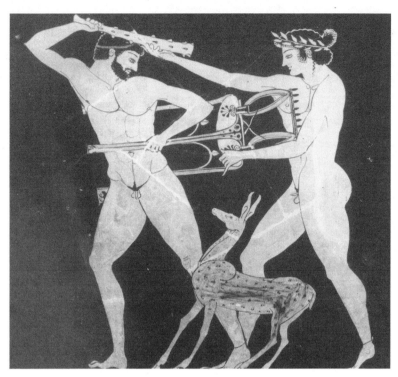

Herakles and Apollo fight for possession of the tripod.

fallen in love with his queen. Certainly she bore him a son, Lamos (or Agelaos, according to Apollodorus 2.7.8), before she set him free.

He may have assumed the woman's role with Omphale, but he also achieved several typical feats of courage during his period of servitude. He killed a giant snake that was plaguing the land, and he sacked the city of Omphale's enemies, the Itones. He also got rid of the brigand Syleus, who was in the habit of forcing passers-by to hoe his vineyard for him. Herakles killed Syleus with his own hoe, then set fire to his vines and killed his daughter Xenodike too – though a late story said that he became her lover, and when he went away she died of longing for him.

Another ruffian who preyed on passing strangers was

Lityerses, a bastard son of King Midas of Phrygia: he forced travellers to compete with him at harvesting and he always won the contest. When his victims flagged, he whipped them, and at the end of the day he cut off their heads with his scythe and bound their bodies into a corn stook, singing a jolly reaping song as he did so. Now Herakles took up his harvesting challenge, and it was Lityerses who was whipped and beheaded.

Another famous encounter, though this time with a comic outcome, was with two ape-like brothers called the Kerkopes. A fragment of an early epic (*Kerkopes*) describes them as 'liars and cheats, well versed in all kinds of mischief, complete rogues', and adds: 'Far over the earth they wandered, forever deceiving men as they travelled.' Their mother had warned them to be wary of a certain *Melampygos*, 'Black-bottom', who turned out to be Herakles, though they realized this too late. They had found him asleep and had tried to steal his weapons, but he woke up and caught them, then hung them by their ankles from a pole carried over his shoulders. From this vantage point they recognized Herakles, from his tanned and hairy buttocks, as the *Melampygos* against whom their mother had warned them, but, nothing daunted, they made him laugh so much with ribald jokes at his own expense that he set them free.

REVENGE FOR OLD GRUDGES

Once Herakles' servitude to Omphale was over, he decided that the time had come to settle some old scores. First he mustered an army and sailed to Troy, to take revenge on Laomedon for refusing him his agreed reward, after he had saved Hesione from the sea-monster. They captured the city and killed Laomedon and most of his sons. Herakles' friend Telamon, king of Salamis and father of the Great Ajax, was the first to breach the Trojan walls and enter the city. Herakles would have taken umbrage at this slur on his own supremacy, had not the quick-witted Telamon swiftly gathered up some stones and built an altar to 'Herakles the Glorious Victor' (*Kallinikos*).

After the defeat of the city, Herakles rewarded Telamon by giving him Laomedon's daughter Hesione as his concubine (she would bear him a son, Teukros, who would fight alongside the Great Ajax in the Trojan War). The only son of Laomedon to survive was Podarkes, renamed Priam, who alone had advised his father to pay the agreed reward. Herakles left Priam as the new king of Troy and sailed away.

Hera had not forgotten her jealousy and resentment of Herakles, and she now sent great storms against his ships which drove them far south to the island of Kos. Here he and his men were attacked by the natives, who thought they were pirates. All ended well for them, for they captured the main city of the island, and Herakles not only killed the king of the Koans but fathered a son, Thessalos, on Astyoche, the daughter of the dead king, so that the island was thereafter ruled by his descendants. Zeus, however, was so angry at this latest act of spite by Hera against his dearest son, that he suspended her for a while from Olympos, her hands bound with a golden chain and with anvils tied to her feet. Soon after this Herakles performed an indispensable service for the gods, when Athene fetched him from Kos and he helped them win their great battle against the monstrous Giants (p. 49).

Herakles' next campaign was against Augeias, king of Elis, who had refused to pay him the agreed fee for cleaning out the Augeian Stables. Augeias heard of his approach and mustered an army of his own, under the leadership of the Siamese twins Eurytos and Kteatos, sons of Poseidon and Molione (the wife of Aktor, brother of Augeias). They were often called simply the Molionides (or Moliones) after their mother, and were usually imagined as each having one head, two arms and two legs, while sharing one torso between them. They were at first a match for Herakles, even killing his half-brother Iphikles in battle, so that he and his men suffered heavy losses and were forced to retreat. Undeterred, Herakles ambushed and killed the twins at Kleonai, then had no trouble in capturing Elis. He put Augeias and his sons to death, then recalled his supporter Phyleus from his exile in Doulichion and made him king in his father's place. Before leaving Elis, Herakles instituted the Olympic Games, the greatest of Greek festivals, held there every four years in honour of Zeus.

He still had grudges to settle, so his next attack was against Neleus, who had refused to purify him for the murder of Iphitos. Herakles led an armed force down to Pylos in the south-western Peloponnese and there killed Neleus and eleven of his twelve sons in battle. (The youngest son, Nestor, survived because he was away from home at the time. He would in due course take over the throne, ruling on at Pylos until well after the Trojan War.)

The eldest son, Periklymenos, posed an especial challenge for Herakles, since he had been given by his grandfather Poseidon the power of changing his shape at will. As the Hesiodic *Catalogue of Women* describes it (fr. 33): 'At one time he would appear among the birds as an eagle, and then at another he would be an ant, a wonder to see, and then again a bright swarm of bees, and then a terrible relentless snake.' He changed his shape repeatedly during the battle with Herakles, becoming, according to Apollodorus (1.9.9), a lion, a snake and a bee, but what shape he had taken at the point of his death we do not know. The Hesiodic fragment says that he died when he perched on the yoke of Herakles' chariot, planning how to bring his opponent down, and was shot by one of Herakles' unerring arrows after Athene had pointed him out – but the name of his particular transformation is missing from the surviving scrap of papyrus that tells the story. An eagle, a fly and a bee have all been suggested. An insect is perhaps the most likely, given that Athene needed to point him out to Herakles, though the eagle might seem a more attractive option, as in Ovid's version (*Metamorphoses* 12.556–72), where Periklymenos tears at Herakles' face with his talons, then soars high in the air. It is then that Herakles shoots him.

So Herakles' revenge against Neleus was very thorough, but it brought in its train another grievance, this time against Hippokoon, the king of Sparta, and his twelve or twenty sons. They had fought on Neleus' side in the great battle, and had moreover murdered Herakles' cousin Oionos because he threw a stone at their savage dog, a huge Molossian hound. So now Herakles avenged these offences by killing Hippokoon and all his sons. Since Tyndareos, the rightful king of Sparta, had earlier been driven out by Hippokoon, Herakles made him king once again in the usurper's place.

Herakles had asked Kepheus, the king of Tegea in Arcadia, to come with his twenty sons on this expedition against Sparta. Kepheus had at first refused, fearing that Tegea would be attacked by Argive enemies in his absence, but Herakles had reassured him by entrusting to his daughter Sterope a bronze jar containing a lock of the Gorgon Medusa's hair, once given him by Athene. This, he said, would put all enemies to flight if she held it up from the city walls. His fears set at rest, Kepheus joined the campaign along with his sons, and Tegea did indeed remain safe – but in the battle against Hippokoon, Kepheus and all his sons were killed.

Herakles had one further encounter with Kepheus' family before he left Tegea – with the king's sister, Auge. Their father Aleos had appointed Auge virgin priestess in the temple of Athene, but Herakles either seduced or raped the girl and left her pregnant. In due course she bore a son, but she kept his birth a secret and hid him in the temple precinct. Unfortunately the land was struck with plague and famine because of this sacrilege, and when Aleos learnt from an oracle that the temple had been profaned, he searched the precinct and found the baby. Auge's secret was out. Her angry father had the infant left on Mount Parthenion to die, and he gave Auge to the navigator and slave-trader Nauplios, to be either drowned or sold overseas. Nauplios, however, took pity on her and gave her to Teuthras, the wealthy king of Mysia, who married her. The baby too was saved, for he was suckled by a doe until some shepherds found him. They took him home and brought him up, calling him Telephos, supposedly because he had been suckled by the teat (*thele*) of a deer (*elaphos*).

On reaching manhood, Telephos questioned the Delphic Oracle about his parents and was told to go to Mysia. Here he was reunited with his mother. Teuthras adopted him, and he eventually succeeded to the Mysian throne. He would play a crucial part in the Trojan War (p. 316). Telephos was said by Pausanias (10.28.8) to be of all Herakles' many sons the one most like his father.

MARRIAGE TO DEIANEIRA

Now Herakles' thoughts turned once again to marriage. The beautiful Iole had been denied him by Eurytos, and he was still intending to have his revenge for that slight, but now he journeyed to woo Deianeira, daughter of Oineus, king of Kalydon, and sister of the hero Meleagros. Deianeira had another suitor, the god of the river Acheloos, which flowed along the western borders of Aitolia. This was the greatest of Greek rivers (Homer calls it the 'king of rivers', *Iliad* 21.194); nevertheless the river-god seemed a terrifying suitor to Deianeira, for like other water-divinities he had the power to change his shape, and he wooed her in three monstrous manifestations.

'He came in three shapes to ask my father for my hand,' says Deianeira in Sophocles' tragedy *Women of Trachis* (10–17), our most detailed source for this last part of Herakles' life.

'Now he was manifest as a bull, now a shimmering, coiling snake, now with a man's body and a bull's head, and from his shaggy beard flowed streams of water from his springs. Expecting a suitor like that, I was always praying, poor creature, that I might die before ever I came near his bed.'

Small wonder that she was deeply relieved when a far more normal suitor appeared – Herakles, who proceeded to wrestle with Acheloos for her hand, while she sat watching in dread lest the wrong combatant win.

But all was well. Even though the river-god fought mightily and changed his shape repeatedly, Herakles at last vanquished him, breaking off as he did so one of the god's horns. To recover this, Acheloos gave in its place the precious horn of Amaltheia, the 'Horn of Plenty', a cornucopia that provided limitless food and drink for its possessor (no doubt a very welcome gift for a man of Herakles' appetites).

So Deianeira married Herakles. Over the years she would bear him several children, including Hyllos, their eldest son, and a daughter, Makaria. They lived at Kalydon until an unfortunate accident forced them to seek a new home. During a banquet at the palace, Oeneus' cupbearer Eunomos caused Herakles some trivial annoyance when he was serving him, and Herakles hit out at the boy. He had no intention of serious hurt, but such was his strength that Eunomos dropped dead. After this accidental homicide, Herakles left Kalydon with Deianeira and went to live with his good friend Keux, the king of Trachis.

On the journey they had to cross the river Euenos, where

they came across one of the Centaurs who had earlier escaped from Maleia and the wrath of Herakles. This was the Centaur Nessos, who was acting as a ferryman for travellers needing to cross the river. Herakles could wade across the stream alone, but he willingly paid for Deianeira to be carried on the Centaur's back. During the crossing, Nessos tried his best (luckily failing) to rape her, so Herakles shot him with one of his unerring arrows, tipped with the poisonous blood taken from the Hydra of Lerna.

Even as Nessos lay dying, he was planning how to get revenge on his murderer. He told Deianeira to gather some blood from around the arrow-wound, assuring her that it would act as a potent love-charm if ever she used it on Herakles, so much so that he would never love another woman more than her. (And this was true, for he would be dead.) The credulous Deianeira did as Nessos said, unaware that mixed with the Centaur's blood was the Hydra's deadly venom. She put the 'love-charm' away in her new home and kept it carefully for many years, in case it might ever be needed.

Herakles and Deianeira would live at Trachis for the rest of their lives. During this time Herakles purged the world of one last great malefactor who preyed on mankind. This was Kyknos, son of the war-god Ares, a bloodthirsty brigand who waylaid travellers bringing offerings to Apollo's temple at Pagasai, in Thessaly. He always challenged them to fight in single combat, and he always won, then he not only stole the often precious gifts that his victims were carrying, but cut off their heads and used their skulls to build a temple to his father Ares.

Kyknos finally met his match in Herakles, an encounter described in the Hesiodic poem *The Shield of Herakles*. He waylaid Herakles and his charioteer Iolaos in Apollo's grove and issued his usual challenge, planning to steal their splendid armour. Herakles, urged on by Apollo, was only too happy to fight the villain, and he killed him with a spear through his neck. Ares had been standing by in support of his son and now rushed forward to avenge him, but Herakles forced the war-god himself to the ground with a spear-thrust to the thigh. Ares escaped to Olympos, though some say that the two fought until Zeus flung a thunderbolt to separate them.

Keux saw to the burial of Kyknos, for he had been the king's son-in-law, married to his daughter Themistonoe. Apollo, however, was still resentful about all his lost offerings, so he made the river Anauros flood its banks and wash away the brigand's grave.

DEATH AND APOTHEOSIS

Eventually Herakles decided that the time had come to avenge himself on Eurytos for refusing him Iole. He returned to Oichalia with an army, sacked the city and killed Eurytos and his surviving sons, then carried off the beautiful Iole as his concubine.

The aftermath of this fateful revenge is dramatized in Sophocles' *Women of Trachis*, where Herakles is about to return home triumphant after sacking Oichalia. He sends ahead of him a group of slaves that includes Iole. Deianeira, seeing the girl's beauty and knowing that she herself is an ageing woman, is afraid that Herakles will now no longer love her, so at last she takes out Nessos' 'love-charm' from its hiding place. She smears it on a fine robe and sends it to her husband, hoping in this way to win back his love, and with no idea that her gift is covered in a deadly poison.

Before Sophocles' detailed dramatization of her story in the fifth century BC, Deianeira seems to have been seen, as far as we can tell, as a bold-hearted and aggressive woman. Hints of this original character survive only in comments such as that of Apollodorus (1.8.1): 'She drove a chariot and practised the arts of war.' It is also likely that this earlier Deianeira deliberately murdered Herakles out of jealousy and rage at his infidelity, with full knowledge of what her poisoned robe would do to him. But in Sophocles everything is quite different, for his Deianeira is a gentle, timid and loving woman, whose only aim is to have Herakles love her again.

The herald Lichas carries the robe to Herakles, who together with his son Hyllos is preparing to sacrifice to Zeus on Cape Kenaion in Euboia. At once Herakles puts on the robe, and soon the poison begins to eat into his flesh like acid. In his torment, he seizes Lichas by the foot and flings him to his death on a rock projecting from the sea. This agony of Herakles in the poisoned robe would provide poets with an allusion for unendurable pain: in Shakespeare's *Antony and Cleopatra*, Mark Antony, whose family claimed descent from Herakles (also known as Alcides after his grandfather Alkaios), cries out when all is lost (IV.xii.43–7):

> 'The shirt of Nessus is upon me. Teach me,
> Alcides, thou mine ancestor, thy rage.
> Let me lodge Lichas on the horns o' th' moon,
> And with those hands that grasp'd the heaviest club
> Subdue my worthiest self.'

Hyllos brings his father home in his death agonies, having of course no idea of Deianeira's good intentions: he simply sees the ghastly effects of her lethal gift. He tells his mother that Herakles lies dying and curses her harshly for his murder. Deianeira, with the terrible knowledge that she has caused the death of her beloved husband and is now hated by her son, goes indoors to her marriage bed and there in utter despair stabs herself fatally with a sword. Too late Hyllos learns her true motives and bitterly reproaches himself for his too hasty anger.

Herakles, carried on stage in torment, instructs Hyllos to

have him taken to Mount Oita and there to burn him on a funeral pyre. As the play ends he is borne out to his fiery death, his final words displaying the fierce courage and endurance that he has shown throughout his arduous life (1259–63):

'Come, my hard soul,
fit on a bit of steel set with stones,
come, cease your cry,
and fulfil your reluctant task
like an act of joy.'

It is the utmost irony that Herakles, who was a match for any living being, man or monster, is finally brought to death by a woman, out of love.

So Herakles, in agony, had his funeral pyre built on Mount Oita and lay on it, ready for death. No one was willing to set light to it, but at that moment the Argonaut Poias, king of Malis, passed by, looking for his sheep. He agreed to light the pyre, and Herakles rewarded him with his great bow and unerring arrows (which Poias would later pass on to his son, Philoktetes, and they would play their part in the taking of Troy by the Greeks). The pyre burned, a clap of thunder broke from heaven, and Herakles was taken up to Olympos and made immortal among the gods.

At last Hera gave up her anger against him and the two were reconciled. She even bestowed on him her daughter Hebe, the goddess of youth, to be his immortal wife. To honour his son, Zeus set in the stars the constellation named after him, depicting Herakles as a kneeling man and commemorating his battle with the Ligurians, when in the most desperate straits he was brought to his knees, but still fought valiantly on.

THE RETURN OF THE HERAKLIDS

Although Herakles had been born at Thebes in Boiotia, he would have ruled Mycenae and Tiryns, the kingdom of his forefathers, but for Eurystheus, and he had always regarded these Peloponnesian cities as his rightful inheritance. Eurystheus too was aware that Herakles' descendants (the 'Heraklids') would have a claim to these lands, so he decided to kill all Herakles' children now that they no longer had the protection of their invincible father. Together with their grandmother Alkmene they were living with Keux, the king of Trachis, but Keux felt himself too weak to oppose the cruel Eurystheus, who was threatening war, so he sent them all to Athens, to the protection of the powerful Theseus (or his sons Akamas and Demophon). Here Eurystheus followed them with his Argive army, and found that the Athenians were offering to fight for the Heraklids against the invader.

When an oracle proclaimed that Athens would prevail in battle only if a virgin of noble birth were sacrificed to Persephone, Herakles' daughter Makaria offered to give up her life. 'I am ready to give myself in sacrifice and die,' she says in Euripides' drama *The Children of Herakles* (501–32):

'For what can we say, when Athens is prepared to face great danger for our sake, if we ourselves lay this burden on their shoulders, and then shrink back from death when we have power to bring them victory? Never! We should deserve contempt if we, born of the great Herakles, show ourselves cowards . . . Lead me to the place where I must die. Garland me and perform the rite, if so you will. Defeat your enemies. Willingly, with no hesitation, I offer my life and pledge myself to death for my brothers' sake.'

So Makaria died and the Athenians duly defeated the Argives, killing all of Eurystheus' sons. Eurystheus himself fled from the field of battle, but he too was caught and killed. According to this same play, Herakles' old henchman Iolaos prayed to Zeus and to Hebe, goddess of Youth, that for just one day he might be young again to take revenge on Eurystheus for his persecutions. His prayer was granted. He pursued and captured his old enemy and brought him back in chains to Athens, where Alkmene, bitterly resentful of all the wrongs Eurystheus had done her family, insisted on his death. In Apollodorus' version (2.8.1) it was Hyllos who caught him, then cut off his head and carried it back to Alkmene. She gouged out his eyes with weaving pins.

With Eurystheus' power over the Heraklids at an end, it now seemed a good opportunity for them to re-establish themselves in the Peloponnese. Hyllos led the other Heraklids southwards and they succeeded in taking many Peloponnesian cities, but a year later a plague broke out, and an oracle declared that their invasion had been premature. They withdrew, and when they questioned the Delphic Oracle and were instructed to return only at 'the third harvest', they obediently waited for three years. Unfortunately the Oracle meant not three years but three generations, so their next attack too was a failure. Once again Hyllos led a force into the Peloponnese, and here Echemos, the king of Tegea in Arcadia, offered himself as champion of the defending Arcadian forces. He killed Hyllos in single combat and once again the Heraklids withdrew.

However Hyllos had married Iole, according to his father's last wishes, and she had borne him a son, Kleodaios, so the family line continued. A hundred years later Hyllos's three great-grandsons, Temenos, Kresphontes and Aristodemos, once more consulted the oracle and understood at last the true meaning of 'the third harvest'. Another expedition was launched. After various initial difficulties, including the death of Aristodemos, who was struck by lightning, the Heraklids set out for the last time to conquer the Peloponnese. They were accompanied by the Dorians (descendants of Deukalion through his son, Hellen), who had become their allies out of gratitude for Herakles' once helping them in a dispute with the Lapiths.

The oracle had advised them to take 'the three-eyed one' as their guide, so when they met an Aitolian named Oxylos, who was riding a one-eyed horse or driving a one-eyed mule, they saw in this combination the oracle's fulfilment. Oxylos agreed to lead them through the Peloponnese, but he was careful to stay away from fertile Elis, a land that he hoped to have for himself, and took them instead through mountainous Arcadia.

This time the invasion was successful and the Heraklids took possession of the main Peloponnesian cities. Having granted the land of Elis to Oxylos in recognition of his services, just as he had hoped, the leaders agreed to decide the ownership of the three chief regions by drawing lots, the first to have the Argolid, the second Sparta and Lakonia, and the third Messenia. Kresphontes was anxious to own fertile Messenia and won it by a trick: when the others threw pebbles into a pitcher of water, he threw in a clod of earth, so that his lot dissolved and the other two lots were drawn out first. Temenos received the Argolid; the two sons of Aristodemos, Prokles and Eurysthenes, drew Lakonia, where in due course they became founders of the two royal houses of Sparta; and Kresphontes won the land he wanted. The Heraklids had now reclaimed what they saw as their territorial birthright – but power struggles within their ranks brought death to two of the expedition's leaders.

Temenos thought so highly of the Heraklid Deiphontes that he married him to his favourite daughter, Hyrnetho, and made him his chief adviser. This made Temenos's own sons afraid for their inheritance, so they killed their father and seized the throne. Deiphontes and Hyrnetho took refuge in Epidauros, but the sons of Temenos still felt aggrieved and they tried to hurt Deiphontes by persuading Hyrnetho to leave him. She refused, for she loved her husband and had borne him three sons and a daughter, and was even now pregnant with their fifth child. So her brothers kidnapped her, and handled her so roughly when Deiphontes tried to rescue her that both she and her baby died. Deiphontes buried her in an olive grove at Epidauros, where cult honours were later paid to her. He himself was made king by the Argives in preference to the sons of Temenos.

Kresphontes too died by violence. He married Merope, the daughter of Kypselos, king of Arcadia, and had three sons by her, but he and his two eldest sons were killed by a rival Heraklid, Polyphontes, who led a revolt against him and seized the throne. Fortunately his youngest son, named Kresphontes after him, was saved by Merope and brought up by Kypselos. The aftermath was dramatized in Euripides' *Kresphontes*, and although the play has been lost, the story can be reconstructed from fragments (with the help of Hyginus's *Fabula* 137).

Polyphontes forced Merope to marry him, but he was always afraid that her son would return and take revenge for his father's murder, so he promised a large reward to anyone who would kill Kresphontes. Just as he feared, the boy grew up and returned to Messenia to avenge his father and brothers. Quite unrecognized, he went to Polyphontes under a false name and said that he himself had killed Kresphontes and was now claiming the reward. Polyphontes, with no idea of the deception, gratefully gave him hospitality, but while the boy was asleep, Merope, believing that he had indeed killed her son, crept up with an axe to murder him. (This highly dramatic scene may well have occurred on stage in Euripides' play.)

Luckily Kresphontes was recognized by an old servant, who stopped Merope just in time. Mother and son were joyfully reunited and together they plotted revenge on Polyphontes.

Merope, pretending to be reconciled to the death of her son, suggested a sacrifice in thanks for his supposed death to which the young stranger would be invited. The delighted king agreed. During the ceremony, Kresphontes was given a weapon to kill the sacrificial victim, but he killed Polyphontes instead and thus regained his father's throne and kingdom.

8

THESEUS, ATHENS AND CRETE

Theseus was the great national hero of Athens. Like Herakles he had a cycle of heroic deeds to his name, many of which are similar to those of Herakles himself. Theseus too rid the world of monsters and brigands, fought the Amazons, and journeyed down to the Underworld. These exploits are regularly depicted on Attic vases from the last years of the sixth century BC. There may well have existed an earlier epic poem about Theseus, celebrating his heroic deeds – but if so it has been totally lost. Our most complete source for the legend is the late but detailed *Life of Theseus* by Plutarch (early second century AD).

Before focusing on this greatest Athenian hero, however, we should first trace the mythical history of Athens and her early kings.

THE KINGS OF ATHENS

The Athenians prided themselves on being autochthonous (literally 'sprung from the earth') – an indigenous people who had inhabited their land from very ancient times. Their earliest king was Kekrops, who showed his chthonic origin by having the normal body of a man, but with the tail of a serpent instead of human legs.

During his reign there took place a contest between Athene and Poseidon to decide who should be the patron-deity of Attica. To demonstrate their divine powers, Poseidon struck the Acropolis with his trident and produced a well of seawater, while Athene planted an olive tree on the hill, taking Kekrops as the witness of her deed. Athene's gift was judged the more valuable (and certainly the olive became a mainstay of the Attic economy), so the country became hers and she named the city Athens after herself. Poseidon was so angry that he sent a flood to cover most of the land, though he later became reconciled when he too was worshipped on the Acropolis. In historical times, as the traveller Pausanias records (1.26.5, 1.27.2), the print of Poseidon's trident on a rock could still be seen within the Erechtheum, as could the well of seawater, which gave out the sound of waves whenever the wind blew from the south. Athene's olive tree too was still flourishing. It had been destroyed by the Persians when they fired Athens in 480 BC, but was said to have miraculously put on a metre or so of new growth on the very day that it was burnt.

Three daughters were born to Kekrops: Aglauros, Herse and Pandrosos. Aglauros was loved by the war-god Ares and bore him a daughter, Alkippe. She was raped by Halirrhothios, a son of Poseidon, but Ares caught him in the act and killed him. The war-god was then charged with murder by Poseidon and was tried by a tribunal of the other gods. He was acquitted. This, the first-ever trial for the shedding of blood, was held on the hill to the west of the Acropolis, thereafter known as the Areopagos (the 'Hill of Ares'), on which murder trials were held in historical times.

Kekrops' three daughters are best remembered for the part they played in the story of Erichthonios. He was the son of Hephaistos and (in a sense) Athene, though like Kekrops he was born from the earth. Athene went to the smith-god's workshop for some weapons, but when Hephaistos saw her, he forgot all about his craft and was afflicted with a fit of uncontrollable passion. He tried to embrace her, but the virgin-goddess would have none of it and ran away. In spite of his lameness, the god caught her and did his best to ravish her, and in the struggle his semen fell on her thigh. Athene wiped it off with a scrap of wool and threw it on the ground in disgust, where it impregnated the earth. When the time came for the child to be born, Gaia (Earth) gave him to Athene, who thus became his adoptive mother.

Athene called the baby Erichthonios (from either *eris*, strife, or *erion*, wool, and *chthon*, earth). She put him in a chest and entrusted it to Kekrops' three daughters, giving them strict instructions not to open it. The girls were naturally full of curiosity, and although sources differ as to exactly who opened the chest, one or more of them did so, and all three of them paid the price for this disobedience. Terrified by what they saw inside, either a snake coiled around the baby, or the baby himself formed as half-child and half-serpent, they went mad and hurled themselves from the Acropolis to their deaths on the rocks below. Some say the snake killed them.

Ovid (*Metamorphoses* 2.708–832) tells a different story, probably of Hellenistic origin, in which the girls lived on after disobeying Athene. Herse was returning home from a festival when she happened to catch the eye of Hermes, and the god thought her so beautiful that he went to the girl's home to woo her. Here Aglauros intercepted him, but promised to help him win her sister so long as he fetched her a fortune in gold. Athene, however, was still angry with Aglauros for disobediently open-ing the chest, so she afflicted the girl with envy of her sister's good fortune. When Hermes returned, Aglauros barred his way to Herse's room. Nothing deterred, the god opened the door with his wand and turned Aglauros to stone, stained black by her dark thoughts. Ovid says no more about Hermes' union with Herse, but other sources say that she bore the god a son, Kephalos. He was so beautiful that Eos, the goddess of Dawn, carried him off and had by him a son, Phaithon, who became an attendant in Aphrodite's temple. (Eos later carried off another, more famous Kephalos as her lover: p. 539.)

Nothing is recorded of how Kekrops reacted to these various

events. To the Athenians he was simply their archetypal ancestral figure, and he was credited, among other things, with introducing the first laws and the building of cities, with establishing monogamous marriage, and with recognizing the supremacy of Zeus among the gods.

Kekrops was followed by two more earth-born kings, Kranaos and Amphiktyon, both of whom are little more than names in a king-list. Kranaos, ruling at the time of the Great Flood, was said to have named the land Attica after his daughter Atthis. He was deposed by his son-in-law Amphiktyon, who in turn was deposed twelve years later by Erichthonios, now grown to maturity, having been reared by Athene herself on the Acropolis.

During his reign, Erichthonios promoted the cult of Athene, setting up her ancient wooden image on the Acropolis and instituting the Panathenaia, her principal festival. His son, Pandion, succeeded him. It was during Pandion's reign that the worship of Dionysos was instituted in Attica, and Dionysos himself gave a vine branch to a humble farmer named Ikarios and taught him how to make wine. Wishing to share the pleasures of this glorious boon, Ikarios gave some wine to a group of shepherds, who drank it down neat with great delight. They soon became intoxicated and thought that Ikarios had poisoned them, so they clubbed him to death and buried his body beneath a tree. His daughter Erigone searched everywhere for him, but without success, until his dog Maira led her to the grave and dug away the loose earth. Seeing her father dead, Erigone hanged herself from the tree in her grief. The dog, also overcome by sorrow, jumped into a well and drowned.

Dionysos was so angered by these deaths that he sent a madness on Athenian girls that made them, like Erigone, hang themselves from trees. Eventually the Athenians discovered from the Delphic Oracle the cause of this madness, and at once they sought out the murderous shepherds and hanged them. They also instituted an annual festival at the time of the grape harvest, the *Aiora* ('Swinging'), during which girls swung on ropes suspended from trees with their feet resting on small platforms, and this is how swings came to be invented. Dionysos immortalized his followers by putting Ikarios in the sky as the constellation Boötes ('the ploughman'), Erigone as Virgo, and the faithful dog Maira as Canis Minor, the Lesser Dog.

Pandion had twin sons, Erechtheus and Boutes, and two daughters, Prokne and Philomela. (For the grisly legend surrounding these two girls and Tereus, the king of Thrace, see p. 457). On their father's death, the two sons divided his inheritance between them: Boutes received the priesthood of Athene and Poseidon, while Erechtheus became king. He was often confused with his grandfather, Erichthonios, and originally the two were most probably one and the same. Homer, for instance (*Iliad* 2.546–51), says that Erechtheus was born from the earth, and that Athene brought him up and installed him in her sanctuary – all of which applies more appropriately to Erichthonios.

Erechtheus had three sons, Kekrops, Pandoros and Metion, and seven daughters. We know the names of four of these girls, all of whom were married: Oreithyia, Prokris, Chthonia and Kreousa. Oreithyia became the wife of Boreas, god of the rough and wintry North Wind. At first he had pleaded for her favour, thinking that he could win her with gentleness. When this proved to no purpose, bristling with rage he reverted to his normal violent temper, and swooped upon her while she was dancing on the banks of the river Ilissos. He swept her up in a cloud of wind and carried her off to his home in Thrace. Here she bore him several children, including twin sons, Zetes and Kalais. They were known as the Boreadai, and being winged like their father were the swiftest men on earth. Some said that their wings grew from their shoulders, some from their temples and their feet, and they had long, dark hair that streamed behind them as they flew, dark as their father's storm clouds. As we have seen, they took part in the voyage of the Argonauts, where on their swift wings they drove off the monstrous Harpies (p. 146).

As for the other girls, Prokris was married to Kephalos (p. 539), Chthonia to her uncle Boutes, and Kreousa to Xouthos (see below); and according to a famous Athenian legend, dramatized in Euripides' tragedy *Erechtheus* (now lost apart from fragments), there were also three unnamed and unmarried daughters who died for the sake of their city when Athens was at war with neighbouring Eleusis. Erechtheus was told by an oracle that he must sacrifice one of his daughters if he wished to make Athens victorious, so one of them was chosen. She was duly put to death, but the other girls killed themselves as well, true to an oath they had all taken to die together. The Athenians then defeated the Eleusinians and killed their leader Eumolpos, a son of Poseidon. Now the god was angry at the death of his son, so, unfortunately for Athens, Erechtheus also died: he was slain by a blow from Poseidon's trident and engulfed in the earth.

It was usually said that Erechtheus was succeeded by his son, a second Kekrops, but in Euripides' unconventional version of the myth in his extant *Ion*, it was Kreousa's husband Xouthos who became king. When the play opens, Xouthos and Kreousa, married for many years, have come to Delphi to consult the oracle about their long childlessness. Only Kreousa knows that she has already borne a child, a son to Apollo, before her marriage.

She was picking flowers near the Acropolis when Apollo saw her. 'You came to me, your hair gleaming with gold,' she recalls (887–8), the image of the beautiful and cruel god forever lodged in her memory. He dragged her into a nearby cave and raped her. She said nothing to her parents about her pregnancy, and in due course she gave birth to her son, alone and in secret, in that very same cave. And there she sadly left him, wrapped in a shawl and lying in a cradle. Later she went back and found that the baby was gone, and ever afterwards she grieved for his loss, believing that he had been carried off and eaten by wild beasts.

Unknown to Kreousa, Apollo had cared for his son. He had sent Hermes to carry baby and cradle to his temple at Delphi, and here Apollo's priestess found the infant and brought him up in the god's service. He was called Ion, and grew up believing himself an orphan.

Now in the play Xouthos consults the oracle and is told that he already has a son, who will be the first person he meets on leaving the temple. He meets Ion, and with perfect faith in the oracle's words he greets him joyfully as his son. Ion at first thinks that this stranger must be mad, but eventually matters are straightened out and they come to the conclusion that Ion must be Xouthos's illegitimate son, born as the result of some youthful indiscretion. Both agree that they must tell the news to Kreousa with great tact.

Before they can do so, Kreousa is told by her servants that Xouthos is intending to bring into the family a bastard son. This boy would in due course supplant the line of Erechtheus on the throne of Athens, so Kreousa decides to kill him. She sends a servant to poison Ion's wine at a celebratory feast given by Xouthos, but the wine is spilt, and when Ion sees a dove drink it and die in agony, he realizes that someone has tried to murder him.

Forcing the truth from the servant, he goes to kill Kreousa, and is on the point of doing so when the priestess intervenes. She brings out the cradle in which Ion was found as a baby and Kreousa, recognizing it at once, joyfully claims Ion as her lost son. To prove it, she describes one by one the little items she left in the cradle with her child – a piece of weaving, a golden necklace, an olive wreath – and one by one Ion, in wonder, lifts them out. Mother and son are finally reunited with great joy: she has her child back again, and he at last has the mother he never knew and always missed. Xouthos remains content in the belief that he is Ion's father, and at the end of the play the family return in great happiness to Athens.

After the second Kekrops' rule, the next king of Athens was his son, a second Pandion, but he was deposed by his uncle Metion and took refuge in Megara. He married the daughter of Pylas, the local king, and in due course became king himself. He had four sons, Aigeus, Nisos, Lykos and Pallas. On his death Nisos succeeded him on the throne of Megara, while the other three brothers marched against Athens and drove out the sons of Metion. Aigeus now became king of Athens. He married twice, but neither marriage produced any children, let alone a son to succeed him, so eventually he went to the Delphic Oracle for advice. Now at last we come to Theseus.

THESEUS

The Delphic Oracle gave its usual riddling type of answer to Aigeus's inquiry about his lack of an heir. 'Loose not the protruding mouth of the wineskin, best of men, until you come to the heights of Athens,' it replied. Aigeus was quite at a loss, so he went to visit a friend of his who was renowned for his wisdom: Pittheus, a son of Pelops and Hippodameia and now the king of Troizen. Pittheus realized that the wineskin was a phallic symbol and understood the oracle's meaning at once: Aigeus must not make love to any woman until he returned to his wife in Athens, for the next time he had sex he would conceive the son he wanted.

Pittheus had no sons and only one daughter, Aithra, so he

now saw the chance to have a grandson with Aigeus's royal blood in his veins. He pretended non-comprehension of the oracle, then made his guest drunk and enticed him into sleeping with Aithra. In the morning Aigeus departed for home, but before he left, he hid a sword and a pair of sandals beneath a huge rock. He told Aithra that if she bore a son, who on reaching manhood could lift the rock, she should send him with these tokens of paternity to Athens.

In the course of time she did indeed bear a son, Theseus, though some said that his real father was the god Poseidon, who had visited Aithra's bed on the same night as Aigeus. (Others said that this was a story invented by Pittheus to save his daughter's reputation.) But whether his father was mortal or god, Theseus was born to Aithra in Troizen, and was brought up there by his mother and grandfather.

Only one story is recorded of his childhood, and this fore-shadows his future heroism. One day his kinsman Herakles came to dinner, and before settling down to eat he took off his great lion-skin and laid it on the ground. The children of the palace, seeing it lying there, thought it was a real lion and fled, shrieking, except for Theseus, who boldly seized an axe and attacked it.

When Aithra judged that the time was right, she told Theseus about his father Aigeus and showed him the rock. He lifted it with ease, then set out to walk to Athens with his father's sword and sandals. His mother and grandfather, knowing that the land-route was plagued by brigands and ruffians of all descriptions, begged him to make a safe journey by sea, but Theseus refused. He had always hero-worshipped Herakles, and now, fired with a desire to win renown by emulating his valorous deeds, he was only too eager to be faced with challenge and danger.

On the road to Athens

His hopes were fulfilled, and on the road to Athens he despatched a whole series of villains by using against them their own methods of murder. He met his first challenge before he had journeyed far from Troizen. At Epidauros there lurked a brigand called Periphetes, a son of Hephaistos and known as the 'Club-bearer', because he always carried a club of bronze with which he would beat to death any travellers who passed by. Apollodorus (3.16.1) mentions that he was weak on his legs and used his club as a crutch, so we may imagine that he would hobble along like a cripple until within striking distance of his unsuspecting victims, then with a sudden blow he would fell them to the ground. He made the mistake of accosting Theseus, who wrested the club from him and cracked open his skull. The club took Theseus' fancy, so he kept it for his own use, and just as Herakles always wore the skin of the Nemean Lion as the evidence of his first Labour, so Theseus carried the club of Periphetes as a reminder of his first trial of strength.

His next encounter, as he came to the Isthmus of Corinth, was with Sinis the 'Pine-bender', so called because of the manner of death he inflicted on travellers. Either he bent down two adjacent pine trees and tied a man's arms to one tree, his legs to another, then let the trees spring up again so that they tore his wretched victim in two. Or he forced a man to help him bend a single pine tree down to the ground, then suddenly released it so that his victim was catapulted high into the air and crashed down to his death. Theseus overcame Sinis and killed him with his own pine trees. The brigand's beautiful daughter, Perigune, had hidden fearfully among some rushes and wild asparagus, vowing never to destroy such plants if only they would protect her now. But she emerged of her own accord once Theseus had promised to do her no harm. He took her to his bed, and in due course she bore a son, Melanippos (a minor Attic hero who had a shrine at Athens). Her descendants always revered such plants as had once sheltered their ancestress.

Next on his journey Theseus dispatched Phaia, the ferocious wild sow of Krommyon. Like so many of the creatures that Herakles killed, this was the offspring of the monsters Typhon and Echidna, and was named Phaia, 'Grey One', after the old woman who reared her. A late and rationalizing tradition changes the story somewhat, suggesting that Phaia was no wild beast, but instead a female brigand of Krommyon, a murderous and depraved woman who was called the Sow because of her mode of life. Either way, she met her end at the hands of Theseus.

As he crossed the Isthmus of Corinth, he passed along some high cliffs rising sheer from the sea, and here he met Skeiron, a brigand who forced all passing travellers to wash his feet. As they stooped to do so, he would kick them off the cliffs and down into the sea below, where they were eaten by a giant turtle. When he tried his trick on Theseus he suffered the same fate as his victims, for Theseus bent down as if to obey him, then caught him by the feet and flung him into the sea, where the turtle ate him.

Passing through Attica, Theseus was confronted by Kerkyon, a son of Poseidon and the king of Eleusis, who forced all passers-by to wrestle to the death with him. Like the other evildoers on the road, he had killed every one of the men he had so far accosted – until he was unwise enough to challenge Theseus, who lifted him high in the air, then dashed him hard to the ground and killed him.

Another legend concerning Kerkyon further demonstrates his cruelty. Hyginus (*Fabula* 187) tells the sad story of his daughter Alope, which is probably taken from Euripides' tragedy *Alope*, now lost. She was loved by Poseidon and became pregnant, but she was scared of her father's anger and so she kept her condition a secret. At last her son was born, and now she was even more afraid, so she dressed him in warm clothes and left him out in the countryside to die. He lived because a mare suckled him – no doubt sent by Poseidon to care for his son.

Soon a shepherd found the baby and took him home, then gave him to another shepherd, but the two of them quarrelled about who should take the fine clothes that the child was wearing. Unable to settle the matter, they asked Kerkyon to arbitrate, and he recognized the clothes as made from a dress of his daughter. So the truth came out. He locked Alope away and left her to die, then exposed the baby for a second time. Once again the mare came and suckled him, and once again some shepherds found him and took him home. This time he was reared to manhood. He was called Hippothoon, 'Horse-swift', a name recalling both the mare that saved him and his father Poseidon, god of horses. Later, when Theseus had come into power at Athens, he made Hippothoon king of Eleusis.

Theseus had one final challenge to deal with before he reached his destination. Soon after he left Eleusis he encountered Prokroustes, 'Beater', so called because of the way he treated wayfarers who were unwary enough to accept his hospitality. He had two beds, one long and one short, and he would force his victims to lie on one of them, then adjust their size to fit the bed, either lopping off their extremities or hammering them out to length. Theseus too was invited in by Prokroustes, where he applied the same treatment to his host. (It is not recorded which kind of death he meted out to him, and on vase-paintings of the scene Theseus sometimes wields an axe, sometimes a hammer.)

Soon after this he arrived in Athens.

Father and son

Aigeus was by now an old man. His whole city was rife with disorder and unrest, and he himself was living in a state of constant fear because his brother Pallas and his fifty sons were threatening to seize the throne. When Theseus came to his father's palace, he did not at once show Aigeus the tokens of paternity and the king had no reason to recognize him. One person guessed who he was, however, and this was the sorceress Medea. She had been living with Aigeus since she was banished from Corinth, and she had borne him a son, Medos. Now she saw Theseus as a threat to her prospects, so she decided that one way or another he must die.

Because of Aigeus's fears of conspiracy, Medea had no trouble in filling his mind with suspicions of this young stranger. Aigeus thought it best to set Theseus some task of valour from which he was unlikely to return alive, so he sent him to get rid of the ferocious Bull of Marathon that was ravaging the countryside. This bull had originally been known as the Cretan Bull, when it was captured by Herakles as his seventh Labour for Eurystheus and taken to Mycenae (p. 199). From there it had made its way to Attica, where it soon became a plague to the inhabitants. Theseus was happy to be tackling a task that would bring so much benefit to the people of Attica, and no doubt happy too because he was attempting a feat of strength that had been accomplished by Herakles before him.

As he travelled to Marathon, he was given shelter by an old woman named Hekale, who treated him kindly and promised to sacrifice in thanksgiving to Zeus if he returned safely from his task the next day. Theseus mastered the bull, just as Herakles had done, and drove it back to the city. On his way he called on Hekale to announce his success and was sad to find her dead. Because of her kindness and hospitality, he later instituted a local ceremony to honour her memory.

Back in Athens, Theseus drove the bull alive through the city for everyone to see, then sacrificed it to Apollo and returned triumphant to his father's palace. Medea still cherished her murderous intentions, so she mixed a cup of poison made from the deadly aconite and persuaded Aigeus to offer it to Theseus at a feast. Just as the unsuspecting youth was about to drink, Aigeus recognized the sword that he was carrying and dashed the cup from his lips. Father and son joyfully made themselves known to each other. Medea, with her schemes exposed, fled from Athens for ever. She eventually returned with Medos to her birthplace of Kolchis, where she restored her father Aietes to the throne from which his brother Perses had deposed him. Presumably she lived out the rest of her life there. Her death is not recorded.

Aigeus announced publicly that Theseus would be his successor on the throne of Athens. Pallas and his fifty sons, who had hoped to inherit the kingdom when Aigeus died childless, broke into open rebellion. Theseus, with his father's support, crushed the revolt.

Soon afterwards, the tribute owed by Athens to Minos, king of Crete, for the death of his son Androgeos became due. Androgeos had been a fine athlete who had won many victories at Athens' Panathenaic festival, but unfortunately this had led to his death, though there are several versions of how it came about. Either his defeated rivals ambushed and killed him; or Aigeus was so impressed by his prowess that he sent him against the Bull of Marathon and it gored him to death; or he became friends with the sons of Pallas, and Aigeus, fearing an alliance that might threaten his rule, had him assassinated. Whichever the cause of Androgeos' death, the result was always the same: his father Minos wanted revenge, so he claimed from Athens a tribute of seven youths and seven girls, to be shipped periodically to Crete and fed to the Minotaur in the Labyrinth.

This time Theseus made one of the company, intending to kill the Minotaur and put an end to the tribute for ever. Before following the story to its conclusion, however, we should first trace the earlier history of Crete, and of Minos and his wife Pasiphae.

Crete: Europa, Minos and Pasiphae

This story begins, as so often, with a love affair of Zeus. As we have seen (p. 161), Agenor, the son of Poseidon and Libya, left his home in Egypt and migrated to Phoenicia, where he founded a kingdom of his own. There he had a family of several sons and one daughter, Europa. Her beauty caught the ever-wandering eye of Zeus, and one day, when she was picking flowers with her friends near the seashore, the god came down

Europa seduced by Zeus in the guise of a bull.

to earth disguised as a beautiful bull, white as untrodden snow and with horns shining like jewels. At first the girls were afraid, but when they saw how tamely he ambled about among them, and how mild and gentle he really was, they fed him flowers, and stroked him, and hung fresh garlands on his horns. When at last he lay down on the sand, Europa, with all fear gone, climbed upon his back. At once he leapt up and plunged into the sea, carrying her far out into the ocean. Her friends never saw her again.

Zeus carried Europa over the sea to Crete and there she bore him three sons, Minos, Rhadamanthys and Sarpedon. She married Asterios, the king of Crete, and he brought up her sons by Zeus as his own family. Sarpedon later migrated to Lycia, and Rhadamanthys went to rule over islands in the southern Aegean, where such was his reputation for wisdom and justice that after his death he was made one of the judges in Hades. Minos succeeded Asterios as king of Crete (though not without opposition: see below). As for the bull whose form Zeus took to abduct Europa, it was immortalized in the heavens as the constellation Taurus, and Europa herself would give her name to the continent of Europe – appropriately, since the Minoans, named after her son Minos, would form the first great civilization in European history (p. 254).

Minos married Pasiphae, a daughter of the Sun-god Helios. She bore him four sons, Katreos, Deukalion, Glaukos and Androgeos, and five daughters, Ariadne and Phaidra (both of whom would be loved by Theseus), Akakallis, Xenodike and Euryale (who would become by Poseidon the mother of the great hunter Orion). Two of the children died: Androgeos, who, as we have seen, was killed at Athens, and Glaukos – who died but was then miraculously restored to life by the clever seer Polyeidos. As a small child, Glaukos had been chasing a mouse when he fell into a storage-jar full of honey and was drowned. His distraught parents searched everywhere for him, but unavailingly, until Polyeidos correctly interpreted the omen of an owl (*glaux*), perched near the storage-room and plagued by bees, and found the boy's drowned body in the honey-jar.

Now Minos quite unreasonably demanded that his son be brought back to life, and he locked the seer up with the corpse until he could achieve this. At first Polyeidos was completely at a loss. Then by chance a snake came slithering across the floor and he killed it, fearing that it meant harm. A second snake appeared, carrying a herb which it put on the dead snake's body, and, to the seer's amazement, the corpse came back to life. Polyeidos lost no time in using the herb on Glaukos, and at once the boy too revived and was restored to his parents.

So this grief at least was turned into joy, but Pasiphae's life was not without other sorrows. Minos proved to be a serially unfaithful husband and fathered several illegitimate children. He even tried to rape Britomartis, the Cretan equivalent of the goddess Athene. Eventually Pasiphae grew so angry at his promiscuity that she bewitched him (she was, after all, the sister of the enchantress Circe): she gave him noxious drugs that made him ejaculate snakes and scorpions whenever he had intercourse, and this made him somewhat less attractive to women. Yet perhaps most traumatic of all for Pasiphae were the events resulting from the death of Asterios and the subsequent dispute over the kingship.

Asterios had died childless, and because Minos was not of his blood he had no automatic right to the throne. Nevertheless he declared to his rivals that the gods supported his claim, and to prove it he said that whatever he prayed for would be fulfilled. He then called on Poseidon to send him a bull from the sea, promising to sacrifice it when it appeared. The god answered his prayer. A magnificent white bull came out of the sea, and Minos won his kingdom.

Unfortunately the bull was so beautiful that Minos could not bear to kill it, so he put it with his herds for breeding and sacrificed another in its place. This broken vow angered the sea-god so much that he inflicted on Pasiphae an ungovernable passion for the bull. Nothing would satisfy her but to mate with the beast – and she had just the man staying in the palace who could help her do so.

This man was the brilliant inventor and master-craftsman Daidalos, an Athenian who had been forced to leave Athens after murdering his nephew Perdix, who was also his apprentice. Perdix had proved to be even more ingenious than his master. He is credited with three inventions: the iron saw, which he made by copying either the backbone of a fish or the teeth in a snake's jawbone, the geometrician's compasses, and the potter's wheel. Eventually Daidalos grew so jealous of his nephew's accomplishments that he killed him, flinging him to his death from the Acropolis.

Athene, who had loved the boy for his skill, took pity on him and turned him into a partridge (*perdix*). Ovid (*Metamorphoses* 8.236–59) explains that this is why the partridge, remembering that terrible fall, always flies low and makes its nest on the ground. Years later, when Daidalos was sorrowfully burying his son Ikaros, also dead from a fall, a nearby partridge flapped its wings and uttered cries of joy.

For his crime Daidalos appeared before the court of the Areopagos and was exiled, which is how he came to be in Crete at just the right time for Pasiphae. When she told him of her lust for the bull, he fashioned a hollow wooden cow, realistically covered with hide, and set it in a meadow. Pasiphae crouched inside the cow, waiting until the bull, completely taken in by so deft an imitation, coupled with her. The fruit of their union was named Asterios but was better known as the Minotaur (*Minotauros*, 'Bull of Minos'), a monster with a human body and the head and horns of a bull.

It might well be argued that Pasiphae was not to blame in all this, since everything had been brought about by Minos's broken vow to Poseidon. And in fact it was so argued in Euripides' tragedy *Cretans*, now mostly lost, which dramatized Pasiphae's passion and the birth of the Minotaur. In a surviving fragment of the play, Pasiphae defends her behaviour, arguing that such an extraordinary lust as hers must have been inflicted on her by some god, angry with Minos himself. 'What did I see in a bull that could eat at my heart with such a shameful affliction?' she asks sarcastically. 'Was he such a fine sight in his clothes, and did such a brilliant light flame from his red hair and his eyes, and burnish his ruddy cheeks? Was he not a graceful bridegroom?' No, she goes on, the fault was all with Minos, who caused Poseidon's wrath. She herself was innocent, her crime involuntary.

Nevertheless Minos was so appalled by his wife's deed and her monstrous offspring that he commissioned Daidalos to build a vast underground maze, so cleverly devised that anyone going in would be quite unable to find the way out again: the Labyrinth. In here the Minotaur could be shut away for ever.

Time passed. The Minotaur grew, fed on human flesh. At some stage Androgeos was killed while at Athens, and Minos responded by declaring war. He first captured Athens' ally Megara, the city of which Nisos, the brother of Aigeus, was king. Nisos had in his hair either a red tress, or a single red hair, on which his life depended. His daughter Skylla betrayed him (some say that she had fallen in love with Minos, others that Minos bribed her with a necklace of Cretan gold) and she cut off the precious hair while Nisos was asleep. At once he died, and now Megara could be taken. Skylla no doubt expected gratitude from Minos, but instead he was disgusted by her treachery. He tied her to the stern of his ship and dragged her behind it until she drowned. Ovid tells us (*Metamorphoses* 8.6–151) that Nisos was turned into a sea eagle, and Skylla into a seabird forever pursued by her vengeful father.

Despite the taking of Megara, the war with Athens lingered on. Eventually Minos prayed to his father Zeus that he might get his revenge in some other way. Zeus sent a famine and a plague on the city, and an oracle told the Athenians that to be saved they must grant Minos whatever satisfaction he demanded. He chose a regular tribute of seven youths and seven girls to be sent periodically to Crete (different sources say either annually or every nine years) as food for the Minotaur.

Two payments of tribute had been made, and the third was now due, when Theseus set off for Crete as one of the Minotaur's offerings. Some say that Minos came to Athens in person to select his victims, and Theseus was his first choice because of his strength and beauty. In the more usual version the selection was by lot, and Theseus himself volunteered to be one of the company, thinking it right that he should share the fate of his fellow citizens, even though he was the king's son and heir to the throne. But however he was chosen, certainly he set off with the firm intention of killing the Minotaur and putting an end to the cruel tribute forever.

Theseus and the Minotaur

The ship that carried the fourteen chosen victims had a black sail to suit its sorrowful mission, and Theseus promised his father that if he survived his perilous adventure, he would change the black sail of mourning to a white or scarlet sail as a sign of his safe return. Thus, when the vessel was approaching Athens, Aigeus would know at once whether his son still lived.

On the outward journey Minos, with his usual amorous inclinations, took a fancy to one of the girls, Eriboia, and began to stroke her cheeks. Bacchylides (*Ode* 17) relates how Theseus defended her, claiming that as a son of Poseidon, and thus Minos's equal, he had every right to oppose him. Minos called for a sign from his own father, Zeus, who at once flashed down a thunderbolt. The king then flung his golden ring into the sea, Poseidon's domain, challenging Theseus to prove his paternity by retrieving it. Without hesitation Theseus dived into the water, while the ship sped onwards (92–116):

The young Athenians trembled as the hero sprang into the sea, and they shed tears from their tender eyes, expecting disaster to follow, but sea-dwelling dolphins swiftly carried great Theseus to the palace of his father, god of horses. There he saw with awe the glorious daughters of blessed Nereus. From their shining limbs glistened a light bright as fire, and around their hair were twisted ribbons braided with gold, as they danced delightedly on lissom feet. And in the lovely palace he saw his father's dear wife, beautiful Amphitrite, in all her majesty. Around him she cast a crimson cloak and set on his thick hair an exquisite garland, dark with roses, which artful Aphrodite had once given to her at her wedding.

The dolphins swiftly carried Theseus back to the ship, and to the amazement of Minos he emerged from the sea, unwetted, and carrying his divine gifts. He had survived this ordeal with honour, but he knew that a far greater challenge was awaiting him in the Labyrinth on Crete.

Luckily for Theseus, Minos's daughter Ariadne fell in love with him, just as Medea had fallen in love with Jason, and she helped him to achieve his aim. Daidalos, the builder of the Labyrinth, was still living in the palace, so she begged him to tell her how Theseus could escape if he survived his encounter with the Minotaur. Daidalos gave her a clew, a large ball of thread, which would guide him back to the outside world again.

Theseus tied one end of this clew firmly to the entrance, then unwound the thread as he wended his way into the innermost depths of the maze.

Theseus about to kill the Minotaur.

There he found the Minotaur. They fought, and the Minotaur died, though sources disagree as to how Theseus killed him. Apollodorus says that he used only his bare fists, and this seems the most likely, since the creature's victims would surely have been sent unarmed into its lair; though in the many vase-paintings of the seventh and sixth centuries BC, when the myth was at the height of its popularity, Theseus fights with sword, or club, or spear, while the Minotaur sometimes uses rocks to fight back. Better to agree with Apollodorus, and to imagine hand-to-hand combat, a hard and bloody fight to the death in the hot darkness.

In whatever way it happened, the outcome of the encounter was always the same, with the Minotaur dead and Minos' cruel tribute ended. Theseus escaped from the Labyrinth by following his thread back to the entrance, then sailed away from Crete with the other young Athenians, having first knocked holes into the bottom of the Cretan ships to prevent pursuit. He took Ariadne with him, for he had promised her marriage in return for her invaluable help.

Yet it did not happen thus, for when they came to the island of Dia, later called Naxos, Theseus abandoned her. Sometimes it was said that he did so from choice, perhaps because he had fallen in love with another girl; a Hesiodic fragment (298) mentions Aigle, the daughter of the Phokian hero Panopeus. In the later tradition it was usually agreed that Theseus acted on the command of the gods, because Dionysos wanted Ariadne for his wife.

Ariadne awoke in the morning to find herself alone and to see her lover's ship speeding into the distance, but she was not desolate for long. Dionysos arrived in his chariot drawn by panthers, accompanied by his revelling entourage of satyrs and maenads, and he carried Ariadne off to Olympos, where he made her immortal. As a wedding present, he gave her a golden crown, made by Hephaistos, that was later set among the stars as the Corona Borealis. Ariadne would bear Dionysos four sons, Oinopion, Staphylos, Thoas and Peparethos.

Theseus sailed onwards, stopping at the island of Delos to sacrifice to Apollo in thanksgiving for the success of his mission on Crete. He and his companions celebrated their survival by dancing the Crane Dance, the intricate movements of which imitated the winding passages of the Labyrinth. This dance became traditional at Delos and was still being performed by the Delians well into the historical period. From Delos, Theseus sailed home to Athens, but he quite forgot to hoist a white or scarlet sail to show his father that he was safe. Aigeus, looking eagerly out to sea from a headland, saw the distant black sail and flung himself in despair into the sea – which ever afterwards has borne his name, the Aegean.

Meanwhile, in Crete, Minos was so furious at the help given to Theseus by Daidalos, and at the subsequent loss of his daughter, that he imprisoned Daidalos himself in the Labyrinth, and with him his young son Ikaros, borne to him by a slave-girl living in the palace. They escaped, and Daidalos fashioned wings of wax and feathers with which he and his son could fly away from Crete to freedom. He gave Ikaros careful instructions on how to fly safely: he must keep midway between earth and heaven, neither too low, where the sea-spray might weigh down his wings, nor too high, where the flaming sun might scorch them.

They took off, and Daidalos watched his son as anxiously as any parent bird its fledgling. At first all went well as they flew far out over the sea, but then Ikaros grew carried away with the joy of flight, and forgetting all his father's warnings he soared higher and higher towards the sun. Finally he came so close that the wax of his wings melted and he plummeted headlong into the sea below, still calling for his father even as the waters engulfed him. The stricken Daidalos retrieved his body and buried it on a nearby island, ever afterwards called Ikaria, just as the sea was renamed the Ikarian Sea in honour of the dead boy, and still bears his name.

Perhaps, for Ikaros, it was worth it. He was doing what mankind, seeing the effortless flight of birds, has always longed to do. It is a modern poet, W. B. Yeats, who best captures what Ikaros may, for a brief eternity, have felt, in *An Irish Airman Foresees His Death* – a very different context, but one that echoes the exultation of Ikaros's flight to the sun:

> Nor law, nor duty bade me fight,
> Nor public men, nor cheering crowds,

A lonely impulse of delight
Drove to this tumult in the clouds;
I balanced all, brought all to mind,
The years to come seemed waste of breath,
A waste of breath the years behind
In balance with this life, this death.

Ovid writes of the people who may have watched Daidalos and Ikaros as they flew across the sky (*Metamorphoses* 8.217–20):

Perhaps some fisherman, wielding his quivering rod, or a shepherd leaning on his crook, or a ploughman resting on his plough handle caught sight of them and stood stupefied, thinking these must be gods who could fly through the air.

When Pieter Brueghel the Elder painted *Landscape with the Fall of Icarus* (1567), he put in the fisherman, the shepherd and the ploughman, but showed them all going about their work quite indifferent to the tiny figure of Ikaros disappearing into the sea: as the proverb says, no plough stops for a man who dies. The myth has always been a potent source of inspiration for artists and has had many different interpretations, but with Ikaros's flight remaining a powerful symbol of man's soaring aspirations. As the eighteenth-century French poet Phillippe Destouches writes:

Le ciel fut son désir, la mer son sépulture:
Est-il plus beau dessein ou plus riche tombeau?

Daidalos travelled to Sicily and took refuge at the court of Kokalos, king of Kamikos. Minos set out to track him down and travelled far and wide in search of him, taking with him a spiral seashell and promising a great reward to anyone who could pass a thread through it. He believed (and quite rightly) that no one but the clever Daidalos would be able to solve the problem. When he brought the shell to the court of Kokalos, Daidalos (perhaps remembering Theseus' escape from the Labyrinth) bored a tiny hole in the shell, then tied a thread to an ant and induced it to pass through the spiral. Kokalos gave the threaded shell to Minos, who knew at once that Daidalos must be here and demanded that he be surrendered. The king promised to hand him over. But that night Minos was killed by Kokalos' daughters while in his bath. They had grown so fond of Daidalos, delighting in their clever guest's artistic skill, that they did not want to lose him, so they scalded Minos to death with boiling water (some say pitch), flooding it through a system of pipes installed by Daidalos himself.

Despite his inglorious end, Minos had been a great and respected king, famous for his vast sea power. This may well be a folk memory of the glorious Bronze Age culture centred in Crete (c. 3500–1100 BC), which has been called Minoan after him, a term coined by Sir Arthur Evans after his excavations at Knossos beginning in 1900. Like his brother Rhadamanthys, Minos was renowned for his wisdom and justice as a lawgiver and after death he became, with him, one of the judges over the souls of the dead in Hades.

As for Daidalos, he too was held in honour after his death, and to the ancients his name became synonymous with ingenuity and fine craftsmanship. They saw evidence of his work in many remarkable buildings and art works throughout the Greek world, and even in Egypt. Homer (*Iliad* 18.590–92) is the first to mention him as the maker of a dancing-floor for Ariadne at Knossos; and perhaps Virgil's reference is the most poignant (*Aeneid* 6.14–33), when he says that Daidalos built Apollo's great temple at Cumae and adorned it with scenes depicting the birth and death of the Minotaur. 'And you too, Ikaros,' adds Virgil, 'would have had a great part in this splendid work, but for Daidalos's grief. Twice he tried to shape your fall in gold, and twice his hands, a father's hands, dropped helpless.'

Theseus, king of Athens

Theseus returned to an Athens in mourning for her dead king, and to the personal duties of preparing the funeral rituals for his dead father. He himself now began his reign as king of Attica, and was always afterwards honoured as a wise and statesmanlike ruler who laid the foundations of democracy. His greatest political achievement was to unify the many small, independent communities of the land into one state, with Athens at its head. We see him in action in fifth-century tragedy, where he appears as a heroic champion of justice, the strong and compassionate ruler of a great city. In Sophocles' *Oedipus at Kolonos* he protects the old, blind Oedipus and his daughters and gives them sanctuary. In Euripides' *Suppliant Women*, dramatizing the aftermath of the attack of the Seven against Thebes, Theseus forces the Thebans to give up the Argive dead for burial. In Euripides' *Madness of Herakles*, he befriends the broken, desperate Herakles after he has tragically murdered his wife and children, and offers him refuge in Athens.

Like any great hero of his generation, Theseus was said to have gone on the voyage of the Argonauts and the hunt for the Kalydonian Boar. With him went his dearest friend, Peirithoos, son of Ixion and king of the Lapiths of northern Thessaly. They had met while Peirithoos was raiding a herd of Theseus' cattle. Theseus had gone in pursuit, intending to fight the thief, but as soon as the two came face to face, they were both so struck with mutual liking and admiration that they joined hands and swore an oath of lifelong friendship.

They shared many a testing experience over the years. One such was the occasion of Peirithoos' wedding to Hippodameia, when the famous battle between the Lapiths and the Centaurs took place. The Centaurs, as we have seen (p. 196), were an unruly and dangerous tribe of creatures. When Peirithoos first became king of the Lapiths, the Centaurs challenged his rule on the ground that as Ixion's grandsons they had a right to a share in the kingdom. The dispute was settled peacably and the Centaurs were given Mount Pelion as their territory. Now Peirithoos invited them to his wedding-feast, along with many other guests, including Theseus.

All went well at first while the Centaurs, who were unfamiliar with wine, drank milk; but soon they smelled the new and attractive fragrance of the wine and grabbed some for themselves, swilling it down greedily. Before long they became drunken and randy. They seized the Lapith women – one of them, Eurytion, even tried to carry off the bride – and a violent and bloody battle broke out.

Both sides had many casualties. Many Centaurs fell to Theseus, fighting alongside Peirithoos. One of the Lapith fatalities was Kaineus, who had originally been a woman, Kainis, famous for her beauty. She had rejected all her many suitors, but one day, when she was wandering over a lonely part of the seashore, Poseidon came out of the sea and raped her. Afterwards he offered to give her whatever she might wish for, and she asked to become a man, so that she might never again have to undergo such an outrage. The god granted her wish, and as an additional gift he made her body invulnerable to weapons and promised that she would never die by the sword. Thus Kainis became Kaineus, and he even married and had a son, Koronos.

Now at Peirithoos' wedding Kaineus fought and killed several Centaurs. The Centaurs did their utmost to kill him too, thrusting their swords at him and hurling spears, but their weapons had no effect on his invulnerable body and fell away blunted. Eventually they managed to despatch him by striking him with the trunks of pine trees until he was hammered into the ground

Finally, after a long and savage struggle, the Lapiths were the victors. This battle would become a favourite subject in ancient art and is depicted most powerfully in sculpture, such as on the Parthenon metopes, the west pediment of the Temple of Zeus at Olympia, and the frieze from the Temple of Apollo at Bassai. It seems to have symbolized the triumph of Greek civilization over bestiality and the forces of barbarism. The Lapiths drove the surviving Centaurs out of Thessaly and into the Peloponnese, where they next fought with Herakles – to their cost (p. 196).

Peirithoos also accompanied Theseus when, like Herakles, he went on an expedition against the Amazons. Theseus carried the Amazon queen Antiope (sometimes called Hippolyte) back to Athens as his mistress, hotly pursued by the rest of the warrior-women. A great horde of these laid siege to the Acropolis itself, but Theseus and his army vanquished them in a fierce battle and most of them were killed. Antiope stayed with Theseus and bore him a son, Hippolytos.

Some years later Theseus married Phaidra, the daughter of King Minos and thus the sister of the abandoned Ariadne. Minos by now was dead and the match was arranged by his son Deukalion, who presumably had forgiven Theseus' earlier desertion of his sister. Antiope felt so resentful of this marriage that during the wedding celebrations she led out her Amazon companions armed for battle, threatening to kill the assembled guests. In the ensuing struggle, Antiope herself was killed.

Phaidra bore Theseus two sons, Akamas and Demophon, who would in due course become kings of Athens. The fifty sons of Pallas saw that their hopes of legitimately inheriting the throne had now virtually disappeared, so they made a final desperate attempt to depose Theseus. He and his supporters killed them all.

Because Theseus had spilt the blood of kinsmen, he was exiled from Athens for a year, so he took his wife and family to his other kingdom of Troizen, inherited from his grandfather Pittheus. Here his son Hippolytos was living. Phaidra fell in love with her stepson and tried to seduce him, but he spurned her advances, so to get her revenge she lied to Theseus that Hippolytos had tried to rape her. Theseus cursed his son, calling on Poseidon to kill him, and the god sent a bull from the sea which terrified Hippolytos's horses. He was thrown from his chariot and dragged to his death, entangled in the reins. Phaidra, her treachery exposed, hung herself. (For a more detailed treatment of this legend, see p. 470.) The traveller Pausanias (1.22.1–2, 2.32.1–4) saw the graves of both Phaidra and Hippolytos at Troizen, and near them a myrtle tree, its leaves pierced with holes. It was said that Phaidra had made these with her hair-pin, when, day after day, in an agony of frustrated love, she watched Hippolytos exercising on the race-course nearby.

Peirithoos too was by now a widower, so the two friends planned what turned out to be one final enterprise together. They agreed to help each other win new wives – but not just any wives, for they were aiming high: they both wanted to marry a daughter of Zeus. First of all they carried off Helen, the beautiful daughter of Zeus and Leda, wife of King Tyndareos of Sparta. They drew lots for Helen and Theseus won. They left her in the charge of Theseus' mother, Aithra, at Aphidnai in Attica, then set off together to win a bride for Peirithoos. He, foolish man, had chosen Persephone, the daughter of Zeus and Demeter and the wife of Hades, king of the Underworld. In their absence, Helen was rescued by her two brothers, Kastor and Polydeukes. They took her back home to Sparta, along with Aithra, who was made Helen's slave.

So Theseus and Peirithoos had lost one of their chosen wives, and they fared no better with the other. They descended to the

Underworld through the entrance at Tainaron in the Peloponnese, and at first all seemed to be going well, for Hades greeted them with friendliness and invited them to take a seat. They did so, but these were no normal seats. Once they sat down, they could no longer stand up again, because the seats stuck to their flesh and they were held fast by coiling snakes. Besides which, these were seats of forgetfulness and they lost all will to move.

So there they stayed, and would both have remained there for ever had not Herakles come to the Underworld to fetch its guard-dog, Kerberos, as his twelfth Labour for Eurystheus. Finding the two friends fast in their seats, he took Theseus by the hand and pulled him to his feet (though it was said that he left part of his buttocks behind, and this is why the Athenians, his descendants, had small bottoms, inherited from their ancient king). But when Herakles set about freeing Peirithoos, the ground shook and he had to stop. So Theseus returned to the land of the living, while Peirithoos had to stay fixed to his seat in the Underworld for ever. It could have been worse: there exist traces of a version in which he was devoured by Kerberos.

When Theseus eventually returned to Athens, he found that Menestheus, the great-grandson of Erechtheus, had been made king in his place, and that his own sons, Akamas and Demophon, had fled for refuge to Elephenor, king of the Abantes in Euboia. Theseus himself found a new home with Lykomedes, king of the island of Skyros. But Lykomedes, although he pretended friendship, was really Theseus' enemy, either because he was afraid of him, or because he secretly supported Menestheus. He took Theseus to the highest point of his island and pushed him off a cliff to his death.

So Theseus, like his enemy Minos, had a somewhat ignominious end, but – also like Minos – he was ever afterwards held in honour. He was certainly Athens' greatest hero, and to the Athenians he was on a par with Herakles, the greatest hero of them all. During the Persian Wars, the Athenians were quite sure that they saw Theseus' apparition, clad in full armour and charging ahead of them against the barbarians, at their victorious battle of Marathon (490 BC). In 475 BC the Athenian general Kimon went to Skyros and brought back what he believed to be Theseus' bones, a skeleton of gigantic size that he had found buried with a bronze spear and sword. These were ceremonially reinterred in a special shrine, the Theseion, in the heart of Athens.

Aftermath

Later kings of Crete

King Minos of Crete was succeeded by his eldest son Katreos, who himself had four children – a son, Althaimenes, and three daughters, Apemosyne, Aerope and Klymene. When Katreos inquired of an oracle how his life would end, he was told that one of his children would kill him, so Althaimenes and Apemosyne emigrated to Rhodes, while Katreos gave Aerope and Klymene to Nauplios, the navigator and slave-trader, to be sold overseas. Nauplios disobeyed him and spared both girls. He married Klymene himself, and gave Aerope as wife to Atreus.

In Rhodes, Althaimenes founded a town called Cretinia, named in memory of his homeland, and also a shrine of Atabyrian Zeus on the top of Mount Atabyria, from which, on a clear day, Crete could be seen. Not long afterwards he murdered his sister Apemosyne. Hermes desired her, but she ran too fast for him to catch her, so the god resorted to a trick: he spread fresh hides in her path so that she slipped and fell, and there he raped her. (This is a very unusual story, for Hermes was normally seen as a kindly god.) She told Althaimenes what had happened, but he thought that she was concealing a liaison with some mortal lover and kicked her to death.

Althaimenes had resolved never to return to Crete in case he should kill his father. Yet an oracle's predictions must come true, so when Katreos grew old, he himself came to Rhodes to find his son. On landing at a deserted spot he was attacked by cowherds, who thought that he and his men were pirates. He tried to explain, but the barking of the dogs drowned out his words, and the cowherds stoned him until Althaimenes appeared. He failed to recognize his father and killed him with a javelin, so the old oracle was fulfilled. When Althaimenes realized what he had done, he prayed to the gods and was swallowed up by the earth.

Katreos was succeeded by his brother Deukalion (who arranged the marriage between Theseus and Phaidra), and Deukalion by his son Idomeneos. We see Idomeneos in action in the *Iliad*, where he has led the Cretan contingent of eighty ships to the Trojan War, with his nephew Meriones as his second-in-command. Idomeneos is older than most of the other Greek leaders, his hair flecked with grey, but he is also a great warrior, staunch and courageous on the battlefield (13.470–76):

> No childish fear gripped hold of Idomeneos,
> but he stood firm, like some great mountain boar
> who, trusting in his strength, stands up
> to a great rabble of men coming against him
> in a lonely place. He bristles up his back,
> and his eyes shine with fire; he grinds his teeth
> in his longing to fight off the dogs and men.
> Thus did spear-famed Idomeneos stand firm,
> and he would not give way . . .

He survived the war and was one of the warriors in the Wooden Horse. After Troy fell he sailed safely home to Crete, and Diodorus (5.79) says that he was buried at Knossos, sharing a tomb with Meriones, and that the Cretans held the two heroes in especial renown, offering up sacrifices to them and calling on their aid in times of war.

Other legends tell of his exile from Crete. Apollodorus (*Epitome* 6.10) relates how his wife Meda had taken a certain Leukos as a lover. Leukos killed both Meda and her daughter, then seized power as a tyrant, and so successfully that when Idomeneos returned home to Crete, Leukos drove him into exile.

Servius, the commentator on Virgil, is our main source for an even more tragic story about Idomeneos' homecoming. Struck by a violent storm on his voyage home, he vowed that if he arrived safely he would sacrifice to Poseidon the first living creature that he met on landing. This turned out to be his own son, who was waiting to welcome him. When he sacrificed the boy to fulfil his vow, a plague broke out, and his people, believing this to be a divine judgement, banished him and he settled in Italy. Idomeneos was the last descendant of Europa to rule in Crete.

The last kings of Athens

Menestheus, who had usurped the throne from Theseus, led the Athenian contingent of fifty ships to the Trojan War. Akamas and Demophon went to the war too, their main object being to rescue their grandmother Aithra, who had been taken to Troy as Helen's slave. When Troy at last fell to the Greeks, they took Aithra home again to Athens and reclaimed their kingdom.

Another legend has one or other of the brothers entangled on the way home with a Thracian princess, Phyllis, who brought her father's kingdom to their marriage as dowry. In one version, Akamas (or Demophon) grew tired of Thrace after a while and wanted to go home again. Phyllis begged him to stay, but despite her entreaties he set off, promising to return to her within a certain time. As he left, Phyllis gave him a casket, telling him that it contained objects sacred to the Great Mother, Rheia, and that he must never open it unless he gave up all intention of coming back to her.

Time passed and Akamas did not return. Eventually Phyllis abandoned all hope of ever seeing her dear husband again and killed herself. Akamas, meanwhile, had settled in Cyprus. One day he opened the casket, and what he saw inside terrified him so much that he leapt on his horse and galloped wildly away. He was thrown, and died by falling on to his own sword.

Demophon's grandson Thymoites was the last king of the line of Theseus to rule at Athens. He was supplanted by Melanthos, a descendant of Nestor, king of Pylos in Messenia. Melanthos's son Kodros succeeded him and became the last king of Athens. During Kodros's reign the Dorians invaded Attica, because an oracle had promised them victory so long as Kodros was left alive. They took great care not to injure him, but he learnt of the prediction and sacrificed himself for his country: disguising himself as a woodcutter, he picked a quarrel with some enemy soldiers and was killed. When they found out what they had done, the Dorians marched home again, sure that they would now be defeated. No one was thought worthy to succeed so noble a king, and monarchy at Athens was replaced by archonship.

9

THE THEBAN SAGA

We have seen how one branch of the family of Io, the descendants of her great-grandson Belos, settled in Argos (Chapter 5). The descendants of her other great-grandson, the Phoenician king Agenor, formed the royal line of the great city of Thebes.

Thebes was the leading city of Boiotia, the plainland area of central Greece, ringed by mountain ranges that included Parnassos, Helikon and Kithairon. All were mythologically significant. Parnassos and Helikon were favourite haunts of the Muses, and Parnassos was the site of Delphi and its famous Oracle, important in real as well as mythological terms. Kithairon was where Aktaion and Pentheus were torn to pieces, one by his own hounds and the other by maenads, led by his own mother; and where the baby Oedipus, the doomed son of Laios and Jocasta, was supposedly left out to die. And although, historically, Thebes and Athens were often hostile to one another, the myths of Thebes were tremendously inspirational to the Athenian dramatists and provided the plots of many Greek tragedies, including two of the most famous of them all: Sophocles' *Oedipus the King* and *Antigone*.

KADMOS AND THE FOUNDING OF THEBES

The legendary founder of Thebes was Kadmos, one of the sons of Agenor. When Kadmos's sister Europa was carried off by Zeus in the form of a bull (p. 243), Agenor sent his sons out into the world to search for her. None of them found her, and none returned home again, for when, after wandering far over the earth, they at last gave up their unsuccessful quests, they all chose to settle elsewhere.

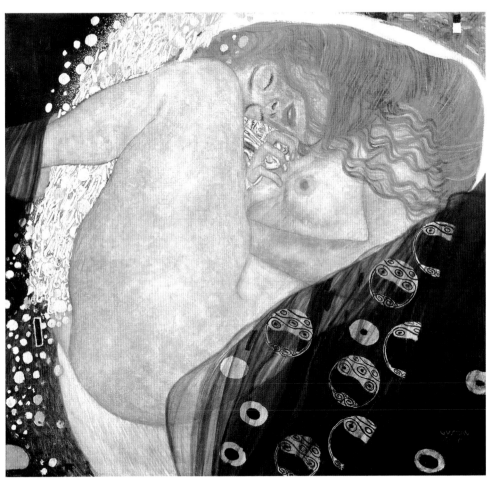

1. Zeus comes to Danae in a shower of gold (p. 168).

2. A startled Daphne finds herself turning into a laurel tree, just as Apollo reaches out to grasp her (p. 521).

3. A savage Kronos (Saturn) devours one of his sons (p. 40).

4. Hera, Aphrodite and Athene await the judgement of Paris and the award of the golden apple for the fairest (p. 309).

5. Embrace of Cupid (Amor) and Psyche (p. 547).

6. Oedipus, on the verge of answering the riddle of the Sphinx (p. 275).

7. The Sabine Women courageously intervene to make peace between their warring husbands and fathers (p. 501).

8. The newly born Aphrodite (Venus) is wafted ashore by wind-gods, amid a cascade of roses, while one of the Graces waits to receive her (p. 28).

9. Greek warriors hide within the Wooden Horse, while the Trojans debate whether or not to take it inside their city gates (p. 372).

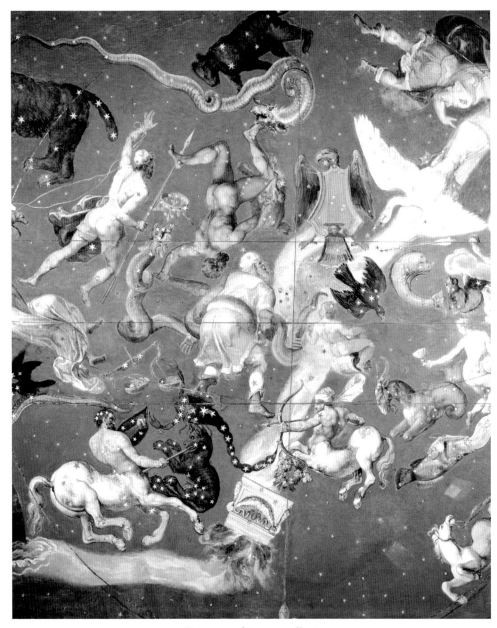

10. Heaven and its constellations.

Kadmos's search took him to Delphi, where he consulted the all-seeing Delphic Oracle for advice. He was told that he should no longer be concerned about his sister, but should instead follow a cow that had a white mark like the orb of the full moon on both flanks. He must go wherever she led him and found a city wherever she first lay down to rest. He travelled through Phokis searching for the prophesied cow and, when he finally found her, followed her through the whole of Boiotia before she at last sank to the ground in weariness. This, then, was to be the site of his city.

Kadmos wished now to sacrifice the cow to Athene, so he sent some of his companions to draw fresh water from a nearby spring, not realizing that it was sacred to the war-god Ares – and that a monstrous dragon, said to be the offspring of Ares himself, lurked there as its menacing guardian. According to Ovid (*Metamorphoses* 3.32–45):

It had a wonderful golden crest, its eyes flashed fire, its body was all puffed up with poison, and a three-forked tongue flickered from a triple row of teeth . . . It was as huge as the Serpent that lies between the two Bears in the sky.

Not surprisingly the dragon killed most of the men. This so enraged Kadmos that he fell on it in fury, and fought long and hard until the serpent lay dead. On the advice of Athene he sowed some of its teeth in the ground, though to his alarm a host of armed warriors at once sprang from the earth. He flung stones at them, so that each of them thought himself under attack from the others, and they all turned and fought among themselves. Only five of them survived. These were known as the *Spartoi*, the 'Sown Men', and they became the ancestors of the noble families of Thebes.

To atone for the slaughter of Ares' dragon, Kadmos had to serve the god for eight years. At the end of that time he built his city in the place where the cow had first lain down to rest and named it Kadmeia (it would later be called Thebes). Zeus honoured Kadmos by giving him a goddess for his bride: Harmonia, the daughter of Ares and Aphrodite. All the gods attended the wedding and brought gifts, celebrating this union of divinity and mortal, just as they would later come to the marriage of the sea-goddess Thetis to the mortal Peleus. Kadmos presented Harmonia with a beautiful robe and a necklace made by Hephaistos, both of which became prized family heirlooms that would play a crucial part in the later history of Thebes. We learn from Pausanias (9.12.3) that in his day (the second century AD) the Thebans would point out not only where Kadmos's house once stood on the acropolis of Thebes, but also the ruins of Harmonia's bridal-chamber and the very spot where the Muses sang during the wedding-feast.

The union proved to be a long and happy one, which was a very real blessing, since alliances between mortal and divinity were usually fraught with pain – for the mortal. Nevertheless, the couple had much grief to suffer because of the tragedies that beset their family. They had five children: four daughters, Semele, Ino, Autonoe and Agaue, and a son, Polydoros. Semele was loved by Zeus, who fathered on her the god Dionysos. But she was tricked by the jealous Hera into asking her lover to appear to her in all his divine glory – which he did, and she was burnt to death in the flame of the lightning flash (p. 103). Even as she died, Zeus snatched the unborn child from her womb and stitched him into a gash cut in his own thigh. There the baby grew until he could be born full term.

Zeus then entrusted the infant Dionysos to Semele's sister Ino and her husband Athamas, king of Orchomenos. They already had two sons of their own, Learchos and Melikertes, and now they willingly took in the motherless baby. They dressed him as a girl to hide him from Hera, but eventually she learnt the truth and punished them by driving them mad. Athamas, thinking that Learchos was a deer, hunted him down and shot him dead. Ino flung Melikertes into a cauldron of boiling water, then leapt into the sea, carrying her dead child in her arms, and drowned. Some good came out of tragedy, for Ino and Melikertes were transformed into the sea-deities Leukothea ('White Goddess') and Palaimon; they lived with the Nereids and came to the aid of sailors in distress. Nevertheless they were still lost to Kadmos and Harmonia.

Artemis watches Aktaion torn to pieces by his own hounds.

Their third daughter, Autonoe, was married to Aristaios, the son of Apollo and the nymph Kyrene. The couple had a son, Aktaion, whose tragic fate, as we have seen (p. 87), was to be turned into a deer by Artemis and then to be torn to pieces by his own hounds. Nor was Aktaion the only grandson of Kadmos and Harmonia to suffer a ghastly death. Their daughter Agaue married Echion, one of the Sown Men, and they too had a son, Pentheus. When Kadmos felt himself too old to rule, he handed over the kingship to Pentheus, now a young man, and it was at this point that Dionysos returned to Thebes, the place of his first 'birth'. He learnt that Agaue and her sisters, far from recognizing his godhead, refused to believe that he was a son of Zeus. They were saying that Semele had been seduced by some mortal man, then lied that her lover was Zeus to cover the shame of her pregnancy. So Dionysos punished them by making them mad, along with all the other women of Thebes: they left their homes and families and lived wild on Mount Kithairon, driven to worship the god as maenads.

When Pentheus too refused to recognize this new god, despite the urgings of old Kadmos and the blind seer Teiresias, Dionysos inflicted him with madness and lured him up the mountain dressed as a Bacchant (p. 473). Here the women tore him to pieces under the delusion that he was a mountain lion, with his mother Agaue the first to lay violent hands on him. She carried his head home in triumph, still believing it to be that of a lion, and it was the sad task of Kadmos to gather up the torn fragments of his grandson's body and to bring his daughter gently back to sanity and grief.

After Pentheus' tragic death, Kadmos and Harmonia left Thebes forever and went to live in Illyria in north-western Greece, and here, it was sometimes said, a last son, Illyrios, was born to them. Here too Kadmos led his people to victory in various wars of tribe against tribe until he finally ruled over the whole of Illyria. Harmonia, in spite of her original divine status, shared a common fate with Kadmos, for at the end of their lives they were both transformed into snakes. This may sound odd, but it could be seen as both an honour and a symbol of their heroic status, since the souls of heroes were thought to live on in the bodies of benevolent snakes. They were sent by Zeus to live a blessed life forever in the Elysian Fields, and after his death Kadmos was honoured throughout Greece as the man who brought civilization to the Greek people by giving them the alphabet, invented by the Phoenicians, and thus the art of writing.

Later rulers: Labdakos, Amphion and Zethos, and Laios

After Kadmos left Thebes, his son Polydoros ruled the city, but he died while his own son Labdakos was still an infant. Now two sons of one of the 'Sown Men', Chthonios, come to the fore: Nykteus and Lykos. Polydoros had married Nykteus' daughter Nykteis, so when Labdakos was left fatherless, it was natural that his grandfather Nykteus should take over the rule of Thebes as regent.

Nykteus had another daughter, Antiope, whose story was dramatized in Euripides' famous tragedy *Antiope*, now existing only in fragments. The girl grew up to be so beautiful that even Zeus desired her, so he came to her in the guise of a satyr and raped her, leaving her pregnant with twins. She fled from her father's anger to Sikyon where the king, Epopeus, took her in and married her. Nykteus killed himself from shame and grief, but before he died he charged his brother Lykos with the task of punishing both Antiope and Epopeus.

Lykos now became regent of Thebes in his brother's place and he set about fulfilling Nykteus' dying wish. He led an army against Sikyon and subdued it, then killed Epopeus and carried Antiope off captive. On the journey back to Thebes she gave birth to twin sons in a herdsman's dwelling on Mount Kithairon. Lykos left them behind to die, but the herdsman brought them up, calling them Amphion and Zethos.

On his return to Thebes, Lykos gave Antiope as a slave to his wife Dirke, who kept her imprisoned and treated her cruelly for many long years. At some stage during this time Labdakos came of age and took over the rule of Thebes, but he too died young, leaving a one-year-old son, Laios, so once again Lykos became regent.

One day Antiope's bonds were miraculously loosened

and she escaped from her imprisonment. She went to the herds-man's dwelling and found her sons, begging them to take her in, but they did not recognize her and turned her away. Alone and unprotected, she was recaptured by Dirke, who was worshipping Dionysos on Mount Kithairon. Dirke, in her mae-nadic frenzy, was about to tie Antiope to a wild bull by her long hair when Amphion and Zethos arrived in the nick of time, having been told by the herdsman that this was indeed their mother. They tied Dirke to the bull in her place and she was torn and trampled to death by the maddened beast. Her body was flung into the stream that was then named Dirke after her.

The brothers drove Lykos from Thebes (though some say they killed him), and they also banished Laios, the legitimate heir to the throne in the Kadmeian line. He found a home with Pelops, the king of Pisa in Elis, and Amphion and Zethos jointly took over the rule of Thebes.

Although they were twins, their natures were very different. Zethos was a down-to-earth man, skilled in the practical pur-suits of agriculture, cattle-breeding and war. Amphion was a brilliant musician and could play so enchantingly on his lyre, given him by Hermes, that animals and birds and even stones followed him. The two of them set about fortifying their city, with each brother using his own particular skill to build massive walls around Thebes. Zethos's strength and practical ability paid dividends, but Amphion's musicianship even more so, for when he played his lyre, the stones of their own accord fitted themselves into place. The brothers gave the walls of their city seven gates, one for each of Amphion's lyre-strings, and they changed its name from Kadmeia, named after Kadmos, to Thebes, after Zethos's wife Thebe.

Amphion married Niobe, daughter of the Lydian king, Tantalos, and their marriage was blessed with many children.

The number varies from author to author, usually with the total figure made up of an equal number of males and females. Homer, for instance, said that they had twelve children, six sons and six daughters; seven and seven said Aeschylus, Sophocles, Euripides, Apollodorus and Ovid; nine and nine said Sappho; ten and ten said Bacchylides and Pindar; while Hesiod said both ten and ten, and elsewhere nine and ten. Yet although the numbers varied, the aftermath was always the same: Niobe boasted that she was superior to the goddess Leto, who had only two children, whereupon the offended mother sent her son and daughter to earth to avenge the insult. Apollo shot all Niobe's sons while they were out hunting on Mount Kithairon, and Artemis shot all her daughters inside the house. Niobe, in her grief, went back to her father's land, and there she was turned into a rock on Mount Sipylos, an image of everlasting sorrow with water flowing down her face like tears. She remains to this day a symbol of loss and grief.

Amphion too died: either he was killed along with his sons, or he committed suicide from grief, or he tried to take vengeance on Apollo and was shot by the god while attacking his temple. Zethos by now was also dead. In one version of the myth he had been married, not to Thebe, but to Aedon, the daughter of Pandareos, who had borne him one son, Itylos. Aedon so much envied the many children born to her sister-in-law Niobe that she tried during the night to kill Niobe's eldest son in his sleep, but in the darkness she mistook his bed and killed Itylos. Distraught at what she had done, she begged the gods to turn her into a bird and they answered her prayer. She became a nightingale, and now night and day she could sing out her never-ending sorrow for her dead son. Zethos died of grief.

With both brothers dead, Laios, the son of Labdakos and the legitimate heir to the throne, could return from Pisa to become the king of Thebes. Unfortunately he incurred a fateful curse on his house. While in Pisa he had been teaching the young son of Pelops, Chrysippos, to drive a chariot and had fallen in love with the boy. He carried him off to Thebes to make him his catamite, and Chrysippos was so ashamed that he killed himself by falling on his sword. Pelops, who loved his son dearly, laid a curse on Laios that led to his death, for Zeus heard the curse and ordained that as punishment Laios would be killed by his own son.

Laios married Jocasta, daughter of the Theban Menoikeus. For a long time they remained childless, so Laios took the natural step of consulting the Delphic Oracle. Instead of getting the helpful advice he hoped for, he was given the horrifying prediction that if he had a son, that son would kill him. For a time he kept away from his wife's bed, but one night, inflamed with wine, he forgot the oracle's warning and made love with Jocasta. In due course she bore him a son. Before the baby was three days old, Laios pinned his ankles together and gave him to a herdsman, with instructions that he be cast out to die on Mount Kithairon.

Laios now felt secure; but although he never knew it, his son was still alive, for the herdsman took pity on the helpless infant and gave him to a second herdsman, also pasturing his flocks on the mountain. This man took the baby back to his home city of Corinth. Here the childless king and queen, Polybos and Merope, adopted the infant, calling him Oedipus ('Swollen Foot') because of the wounds in his ankles. They brought him up to believe that he was their true son.

THE TRAGEDY OF OEDIPUS

The story of Oedipus is one of the best known of all legends. From fifth-century Greek tragedy we know him as the man who unwittingly killed his father, then married his mother and had four children by her. When the incest was discovered, she committed suicide and he blinded himself, then wandered through the world as a polluted exile until his death.

Originally, however, Oedipus's story was rather different. In ancient epic he killed his father and married his mother – these are the immutable basics of his story – and his mother, when the truth was discovered soon after their marriage, committed suicide. But as far as we can tell from scattered epic references to the myth, Oedipus ruled on at Thebes, married again and had his four children by a second wife, Euryganeia. He died in battle while still active and in power, and was given splendid funeral games as the mark of respect due to a great hero. So originally there were no children born of incest, no self-inflicted blindness, no exile. This is all very different from the legend in Sophocles' seminal tragedy *Oedipus the King* (*Oedipus Tyrannos*, often known by its Latin title of *Oedipus Rex*), which gives the canonical version of Oedipus's story.

There were of course many other accounts by other authors. These include a tetralogy on the legend by Aeschylus, produced in 467 BC, consisting of three tragedies, *Laios*, *Oedipus* and *The Seven Against Thebes*, and a satyr play *Sphinx*. Only the third tragedy is extant, dramatizing the effects of Oedipus's curse on his sons, which results in the tragic and ultimately fatal conflict of the two brothers over the rule of Thebes. Fragments of the other plays remain and we know, for instance, that the oracle told Laios that for his city's sake he must never have children, but one night, overcome by lust, he fathered his doom-laden son. In Euripides' *Oedipus*, now lost, Oedipus was blinded, not by his own hand, but by the servants of Laios. And in his *Phoenician Women*, Jocasta did not kill herself when she learnt about her incestuous marriage, but is alive in the play to try and make peace between Eteokles and Polyneikes, who are fighting over the rule of Thebes. Here she dies only after her sons have killed each other, when in her grief she commits suicide over their corpses.

Yet interesting as these variants are, it was Sophocles' version that became the definitive account of Oedipus's story. His *Oedipus the King* is without doubt one of the most celebrated plays of all time, cited by Aristotle in his *Poetics* as a model of dramatic craftsmanship. It overshadows all other treatments of the myth, both before and after. (It also famously gave Freud the name 'Oedipus Complex' for a boy's attraction to his mother and repressed hostility towards his father, who is seen by the child as a rival for his mother's love, all of which causes psychological problems later in life.)

Although the play opens when Oedipus has already been ruling Thebes for many years, the vital background to the dramatic action is made clear as the tragedy progresses. Oedipus grew up in Corinth, fully believing that Polybos and Merope were his real parents, but one day, when he was a young man, a drunkard taunted him with not being their true child. They reassured him, but doubts still gnawed at his mind, so he consulted the Delphic Oracle in the hope of learning the truth. And just as Laios's innocent query unleashed a terrifying prediction, so was Oedipus's question left unanswered and he was told instead that he was destined to kill his father and have sex with his mother.

Oedipus at once resolved never for the rest of his life to return to Corinth, and he set off in a quite different direction, travelling towards Thebes. Near Daulis, at a narrow place where three roads meet, a man in a chariot tried to force him off the road, hitting out at him with a goad. Oedipus struck back in anger and killed the man, then killed most of his attendants too – all but one servant who managed to escape with his life. The man in the chariot was Oedipus's real father, Laios, who had been on his way once again to consult the Delphic Oracle. Neither father nor son had recognized the other.

Oedipus went on to Thebes, where he found the terrible Sphinx preying on the citizens. She was a monster with the head of a woman, the body of a lion and the wings of a bird, and she sat on Mount Phikion outside the city, challenging all the Thebans who passed by to answer her famous riddle, given her by the Muses. 'There is on the earth a two-footed, four-footed, three-footed creature with a single name; and alone of all beings that travel on land or in the air or sea, it changes its form. When it goes on most feet, then the speed of its limbs is slowest.' She snatched up and devoured anyone who failed to give her the correct answer.

She had been sent, it was said, by one of the gods – most commonly Hera because the Thebans had dishonoured her, as goddess of marriage, when they failed to punish Laios for his abduction of Chrysippos. An oracle declared that the Thebans would never be rid of the Sphinx until her riddle was solved, so many men tried to answer it, and failed, and died. At last in desperation Kreon, the brother of Laios's widow Jocasta, ordained that whoever could give the right answer to the riddle would be rewarded with the rule of the kingdom and the hand of Jocasta in marriage.

It was at this point that Oedipus arrived in Thebes, and he eagerly confronted the monster (Plate 6). Sophocles does not go into explicit detail about their encounter, so to imagine this we turn to Seneca, whose *Oedipus* is based on Sophocles' tragedy. Seneca puts into Oedipus's mouth a typically grisly and emotive description of the episode (91–102):

'I faced that abominable witch, though her jaws dripped blood and the ground beneath was white with scattered bones. As she sat on her high crag with outstretched wings, waiting to seize her prey and lashing her tail like a lion, savage in her wrath, I asked her riddle. A terrible sound rang out from above and she snapped her jaws, tearing at the rocks, impatient to claw out my living heart, then spoke her cryptic words and set the baited trap. But the grim riddle of the monstrous bird I solved.'

The answer was 'man', who crawls on all fours in infancy (when he is slowest), walks erect on two legs when grown, and uses a stick as a third leg in old age. The defeated Sphinx hurled herself down from the citadel to her death, and Oedipus was greeted as a hero and rewarded with the kingship of Thebes. He also married the widowed queen, his real mother – again with neither recognizing the other. They lived happily together for many years and had two sons, Eteokles and Polyneikes, and two daughters, Antigone and Ismene. Eventually a terrible plague descended on Thebes.

This is the point at which *Oedipus the King* opens. Oedipus is determined to cure his afflicted city, and he has already sent Kreon to consult the Delphic Oracle. Kreon returns with the answer that the plague will end only when the man who murdered Laios has himself been killed or banished. Oedipus undertakes at once to discover the murderer. He puts a solemn curse on the unknown killer and questions Kreon to find out more about Laios's death. He also questions the blind seer Teiresias in a scene rich in irony. The prophet, although physically blind, knows that Oedipus himself is the polluter of Thebes, the very man for whom he is seeking, while Oedipus, although his eyes can see, is mentally blind to the truth. He is also too angry to listen to what Teiresias tells him, convinced that the seer and Kreon are in league together and plotting to depose him.

Jocasta tries to make peace and calm Oedipus's anger, and in doing so she mentions that Laios was killed at a place near Daulis where three roads meet. Oedipus remembers his chance encounter with the unknown traveller and is shocked to realize that he himself may well have been the murderer of the king.

To find out the truth, he sends for the one servant of Laios who survived the massacre and has since lived far out in the Theban countryside.

Jocasta prays to Apollo that Oedipus may find peace from his fears, and as if in answer to her prayer a messenger arrives from Corinth, announcing that Polybos is dead from old age. At first this is heartening news, for it seems to mean that, despite the oracle, Oedipus could not after all have killed his father. 'O prophecies of the gods,' cries Jocasta (946–7), 'Where are you now?'

Yet the messenger also happens to be the very man who long ago carried the baby Oedipus to Corinth. So when Oedipus expresses his fear that he could still be in danger of having sex with his mother, the old man reassures him that Polybos and Merope were not his real parents, but had merely adopted him. He himself, he says, was given the baby, with its pitiful, pierced ankles, by another herdsman on Mount Kithairon – one of Laios's men.

Now the hunt for Laios's killer is forgotten as Oedipus seeks to find out his real parentage. Jocasta has realized the truth and she desperately implores Oedipus not to pursue the matter any further. He dismisses her pleas, believing her merely afraid that he will prove to be lowborn. She goes indoors, where in the depths of her shame she will hang herself.

Another old man arrives, the single eyewitness of Laios's murder. He proves to be none other than the herdsman who carried the baby Oedipus from the Theban palace to his supposed death, and out of pity saved him. Oedipus wrings the full truth from him, at the last minute guessing that what he is about to hear will be the worst possible knowledge. 'I am on the brink of terrible words,' cries the herdsman. 'And I of terrible hearing,' replies Oedipus. 'Yet I must hear' (1169–70). This is what makes him one of the great heroes: not the physical might to battle monsters, like Herakles, but his qualities of mind and will – the intelligence to answer the Sphinx's riddle in the first place, and now the unswerving resolve to discover the truth, and the courage to face it, whatever it may be.

So at last he learns that he himself is the unknown killer for whom he has been searching and, worse even than this, that Apollo's appalling oracle has come true. Distraught, he goes indoors, and here he finds Jocasta dead by her own hand. He does not kill himself, for this would instantly bring him into the company of his dead parents in the Underworld – and he cannot yet bear to face the mother who shared his bed and the father he killed. So he tears out the long golden pins from Jocasta's robe and in his anguish gouges out his eyes, the eyes which could see, but had nevertheless been blind to the truth. At the end of the play, a blinded but unbroken man, he is ready to go into exile, leaving Thebes forever, in obedience to the commands of Apollo. Kreon takes over the rule in his place.

The sequel to these events is recorded in Sophocles' tragedy *Oedipus at Kolonos*, written at about the age of 90 just before his death in 406–405 BC. Here Oedipus at last reaches the end of his long sufferings, when in a moving and mysterious death he is taken from earth by the gods. He has wandered as a blind and miserable outcast for many years, guided by his faithful daughter Antigone. Now, weary of life, he comes to Kolonos in Attica (the birthplace of Sophocles himself) and reaches the sacred precinct of the Eumenides, which he knows from an oracle of Apollo is the place where he will die. King Theseus gives him sanctuary, supporting him against Kreon and his own son Polyneikes, both of whom try in vain to make him return to Thebes to help in the dispute over the Theban throne (see below). In return, Oedipus prophesies that the place of his death will forever bring blessings from the gods on Attica.

At the end of the play, Oedipus's coming death is announced

by peals of thunder. No longer needing guidance, the old blind man walks confidently into the depths of the sacred grove, and there the voice of a god rings out: 'Oedipus, Oedipus, why do we linger. Long indeed have you been made to wait' (1627–8). At a spot known only to Theseus, Oedipus mysteriously disappears from human sight. He has at last found the death he longed for.

THE SEVEN AGAINST THEBES

The expedition of the Seven against Thebes was one of the great mythological campaigns of the ancient world, by no means as large as the expedition of the Greeks against Troy, immortalized by Homer in the *Iliad*, but still one in which many great heroes and their followers took part. Sadly, the epic *Thebais* which told the story at length is lost, apart from a few tiny fragments, so the myth must be pieced together from other sources. Here Apollodorus (3.6), as so often, is helpful. And since this dramatic story was a favourite with the Greek tragedians, we are also fortunate to have several of the relevant plays extant.

It all began when the two sons of Oedipus, Eteokles ('True Glory') and Polyneikes ('Much Strife'), quarrelled over the rule of Thebes. Kreon had been regent until they came of age, but then both brothers wished to be king, and there are various accounts of how they settled the matter. Either they agreed that they would each have alternately a year in power, then a year in exile, and Eteokles took the first year as king, but refused to give up the throne when the year was over. Or Eteokles simply took the throne and drove Polyneikes out. Or the brothers made a bargain that one of them would rule while the other left Thebes for ever, taking a large share of the property. When they came to draw lots, it was Eteokles who won the kingship and Polyneikes who left Thebes with many possessions. (These included the beautiful necklace and robe of Kadmos's wife

Harmonia, each of which would play a fateful part in the subsequent story.) Unfortunately Polyneikes later changed his mind and decided that he still wanted to be king. Whatever the details, the end result was the same: Polyneikes, finding himself exiled from his homeland, resolved to win the throne of Thebes by force.

He had taken refuge with Adrastos, the king of Argos, arriving at the very same time as another exile, Oineus's son Tydeus, who had been banished from Kalydon for murder. One fateful night, Adrastos was awakened by the two young men fighting for possession of a bed in the palace porch, and at once he was reminded of an oracle that said he must yoke his daughters in marriage to a lion and a boar. Either the two men were fighting like these same wild beasts; or they had on their shields the emblems of a lion (Polyneikes) and a boar (Tydeus); or they were clad in the skins of those animals; or the creatures were symbols of their homelands, the lion standing for the lion-bodied Sphinx of Thebes and the boar for the Kalydonian Boar. Whatever the reason, Adrastos remembered the oracle and married his daughters to the young men, Argeia to Polyneikes and Deipyle to Tydeus.

The couples settled at Argos, but Adrastos promised his new sons-in-law that he would restore them to their lost kingdoms. First of all he would help Polyneikes to recover Thebes. He mustered a large army of seven champions and their followers, the 'Seven against Thebes' – though there is no fixed canonical list of the Seven. Apollodorus (3.6.3) lists the nine champions who appeared in the varying sources, most of them being related by blood or marriage to Adrastos himself. These were his sons-in-law Polyneikes and Tydeus; his brother Mekisteus; his brother-in-law, the seer Amphiaraos; his brother (or nephew) Hippomedon; his nephew Kapaneus; Kapaneus's brother-in-law Eteoklos; Parthenopaios, who was in early epic Adrastos's brother, and later an Arcadian chieftain, son of the huntress Atalanta – and of course Adrastos himself.

All willingly joined the expedition except for Amphiaraos. He was the greatest seer of his day and could foretell that the expedition was doomed to failure and its leaders, all but Adrastos, to death. Not unnaturally he refused to join and he tried to discourage all the others from doing so. Old Iphis, the father of Eteoklos, now advised Polyneikes that all would be solved if he could bribe Eriphyle, Amphiaraos's wife and Adrastos's sister, into supporting the campaign. Once, in a long ago quarrel, Amphiaraos had agreed that any dispute he had with Adrastos should be settled by Eriphyle; so now Polyneikes offered her, in return for her help, the enchanting necklace given by the gods to his ancestress Harmonia. Eriphyle greedily took the necklace and forced her husband to join the expedition. Before he left home for the last time, he charged his two sons, Alkmaion and Amphilochos, to avenge his certain death.

The army set out for Thebes. They stopped at Nemea for water, and here they encountered a slave woman, Hypsipyle, who had once been queen of the island of Lemnos when Jason and the Argonauts sailed in (p. 141). The other Lemnian women had killed all their menfolk, while Hypsipyle alone had spared her father, the king, and had secretly sent him to safety. Later, on discovering this treachery to their cause, the angry women had sold her into slavery and she had been bought by Lykourgos, the king of Nemea. Now she was nurse to the king's baby son, Opheltes, and when Adrastos and his party asked her for water, she left the baby lying on a bed of parsley while she showed them the way to a spring.

They returned to find the child dead, bitten by a snake that had coiled itself around his little body. The seer Amphiaraos interpreted this as an omen pointing to the failure of the expedition, so they killed the snake and buried the child under

Polyneikes bribes Eriphyle with the necklace of Harmonia.

the name of *Archemoros*, 'Beginner of Doom'. In his honour they founded the Nemean Games, at which thereafter the judges wore dark-coloured clothing in mourning for Opheltes and the victors were rewarded each with a crown of parsley. Here at these first contests, says Apollodorus, Adrastos won the horse race, Eteoklos the foot race, Tydeus the boxing match, Amphiaraos the jumping and the discus throwing, Laodokos (otherwise unknown) the javelin throwing, Polyneikes the wrestling match, and Parthenopaios the archery contest.

Despite this portent of disaster, the army continued on its way. (As for Hypsipyle's fate, according to Euripides' partially preserved play *Hypsipyle*, her two sons Euneos and Thoas rescued her from slavery and took her safely back to Lemnos.) When the army drew near Thebes, they sent Tydeus ahead into the city to demand that Eteokles surrender the throne to Polyneikes. Tydeus delivered the message, then gave the Thebans a foretaste of his prowess by challenging all comers to single combat. He defeated every opponent. Despite this demonstration, Eteokles refused to pay any heed to Tydeus's demands and even sent out fifty armed men to ambush him as he left the city. He killed them all apart from Maion, the son of Haimon and grandson of Kreon.

The Argive army now moved in against Thebes. Adrastos assigned one of his champions to attack each of the city's seven gates, and Eteokles stationed his best men to defend them. This prelude to battle is powerfully dramatized in Aeschylus's *Seven Against Thebes*, where the tension steadily mounts as Eteokles hears who of the enemy is attacking each of the seven gates and assigns, one by one, his best fighters to defend them. Finally he hears that at the seventh gate, the gate that he himself must defend, Polyneikes waits. So the brothers will meet in mortal combat, and one or both must die.

In Euripides' tragedy *The Phoenician Women*, which also dramatizes the Argive attack on Thebes, Eteokles asks the blind prophet Teiresias for advice on how best to overcome the enemy. The seer predicts that Thebes can be saved only by a sacrifice to the war-god Ares of a virgin male descended from the 'Sown Men'. The only young man who answers this description is Menoikeus, the unmarried son of Kreon. Menoikeus is willing to die to bring victory to his city, but Kreon cannot bear to lose his son, even for Thebes, so he tries to persuade him to go away to safety. Menoikeus agrees to do so, then secretly climbs to the top of the city, and here, thrusting his sword into his throat, he plunges down from the battlements. After this noble act the Thebans go confidently into battle.

They were right to be confident. Although accounts of the battle positions vary and the order of events during the fighting is confused, the outcome was never in question: the attackers were decisively routed. Some died in single combat. Partheno-paios was crushed by a huge stone hurled down from the battle-ments by Periklymenos. Kapaneus scaled the walls on a long ladder, boasting that not even the lightning of Zeus could stop him taking the city, but as he crested the wall a thunderbolt blasted him to his death.

Tydeus, who was a favourite of the goddess Athene, killed his opponent Melanippos, but at the same time was himself mortally wounded. Athene came to him as he lay dying, mean-ing to make him immortal, but Amphiaraos, with his seer's powers, knew what she intended and aimed to stop her. He still bore a grudge against Tydeus for helping to initiate the calamitous expedition, so he now cut off Melanippos's head and gave it to the dying man. Tydeus savagely split the head open and began to gulp down his enemy's brains, a sight so barbaric that the disgusted goddess kept back her gift of immor-tality and allowed her former favourite to die a mortal's death.

Amphiaraos himself met a unique end as he was fleeing in his chariot: Periklymenos was about to hurl a spear into the seer's back when Zeus, taking pity on him, split open the earth ahead of him with a thunderbolt, and Amphiaraos was swallowed up, chariot, charioteer, horses and all, and in this fashion descended to the Underworld.

Finally the entire purpose of the expedition was brought to nothing when Polyneikes and Eteokles met in single combat, and each fell dead on the other's sword. In Euripides' *Phoeni-cian Women*, their mother Jocasta (who here did not commit suicide when she discovered her incest, as in the usual myth) tries to make peace between her sons before it comes to this. She fails, and they fight and kill each other, and it is only now that she kills herself – not from shame, as in other versions, but from grief (1455–9):

And when their mother saw them dead, it was more than she could bear. She snatched up a sword that lay beside the corpses and did a fearful thing: right through her throat she thrust the iron blade, and now she lies between her beloved sons, with a lifeless arm embracing each.

As Amphiaraos had foretold, Adrastos alone of all the champions survived. His mount on the expedition was the divine horse Areion, the offspring of Poseidon *Hippios* (Horse Poseidon) and Demeter, born after the goddess caught the eye of Poseidon when she was wandering the earth, seeking her lost daughter Persephone. Demeter changed herself into a mare to escape the god's amorous intentions and hid among a herd of horses, but the god became a stallion and mounted her. Their offspring Areion was fabulously swift, and now he saved his master's life by carrying him from the battlefield to safety.

With Eteokles dead, the rule of Thebes fell once again to Kreon, who now, contrary to custom, refused to let Adrastos and the surviving Argives bury their dead. The aftermath of this command is dramatized in Euripides' *Suppliant Women*, where Adrastos and the widows and children of the dead champions come to Athens to beg Theseus to intervene on their behalf. Theseus leads an Athenian army against the Thebans and forces them to give up the corpses of the enemy dead.

The bodies are brought back to Eleusis for burning and burial, and here, in a daring *coup de théâtre*, Euripides has Euadne, the wife of Kapaneus, fling herself into the flames of her husband's funeral pyre. 'To die a death with the one you love is the sweetest death of all,' she cries from high above the pyre, 'and this may the gods grant me!' Her old father Iphis cannot reach her to save her, so he does his best to dissuade her from dying, but fails. 'I let my body go,' she says to him, 'my end is a grief to you, but to me, and to my husband with me in the fire, a joy.' And with this, she falls into the flames.

Another Greek tragedy, one of the most famous of them all, also dramatizes the aftermath of the Argive attack on Thebes, when Kreon decrees that, of Oedipus's two dead sons, Eteokles will be given honourable burial, while the traitor Polyneikes will be left unburied as a prey for the birds: Sophocles' *Antigone*.

THE TRAGEDY OF ANTIGONE

Antigone plays a minor part in several of the fifth-century Greek tragedies. She makes her first appearance in Aeschylus's *Seven Against Thebes* (467 BC), where she and her sister Ismene lament the deaths of their two brothers at each other's hands. In Sophocles' *Oedipus the King* (date uncertain), the two girls, here very young, have non-speaking parts in which they come on stage at the end of the play to be with their broken, blinded father. At the end of Euripides' *Phoenician Women* (409 BC), Antigone leads Oedipus into exile. And in Sophocles' *Oedipus at Kolonos*, as we have seen, Antigone has looked after her father for many years while he wandered in exile, a blind outcast, and now they reach Athens and the place of Oedipus's final, mystical release from his sufferings when he is taken to the gods. But it is in Sophocles' seminal *Antigone* (possibly 442 BC) that she achieves her definitive character, enduring and inspirational, as the voice of individual conscience and family loyalty in defiance of law and state.

When the play opens, the battle that has raged around Thebes is over and the Argive army has departed. Polyneikes and Eteokles lie dead, and Kreon, who is now ruling, has decreed that Eteokles, the defender of the city, will be given honourable burial, while the corpse of the attacker Polyneikes, a traitor to his country, will be left lying in the plain as a prey for the birds. The penalty for disobedience to this decree will be death.

Yet to Antigone both men are her brothers, regardless of their political actions, and both of them equally deserve burial. She has resolved to bury Polyneikes herself, and she tries to persuade Ismene to help her. Ismene serves as a foil to the fearless and determined Antigone: she is the cautious and timid sister, who sympathizes with Antigone's resolution to bury Polyneikes in defiance of Kreon's edict, but feels herself too weak to take any part in the deed. 'We must remember that we are women,' she says, 'and we are not meant to fight against men. Remember too that we are ruled by those who are stronger, and so must obey this decree, and other things even more painful . . . I shall obey those in authority, for there is no sense in actions that exceed our powers' (61–8).

'Do what you please,' responds Antigone (71–7), 'but I shall bury him. And if I die in doing it, that will be fine. I shall lie, convicted of a righteous crime, a loved sister beside a loved brother . . . But if you so choose, you must dishonour what the gods hold dear.'

So quite alone Antigone scatters on her brother's body the sprinkling of earth that will suffice for token burial. She is captured in the act and brought to Kreon, and despite the threat of death hanging over her, she proclaims the eternal validity of her principles in defiance of Kreon's edict (450–69):

'Your edict did not come from Zeus, and Justice who dwells with the gods below made no such law for mankind. I did not think your orders strong enough to outrun the gods' unwritten and unfailing laws, you being only a man. Those laws are not of today, nor yesterday, but everlasting . . . I knew that I should have to die, of course, even without your edicts. And if I am to die before my time, so much the better ... For me to meet my fate will be no pain. But if I had let my mother's son lie there unburied, then I'd have cause to grieve as now I grieve not.'

Even though it has turned out to be his own niece who defied his edict, Kreon is still determined to carry out his threat of death, so he sends Antigone away to be walled up alive in a tomb. Ismene, although she has played no part in burying Polyneikes, is willing to die along with her sister, but Antigone will have none of it. 'Don't try to share my death,' she says, 'and don't lay claim to something you had no hand in' (546–7). She is taken away alone to her living burial.

Yet however misguided Kreon may be in stubbornly enforcing his edict, he is doing his best to govern his city lawfully. He is acting from good intentions and, he fully believes, in the interests of Thebes – which to him is the most important consideration. 'The man who considers a friend more important than his own country,' he says, 'I count him as nothing' (182–3). Yet he is wrong to bury the living, just as he is wrong to leave unburied the dead. His son Haimon, who is betrothed to Antigone, tells him how mistaken he is, and that the whole city censures his action, but he refuses to listen, and rages at his son for seeming to take sides against him. The blind seer Teiresias tells him that the gods disapprove and are rejecting all Theban sacrifices, but still Kreon obstinately stands firm. It is only when the Chorus of Theban elders remind him that never yet has Teiresias prophesied falsely that he gives way.

He is too late. He goes to release Antigone, stopping to bury Polyneikes on the way, and by the time he gets to the tomb Antigone has hung herself. Haimon is with her. He has just discovered her body, and now has only hatred and fury for his father. A messenger describes the scene (1231–41):

'With wild eyes, the boy glared at his father, wordlessly spat in his face, then drew his two-edged sword. His father jumped back to evade him and he missed his aim. Then the wretched boy, enraged with himself, pressed his body against the sword and drove half its length into his side. Still living, he clasped the girl in a feeble embrace and coughed out a sharp jet of blood that sprinkled her white cheek. He lies, a corpse enfolding a corpse, achieving his marriage rites, poor boy, in the house of Hades.'

Nor is this the whole tragedy for Kreon: his wife Eurydike has heard the messenger's report of Haimon's death, and she now takes her own life too, cursing her husband with her dying breath. So Kreon is left alive at the end of the play, desolate, to mourn too late the chain of disaster and bereavement brought about by his own blindness and obstinacy.

Teiresias, the blind Theban prophet

Teiresias is a recurring figure in the Theban saga – not surprisingly, for he was reputed to live for seven generations – so a few words on the city's famous blind seer would be appropriate before that saga comes to its close. He was a descendant of Udaios, one of the original 'Sown Men', and son of the nymph Chariklo. Various stories are told to account for his blindness. Some said that the gods blinded him because he revealed their secrets to men. Others said that he came one day, hot and weary from the hunt, to drink from a spring on Mount Helikon, and there he inadvertently saw Athene bathing naked with his mother, who was a favourite companion of the goddess. At once Athene cried out in anger and struck him blind; then in response to Chariklo's anguished entreaties, she gave him in reparation the gift of prophecy, the power to understand the speech of birds, and a staff with which he could guide himself as well as if he still had sight. She also promised him a long life, and after his death the retention of his mental powers undimmed among the dead. (Accordingly, Homer makes Odysseus consult the great seer in the Underworld, travelling down to the land of the dead to seek advice on his dangerous journey home: p. 402.)

In yet another version (although its details vary) Teiresias saw two snakes copulating, either on Mount Kithairon near Thebes or on Mount Kyllene in Arcadia. He struck out at them, and was turned from a man into a woman. Later he saw the same snakes copulating again, and again he struck out, and this time was turned back into a man. These experiences obviously gave him a unique insight into the natures of both male and female, so when Zeus and Hera were arguing as to whether men or women found more enjoyment in the sex act, they turned to Teiresias for the answer. His reply was that a woman's delight was nine or ten times greater than a man's, and this won Zeus the argument. The infuriated Hera promptly struck Teiresias with blindness, but Zeus awarded him in consolation the gifts of prophecy and a long life.

THE EXPEDITION OF THE EPIGONOI ('AFTER-BORN')

Ten years after the attack of the Seven against Thebes, a second expedition took place: encouraged by Adrastos, the sons of the first attackers, the Epigonoi, rallied to avenge their fathers. This time the attack on Thebes was a success.

The warriors who with Adrastos led this second army were Aigialeus, son of Adrastos, Thersandros, son of Polyneikes, Diomedes, son of Tydeus, Alkmaion and Amphilochos, sons of Amphiaraos, Sthenelos, son of Kapaneus, Promachos, son of Parthenopaios, Euryalos, son of Mekisteus, Polydoros, son of Hippomedon, and Medon, son of Eteoklos.

The young men consulted the Delphic Oracle, which promised them victory if they made Alkmaion their leader. At first he and

Amphilochos were unwilling to take part, just like their father in the earlier expedition, but once again their mother Eriphyle was bribed to intervene. She had sent her husband Amphiaraos to what she knew would be his death, all for the sake of the necklace of Harmonia, offered to her by Polyneikes. Now Thersandros, Polyneikes' son, offered her Harmonia's beautiful robe. She took it and persuaded her sons to join the campaign, even though she knew that they were risking their lives. (But this time she would get her just deserts, for her sons would return victorious and Alkmaion would avenge their father by killing their mother – so her glorious finery did her little good.)

Under the leadership of Alkmaion the army marched on Thebes. The Thebans came out to meet them, led by Laodamas, son of the dead Eteokles, and were routed by the Argives. It was usually said that the only one of the Epigonoi to die, killed by Laodamas, was Aigialeus, just as his father Adrastos had been the only one to survive the first expedition. (This time Adrastos too would die, out of grief for his dead son.) Laodamas himself was killed by Alkmaion. The Thebans fled to safety within the walls of their city, then on the advice of Teiresias they stole away under cover of night. The ancient seer accompanied them, but on his journey he stopped near Haliartos at the spring of Telphousa, and drank from it, and died.

Ten years on from their fathers' defeat and death, the Epigonoi entered Thebes in triumph. They razed the walls to the ground and pillaged the city, sending a part of their booty to Apollo at Delphi. This included a thank-offering of Teiresias's daughter Manto, since they had vowed that they would dedicate to the god the 'fairest of the spoils' if they were victorious.

Thersandros now took the throne that his father Polyneikes had been so eager to win, but Thebes would never again have the strength that once it had. Homer, describing the Greek forces that went to the Trojan War (*Iliad* 2.505), mentions only *Hypothebai*, 'lower Thebes', and not the once great citadel.

Yet this is not quite the end of the story. There is still the fate of Alkmaion to recount, as well as that of those ill-omened Theban heirlooms, the robe and necklace of Harmonia.

HARMONIA'S ROBE AND NECKLACE

After the fall of Thebes, Alkmaion and Amphilochos returned safely home to Argos, where Alkmaion, prompted by the Delphic Oracle, killed their treacherous mother Eriphyle. Amphiaraos was avenged. Unfortunately Alkmaion was now driven mad by his mother's Furies, those avengers of kin-murder, just as Orestes would be after the murder of his mother Klytaimnestra.

Alkmaion wandered from place to place, and eventually was taken in and purified by Phegeus, the king of Psophis in northern Arcadia, whose daughter Arsinoe he now married. As a wedding gift he gave her Harmonia's robe and necklace, recovered from Eriphyle on her death. All was not yet well, however, for the land of Psophis became barren from harbouring a matricide, so once again Alkmaion wandered onwards. Eventually he arrived at the mouth of the river Acheloos, where the river-god not only purified him but married him to his daughter Kallirhoe ('Fair-flowing). She bore Alkmaion two sons, Akarnan, after whom the land was named Akarnania, and Amphoteros.

All was now well – until Kallirhoe heard of the magnificent robe and necklace of Harmonia and wanted them for herself, threatening that she would leave Alkmaion if he did not give them to her. So away he went reluctantly back to Psophis. He obtained the heirlooms by lying to Phegeus, saying that he would be cured of his madness only if he dedicated the gifts at Delphi. When one of his servants revealed the truth, Phegeus ordered his sons to kill Alkmaion. They did so, then buried him in a grove of cypress trees. When the traveller Pausanias saw Alkmaion's tomb in its bleak upland valley, he said (8.24.7) that the cypresses surrounding it were so tall that even the nearby mountain was overshadowed by them, but the local people refused to cut them down since they were sacred to Alkmaion.

Even though Alkmaion was dead, the cycle of killings continued, for Kallirhoe, hearing of her husband's murder, prayed to Zeus to make her sons grow up quickly, that they might lose no time in avenging him. Zeus, who loved her, granted her prayer and at once the boys became men. They killed the sons of Phegeus, then Phegeus and his wife as well. Finally, at the command of Acheloos, they dedicated the death-bringing robe and necklace of Harmonia at Delphi, and now at long last the beautiful objects could cause no more harm among men.

THE TROJAN WAR

Troy, a rich and powerful city lying in the north-western corner of Asia Minor, a few miles from the southern entrance to the Hellespont, was the site of the greatest war in classical mythology, fought because Paris, prince of Troy, abducted Helen, wife of King Menelaos of Sparta, and carried her off to his home. A huge Greek army, led by King Agamemnon of Mycenae, sailed to Troy to reclaim her. They besieged Troy for ten long years, and at the end of that time they captured the city and put it to the torch.

In ancient times a cycle of eight long epic poems related the events of the Trojan War from start to finish. Of these eight, only the *Iliad* and the *Odyssey* of Homer are extant, the *Iliad* telling of the wrath of Achilles during the tenth year of the war, the *Odyssey* describing the return home to Ithaca of Odysseus, and his defeat of the Suitors who were harassing his wife Penelope. The other six epics – poems from the 'Epic Cycle' by poets other than Homer – narrated all other events relating to the war. The *Kypria* covered the early years prior to the action of the *Iliad*; the *Aithiopis*, the *Little Iliad* and the *Sack of Troy* covered the later events and the fall of Troy. The *Returns* told of the homecomings of the Greek heroes other than Odysseus, and the *Telegony* of what happened to Odysseus after his exploits in the *Odyssey*.

These other epics no longer exist, apart from fragments. Yet all is not lost when we come to piece together the events of the whole war, for Proclus's brief summaries of the poems are helpful, as are the narratives in Apollodorus, and we can fill in the details from a whole variety of other sources (including the

Iliad and the *Odyssey* themselves, each of which tells of events in both past and future).

One of the greatest stories of archaeology is how Heinrich Schliemann was determined to prove the truth of the *Iliad* and of the Trojan War, and in the second half of the nineteenth century excavated the great mound of Hisarlik in modern Turkey, rediscovering Troy. Of the nine levels which Schliemann defined, Troy VI and VII are the cities that date from the Mycenaean age. Fallen masonry and traces of fire show that Troy VI was violently destroyed around 1270 BC, and Troy VIIa around 1190 BC, though here traces of human bones too have been found in streets and houses.

Other excavators have succeeded Schliemann, and excavations at Troy are still continuing, though there have always been, and no doubt always will be, those who deny that Troy ever existed. Let us give the last word here to Byron, writing in *Don Juan* (C. IV. ci): 'I've stood upon Achilles' tomb, / And heard Troy doubted; time will doubt of Rome.'

THE KINGS OF TROY

Before focusing on the Trojan War itself, we must turn from the end of Troy to its beginnings, with a brief survey of the city's kings and early history.

The first in the not-so-very-long line of Trojan kings was Teukros, son of the river-god Skamandros, the chief river of the Trojan plain, and Idaia, a nymph of Mount Ida. Teukros married his daughter Bateia to Dardanos, who was a son of Zeus and Elektra, one of the seven Pleiades. Dardanos had come from the island of Samothrace, and he now founded a settlement in the foothills of Mount Ida, calling it Dardania after himself. He was succeeded by his son Erichthonios, who according to Homer was the wealthiest of mortals because of his herds of splendid horses. Indeed, Troy was always famous for its horses:

Homer calls it 'the land of fine horses' and refers to the Trojans in general, and the great Trojan hero Hektor in particular, with the epithet 'horse-taming'; but Erichthonios' horses were especially wonderful (*Iliad* 20.221–9):

> Three thousand mares had he, that fed on the grasslands,
> mares that joyed in their young foals. And as they grazed,
> Boreas, the North Wind, desired them, and made himself
> into a dark-maned stallion, and coupled with twelve mares,
> and they, conceiving, bore to him twelve young horses.
> These, when they frisked across the grain-giving land,
> would run along the topmost ears of corn, not breaking them,
> and again, when they sported over the wide sea's waves,
> would gallop above the crests of the salt grey breakers.

Erichthonios married Astyoche, the daughter of another river-god of the Trojan plain, Simoeis. Their son Tros would in due course give his name to Troy, the Troad and the Trojans.

Tros married Kallirhoe, another child of the river-god Skamandros, and had three sons by her. One of these, Ganymede(s), was so beautiful that he was taken up to Olympos by the gods, to be the cupbearer of Zeus. A sexual element creeps into the later myth, when Zeus's interest in Ganymede becomes erotic and the boy is snatched up by an eagle, either a servant of Zeus, or Zeus himself in disguise. In the early *Homeric Hymn to Aphrodite*, however, there seems to be no hint of this erotic element. Ganymede was carried up to Olympos by a whirlwind, and his father had no idea where he had been taken (207–17):

> ... and unceasing grief filled the heart of Tros,
> and he mourned his dear son always, time without end,
> until Zeus pitied him and gave as recompense
> high-stepping horses, the kind that carry the gods.
> These he gave as a gift, and at his command

Hermes, the messenger-god, told how the boy
would now be deathless and ageless like the gods.
And when Tros heard these tidings sent by Zeus
he mourned no longer, but was glad in his heart,
and joyfully rode his storm-swift horses.

They were 'the best of all horses beneath the dawn and the sun', says Homer (*Iliad* 5.265–7). According to the Epic Cycle's *Little Iliad*, another gift was that of a golden vine, wrought by Hephaistos, which would later play a part in the Trojan War (p. 371). Zeus immortalized Ganymede among the stars as the constellation Aquarius, the Water-carrier.

A second son of Tros was Assarakos, who stayed in Dardania and became the progenitor of the Romans, since his great-grandson Aeneas would sail to Italy after the fall of Troy and there found the Roman race (Chapter 14). The third son, Ilos, left Dardania and founded Troy itself. First he went to take part in games held by the king of Phrygia, where he won the wrestling contest. His prize was fifty youths and fifty young girls, but the king, in obedience to an oracle, also gave him a dappled cow and told him to found a city wherever the cow first lay down.

Ilos followed the cow until they came to a hill, sacred to the goddess Ate, which rose out of the broad plain between Mount Ida and the sea. Here the cow at last lay down to rest, so here Ilos founded his city. It would be called Ilios/Ilion after Ilos himself and Troy after his father. When Ilos prayed for a sign of approval from Zeus, a wooden statue of Pallas Athene miraculously fell at his feet out of the sky, so at this very spot he built Troy's great temple of Athene to house the image. The statue was known as the Palladion, and was believed to have the power of making impregnable the city that possessed it. Thus, as long as it stayed safe in Athene's temple, Troy would never fall.

After his death, Ilos was buried out on the Trojan plain and his tomb became a familiar landmark near Troy. He was succeeded by his son Laomedon who, like his grandfather Tros, married a daughter of the river-god Skamandros, Strymo. Like his grandfather too he lost a son to the gods because of the boy's beauty: Tithonos was desired by Eos, the amorous goddess of Dawn. She carried him off to her home in Ethiopia, in the farthest east and by the river of Ocean. Here she bore him two sons, Memnon and Emathion, who became kings, respectively, of Ethiopia and Arabia. And every morning 'Dawn arose from her bed, from the side of proud Tithonos, to carry light to the immortals and to men', as Homer puts it (*Iliad* 11.1–2, *Odyssey* 5.1–2).

Once again the *Homeric Hymn to Aphrodite* (218–38) recounts the sequel: because of her love for Tithonos, Eos asked Zeus to grant him eternal life, and Zeus did so. But the unhappy goddess had forgotten to ask for her lover eternal youth as well, so as the years passed by he grew older, and greyer, and more shrivelled. When the first grey hairs sprouted from his head and his chin, Eos abandoned his bed though she still tended him, giving him food and ambrosia and lovely garments.

> But when hateful old age completely weighed him down,
> and he could no longer move nor lift his limbs,
> this seemed to her in her heart the wisest plan:
> she laid him down in a room and closed on him
> the shining doors, and there, with all the strength
> that once he had in his supple limbs now gone,
> he babbles eternally.

A different and happier ending was later given to the story and recorded by ancient scholars: Eos changed Tithonos into a cicada, that most vocal of insects, so that she might have the pleasure of her lover's voice forever sounding in her ears. Yet perhaps the sadder ending is the one more likely to appeal to poets, and this is the one that Tennyson adopts for his early poem *Tithonus*, where he makes verbal music of Tithonos's long ageing:

> The woods decay, the woods decay and fall,
> The vapours weep their burthen to the ground,
> Man comes and tills the field and lies beneath,
> And after many a summer dies the swan.
> Me only cruel immortality
> Consumes: I wither slowly in thine arms,
> Here at the quiet limit of the world,
> A white-hair'd shadow roaming like a dream
> The ever-silent spaces of the East,
> Far-folded mists, and gleaming halls of morn . . .

We hear nothing in ancient literature of Laomedon's grief for his lost son, which is perhaps unsurprising in a man renowned most of all for his arrogance and treachery to gods and mortals alike. In his reign Troy was fortified, and he was lucky enough to have two gods build the great walls for him: Apollo and Poseidon, who came to earth disguised as men. Either they were obliged to serve a mortal for a whole year as a punishment for rebellion against Zeus, or they wished to test Laomedon's reputation for bad faith. Certainly he proved himself dishonourable, for once the walls were built, he refused to pay the agreed wage. In Homer we see the treacherous and violent king in action, when Poseidon describes the end of that long, hard year of labour (*Iliad* 21.450–7):

'But when the changing seasons brought round the glad time for payment, then outrageous Laomedon robbed us of all our wage and sent us away with menaces, threatening to bind us hand and foot and to sell us as slaves in far-off islands. He even said he would peel off our ears with a cleaver. So we went away with rage in our hearts, angry about our wage which he promised and would not pay.'

To punish Laomedon, Apollo sent a plague on the land, and Poseidon a flood and a fearsome sea-monster that preyed on the people. Oracles foretold that deliverance would come only if the king gave his daughter Hesione to be devoured by the monster. So he chained her to the rocks by the sea-shore, and there she waited for the beast to come for her. Fortunately at this moment Herakles came sailing by, on his way home from the land of the Amazons. He offered to kill the sea-monster, in return for the divine horses once given to Tros as recompense for the loss of Ganymede, and Laomedon agreed.

Herakles fulfilled his part of the bargain. According to Hellanicus, he leapt in full armour into the jaws of the beast and entered its belly, then destroyed it by hacking and hewing at it from within. But now, with the monster dead, Laomedon once again went back on his word. He refused to give up his immortal horses, and Herakles sailed away empty-handed, vowing revenge.

In due course he returned with an army. They breached the walls of Troy and killed Laomedon and all his sons except Podarkes, who alone had advised his father to honour his agreement. Herakles gave Hesione as the prize for greatest valour to his ally Telamon, the king of Salamis, who had been the first to breach the city walls. Hesione was allowed to choose one of the Trojan captives to be set free, so she chose her brother Podarkes, ransoming him with her veil, after which his name was changed to Priam (from the Greek verb *priamai*, 'to buy') and he became king of Troy. He rebuilt the city, making it larger and stronger than ever before, and ruled in peace for many years.

Priam was the most famous, the most powerful – but also the last – of this line of horse-loving kings. Towards the end of his long and prosperous reign the Trojan War took place, and despite all the divine favour that the Trojans had enjoyed, at the end of the war their city fell to the Greeks and was put to the torch. Priam himself was murdered on the altar of Zeus in the courtyard of his own palace. By this time his many sons were dead, including the great Hektor, bulwark of the Trojans, and now Hektor's little son Astyanax was flung from the city walls. With him died the royal line of Troy.

The story of the Trojan War must be told in detail. Before the war could begin, however, there were three key figures who had first to be born: Helen, daughter of Zeus, who was the most beautiful woman in the world; Paris, whose abduction of Helen set the war in motion; and Achilles, who was the war's greatest warrior.

THE BIRTH OF HELEN, DAUGHTER OF ZEUS

Zeus had his own reasons for causing the Trojan War, as a fragment from the lost *Kypria*, the first work in the Epic Cycle, explains:

There was a time when the many tribes of men, though they were wide-dispersed, weighed down the broad and deep-bosomed earth. Zeus saw it and took pity, and in his wisdom resolved to lighten the all-nurturing earth of men by causing the mighty strife of the Trojan War, so that the load of death might empty the world. And so the heroes died at Troy, and the plan of Zeus was accomplished.

The birth of Helen was all part of this plan.

Her mother was usually said to be Leda, wife of the Spartan king Tyndareos. Zeus took the form of a swan, then cunningly flew into Leda's arms for protection from an eagle that was pursuing him. The result of their union was an egg, from which was born the beautiful Helen. Three more children were also born to Leda – Kastor and Polydeukes, known as the Dioskouroi ('Boys of Zeus'), and Klytaimnestra, who grew up to marry, and later murder, Agamemnon, the king of Mycenae. Helen and Polydeukes were the immortal children of Zeus, while Kastor and Klytaimnestra were the mortal children of Tyndareos.

Euripides' *Helen*, a play first produced in 412 BC, is our earliest source for the story of Leda and the swan. Helen herself

Zeus, in the form of a swan, rapes Leda.

explains her background (16–21): 'My homeland is famous Sparta, and my father Tyndareos. But the story goes that Zeus took the likeness of a swan, then flew to my mother's lap to escape from a pursuing eagle and thus had his crafty way with her. If', she adds, 'that story is true.'

In the earliest recorded tradition, however, Helen's mother

was not Leda but Nemesis, the goddess of Retribution, as another fragment from the *Kypria* relates:

Helen, a marvel to men, was born to lovely-haired Nemesis after she was cruelly forced to join in love with Zeus, the king of the gods. For Nemesis tried to escape him, unwilling to lie in love with Zeus the Father, son of Kronos. Vexed in her heart with shame and anger, she fled over the earth and the black barren water, and Zeus pursued, for he longed in his heart to have her. Now she took the form of a fish and sped through the waves of the loud-roaring sea, and now along the river of Ocean and the far ends of the earth, and now she fled across the furrowed land, always turning into such dreadful creatures as the dry land fosters, that she might escape him.

This *Kypria* fragment tells us no more, and it is Apollodorus who records the sequel (3.10.7): when Nemesis finally became a goose, Zeus turned himself into a swan and mated with her. In due course Nemesis laid an egg and left it in a wood, where a shepherd found it and brought it to Leda. She put it carefully in a chest until it hatched, then brought up Helen as her own daughter. This is probably the story that was known to Sappho, since she says in one of her fragments (fr. 166), 'They say that long ago Leda once found an egg, blue like a hyacinth.'

So whichever of the two, Leda or Nemesis, may have been Helen's mother, it was always Leda who looked after the egg until it hatched. Helen's famous egg could still be seen in Sparta in the second century AD, as the traveller Pausanias records (3.16.1). When he visited the temple of the Leukippides, he saw the egg hanging by ribbons from the temple roof.

And it was always Leda who brought Helen up, in the royal palace at Sparta. The years passed, and news of Helen's beauty and divine birth spread far and wide. When she was still young, perhaps even as young as seven or eight, she was abducted by the Athenian king Theseus and his comrade Peirithoos, both of whom were planning to marry a daughter of Zeus (p. 258). Luckily Helen was soon rescued by her brothers Kastor and Polydeukes and taken unharmed back to Sparta.

When Helen reached the age to marry, the greatest heroes from all over Greece gave bride-gifts to Tyndareos in the hope of winning her hand. The Hesiodic *Catalogue of Women* gave a list of these suitors, of which a few names are recoverable from the surviving papyrus fragments. These include Protesilaos of Phylake, Idomeneos from Crete, Menestheus of Athens, Alkmaion and Amphilochos, sons of the seer Amphiaraos, Thoas from Aitolia, Elephenor of Euboia, Podarkes from Thessaly, and Menelaos, the brother of Agamemnon. Ajax, the son of Telamon ('the Great Ajax'), had no presents to give, but he promised great herds of sheep and cattle that he would steal from his neighbours. The canny Odysseus gave no gifts at all because he believed that he had no chance of winning Helen – so he saved himself the expense. (Besides which, he had his eye on another bride, Tyndareos's niece, Penelope.) Two other great heroes took no part in the contest: Agamemnon, because he was already married to Helen's sister, Klytaimnestra, and Achilles, because he was too young.

In general we can assume that most of the Greek leaders named in the *Iliad* as fighting at Troy would have tried to win Helen. Tyndareos was afraid of trouble from the disappointed suitors once one had been chosen above the others, so on Odysseus' suggestion he made them all swear an oath to respect his choice, and to come to the aid of the lucky husband in the event of any future threat to the marriage. They willingly took this vow, standing on the pieces of a sacrificed horse, says Pausanias (3.20.9), so as to make their oaths more binding – and it was these oaths which later obliged them to fight at Troy when Helen was carried off by Paris.

Menelaos was the chosen suitor, because he gave the most

bride-gifts says the *Catalogue*. (No doubt his rich and powerful brother Agamemnon helped him out.) So Helen and Menelaos were married, and Tyndareos adopted his new son-in-law as his successor on the throne of Sparta. A daughter was born to the couple, Hermione, who had 'the beauty of golden Aphrodite' according to Homer (*Odyssey* 4.14). The years passed, and Helen lived on tranquilly at Sparta, but the gods had already intervened in human affairs and she was waiting, though she did not know it, for Paris.

THE BIRTH OF PARIS TO PRIAM AND HECUBA

Priam, as an eastern monarch, had a number of wives and many children. Towards the end of the *Iliad* he says pathetically to Achilles (24.493-7):

> 'I have had the finest sons in far-spread Troy,
> but I say that not one of them is left to me.
> Fifty were my sons, the day the Greeks came here,
> nineteen born to me from a single mother,
> and the others born of women in my palace.'

This single mother, Priam's chief wife, was Hecuba, and most of the Trojan heroes who played a significant part in the war were her sons. These include Hektor, the mightiest warrior on the Trojan side, Troilos, who would die young, the seer Helenos, and Deiphobos. Hecuba had daughters too, including Kassandra (who, like her twin Helenos, had prophetic powers), Polyxena, Laodike and Kreousa. The Trojan War, or war's aftermath, would bring death to all of these children apart from Helenos. And there was one more son who was the cause of the war: Paris, also known as Alexandros.

When Hecuba was pregnant with Paris, she dreamt that she gave birth to a flaming torch which set light to the whole of Troy, or – in the earliest surviving account, Pindar's *Paean* 8 –

to a hundred-handed Fury, breathing fire, that razed the city to the ground. This clearly portended that Hecuba's coming child would bring complete destruction on the city, so, when Paris was born, Priam gave him to one of his shepherds, Agelaos, to be abandoned on Mount Ida, where either the baby would die of exposure, or wild beasts would kill him. And this might well have been his fate, for a she-bear found him – but instead of killing the infant, she suckled him for five days. When at the end of that time Agelaos found him alive and well, he realized that the gods must intend the boy to live, so he took him home to his farm and brought him up as his own son. Paris grew up to be a herdsman on Mount Ida.

Yet this very occupation led him back to Troy, and to his family. One day Priam's servants carried off his favourite bull to be a prize at funeral games in honour of a long-dead son (none other, ironically, than Paris himself), and Paris, unwilling to lose the bull, went to Troy to compete in the games and win it back. He succeeded, for he was a strong and athletic youth, defeating all comers, including his own brothers. This victory by an unknown outsider, apparently a mere commoner, naturally caused some resentment, and one of Paris's brothers, Deiphobos, was so angry that he drew his sword to attack him. Paris fled for sanctuary to the altar of Zeus, and there Kassandra saw him. By her visionary powers, she recognized him as her brother, believed dead.

Kassandra had been given the art of prophecy by the god Apollo: he had fallen in love with her and had promised her the power of second sight in return for her sexual favours. She agreed, and Apollo fulfilled his promise, but she then went back on her word and rejected the god's advances. He left her with the power to foretell the future truly, but turned the blessing into a curse by condemning her always to be disbelieved. So now when she recognized Paris, and predicted that to take him back within the family would bring disaster on the city, her words were ignored.

Euripides presented what must have been a moving version of the recognition of Paris in his lost tragedy *Alexandros*. We know from surviving fragments of the play that Hecuba, still grieving for her dead baby years after his loss, was urging Deiphobos on to kill Paris when, in the nick of time, she somehow realized that this was her long-lost child, and mother and son were joyfully reunited.

Priam and Hecuba now welcomed Paris home as part of the family, with no more thought of the old ominous dream. Now, as prince of Troy instead of a humble herdsman, he was in a position to visit Sparta and win Helen's love, promised to him by Aphrodite (p. 310).

THE BIRTH OF ACHILLES TO PELEUS AND THETIS

Thetis was a sea-goddess, a Nereid, one of the many daughters of Nereus, the Old Man of the Sea. She was so beautiful that Zeus himself desired her, but she rejected his advances out of respect for the feelings of his wife Hera. Poseidon too would have liked to win Thetis's love, but when a prophecy foretold that she was destined to give birth to a son who was greater than his father (p. 131), both gods gave up their suit, deciding that it would be safer if she were married off to a mortal.

They chose Peleus, the son of Aiakos, king of the island of Aigina, and himself king of Phthia in Thessaly. Peleus was a great hero who had taken part in the Kalydonian Boarhunt and the voyage of the Argonauts. He was strong, courageous and steadfast – and he needed to be so, for Thetis would not willingly yield to marriage with a mortal. He would have to take her by force, wrestling long and hard with her to win her. He lay in wait by the Thessalian sea-coast and caught her by surprise as she came out of the sea, then seized her firmly in his arms as his bride. Being a sea-goddess, she could change her shape at will, and she became in turn, say the various sources, fire, water, wind, tree, bird, tiger, lion, snake and cuttlefish. Resolutely Peleus clung to her through all these transformations, until at last she gave in. She returned to her own shape and agreed to become his wife.

This wedding of goddess and mortal was celebrated on Mount Pelion. The Muses sang, and all the gods attended and brought gifts – all, that is, except Eris, the goddess of Strife, who had not been invited because she was so disagreeable. She appeared nevertheless, and out of spite she threw into the midst of the gathering the 'Apple of Discord', a golden apple inscribed with the words 'for the fairest'. The goddesses Hera, Athene and Aphrodite all claimed the apple, and their dispute would in due course lead to the 'Judgement of Paris', and then to the Trojan War.

Peleus and Thetis had a son, Achilles, who would indeed turn out to be greater than his father. Thetis wanted to make her child immortal, so she began to burn away the mortal part of him inherited from his father by dipping him in the fire at night, and anointing his body with ambrosia during the day. Unfortunately she was interrupted one night by Peleus. He cried out in horror when he saw what she was doing, and she was so angry at his interference that she forsook baby and husband and went back to live in the sea with the other Nereids. A different and later story said that she dipped the baby Achilles into the waters of the river Styx, gripping him by the ankle, and in this way she made his whole body invulnerable except for the ankle by which she held him (his 'Achilles' heel'). An arrow-shot in that one weak ankle would eventually bring about his death.

In due course, Peleus gave Achilles to be educated by Cheiron, the wise and kindly Centaur who lived in the wilds of Mount

Pelion. Cheiron was skilled in archery, medicine, hunting and the arts, especially music, and he trained his young charge in these accomplishments. He fed Achilles on the flesh and entrails of lions and wild boars to instil in him strength and courage, and the boy grew up to be strong, handsome and valiant, and so fleet of foot that he could run down stags without the help of hounds – *podarkes Achilleus*, Homer calls him, 'swift-footed Achilles'.

Although Thetis had abandoned her Thessalian home, she never ceased to watch over her son. As time went by, she recognized the approach of the Trojan War, and she knew that if Achilles went to fight at Troy, he was destined to die. Determined to do what she could to avert this fate, she dressed him as a girl and sent him to live with the women at the court of Lykomedes, king of the island of Skyros.

The secret was in some way betrayed and, when the time was ripe, Odysseus would go to Skyros to penetrate Achilles' disguise and recruit him to the Greek army. In fact Achilles would go eagerly to war at Troy, heedless of his tragic destiny, and taking with him splendid gifts once given to Peleus at his wedding: a suit of fine armour; a stout ash spear given by Cheiron, polished by Athene and with a blade wrought by Hephaistos; and the immortal horses Xanthos and Balios, gifts of Poseidon, god of horses. He would become not only a hero greater than his father Peleus, but the greatest warrior who fought at Troy.

THE JUDGEMENT OF PARIS

After Eris had thrown down the golden apple, inscribed with the words 'for the fairest', at the wedding of Peleus and Thetis, three goddesses laid claim to it: Hera, wife of Zeus and queen of heaven, Athene, goddess of war, and Aphrodite, goddess of love. None of the three was willing to yield, so on Zeus's instructions Hermes took them down to Mount Ida, where Paris was tending his flocks, and told him to award the golden apple to the most beautiful (Plate 4). They all offered Paris bribes: Hera promised him imperial power, Athene victory in battle, and Aphrodite the love of the most beautiful woman in the world, Helen of Sparta. Paris chose Aphrodite.

Our early sources offer few details of this contest of beauty. Homer refers to it briefly when he says (*Iliad* 24.27–30) that Hera, Athene and Poseidon were unyielding in their hatred of Troy and the Trojans 'because of the blind folly of Alexandros [Paris], who offended the goddesses [i.e. Hera and Athene] when they came to his farmstead, and favoured the one who offered him grievous lust [clearly Aphrodite]'. This may sound slightly obscure, but there is no reason to doubt that it refers to the familiar story of the Judgement, especially in view of Hera's and Athene's relentless hostility to Troy throughout the *Iliad*, in contrast to Aphrodite's affection for the Trojans and her continuing interest in the relationship of Paris and Helen.

The contest was also described in the lost *Kypria*, according to Proclus's summary of the poem:

Eris arrives while the gods are feasting at the wedding of Peleus and starts a dispute beteen Hera, Athene and Aphrodite as to which of them is most beautiful. The three are led by Hermes at the command of Zeus to Alexandros on Mount Ida for him to judge, and Alexandros, won over by his promised marriage to Helen, decides in favour of Aphrodite.

Fragments of the poem describe how Aphrodite prepared herself for the contest by dressing in perfumed garments, made for her by the Graces and the Seasons, and dyed with flowers of spring – crocuses and hyacinths and violets and roses and daffodils and lilies – and wearing on her head a woven crown of sweet-smelling flowers.

So these early references are fairly brief, and it is only in fifth-century tragedy that the fuller story becomes a familiar theme, as in Euripides' *Trojan Women* (924–32, with Helen speaking):

Paris judged the group of three goddesses. Athene's gift to Alexandros was that he should overthrow Greece at the head of a Trojan army. Hera promised that, if he judged in her favour, he should rule over Asia and the furthest ends of Europe. Aphrodite praised my loveliness and promised that I should be his, if she were to outshine the other goddesses in the contest of beauty. Consider the obvious outcome: Aphrodite won.

So Paris chose Aphrodite as the fairest and awarded her the golden apple. His destiny – along with that of Troy – was now fixed. This 'Judgement of Paris' has always been a powerful source of inspiration both in literature and art, but perhaps the most poignant reflection on the story can be found in some of the ancient vase-paintings, where Paris is shown trying to run away in fear at the approach of the goddesses. He should have done so, for the war that resulted from his choice would destroy his city and bring death to all his family, and to himself.

PRELUDE TO WAR

Paris's success with Helen was now assured by the promise of the all-powerful goddess of love. He was naturally eager to claim his reward – and as late-come prince of Troy he was in a position to do so. The *Kypria* summary quoted above goes on to tell how he had ships built for his journey to Greece. Kassandra and Helenos could both foretell the disastrous future and they tried to dissuade him from going, but he paid no attention. As soon as he could, he set sail for the Peloponnese.

By this time Menelaos and Helen had been married for a good many years and their daughter Hermione was nine years

old. Menelaos made Paris welcome and entertained him gener-
ously. Paris in turn gave rich gifts to Helen, biding his time. For
nine days his visit was uneventful, but on the tenth day Menelaos travelled to Crete to bury his grandfather Katreos. As he
left, he told Helen to look after their guest and to supply him
with anything he might need. This was Paris's opportunity. He
paid court to Helen, and she, swayed by Aphrodite, was quick
to fall in love with him. They went to bed together and consummated their love, then they left Sparta for Troy, and sailed away
by night in ships piled high with treasures from the palace.
Once in Troy, Helen was accepted by the Trojans as Paris's
chosen bride and the couple formally celebrated their marriage.

When Menelaos returned home and found that Helen had
eloped with their Trojan guest, he at once went for help to
Agamemnon. The brothers sent envoys around Greece, remind-
ing Helen's old suitors of their oaths to defend Menelaos's
marital rights and calling them to war. By this means they
mustered a huge army to fetch Helen back by force, with each
of the suitors leading a contingent of ships and warriors. Agamemnon, who provided the largest contingent of 100 ships,
was commander-in-chief.

Not all came willingly. Odysseus, king of the island of Ithaca,
was by this time married to Penelope and had a baby son,
Telemachos. He was very reluctant to go to war, especially after
learning from a seer that, if he went to Troy, he would not
return home for twenty years, and then only after much suffering. When Agamemnon's envoy, Palamedes, came to recruit
him, he pretended to be mad. Palamedes found him wearing a
madman's cap, and ploughing the land with two different kinds
of animals yoked together – a horse and an ox, or an ox and
an ass – and sowing the furrows with salt instead of seed. But
Palamedes was renowned throughout Greece for his intelligence
and he realized at once that Odysseus was pretending. To prove

him sane, Palamedes threatened little Telemachos, either with a sword, or by putting the baby in front of the ploughshare. Odysseus leapt at once to save his son, thus proving that he was not mad at all, and was then obliged to go to war. He never forgave Palamedes for forcing him to leave his family and his beloved Ithaca, and in due course he would have his revenge.

Having accepted his fate, Odysseus helped to recruit other leaders. It was he who went to fetch Achilles from the court of Lykomedes on Skyros where, as we have seen, he was posing as a girl because of his anxious mother's fears. The wily Odysseus tricked Achilles into betraying his identity. Once in the palace he laid out a collection of gifts, feminine trinkets mixed with military weapons. The women reached at once for the trinkets, while Achilles gave himself away by choosing the arms. In another version, he was too clever to be taken in by this ploy and chose the feminine fripperies like all the other women. Odysseus, not to be outsmarted, had a bugle sound a call to arms, and Achilles, thinking that an enemy was at hand, immediately stripped off his women's clothes and seized shield and spear. Either way, his disguise was gone. He now went eagerly to war, accompanied by his dear comrade, Patroklos, and leading his men, the Myrmidons – and leaving behind him in Skyros a son, Neoptolemos (also called Pyrrhos, 'Red-head'), born to Lykomedes' daughter Deidameia.

Other leading warriors included Ajax, son of Telamon and king of Salamis, a huge man of immense strength and courage who carried a massive shield like a tower, seven ox-hides thick and covered with bronze. He was a fighter second only to Achilles, and Homer calls him 'the bulwark of the Greeks' (*Iliad* 3.229). He led twelve ships to the war, and was accompanied by his half-brother Teukros (the son of Telamon and his concubine Hesione), who was a skilled archer. Ajax was known as the Great Ajax, to differentiate him from his namesake the Lesser

Ajax, son of Oileus and king of Lokris in central Greece. The Lesser Ajax led a contingent of forty ships carrying light-armed troops, who used bows and slings instead of the usual heavy arms. He was physically the opposite of his larger counterpart, being small and fleet of foot; an expert spearsman, he was at his most deadly when in pursuit of a fleeing enemy. He was very different in character too, being arrogant, quarrelsome and impious. So, although a good fighter, he was generally disliked by his comrades. He often fought alongside the Great Ajax, with Homer repeatedly referring to the two of them together as the *Aiantes* (Ajaxes).

Another fine warrior was Diomedes, son of Tydeus and king of Argos, who had taken part in the successful attack on Thebes made by the Epigonoi when the sons of the Seven marched on the city to avenge their dead fathers. Diomedes led eighty ships from Argos, with Sthenelos and Euryalos as his subordinates.

The aged Nestor, king of Pylos, came from the south-western Peloponnese with ninety ships and accompanied by his sons Antilochos and Thrasymedes. Nestor was a very old man, by far the oldest of the Greek leaders. Although still a valiant fighter, he was most of all valued for his wise advice – which he was always ready to give in any situation, and often at great length. 'From his tongue flowed words sweeter than honey,' says Homer (*Iliad* 1.249). Nestor also enjoyed telling long, rambling stories about the distant past and his own valorous deeds of long ago, but however long-winded he proved to be, he was always heard out by his comrades with affection and respect. 'By father Zeus, and Athene, and Apollo,' says Agamemnon in the *Iliad* (2.371–4), 'I wish I had ten such advisers among the Greeks, for then the city of Priam would soon fall beneath our hands, captured and sacked.'

Also important was Patroklos, the lifelong friend of Achilles. Patroklos was the son of Peleus' uncle, Menoitios, and the two boys had been brought up together in Peleus' house in Phthia. When the young men set out together to the Trojan War, Achilles tried to comfort Menoitios for his son's departure by saying that he would bring Patroklos back from the war in glory (18.324–8, a 'futile promise' says Homer). Menoitios at that time offered his son advice which throws light on the relationship between the two comrades (11.786–9): 'My child, Achilles is higher-born than you are, but you are the elder; and yet in strength he is by far the greater. You must speak sound words to him and advise him well and guide him.' Yet it would be Patroklos's advice to his friend that would bring about his own death, and thus Achilles' death too.

These warriors, and many others, gathered together their ships and men and assembled on the eastern coast of Greece at Aulis in Boiotia. Homer's catalogue of ships and leaders in the *Iliad* (2.494–759) records that the fleet consisted of 29 contingents of 1,186 ships in all, with 44 leaders from 175 towns or other localities. The whole would have comprised, according to a plausible calculation, about 100,000 men.

At Aulis, while they were sacrificing to the gods to win divine favour for their expedition, there appeared a great portent. A snake glided from beneath the sacrificial altar, 'a terrible serpent with a blood-red back, which Zeus himself had sent forth to the light,' says Homer (*Iliad* 2.308–9). Swiftly it climbed to the topmost branch of a plane tree, where it devoured eight baby sparrows in their nest. The mother sparrow, hearing the piteous cries of her young, fluttered around in helpless frenzy, until the snake caught her by the wing and devoured her too. At once the snake was turned to stone by Zeus. Kalchas, the seer who was accompanying the expedition to Troy, interpreted this portent as meaning that the coming war would last for nine years, and that in the tenth year Troy would be taken.

Then the great fleet set sail.

THE FIRST ATTEMPT TO REACH TROY

The Greeks did not know the exact location of Troy, and after crossing the Aegean they landed too far to the south, in the neighbouring country of Mysia. Believing this to be the Troad, they began to pillage the land. The Mysians attacked them, led by Telephos, their king, and drove them back towards their ships, slaughtering many of them. Telephos himself killed, most notably, Thersandros of Thebes, son of Polyneikes and leader of the Boiotian contingent, but he was soon put to flight by Achilles. As he fled, he caught his foot in a grapevine and fell, and Achilles wounded him deeply in the thigh with his spear.

The Greeks soon realized their mistake, and since they had no quarrel with the Mysians they put to sea once more. Unfortunately their ships were dispersed by a violent storm, so they had to sail back separately to Greece, then reassemble and prepare for a second expedition. Meanwhile Telephos's wound refused to heal. Eventually he learnt from an oracle that it could be cured only by the one that had caused it in the first place, so he too set sail for Greece to appeal for Achilles' help.

He found Achilles in Argos, where the Greeks were reassembling their forces. In a famous scene from the lost *Telephos* of Euripides (a rich source of comedy for the playwright Aristophanes, and delightfully parodied in his *Women at the Thesmophoria*), Telephos arrived among the Greeks disguised as a beggar in rags. To enforce his appeal, he seized Agamemnon's infant son Orestes as a hostage, threatening to kill him if the Greeks refused to help, and promising to show them the way to Troy, if only Achilles would heal him in accordance with the oracle. Achilles was at a loss, until Odysseus pointed out that the oracle referred to the weapon itself, and not to the man wielding it. So Achilles scraped off some rust from his great spear and applied it to the wound, and soon Telephos was miraculously cured. He was now ready to guide the Greeks to Troy.

The fleet mustered at Aulis for a second time, but now they were held there, either by unfavourable winds or by no winds at all. Now Kalchas made a second prophecy: that the goddess Artemis was angry, and would be appeased only by the sacrifice of Agamemnon's virgin daughter Iphigeneia. In our earliest source, the *Kypria* (Homer makes no mention of Iphigeneia's death), the goddess's reason for anger was that Agamemnon had shot a stag and boasted that he was a finer hunter than Artemis herself. Later sources give other reasons: Agamemnon had broken a vow to sacrifice to the goddess the most beautiful thing born in the year of Iphigeneia's birth – which had been the girl herself (Euripides' *Iphigeneia among the Taurians*). Or his father Atreus had promised to Artemis the finest animal among his flocks, then had failed to sacrifice a lamb with a fleece of gold when it appeared (Apollodorus). Yet whatever the reason for Artemis's anger, the result was always the same: Iphigeneia had to die.

And die she did. Agamemnon lured her to Aulis with the promise that Achilles was waiting there to marry her. She came, accompanied by her mother Klytaimnestra. The outcome is movingly dramatized in Euripides' *Iphigeneia at Aulis*, where we see Agamemnon's despair at the need for his daughter's death, and Klytaimnestra's rage when she learns of her husband's real plans, and Achilles' valour as he determines to save the frightened girl, whatever the cost. Iphigeneia herself finally resolves this dramatic conflict by offering herself willingly for sacrifice, so as to salvage the expedition. She says to her father (1552–60):

'I am here at your bidding; but I willingly give my body for my homeland, and for the whole of Greece, to be led to the goddess's altar and there sacrificed, if this is her decree. From what I do, may you prosper, and win victory, and return safe home. Then let no Argive lay a hand on me: silent, unflinching, I will offer my throat.'

And she does so – but at the crucial moment, at the very stroke of the knife, Iphigeneia is gone, and on the altar in her place is a deer in its death throes. As in most versions of her death, beginning with the *Kypria*, Artemis has substituted a deer on the sacrificial altar, and has snatched the girl away to be her priestess in the land of the Taurians.

It is a very different matter in Aeschylus's tragedy *Agamemnon*. The Chorus describe the harrowing sacrifice: how Iphigeneia was gagged, lifted and held horizontal over the altar so that her throat was bare to the knife; and how, although she could not speak, her eyes begged for pity. But here there is no substitution, no deer, no miraculous salvation. Iphigeneia is simply a child, dead – and, as such, an abiding source of rage and grief for her mother Klytaimnestra, who would at last, ten long years later, take a fierce and pitiless revenge on Agamemnon by murdering him on his return home (p. 447).

But this is far in the future. Iphigeneia was sacrificed, the winds blew favourably, and the fleet once again set sail for Troy, this time under the guidance of Telephos.

THE FIRST NINE YEARS OF THE WAR

After safely crossing the Aegean, the Greeks put in at Tenedos, an island near Troy where Tenes was king. He had divine blood in his veins, for his father was Kyknos, king of Kolonai near Troy and son of the sea-god Poseidon, though some said that Tenes was a son of Apollo. He had been born to Kyknos's first wife, Prokleia, a daughter of Laomedon, and in later years had quarrelled bitterly with his father when Kyknos's second wife, Philonome, fell in love with him and tried to seduce him. Tenes

The sacrifice of Iphigeneia.

rejected her, so she took her revenge by accusing him to her husband of making advances to her. She even brought forward a flute-player called Eumolpos as a so-called witness.

Kyknos believed her lies, and he put Tenes and his sister Hemithea in a chest and launched it out to sea. The chest was washed ashore on the island of Leukophrys, so Tenes settled there with his sister, and when he was made king by the inhabitants he renamed the island Tenedos after himself.

Kyknos in due course learnt the truth about the supposed seduction. He stoned the flute-player to death and buried his wife alive in the earth, then sailed to Tenedos to ask his son's forgiveness. The embittered Tenes would have nothing to do with him and severed the mooring-ropes of his ship with an axe. Kyknos drifted away, just as Tenes himself had once done.

When the Greek ships were putting in at Tenedos, Tenes tried to ward them off by bombarding them with stones. Achilles killed him, even though Thetis had forewarned him that on no account must he do so, or else he himself would die at the hands of Apollo. A divine prophecy could never be wrong and, as we shall see, Apollo would in due course play his part in Achilles' death.

It was at this point in the expedition that Philoktetes, king of Malis and leader of the Malian contingent of seven ships, was abandoned by his comrades. He had been bitten in the foot by a snake and the wound festered incurably, so because of the unbearable stench of rotting flesh and Philoktetes' continual cries of agony, he was left behind on the deserted island of Lemnos. But Philoktetes was the keeper of the great bow of Herakles and its inescapable arrows, and ten years later his comrades would need his presence at Troy before the city could be taken. Meanwhile he kept himself from starving by shooting wild birds and animals.

The Greeks now successfully reached Troy, but before they went irrevocably to war with the Trojans, they made one last attempt to regain Helen by peaceful means. Menelaos and Odysseus went into Troy to ask for her return, along with the treasures that had been stolen when she eloped with Paris – but to no avail. Paris had bribed some of the Trojans to withstand any such request, and the more aggressive among them even urged that the two Greeks be killed. The Trojan elder Antenor intervened to save them, and Menelaos and Odysseus left Troy with their lives – but without Helen. War was now inevitable, and the most vocal of the hostile Trojans, Antimachos, would live to regret it, for all three of his sons would be killed during the fighting.

An oracle had predicted that the first warrior to touch Trojan soil would be the first to die, so all the Greeks hesitated to land. Finally Protesilaos, leader with his brother Podarkes of the contingent of forty ships from Phylake, took the initiative and valiantly leapt ashore. He killed several Trojans before himself being killed by Hektor, the eldest son of King Priam and the leader of the Trojan warriors. Protesilaos left behind him, says Homer (*Iliad* 2.700–701), a wife, her cheeks lacerated in mourning, and a home only half-completed.

This young wife was Laodameia, who was inconsolable at her husband's death. Seeing her great grief, the gods took pity on her, and Hermes brought Protesilaos back to earth to be with her for a few hours. On his return to Hades, Laodameia killed herself so that she might go with him. In Euripides' lost tragedy *Protesilaos*, the couple had been married for only one day when the summons came for the expedition to Troy. Here it was Protesilaos who, after his death, appealed to the gods to let him have just one more day with his young bride; and here, too, Laodameia killed herself when he was taken to Hades for the second time.

After Protesilaos's death, the fighting started in earnest and many Trojans were killed. One of the Trojan allies who tried to oppose the Greek landing was Kyknos, a son of Poseidon and probably the very Kyknos who was the father of Tenes. Poseidon had made his son's body invulnerable to human weapons, so when Achilles attacked Kyknos with spear and sword, they made no impression on him at all. Finally Achilles killed him either by hurling a stone at his head, or by forcing him to the ground and throttling him with his own helmet thongs.

Seeing that they were unlikely to be victorious over this

massive Greek army, especially one with the invincible young Achilles at the forefront, the Trojans retreated to the safety of their city. The Greeks established themselves on the Trojan plain, and for nine years they held Troy under siege, skirmishing occasionally with any Trojans who dared to emerge from behind their massive walls.

Because of the sparseness of our sources, we know of only a few noteworthy events during these nine years. One such was the death of Troilos, son of Priam and Hecuba. It was said that Troy was destined never to fall if Troilos reached the age of twenty, so inevitably the Greeks resolved to kill him. References to his murder in extant literature are few, and none of them explicit, but here vase-paintings help us to piece together the details, since from the seventh century BC onwards this was a favourite subject in art. Despite the literary gaps, we see that this was clearly a very popular story.

It seems that Achilles lay in wait for Troilos outside the walls of Troy, then caught and killed him in a sanctuary sacred to Apollo. In Sophocles' lost tragedy *Troilos*, we know that the boy was exercising his horses near Apollo's sanctuary when Achilles ambushed him. Troilos was clearly another horse-loving Trojan like so many of his ancestors – in Homer's only reference to him, where Priam simply mentions him as dead, he is described as 'delighting in horses' (*Iliad* 24.257).

In art we see Achilles lying in ambush at a fountain house, where Troilos's sister Polyxena comes to draw water, accompanied by her brother. Troilos is usually riding one horse and leading another. Achilles leaps out and chases after him, while he gallops away, and the water jar crashes to the ground as Polyxena too runs away in fear. Swift-footed Achilles outruns Troilos's horse and catches the boy – sometimes he drags him from his horse by the hair – then kills him on Apollo's altar. Some scenes even show Troilos savagely decapitated, and many scenes depict a powerful contrast between the huge, attacking warrior and the seemingly small, defenceless boy, here scarcely more than a child. Finally the Trojans attack Achilles over Troilos's mutilated body. Troilos may have had to die if the Greeks wished to take Troy, but this does seem to have been a particularly brutal murder.

Another death – in effect another murder – was that of Palamedes, who had roused Odysseus' implacable enmity by forcing him to come unwillingly to war. In our earliest version in the *Kypria*, Palamedes drowned while he was out fishing, in a death somehow caused by Odysseus and Diomedes. According to the later and more usual story, Odysseus forged a letter under the name of Priam, promising Palamedes a large sum in gold if he would betray his fellow Greeks, and then buried this same amount of gold in his victim's tent. The letter was either dropped in the camp, or planted on a Trojan captive. It soon came to the notice of Agamemnon, who read it, discovered the hidden gold, and handed the apparently guilty Palamedes over to the army to be punished. They stoned him to death as a traitor.

Palamedes' father Nauplios never forgave the Greeks for his son's death. According to Euripides' lost tragedy *Palamedes* (parodied, like *Telephos*, in Aristophanes' comedy *Women at the Thesmophoria*), it was Palamedes' brother Oiax, also serving at Troy, who sent the news of his execution to their father. He inscribed the story on a number of oar-blades, then threw them into the sea in the hope that they would float to Greece. Unlikely as it may seem, one of these oar-blades was eventually washed up in Euboia, where Nauplios found and read it, and swore to avenge his son's death. Years later, when the Greek fleet was sailing home after the fall of Troy, he would have his revenge by luring many of their ships to destruction on the cruel rocks of Cape Kaphereus.

As the nine years of siege passed, the Greeks made forays against other settlements in the region, and against more distant cities and islands, to win food and plunder for the army. Usually Achilles led the raids. One of these assaults was against Hypoplakian Thebe, a small city near Troy. We know rather more about this attack than most because Thebe's king was Eetion, the father of Hektor's wife Andromache, who, in the *Iliad*, herself describes what happened (6.414–24):

> 'Indeed it was godlike Achilles who killed my father
> And sacked the strong-built city of the Kilikians,
> Thebe of the lofty gates. He killed Eetion,
> but honouring him in his heart he left him his armour:
> he burnt him on a pyre in splendid war-gear,
> and built him a burial mound. The mountain nymphs,
> daughters of shield-bearing Zeus, grew elms around it.
> And my seven brothers who lived there in the palace
> they all in one day went down to the house of Hades,
> slaughtered together by swift-footed, godlike Achilles,
> while tending their white-fleeced sheep and lumbering oxen.'

The flocks of sheep and oxen no doubt served well as food for the Greek army. Eetion's wife was also taken captive, until Achilles set her free on the payment of a ransom, but with her husband and seven sons dead, soon she too died.

Lyrnessos, near Troy, was another city that was sacked – significant, because out of the spoils Achilles was awarded the beautiful captive Briseis as his prize. She brings us to Homer's *Iliad*, which brilliantly illuminates events in the tenth and final year of the war.

THE WRATH OF ACHILLES IN THE TENTH YEAR

> Sing, Muse, the wrath of Peleus' son, Achilles,
> the accursed wrath that brought countless sorrows
> to the Greeks, hurled down to Hades the souls
> of many brave heroes, and left their corpses a prey
> for the dogs and all the birds . . .

Thus begins the *Iliad*, the very first word in the Greek being *menin*, 'wrath', the anger of Achilles that will reverberate through the whole work: first anger against Agamemnon over a slight to his honour, and then – after the death of Patroklos at Hektor's hands – an even fiercer anger against the Trojans in general and Hektor in particular. Only at the end of the poem, after Hektor's death, will this wrath ease into acceptance and compassion when old Priam comes into the Greek camp and begs to ransom his son's body.

This anger begins with a violent quarrel between Achilles and Agamemnon over their war-spoils. Just as Achilles received the captive girl Briseis as his prize, so Agamemnon had been awarded Chryseis, daughter of Chryses, priest of the god Apollo. Chryses was distraught at the loss of his daughter, and brought gifts as ransom and begged for her release, but Agamemnon arrogantly drove the old man away under threat of violence. Now, at the opening of the *Iliad*, Apollo is angry because of this slight to his priest, and coming to earth he strikes the Greek camp with plague (1.44–53, a splendid portrayal of this awesome god in action):

> Angered in his heart he strode from the peaks of Olympos,
> carrying on his shoulders his bow and covered quiver,
> and the shafts clashed on the shoulders of the angry god,
> moving in fury. He came as night comes down.

Settling far from the ships he let fly an arrow,
and terrible was the clash that rose from his silver bow.
First he killed the mules and the running dogs,
then shot his piercing arrows against the men,
and the funeral pyres burned thick and kept on burning.
For nine days the shafts of the god fell on the army.

On the tenth day the Greeks hold an assembly, during which the seer Kalchas explains the reason for the plague and for Apollo's wrath. Agamemnon reluctantly accepts that he must give up Chryseis to appease the angry god, but this will leave him without his share of the spoils, which is a slight to his status, so he unwisely says that in recompense he will take the war-prize of some other man, maybe of Achilles himself. The angry Achilles responds to this injustice by threatening to leave Troy and take his ships and men home to Phthia. Agamemnon, furious in his turn, replies (1.177–86):

'Always strife is dear to you, and wars and battles,
and though you are very strong, that is a god's gift.
Go home then with your ships and your comrades,
be king over the Myrmidons. I care nothing for you,
nothing for your anger. But here is my threat to you:
Since Phoibus Apollo has taken away my Chryseis
... I shall come myself to your hut and take away
the fair-cheeked Briseis, your prize, and you will learn
how much greater I am than you.'

Achilles loves Briseis dearly: she is promised to him in marriage (19.297–9), and he calls her his 'dear wife' (9.336). And he says, once she has been taken from him to Agamemnon, 'any man loves the woman who is his, and cares for her, just as I loved this one from my heart, even though I won her by my spear' (9.342–3). But there was more to it than this: a warrior's heroic standing relied not only on words and deeds, but on visible possessions and spoils, so Achilles now feels himself dishonoured by the loss of his prize, as well as pained by the loss of a beloved woman.

He reacts by refusing to fight any more and declares to Agamemnon that they will all regret the loss of their best warrior. 'I swear there will come a time when a longing for Achilles will be felt by the sons of the Achaians [the Greeks], by every one of them,' he cries (1.240–44), 'and on that day, for all your sorrow, you will be able to do nothing to help, when many of them drop and die before man-slaughtering Hektor. Then you will eat your heart out in anger that you did no honour to the best of the Achaians.'

He withdraws from the fighting, taking his Myrmidon followers and his comrade Patroklos with him, and retires to his tent. When Briseis is taken from him, he goes alone to the seashore and weeps. Here his mother Thetis hears his sorrow and comes to him from the deeps of the ocean to comfort him. She agrees to intercede for him with Zeus, asking the great god to grant success to the Trojans in his absence, so that the Greeks will be sure to feel the lack of their supreme warrior. Zeus promises to do so (1.528–30):

> The son of Kronos spoke, and nodded his dark brow,
> and the divine locks waved from the king's immortal head,
> and great Olympos shook.

So we know that before long the tide of battle will turn in favour of the Trojans – though this does not happen immediately.

The Greeks marshal their forces and march in full strength towards Troy, across the meadows of the river Skamandros (1.455–8):

Even as ravening fire burns a vast forest
on a mountain peak, and the blaze shows far off,
so from their splendid bronze, as they marched out,
the dazzling gleam shone through the air to heaven.

Seeing that a major attack is imminent, the Trojans, led by Hektor, rally on a hill outside Troy. But before the armies can begin fighting, Paris steps forward and offers to engage in single combat any one of the Greeks. Menelaos takes up the challenge (somewhat to Paris's dismay), and the leaders agree a truce while they fight their duel. The winner will take Helen with no more argument and the war will be over.

Throughout the *Iliad*, Paris makes an attractive figure as he light-heartedly moves around the battlefield, dressed in a leopard-skin, but his serious brother Hektor does not approve, and he now heaps reproaches on him (3.39–55):

'Evil Paris, beautiful, woman-crazy deceiver,
better you had never been born, or had died unwed.
Truly I would have wished it so. Better by far
than for you to be a disgrace and a cause for scorn.
Surely now the long-haired Achaians laugh aloud,
thinking you our bravest champion because of your beauty,
while there is no strength, no courage in your heart . . .
And would you not stand against warlike Menelaos?
You would learn what kind of man he is, whose lovely
wife you have taken. The lyre would not help you,
nor the gifts of Aphrodite, nor your long hair,
nor your beauty, when you lie low in the dust.'

Yet Paris is far from the cowardly libertine that these lines might suggest. He stands up to Hektor: 'Do not hold against me the lovely gifts of golden Aphrodite,' he replies. 'Glorious gifts of the gods' own giving must never be thrown away, even though a man would not take them by his own choice.' And he certainly has courage, for when he offered to fight any one of the Greeks, he was well aware that he was putting himself in serious danger. In fact, when the duel takes place, he is almost killed by Menelaos, who ends by dragging him by the helmet back into the Greek lines.

Here Aphrodite steps in to save her favourite, spiriting him away from the battlefield to his own bedroom. She summons Helen to join him, and Helen unwillingly obeys the implacable goddess, greeting her lover with disillusioned words (3.428–9): 'So you have come back from the fighting. How I wish that you had died there, beaten under by the stronger man, who used to be my husband.'

Yet she is still in sexual thrall to Paris. He says to her:

'Let us go to bed and find pleasure in love, for never so much before has passion enfolded my heart, not even when I first took you from lovely Sparta, carrying you off in the seafaring ships, and lay with you in love on a rocky island. Not even then did I love you as much as now, nor sweet desire overcome me.' (3.441–6)

And Helen says no more, but goes with him to bed. This was indeed one of the great love stories of all time, and Helen is right to say that the two of them 'would in time to come be the subject of song for men of future generations' (6.357–8).

The Greeks believe that Menelaos was the victor in the duel and they shout for the return of Helen, but before the Trojans can respond, the truce is broken. Inspired by the goddess Athene, who wants war to continue until her hated Troy is razed to the ground, the Trojan ally Pandaros shoots an arrow at Menelaos. The arrow grazes his flesh and draws blood, and at this the Greeks quickly re-arm and attack the Trojans. Now we see the great warrior Diomedes in triumphant battle-action, inspired by Athene herself (5.2–8):

She gave him strength and courage, to be conspicuous
among the Greeks and win the glory of valour.
She made unwearying fire blaze from his shield
and helmet, like the autumn star that beyond all stars
rises brilliant from bathing in the stream of Ocean:
such was the fire she made blaze from his head and shoulders,
urging him into the midst of the throng of battle.

He creates havoc in the Trojan ranks (5.87–94):

He stormed across the plain like a winter-swollen
torrent in spate, sweeping away the dykes
in its swift flood, one that the strong-built dykes
and the walls of fruitful vineyards cannot hold back,
or stay its sudden rise when the rain of Zeus
falls heavy, and many are the lovely works of men
that fall beneath it. Like these the massed battalions
of Trojans were scattered by Diomedes, and many
as they were they could not stand against him.

He is shot in the shoulder by Pandaros, but he retires for only
a moment while his comrade Sthenelos pulls out the arrow,
then he returns to the fighting with his zest for battle even
greater than before (5.135–43):

His heart before had raged to fight the Trojans,
but now a tripled fury seized him, as of a lion
that a country shepherd, guarding his fleecy sheep,
grazed as he leapt the fence of the fold, and has not
killed him, but only stirred up the lion's strength
and cannot help his flock, but the lion enters
the fold and the forsaken sheep flee in fear,
then lie strewn on each other in heaps, when he
in fury leaps out again from the deep yard:
raging so did mighty Diomedes fight the Trojans.

He not only kills many Trojans, including the man who wounded him, Pandaros, but he even attacks the gods themselves. When Aphrodite comes to help her son Aeneas, who has been felled by a great stone, Diomedes wounds her in the wrist so that she flees in pain up to Olympos. Apollo takes over the care of Aeneas, and three times Diomedes surges forward to kill him, three times the god batters back his bright shield. When for the fourth time Diomedes comes on as if he were more than human, then Apollo orders him to give way, and he obeys. Later he comes across the war-god Ares on the battlefield, stripping a corpse, and once more with the help of Athene he attacks him, wounding him in the belly. Ares bellows as loud as 9,000 men, or 10,000, when they forge forward into battle. Then he too flees in pain up to Olympos.

So for the time being, thanks largely to Diomedes' tremendous onslaught, the Greeks still have the upper hand. They begin to advance once again towards Troy, and the anxious Hektor goes back into the city to ask the Trojan women to pray for help in their plight. His mother Hecuba and sister Laodike take a beautiful robe to offer to Athene in her temple, and the priestess Theano, wife of the Trojan elder Antenor, prays for the goddess to save Troy. 'But Pallas Athene rejected her prayer,' says Homer (6.311) – though the women know nothing of Athene's reaction and are hopeful that now all will be well.

On the battlefield Hektor is the greatest of the Trojan warriors – even the mighty Diomedes has quailed before his approach and has moved out of range. Now we see Hektor among his family in Troy, a noble, loving and compassionate man. Going in search of his wife Andromache, he finds her on the city walls with their infant son Skamandrios (named after the chief river of the Trojan plain), also called Astyanax ('lord of the city'), 'a little child, only a baby, the beloved son of Hektor, lovely as a star shining'. Andromache expresses her fears for Hektor's life and begs him not to carry on risking death in battle, but to stay in Troy within the safety of the city walls. His reply shows the honour and sense of duty that keep him fighting, even in what seems to him to be a hopeless war (6.441–9):

'I would be ashamed before the Trojans
and the Trojans' wives, with their trailing dresses,
if like a coward I skulk away from the fighting.
My spirit will not let me, for I have learnt
always to be brave and to fight in the forefront,
winning great glory for myself, and for my father.
But this I know well in my mind and in my heart:
the day will come when sacred Ilion shall perish,
and Priam, and the people of Priam of the strong ash spear.'

Then follows one of the most famous scenes in ancient literature, when little Astyanax cries in fright at his father's fearsome helmet (6.466–74):

Glorious Hektor held out his arms to his son,
but the baby shrank back crying against the breast
of his fair-girdled nurse, scared at the sight of his father,
frightened by the bronze and the horse-hair crest
that he saw nodding dreadfully at the top of his helmet.
His beloved father laughed, and his lady mother,
and at once glorious Hektor took from his head
the helmet, and laid it shining upon the ground,
and kissed his son, and rocked him in his arms.

Hektor prays for the little boy's future (6.476–81):

'Zeus and you other gods, grant that my son
may be like me, pre-eminent among the Trojans,
as strong and brave as I am, a mighty ruler of Troy.

And let them say, as he comes back out of the fighting,
"He is better by far than his father." And let him kill
his enemy, and carry home the bloody spoils,
and bring joy to the heart of his mother.'

But this prayer will not be fulfilled, for Hektor will be killed by Achilles, and Troy will fall, and Hektor's little son will be murdered by the Greeks.

Before he returns to battle, Hektor assures Andromache that he will not be defeated, but she still fears for him and, once he is gone from her, she and her maids weep for him as though he were already dead. He meets Paris at the gates of Troy and they leave the peace of the city and go back out to the battlefield. Paris is eager to fight (6.506–14):

As when a horse, stabled and corn-fed at the manger,
breaks his rope and gallops in thunder over the plain
to where he likes to bathe in a sweet-flowing river,
exulting. He holds his head high and his mane
streams over his shoulders; knowing his splendour,
he is carried on swift knees to his loved pastures;
so came Paris, son of Priam, from the high citadel,
shining in all his armour like the shining sun,
laughing aloud as his swift feet carried him.

The brothers talk of the happy day when war will be over and the Greeks driven away from Troy. Neither will live long enough to know that that day never comes.

There is now once more a temporary truce as Hektor offers to fight any Greek hero in single combat. At first the Greeks all hesitate to take up the challenge. Then Menelaos volunteers, but Agamemnon dissuades him, saying that he will certainly be killed. Finally old Nestor stirs them with tales of his own glorious deeds when young, and nine willing men step forward.

They draw lots to see who will fight, and the Great Ajax is the man chosen.

Hektor and Ajax are well matched and their duel is inconclusive: they fight with spears, and then rocks, and just as they are drawing their swords for close combat, the heralds stop them because of the approach of night. They part in friendship with an exchange of gifts, Hektor giving a sword and Ajax a sword-belt. During the night both armies gather up their dead and cremate them, and the Greeks, on the advice of old Nestor, begin to fortify their camp with an earthen wall and a deep ditch set with spikes.

When battle resumes at dawn, Zeus at last gives the advantage to the Trojan army, led by an invincible Hektor. He storms about the battlefield in his chariot, taunting the Greeks, threatening to burn their ships, and shouting encouragement to his four horses, Xanthos, Podargos, Aithon and Lampos (Chestnut, Whitefoot, Blaze and Bright). The Greeks are driven right back towards their ships and, when night falls, the Trojans are able to camp out on the plain for the first time since the Greeks landed over nine years earlier. Their watch-fires shine out like stars (8.555–65):

> As when in the sky the stars round the gleaming moon
> shine in their splendour, when the air has fallen still,
> and the mountain peaks are clear, and the high headlands
> and wooded glades, and boundless brilliant air
> spills from high heaven, and all the stars shine clear
> to gladden the heart of the shepherd; even so many,
> between the ships and the rolling streams of Xanthos,
> shone the Trojan fires in front of the walls of Troy.
> A thousand fires were burning there on the plain,
> and beside each blazing fire sat fifty men.
> And their horses, champing oats and glistening barley,
> stood each beside his chariot, waiting for dawn.

The Greeks are now trapped behind their defences and are desperately afraid. Now Agamemnon is indeed feeling the loss of his finest warrior, just as Achilles promised. They hold a council, and at the urging of Nestor and the other leaders, Agamemnon agrees to seek a reconciliation. He will promise to give Briseis back to Achilles, with a solemn oath that he has never slept with her, and will offer many other fine gifts: seven tripods, ten talents of gold, twenty shining cauldrons, twelve prize-winning horses, and seven women of Lesbos, especially beautiful and skilled. And there will be yet more gifts if Troy is conquered, including twenty Trojan women, and even the hand of one of his own daughters in marriage, with a great dowry and a kingdom of seven rich cities. Three men – Odysseus, the Great Ajax and old Phoinix, who was Achilles' boyhood tutor – are to go to Achilles' tent to tell him what Agamemnon offers if only he will come back and fight.

They find Achilles playing his lyre and singing, while Patroklos listens. Patroklos, vulnerable and compassionate, is one of the most sympathetic characters in the *Iliad*. Everyone who speaks of him calls him kind, or gentle, or tender. After he is killed, Briseis will say of him, 'I weep your death without ceasing, for always you were kind' (19.300), and Menelaos will sum up this special quality of tenderness: 'poor Patroklos, who was gentle, and knew how to be kindly to all men while he lived' (17.670–72). In some later writers, such as Aeschylus in his lost tragedy *The Myrmidons*, the bond between Patroklos and Achilles would be seen as homosexual love, but there is no trace of this in Homer. Here their sexual relationships are with women, as at 9.663–8 when they both go to bed in their shared tent, but each with his own woman. In Homer their mutual love is the deep devotion of friends.

Achilles welcomes Odysseus, Ajax and Phoinix, and serves them food and drink, but he refuses to return to battle, even when Odysseus describes the bounty that Agamemnon has promised him. Indeed, Achilles makes it clear that he has become disenchanted with the whole war (9.318–27):

'Fate is the same for the man who holds back
and the man who fights his best. In one honour
are held both the cowards and the brave.
Death still comes to the man who does nothing,
as well as the man who does much. I win nothing
for suffering heart-sorrow and forever risking
my life in war. As a bird brings in her beak
to her unfledged chicks whatever she can catch,
while she herself suffers, such was I as I lay
through many nights unsleeping, and spent
full many bloody days in battle . . .'

Still full of anger and wounded pride, he rejects Agamemnon's gifts (9.378–87):

'Hateful to me are his gifts. I value them
no more than a splinter of wood. Not if he gave
ten times or twenty times as much to me
as he has now, and offers more besides . . .
not even if his gifts numbered as sand or dust,
not even so would Agamemnon persuade me,
until he has paid full price for the outrage
he has done me, grieving my heart.'

He says that his mother Thetis has told him that he has a choice of two destinies: he will have either a long and obscure life at home, or death at Troy and everlasting glory. So he will return home at once, because his life is worth more than all the spoils of Troy.

Now old Phoinix tries to win him over with a tearful and passionate plea, remembering earlier days when he loved

Achilles like a son, and succeeds in persuading him not to be so hasty, but to decide in the morning whether he will sail home or stay at Troy. Finally Ajax appeals to him on the grounds of comradeship, and Achilles relents a little more: he will stay at Troy after all, but he will not return to battle until the Trojans fire his huts and ships. So Achilles' stern resolve not to fight any more has indeed been softened by his friends, but because of his pride and outraged honour, he does not relent enough to avoid tragedy. He will pay a painful price.

During the night Hektor sends a Trojan spy, Dolon, to reconnoitre the Greek camp. Homer describes Dolon as 'ugly, but swift of foot, and the only son among five sisters' (10.316–17) – this last probably meant as disparagement, suggesting that he is a sissy. Certainly he is greedy, for he goes on the spying expedition, not out of patriotism, but for the reward that Hektor promises him: the chariot and immortal horses of Achilles. Dolon wears a wolfskin as camouflage and a cap of weasel skins, and these perhaps symbolize his unattractive character, for both animals had a bad reputation in antiquity.

Slinking through the dark land between the two camps, he is captured almost at once by Odysseus and Diomedes, who have set out on a similar expedition to spy on the Trojans. Gibbering with terror, Dolon promises them a rich ransom if they will only let him go, then tells them all he knows about the Trojan camp and the position of the Trojan allies, hoping that this will save his life. He even points out a contingent of allies newly arrived from Thrace, who are all asleep from weariness. He points particularly to the magnificent horses owned by their leader, Rhesos: 'They are the finest horses I ever saw, and the biggest,' he says. 'They are whiter than snow, and they run with the speed of the wind' (10.436–7). But this betrayal of his comrades does him no good, for Diomedes cuts off his head, even as he pleads for his life, and it falls to the ground still speaking.

With Dolon out of the way, Diomedes butchers thirteen of the sleeping Thracians, including Rhesos himself, while Odysseus takes his splendid horses. They escape safely back to camp with their booty, and this minor triumph cheers the Greeks' spirits.

Next day the two armies clash in the greatest encounter of the war so far. Several of the Greek leaders are wounded and put out of action, including Agamemnon, Odysseus and Diomedes. Achilles, watching from the stern of one of his beached ships, sees Nestor bringing in one of the wounded, and he sends Patroklos to find out whom Nestor has rescued. 'And here,' says Homer, 'was the beginning of his tragedy' (11.603) – because Nestor will beg Patroklos to persuade Achilles to fight, or at least (and this is how it will be) to go into battle himself, wearing Achilles' armour, so that the Trojans will give way in fear.

The Trojans, 'fighting like blazing fire', drive the Greeks back behind their ditch and wall. Sarpedon, lord of the Lycians and the mightiest warrior among the Trojan allies, leads his comrades in an assault against the wall, determined to breach it or die in the attempt (12.299–308):

> He went onwards like some mountain lion,
>   one who for a long time has been without meat,
>   and now his fearless heart urges him on
>   to get inside a strong-built sheepfold
>   and go for the sheep flocks. And even though
>   he finds there herdsmen guarding their sheep
>   with spears and with dogs, even so he will not
>   be driven from the fold without some attack,
>   and either he makes his spring and seizes a sheep,
>   or is himself hit first by a spear from a quick hand.
> So now his spirit urged on godlike Sarpedon
>   to rush at the wall and break apart its defences.

He succeeds, and makes the first breach in the wall. 'He opened a pathway for many,' says Homer (12.399).

Another Trojan ally is Asios, the son of Hyrtakos, king of Perkote in the Troad. Asios is proud of his chariot and the huge and fiery horses that carried him to Troy, and against all wise advice he has brought them into the thick of the Trojan attack on the Greek wall. 'Poor fool,' says Homer (12.113–15), 'for he was not going to escape the evil fates, nor ever again go back from the ships to windy Troy, delighting in his horses and chariot.' Soon afterwards he is struck by the Cretan leader, Idomeneos, with a spear-cast to his throat, and he dies, outstretched, in front of his precious horses, which are taken as booty by the Greeks.

Meanwhile Hektor breaks through the Greek gates by hurling a huge stone and smashing them open (12.462–71):

> Then glorious Hektor leapt inside, his face
> like the onset of night. He gleamed in fearful bronze
> that girded his skin, and brandished two spears.
> No one but a god could have come against him
> and stopped him as he burst through the gates,
> his eyes blazing with fire. Turning, he shouted
> to the mass of Trojans to climb over the wall,
> and they obeyed his order. Some climbed the wall
> and others poured in through the strong-built gates.
> The Greeks fled in fear among their hollow ships,
> and the clamour rose unceasing.

The Greeks are now in desperate straits as the two armies re-engage actually within their camp, with frightful carnage on both sides. Yet divine help is at hand, for Poseidon comes among the Greeks to spur them on to greater efforts against the enemy. At first he comes in disguise to escape the notice of Zeus, whose plan is still to give the advantage to the Trojans until – but only until – they have set fire to one of the Greek ships. Up on Olympos, Hera too is planning to thwart Zeus's purpose: she seduces him in a bed of clover, crocuses and hyacinths (p. 58), then has Hypnos, the god of Sleep, shed over him a sweet slumber. Poseidon can now openly rally the Greeks, which he does to great effect. They fight furiously, and the Trojans are driven back across the earthen wall and out of the Greek camp. Even Hektor is wounded when the Great Ajax fells him with a huge rock. He is carried by his comrades out of the fighting, vomiting blood.

Now Zeus wakes and, realizing what has happened, orders Poseidon away from the battlefield. Once more the tide of battle turns, as Apollo comes to help Hektor back into the fighting and the Trojans storm the Greek wall again. Apollo destroys the wall – like a little boy who plays at building sandcastles on the beach, says Homer, then knocks them down again with his hands and feet (15.362–4). The Greeks are pressed right back on to their beached ships. Now the Great Ajax comes into his own. He fights on relentlessly, encouraging his men and striding from ship to ship, like, says Homer, a bareback rider with four horses who jumps from horse to horse as they gallop across the plain (15.679–84). Sweating and weary, he beats off his attackers with a huge pike, fully believing that he is going to die, yet nevertheless ready to battle on until he drops.

At this crucial moment, when the triumphant Trojans are about to set fire to the ships, Patroklos comes to Achilles, weeping with compassion for all their dead and dying comrades. 'Pitiless, you are,' he says to his friend. 'The horseman Peleus was never your father, nor Thetis your mother, but you were born of the grey sea and the high cliffs, so hard is the heart in you' (16.33–5). If Achilles will not fight, he adds, at least he should let Patroklos himself dress in his armour and lead out the Myrmidons into battle, so that the enemy will think it is Achilles and give way in fear. 'So he spoke, begging this in his

Achilles carefully bandages the wounded Patroklos.

great ignorance,' comments Homer, 'for this was his own death and sorrowful fate that he was asking for' (16.46–7).

The Trojans now succeed in firing one of the Greek ships, and Achilles gives in to his friend, saying that he never intended to be angry forever. He tells Patroklos to lead out the Myrmidons, and fight, and save the ships – but to be content with this. He must then come back to the camp and on no account advance against the walls of Troy.

So Patroklos dresses in Achilles' armour and harnesses his horses, the divine Xanthos and Balios (Chestnut and Dapple) and the mortal Pedasos (Pounder). Achilles pours a libation to

Zeus, praying that he will make his friend's heart brave within him to drive the Trojans from the ships; he also prays for Patroklos's safety (16.249–52):

> . . . and all-wise Zeus heard him. The father
> granted one prayer, but the other he refused: he allowed
> Patroklos to beat back war and tumult from the ships,
> but refused to let him come safely back from the fighting.

Patroklos leads out the Myrmidons, who stream from the camp eager to do battle (16.259–67):

> They came swarming out like wasps at the wayside
> when children are in the habit of making them angry,
> forever teasing them in their home by the roadside,
> as children will, and laying up harm for many.
> For if some passing traveller brushes, unknowing,
> against their nest, the wasps with valiant hearts
> all come flying out to defend their young.
> In spirit and fury like these the Myrmidons
> swarmed out from their ships, with ceaseless uproar.

The Trojans, seeing Patroklos, do indeed believe that he is Achilles, and fear fills their hearts. They retreat from the ships, and Patroklos kills many as he sweeps in his chariot across the Trojan plain. His supreme achievement is to attack and kill the mighty Sarpedon, leader of the Lycians and a son of Zeus. The two warriors meet: 'Like two hook-beaked, crook-clawed vultures fight, loud-screaming, above a rocky peak, so now these two, shouting aloud, rushed at each other' (16.428–30).

Zeus watches the battle. Already before this he has fended off death from his beloved son, Sarpedon, and now, knowing that he is destined to be killed by Patroklos, he pities him and wonders whether to save him yet again. Hera rebukes him bitterly, saying that he should not flout the laws of mortality.

and Zeus sorrowfully accepts his son's death. 'And he let fall to the ground a shower of bloody rain in honour of his dear son, whom Patroklos was about to kill on the rich earth of Troy, far from the land of his fathers' (16.459–61).

Their first two spear-casts miss their mark and kill instead Sarpedon's charioteer, Thrasymelos, and Achilles' mortal horse Pedasos, who has galloped long and courageously beside the immortal pair, Xanthos and Balios (16.463–9):

> Patroklos, throwing first, hit glorious Thrasymelos,
> the brave charioteer of lord Sarpedon, striking
> his lower belly and breaking the strength of his limbs.
> Sarpedon threw next and missed with his shining spear,
> but the spear struck the right shoulder of Pedasos
> the horse, who screamed and gasped out his life, falling
> into the dust with a moan, and his spirit fluttered from him.

Automedon, Patroklos's charioteer, quickly cuts the traces of the dead Pedasos; the chariot straightens and the two warriors meet again. Now Patroklos's second cast finds its mark, Sarpedon's heart (16.482–91):

> He fell, as when an oak tree falls, or a white poplar,
> or a tall pine, which carpenters in the mountains
> have hewn down with whetted axe to be a ship-timber.
> So he lay outstretched in front of his horses
> and chariot, roaring and clutching at the bloody dust.
> Like a proud and fiery bull that a lion kills
> when it comes amid a herd of shambling cattle,
> and he dies bellowing, brought down by the lion's jaws,
> so now before Patroklos the lord of the Lycian warriors
> died raging . . .

Now there follows a bloody battle over Sarpedon's body, with the Greeks striving to strip his armour, and the Trojans striving to stop them, until 'no longer could a man, even a shrewd one, have recognized godlike Sarpedon, for he was covered completely from head to toe with weapons and blood and dust, while men still thronged about his corpse' (16.638–41). At last the Greeks succeed in stripping his armour, and now Zeus intervenes, and gives instruction to Apollo (16.667–75):

> 'Go now, beloved Phoibos, and lift Sarpedon
> out of range of the missiles, and cleanse him
> of the dark blood, then carry him far away
> and wash him in a running river, and anoint him
> with ambrosia, and fold him in godlike clothing.
> Then give him to be carried by swift messengers,
> Sleep and his twin brother Death, who soon
> will lay him down in the rich broad land of Lycia,
> where brothers and kinsmen will give him burial
> with grave and stone, the final honour to the dead.'

Apollo does as Zeus bids. Sarpedon is lifted up by Hypnos (Sleep) and Thanatos (Death) and is carried away from the Trojan battlefield to honourable burial in Lycia.

If Patroklos had stopped there, he would have been safe. But now he disobeys Achilles' command and rages towards Troy, killing as he goes, and even attacks the walls of Troy itself (16.702–8):

> Three times Patroklos tried to mount the angle
> of the great wall, three times Apollo drove him back,
> pushing away his bright shield with immortal hands;
> but when for the fourth time Patroklos came on,
> like something more than human, the god cried out,
> threatening him with awesome words of command:
> 'Give way, lord Patroklos! It is not destined
> for this city of proud Trojans to fall to your spear.'

And Patroklos gives way. Hektor draws near, urged on by Apollo, and Patroklos kills his charioteer, Kebriones. The two warriors fight over his body (16.756–61):

> Like two lions who, on a high mountain,
> both of them hungry, and both of high courage,
> fight together over a dead deer, just so
> above Kebriones these two, urgent for battle,
> Patroklos, son of Menoitios, and glorious Hektor,
> were eager to tear each other with ruthless bronze.

Greeks and Trojans join in the battle, fighting with spears and arrows and stones around Kebriones, and all the while (16.775–6):

> . . . he lay in the whirling dust,
> a mighty man mightily brought down,
> his horsemanship all forgotten.

Now Patroklos attacks more Trojans. Three times he charges against them, screaming, and three times he cuts down nine men. When he charges for the fourth time, then Apollo comes against him once more. The god strikes the helmet from his head, splinters his great spear and tears away his shield and breastplate. Patroklos stands bewildered, until he is struck, first by a spear-throw from Euphorbos, and then mortally by a spear-thrust from Hektor (16.823–8):

> As a lion overpowers a tireless boar in combat,
> and the two fight in their pride on a high mountain
> over a tiny spring of water, both longing to drink,
> and the lion beats down the boar as he fights for breath,
> so did Hektor, son of Priam, with a close spear-thrust
> take the life of the mighty son of Menoitios,
> who had killed so many.

Dying, Patroklos prophesies that very soon Hektor will be killed by Achilles – that even now death and destiny are standing beside him (16.855–7):

> And even as he spoke the end of death enfolded him,
> and his soul fluttering from his body went down to Hades,
> mourning her fate, leaving youth and manhood behind.

Menelaos has seen Patroklos killed, and knows that his body must be protected if the Trojans are not to despoil it (17.1–8):

> The son of Atreus, warlike Menelaos,
> came through the ranks of fighters, helmeted
> in shining bronze, and bestrode the body. As over
> a first-born calf the mother cow stands lowing,
> she who has known no children before this,
> so over Patroklos stood fair-haired Menelaos,
> and held his spear and round shield in front of him,
> raging to kill any man who might come against him.

Euphorbos, who gave the first wound to Patroklos, challenges Menelaos, not only because he wants to carry off his victim's armour, but because it was Menelaos who killed his brother Hyperenor. Menelaos now kills Euphorbos too by stabbing him through the neck with his spear (17.50–60):

> He thudded to the ground, his armour clashing upon him,
> and his hair, lovely as the Graces, was wet with blood,
> those braided locks bound tight with silver and gold.
> Like some young olive tree that a man makes thrive
> in a lonely place, and gives it generous water,
> so it grows in beauty, and the breezes from all sides
> shake it, and it breaks into thick, pale blossom;
> but then a sudden wind coming in a great storm
> uproots it and lays its length on the ground, like this

was Panthoos' son, Euphorbos of the strong ash spear,
when Menelaos killed him and began to strip his armour.

Hektor approaches, 'his face like raging fire'. He drives Menelaos back from Patroklos's body and seizes the armour from the man he killed. He is just about to hack off his victim's head when the Great Ajax strides on the scene. It is now Hektor's turn to give way, and Ajax's to protect the naked corpse (17.132–7):

> Ajax covered Patroklos with his broad shield,
> standing fast like a lion defending his young,
> one who, in leading his little ones through the forest,
> comes upon huntsmen. He glares, fierce in his strength,
> and draws down his brows, hooding his eyes.
> Even so did Ajax protect the hero Patroklos.

Patroklos's body becomes the centre of a bloody battle: Hektor, who has by now put on the armour of Achilles that he took from his victim, urges his men on to drag the body away, while the Greeks, rallied by Ajax, strive to protect it. The fighting is prolonged; corpses pile on corpses. 'And the iron tumult went up through the barren air into the brazen heaven.' And outside the battle, the immortal Xanthos and Balios weep for the dead Patroklos (17.426–39):

> The horses of Achilles standing apart from the battle
> wept, since first they learned how their charioteer
> had fallen in the dust at the hands of man-slaying Hektor . . .
> They stayed as still as a gravestone set above
> the tomb of a dead man or woman, so they stood
> motionless, holding firm their lovely chariot,
> bowing their heads to the earth, and warm tears ran
> down from their eyes to the ground as they wept in longing
> for their charioteer, their rich manes soiled with dust.

Meanwhile Antilochos, the eldest son of old Nestor, brings the news of Patroklos's death to Achilles. Overwhelmed by grief and remorse, Achilles now realizes the price that he has paid for all his anger and pride. His mother Thetis hears his cries of anguish from the depths of the sea and comes with her sister Nereids to comfort him. She warns him that if he kills Hektor in revenge, then he too must die, because his death is fated to come soon after Hektor's. Achilles accepts this, since his great love for his friend demands that Patroklos be avenged, even at the cost of his own life (18.98–116):

> 'Then let me die directly, since I was not there
> to stand by my friend when he was killed. And now
> far from the land of his fathers he has died,
> without me there to keep him from destruction.
> Now, since I shall not go back to my native land,
> since I was no light of safety to Patroklos, nor
> to my other comrades killed by mighty Hektor
> in their numbers, but sit here beside my ships,
> a useless burden on the good earth . . .
> now I shall go, to find the killer of that dear life,
> Hektor. And I shall accept my own death
> whenever Zeus and the other immortal gods
> wish to bring it about.'

Achilles is now eager to fight again. His hurt pride is no longer an issue, for his anger against Agamemnon is as nothing compared to the greater rage that he now feels towards the Trojans in general, and Hektor in particular.

He stands in front of the Greek ships with flame blazing around his head, kindled by Athene. Three times he shouts a great war cry and the Trojans scatter in panic, giving the Greeks time enough to pull Patroklos's body safely off the battlefield. Yet despite Achilles' reappearance, Hektor is still full of confidence. He again bivouacs with his men on the plain – against the advice of the prudent Poulydamas, who urges that the Trojans withdraw into their city at once and stay there during the following day, where they can defend Troy from the walls while keeping their distance from the enemy. Poulydamas is the son of the Trojan elder Panthoos and was born on the same night as Hektor – and while Hektor is the better warrior, Poulydamas is the wiser man. Hektor will regret his impatient rejection of Poulydamas's wise counsel when Achilles comes back to the fighting and all too many Trojans are killed.

All night the Greeks mourn for Patroklos. Achilles swears that he will not bury his friend until he has brought Hektor's head and armour to the funeral, and twelve young Trojans to be killed before the funeral pyre. But he cannot fight yet for he has no armour – his old armour, borrowed by Patroklos, is now being worn by Hektor. So Thetis has splendid new armour made for her son by the smith-god, Hephaistos, the like of which has never been seen before. The shield in particular is a fantastically ornate work of art, made of gold and silver and bronze, and covered with countless intricate scenes of human lives in peace and war, all surrounded by the great river of Ocean that encircles the world.

At dawn Thetis brings the new armour to Achilles. His men are afraid to look straight at something so wondrous, but Achilles gazes hard at it, imagining the death of Hektor. His eyes blaze beneath his lids like flame. He then strides up and down the beach, calling the Greeks to an assembly. Here he formally announces the end of his anger against Agamemnon, and the king replies with an apology. All the gifts that he promised Achilles are duly presented, and Briseis is given back, untouched, to her rightful man. Now the Greeks can enter battle once more with their mightiest warrior at their head. They hurry to arm themselves (19.357–68):

As when thick snowflakes flutter from the sky,
cold beneath the blast of the north wind
born in the bright heaven, so now in their numbers
were carried out from the ships the helmets, gleaming
bright, the bossed shields, the plated corselets
and the ashen spears. The shining went up to heaven,
and all around the earth laughed with the flash of bronze,
while a thunder rose from beneath the feet of the men.
And in their midst Achilles armed himself to fight.
A gnashing came from his teeth, his eyes flashed
brilliant fire, and into his heart there came
unbearable grief. Raging at the Trojans he donned
the gifts of the god, wrought by Hephaistos' toil.

As Achilles rides out in his chariot, drawn by the immortal
Xanthos and Balios, he tells his horses to be sure to carry him
safely from the battlefield, not leave him there as they did
Patroklos. Xanthos is given by Hera the power of human speech
for a few brief moments, and he warns his master of his own
imminent death which the horses will be unable to prevent
(19.408–18):

'We shall keep you safe this time, mighty Achilles.
Yet the day of your death is near – not caused by us,
but by a great god and irresistible Fate . . .
We two run swift as the breath of the West Wind
which, men say, is swiftest of all; but for you
it is fated to die at the hands of a god and a mortal.'

The armies approach each other, and the Trojans go weak at
the knees when they see Achilles shining in all his armour. His
driving urge is to reach and kill Hektor, but he slaughters a
multitude of Trojans as he goes. One of those who die is Polydoros, another son of Priam, and at the sight of this Hektor

approaches, eager to avenge his brother. He knows full well that Achilles is the better man and likely to kill him. 'I know that you are brave,' he says, 'and that I am far weaker than you. But all this rests on the knees of the gods, and I may yet, even though I am weaker, rob you of life with a cast of my spear, since my weapon too has before now been found sharp' (20.434–7).

Hektor lets fly his spear, but Athene intervenes and it drops harmlessly to the ground. He is now at Achilles' mercy, but Apollo delays the fatal moment by shrouding Hektor in a thick mist. Achilles tries in vain to reach him before once again creating carnage among the Trojans (20.490–94):

> As inhuman fire rages through the deep glens
> of a dry mountain, and the forest burns to its depths,
> and the blustering wind drives on the flames
> in all directions, so Achilles swept everywhere
> with his spear like some god, harrying Trojans
> as they died, and the black earth ran with blood.

Many Trojans flee into the river Skamandros, and Achilles leaps in after them to continue his massacre. Here he encounters another son of Priam, Lykaon. Once before he captured Lykaon, and ransomed him. Now he catches him again, unarmed, but this time, with his fury against all Trojans blazing within him, there is no thought of ransom. Lykaon goes down on his knees, pleading for his life and clutching the spear that may kill him, but even as he does so he knows that his pleas are useless. 'This time death will come to me here,' he says, 'for I think there is no way I can escape your hands, now that a god has brought me to them.' Still he adds, 'Do not kill me, for I was not born of the same mother as Hektor, who killed your comrade gentle and brave' (21.92–6).

Achilles replies that he has changed since Patroklos was slain: 'Now there is no one who shall escape death if the gods send him into my hands in front of Troy, not one of all the Trojans, and least of all the sons of Priam' (21.103–5). Yet his killing of Lykaon is no mere brutal murder, for Achilles knows that he himself will die too, just as Lykaon now must die, and he is deeply aware of their shared humanity. 'Friend', he calls Lykaon, even as he kills him (21.106–19):

'So, friend, you die too. Why all this lamentation?
Patroklos also is dead, who was better by far than you.
Do you not see what kind of a man I am,
in beauty and stature, the son of a noble father,
and my mother a goddess? Yet even over me
hangs death and mighty fate. And there shall come
a dawn, or an evening, or a noonday, when some man
will take my life in the fighting, whether it be
with a cast of his spear or an arrow from his bow.'
So he spoke, and Lykaon's strength and spirit
collapsed. He let go of the spear and sat back,
both arms outspread, and Achilles, drawing
his sharp sword, struck his collar-bone by the neck,
and the two-edged sword sank full in. He dropped
to the ground, face down, and lay full length,
and out flowed his dark blood, soaking the earth.

Achilles flings Lykaon's body into the river Skamandros and carries on slaughtering the enemy. The river is now running red and is so congested with corpses that the angry river-god cries out in complaint (21.218–20):

'My lovely streams are crowded full with corpses,
and I cannot pour my waters out to the bright sea,
choked with the dead men you so ruthlessly kill.'

Achilles carries on attacking Trojans 'like something more than mortal', so Skamandros breaks his banks and rushes with mountainous waves to drown Achilles, who runs away before him (21.251–69):

> Achilles leapt away the length of a spearcast,
> with the swoop of a black eagle, the great hunter,
> who is the strongest and swiftest of all birds.
> Like this he sped away, and on his chest
> the bronze armour clashed terribly as he fled,
> slipping away from under the rush of the waters.
> But the river came surging after with a mighty roar . . .
> and every time swift-footed godlike Achilles
> would turn and try to fight the river . . . so often
> the great flood of the sky-fed river would strike
> his shoulders from above.

The river-god's rage swells even greater. He calls for help to his brother-river and tributary, Simoeis, and threatens Achilles with death (21.311–27):

> 'Come to my aid with all speed, fill your streams
> with water from your springs, stir up all your torrents,
> stand high in a great wave, and rouse a mighty roar
> of timbers and rocks, so we stop this savage man
> who in his strength is raging like the gods.
> I say that never will his strength avail him, nor
> his beauty, nor his lovely armour, which deep
> in my waters will lie covered over with mud,
> and him I shall wrap in sand, and on him shed
> great heaps of shingle past all measuring,
> nor will the Greeks know where to find his bones,
> so vast a shroud of silt shall I heap on him.
> Here shall be built his tomb – he will have no need
> of a funeral mound and the Greeks to bury him.'

> So he spoke, and rushed in tumult on Achilles,
> raging on high and seething with blood and foam
> and corpses. And the dark wave of the sky-fed river
> rose towering up to overpower Achilles.

Achilles is saved by the goddess Hera. She sends Hephaistos, god of fire, to scorch the turbulent river with flame and dry it up. Skamandros, his waters burning away, fearfully submits, giving up his pursuit and making a solemn vow to Hera (21.374–6):

> 'Never will I ward from the Trojans the day of evil,
> not even when all of Troy is burning with raging fire,
> and the Greeks are doing the burning.'

This will mean that when the Greeks finally enter Troy, and sack the city, and put it to the torch, Skamandros may not loose his lovely waters to save his descendants.

Achilles, free of the river, heads for Troy, and the Trojans flee ahead of him, desperately trying to reach the safety of their city. Now Agenor, the brave son of the Trojan elder Antenor, saves his comrades by stepping out to challenge Achilles. He knows that Achilles will probably kill him, but nevertheless he stands firm (21.573–80):

> Just as a leopard comes out of her deep thicket
> to face the man who is hunting her, and has no fear
> nor any thought of flight when she hears the baying
> of his hounds, and even though he is too quick for her
> and throws or strikes with his spear, yet even then,
> stuck through with the shaft, she does not lose her courage
> until she has fought or died; so noble Agenor
> refused to flee before he had fought Achilles.

Agenor throws his spear, striking Achilles on the leg, but without piercing his armour. He is now at Achilles' mercy, but he is saved by Apollo and spirited away before his opponent can let fly a more deadly cast. The god then disguises himself as Agenor and lures Achilles into giving chase. This allows the Trojans to escape safely into Troy – all except Hektor, who now waits alone outside the city for his own fatal confrontation with Achilles. His parents beg him to come inside the walls to safety, but he stands his ground, determined to atone for his folly in causing so many Trojan deaths, when he kept his men out too long on the plain.

Achilles approaches, brandishing his terrible spear, his armour blazing like a great fire or the shining sun, and the terrifying sight is too much for Hektor: he turns and flees, and Achilles pursues him. They run around Troy, past the two well-springs 'near which are fine broad washing-troughs made of stone, where the Trojans' wives and their lovely daughters used to wash their bright clothes, in the old days, when there was peace, before the coming of the Greeks' (22.152–6) – a pathetic reminder of a peace now forever lost, since Hektor is about to die, and without Hektor, the city's champion, Troy must fall, and the Trojan women be taken into slavery. On Olympos, Zeus weighs the fates of the two men in his golden scales, and Hektor's is the heavier, sinking down towards Hades.

Three times the two adversaries run around Troy, until Athene intervenes and tells Achilles to halt. She takes the form of Deiphobos, another of Priam's sons, and tricks Hektor into thinking that his brother has come to his aid. She urges him on to fight Achilles, saying that the two of them will stand fast against him side by side. So Hektor stops and faces his enemy. Achilles throws first, and misses. Now Hektor throws, but his spear bounces harmlessly back from his opponent's god-made shield. He calls to Deiphobos to hand him another spear – but there is no Deiphobos. Finding himself alone, Hektor all too late realizes the truth (22.297–301):

'So the gods have indeed summoned me to death.
I thought the hero Deiphobos was standing close beside me,
but he is inside the walls, and Athene was tricking me.
And now evil death is right at my side, no longer
far away, and there is no way out.'

'Now my fate is upon me,' he adds, 'but at least let me not die
without a struggle, ingloriously, but in doing some great deed
which men in the future will hear of' (22.303–5). He goes
bravely towards certain death (22.306–12):

He drew his sharp sword, huge and sturdy,
from by his side, and gathering himself he swooped
like a high-flying eagle, who darts to the plain
through the dark clouds to seize a tender lamb
or a cowering hare; even so Hektor swooped,
swinging his sharp sword, and Achilles rushed
at him, his heart within him full of savage wrath.

They meet, and Achilles drives a spear into Hektor's throat,
wounding him mortally. As he dies, Hektor begs that his body
be returned to Priam, but Achilles, still overcome with rage and
hatred, bitterly rejects his plea (22.345–54):

'Do not entreat me, you dog, by knees or parents.
I only wish that my wrath and fury might drive me
to hack your flesh away and eat it raw, for the evil
that you have done to me. So no one can ward off
the dogs from your head, not if they bring here
and set before me ten times and twenty times
the ransom, and promise even more; not if
Priam, son of Dardanos, should offer your weight
in gold; not even so shall your lady mother
lay you on the death-bed and mourn her son.
No, the dogs and birds shall utterly devour you.'

Just as the dying Patroklos prophesied Hektor's death at Achilles' hands, so now with his dying breath Hektor prophesies Achilles' own death at the hands of Paris and Apollo. Then the very same words are used for this death as for the death of Patroklos (22.361–3):

> And even as he spoke the end of death enfolded him,
> and his soul fluttering from his body went down to Hades,
> mourning her fate, leaving youth and manhood behind.

Achilles maltreats Hektor's body, piercing it at the ankles and fastening it with thongs to his chariot, then dragging it in the dust behind him. When the Trojans look down and see that their defender is dead, their cries of grief echo and re-echo through the city. 'It was as if the whole of towering Troy had been torched, and was burning top to bottom,' says Homer (22.410–11) – a true vision of what now must happen.

Andromache is indoors, and she does not at once realize that her husband is dead (22.440–72):

> She was weaving at her loom inside their high house
> a double cloak, crimson and covered with flowers.
> She called through the house to her lovely-haired maids
> to set on the fire a great cauldron, and heat warm water
> for Hektor, for when he came home out of the fighting,
> poor innocent, not knowing the time for baths had passed
> and he was dead, killed by Achilles and grey-eyed Athene.
> But now she heard mourning and wailing from the walls,
> her limbs shook and the shuttle fell from her hand . . .
> she ran from the house like a mad woman, her heart
> leaping in fear, and her maidservants ran with her.
> Then when she came to the tower and the crowd of men,
> she stood on the wall, staring, and saw her husband
> being dragged in front of the city, roughly dragged

by galloping horses towards the ships of the Greeks.
Black night covered her eyes and she fell backwards,
breathing out her life and throwing far away
her shining head-dress – the netted cap, the woven
head-band, and the veil once given to her
by golden Aphrodite, on that day when
shining-helmeted Hektor led her forth
from the house of Eetion . . .

All the people of Troy mourn the death of their champion. Meanwhile Achilles holds Patroklos's funeral. He slaughters twelve Trojan captives before the huge funeral pyre, just as he promised, then holds funeral games in honour of his friend, offering many rich prizes to the contestants. Yet even with Patroklos given full burial rites and Hektor dead, Achilles still burns with anger. For eleven days he carries on dragging his enemy's corpse in the dust behind his chariot, driving around Patroklos's tomb, though the gods pity Hektor and keep his body safe from harm, however much Achilles maltreats it. On the twelfth day they intervene and arrange for Hektor to be ransomed. Zeus sends Thetis to Achilles, to say that it is time for Hektor's body to be returned to his family for burial, and he sends Iris to Priam, to tell him to go to the Greek camp by night, taking gifts, and to beg for the return of his son.

Both men obey, and the *Iliad* ends with a supremely moving scene of pity and reconciliation between these two enemies. Priam bravely goes by night into the enemy camp, taking with him rich gifts in a wagon drawn by mules and driven by his herald, Idaios. The god Hermes, disguised as a handsome young Myrmidon, shows Priam the way to Achilles' tent. The old man goes in alone and finds Achilles there with two of his comrades (24.477–84):

Coming close to Achilles, he clasped his knees,
and kissed his hands, those terrible, murderous hands
that had killed so many of his sons . . .
and Achilles was seized with wonder at the sight
of godlike Priam, and the others wondered too.

Priam urges Achilles to remember his father, Peleus, who is now grown old like Priam himself and will soon be bereaved of his son. Then he speaks of his own pitiful fate (24.493–512):

'I have had the finest sons in far-spread Troy,
but I say that not one of them is left to me.
Fifty were my sons, the day the Greeks came here,
nineteen born to me from a single mother,
and the others born of women in my palace.
Raging Ares brought down dead most of them,
but one was left, who guarded my city and people,
him you killed just now defending his country,
Hektor. Because of him I come to the Greek ships,
to win him back from you, bringing untold ransom.
Honour the gods, Achilles, and have pity on me,
remembering your father. But I am yet more pitiable,
suffering what no other man on earth has suffered:
I have kissed the hands of the man who killed my son.'
So he spoke, and roused in Achilles a passion
of grief for his father. He took the old man's hand
and gently pushed him away. Then the two of them
remembered. Priam, huddled at Achilles' feet,
wept loud for man-slaying Hektor, and Achilles wept
for his own father, and now again for Patroklos,
and the house was filled with the sound of their grief.

At long last Achilles' anger is at an end, replaced by pity when he sees the anguish of the old man. They weep together, then he raises Priam to his feet and seats him on a chair. He accepts the ransom gifts and prepares Hektor's body for return to Troy with his father. Then the two so-called enemies, Greek and Trojan, share food together in peace, and sleep. When Priam wakes, he takes his son's body home. For eleven days there is a truce, agreed by Achilles, in which Hektor can be given the full honours of death. The *Iliad* ends with his funeral, the burial of a noble Trojan (24.784–804):

> For nine days they gathered piles of wood,
> but when the tenth dawn brought its light to men,
> they carried out brave Hektor, their tears falling,
> and set his body on a towering pyre, and lit it.
> When rosy-fingered dawn appeared next day,
> they all collected round glorious Hektor's pyre.
> And when they had assembled there together,
> they first with gleaming wine put out the burning,
> where fire still had strength, and then his friends
> and brothers gathered his white bones, mourning,
> tears pouring down cheeks. They took the bones
> and laid them in a golden urn, shrouding them
> in soft crimson robes, and straightway set it
> in a hollow grave, piling on huge stones
> laid close together. Quickly they heaped a mound,
> with look-outs set on every side, for fear
> the well-greaved Achaians might soon attack.
> Having piled the grave-mound they went back,
> and met together and held a glorious feast
> in the palace of Priam, the god-ordained king.
> Thus they buried Hektor, tamer of horses.

THE LAST MONTHS OF THE WAR

After the brilliant light shed by the *Iliad* over a few weeks in the tenth year of the war, the last few months leading to the fall of Troy seem hidden in relative obscurity. Once again events have to be pieced together from a variety of sources.

After the death of Hektor, the mainstay of Troy, it seemed that when the fighting resumed the city must fall into Greek hands, but now much-needed help came to the dispirited Trojans from some powerful allies, bringing them fresh hope and offering a genuine threat to the Greeks. First to arrive was an army of Amazons, led by Penthesileia, a daughter of the war-god Ares and the Amazon queen Otrere. She killed many Greeks before being herself killed by Achilles. The story goes that, even as Achilles delivered the fatal blow, their eyes met and he fell in love with her; or that he fell in love with her corpse after he had stripped it of its armour. Either way, the love came too late. He was jeered at by Thersites for his emotion, and some say that Thersites even gouged out the eyes of the dead Penthesileia with the point of his spear. Achilles struck him dead with a single blow.

In the *Iliad* Thersites is a man of low birth. According to Homer (*Iliad* 2.212–77) he was the ugliest man at Troy: he was lame, bandy-legged, hump-backed, and had a bald, pointed head. He was not popular, for when he abused Agamemnon (with some justification) for stealing Briseis from Achilles, Odysseus beat and threatened him until he collapsed in pain and fear, and all the army laughed at him. Later sources gave him a noble pedigree, making him a cousin of the warrior Diomedes; and it certainly seems that he was no commoner in the Epic Cycle's *Aithiopis*, for here his death at Achilles' hands led to a serious quarrel among the Greeks. As a result, Achilles had to go to Lesbos, where he sacrificed to Apollo, Artemis and Leto before he could be purified of the murder.

After Achilles' return to Troy, more Trojan allies arrived: a large army of Ethiopians, led by their king, Memnon. He was the son of Eos, goddess of Dawn, and the Trojan Tithonos, and thus the nephew of King Priam. Like his father, he was very beautiful; Odysseus once said that he was the handsomest man he had ever seen (*Odyssey* 11.522). Now he came to Troy, like Achilles the son of a goddess, and wearing, like Achilles, divine armour made by Hephaistos.

His people, the *Aithiopes* or 'Burnt-faces', were identified by Greek historians and geographers with the black Africans who lived to the south of Egypt, but the Ethiopians of mythology were thought to live near the sunrise at the ends of the earth, where their proximity to the burning Sun-god as he arose gave them their dark skins. Thus Memnon's kingdom was usually located in the east. Many ancient writers say that he came from Suza, the old capital of Persia, and from here he marched north-westwards to Troy, erecting as he went several great memorial pillars to mark his route. These, Herodotus tells us (2.106), caused him to be confused with Sesostris, a ruler of Egypt. In fact Memnon had other connections too with Egypt. This was not Memnon's only Egyptian connection. The 'Colossus of Memnon' was the name given to one of the two huge, seated statues at Thebes which mark the position of the now-vanished mortuary temple of Amenophis III (mid-second millenium BC). This colossus was famous in antiquity for giving out a resonant musical note when struck by the rays of the rising sun, as though Memnon were greeting the light of his mother, the Dawn. The Roman emperor Septimius Severus restoring the statue in AD 199, inadvertently silenced it forever.

Memnon's arrival put fresh heart into the Trojans, especially when he stormed into battle and killed many Greeks. One of his victims was Antilochos, the eldest son of Nestor. Paris shot one of Nestor's horses, and when the old man's chariot foundered,

Nestor cried out to his son to rescue him from Memnon, who was dangerously close. Antilochos, rushing to save his father, sacrificed his own life. Since the death of Patroklos, Antilochos had been Achilles' closest friend, and now Achilles, once again raging with grief and anger, came swiftly up to avenge him.

Achilles and Memnon fought a great duel while their two goddess-mothers, Thetis and Eos, each begged Zeus that her son might be the victor. This was a scene dramatized in a lost tragedy of Aeschylus, the *Psychostasia*, where Zeus weighed the souls (*psychai*) of the two heroes to decide who should die, while Eos and Thetis, one each side of the scales of Zeus, pleaded for the lives of their sons. Though this might sound like a particularly dramatic Aeschylean invention, it cannot be so, for the scene occurs on vase-paintings from about 540 BC. Memnon's soul was the heavier, sinking towards Hades, and so at the end of a hard-fought duel it was Achilles who triumphed and Memnon who died.

Eos, grief-stricken, carried Memnon's body from the battlefield and asked Zeus to show her son some special honour. In the *Aithiopis*, Zeus made him immortal, but a later story said that he changed the smoke from Memnon's funeral pyre into birds which circled the pyre and then, separating into two groups, fought and killed each other, falling into the flames as offerings to the hero's soul. Ever afterwards fresh flocks of birds, called *Memnonides*, came once a year to Memnon's tomb, and fought again and died again in his honour. It was also said that the morning dew is formed from the tears shed by the still inconsolable Eos in grief for her dead son.

Memnon was probably Achilles' most formidable opponent of all, so his defeat was his greatest triumph – but it was followed almost immediately by Achilles' own death, when he routed the now despairing Trojans and rushed after them into Troy. Sadly, no early account of exactly what happened exists. We know

A mourning Eos carries the dead Memnon.

from Hektor's dying prediction in the *Iliad* that he would be killed 'by Paris and Apollo in the Skaian Gate', one of the gates of Troy (22.359–60). It seems likely that as Achilles stormed triumphantly through the gate, Paris shot an arrow at him and Apollo guided it to the fatal spot.

So Thetis too lost her son. For all that she is a goddess, the *Iliad* portrays her like any grieving, human mother, when she knows full well that Achilles is doomed soon to die. 'I gave birth to a son peerless and brave,' she says (18.55–60), 'one pre-eminent among men. He shot up like a young plant, and I nurtured him, like a tree grown in a rich orchard. Then I sent him away with the curved ships, to fight the Trojans in the land of Ilion. And never again shall I welcome him, come back home again to the house of Peleus.' Another unforgettable cry of grief comes from Thetis in a fragment of Aeschylus (350) from an unknown play, where she tells how, at her wedding to Peleus, Apollo prophesied falsely that her son would have a long and happy life – Apollo, the very god who would bring about Achilles' death:

> He sang that I would be blest with a son
> who would live a long life, knowing no sorrow.
> He said all this, singing a paean in praise
> of my great good fortune, cheering my heart.
> And I believed the words of Apollo were true,
> rich as he is in holy, prophetic skill.
> But he who sang of this,
> he who was there at the feast,
> he who said these things –
> he it was who killed my son.

After Achilles' death, there was a bloody struggle for his body and divine armour, but at last the Great Ajax hoisted the corpse on to his shoulders and carried it back to the Greek ships, while Odysseus fought off the Trojans from the rear. Homer's *Odyssey* (24.15–94) describes Achilles' funeral rites. At his death, his mother came with her Nereids out of the sea and for seventeen days mourned his loss, along with the nine Muses and the whole Greek army, all weeping. On the eighteenth day they lit his funeral pyre. At dawn on the following day his bones were gathered up and laid alongside those of Patroklos in a golden urn, made by Hephaistos and given to Thetis by Dionysos. The remains of the two friends were laid to rest with those of Antilochos, and a grave mound was heaped high over them on a jutting headland there by the Hellespont, ever afterwards a landmark for sailors.

According to Homer, Achilles went down to live a shadowy existence after death in Hades: in the *Odyssey*, Odysseus met his shade there, in company with Patroklos, Antilochos and the Great Ajax (p. 110). In the *Aithiopis*, Thetis snatched his body away from his funeral pyre and carried it to Leuke (the White Island), later identified with an island in the Black Sea at the mouth of the Danube. Achilles was said to live a blissful afterlife there with Patroklos and other heroes, all immortalized.

After Achilles' funeral, the Greeks held splendid games in his honour, with prizes donated by the gods. His divine armour was offered as a reward for the bravest warrior, and both the Great Ajax and Odysseus laid claim to it. In the epic versions, the question of who most deserved the award seems to have been settled by the Trojans: either Trojan prisoners were asked for their verdict, or Trojan women were overheard talking on the walls of Troy. In later tragedy, a vote was held among the Greek warriors.

The outcome was always the same: Odysseus was awarded the arms, to the rage and disbelief of Ajax, who was convinced that they should have been his. As indeed they should have been – or so it seems from the depiction of the brave and steadfast Ajax in the literature left to us. And even Odysseus himself, when he met the shade of Ajax in Hades, admitted that Ajax surpassed all the Greeks except for Achilles. Odysseus begged Ajax to forget his bitterness over the award of Achilles' arms, but Ajax refused to speak, and stalked away in haughty silence: 'He made no answer, but went off after the other ghosts of the perished dead, into the darkness' (*Odyssey* 11.563–4).

After Odysseus won Achilles' arms, Ajax resolved to avenge this slight to his honour by killing the Greek leaders, but Athene deranged his mind, and instead of killing men he slaughtered the flocks that were kept to feed the army. When his madness left him and he realized what he had done, full of shame and despair he fell on his sword.

As with the death of Achilles, there are all too few details of Ajax's suicide in early literature, but luckily we have Sophocles' later tragedy *Ajax* extant, dramatizing the last day of Ajax's life. When the play opens, Ajax has already killed the animals, and we see him both maddened by Athene and triumphantly believing that he has slain his enemies, and then sunk into despair when he wakes to sanity and reality. Surrounded by bloody carcasses, he cries in anguish (364–76):

> 'Do you see me, the bold, the valiant,
> the one who was fearless in deadly war,
> and now formidable to tame and trusting beasts?
> What mockery! What shame! . . .
> I let my enemies go, and fell
> on horned cattle and splendid flocks
> of goats, shedding their dark blood.'

The only course left is to kill himself: 'Honour in life or honour in death is the only choice for a man of any nobility,' he says (479–80). And because there is now no more chance of honour in life, then he must die. His concubine, Tekmessa, the mother of his little son Eurysakes, begs him not to kill himself, but his heart is resolute, even though he seems to say that he will learn to live with what fate has dealt him (669–77):

> 'Even harsh and mightiest strengths give way.
> Snow-packed winter yields to fruitful summer.
> The vault of endless night at last gives place
> to dawn's white horses kindling radiant light.
> The dread winds' breath slackens and lulls to rest
> the sounding sea. Even all-powerful sleep
> in time must loose his captive. Must not I,
> then, likewise learn to yield?'

Ajax resolutely prepares for death.

Yet Ajax, when he is alone, still cursing his enemies, makes his last prayers to the gods and falls on the very sword given him by Hektor after their duel – a reminder, in a death brought about by shame and dishonour, that he was once a great hero.

Tekmessa discovers his body. She covers it with her cloak, crying out (915–19):

> 'He must not be seen, so I shall cover him
> completely, with this enfolding cloak,
> since no one, loving him, could ever bear
> to see him with the black blood spurting up
> to his nostrils, out of the murderous wound
> he dealt with his own hand . . .'

Then Ajax's half-brother, Teukros, arrives, coming just too late on the scene to prevent the tragedy (992-1001):

> 'Of all the sights I have ever seen
> this to my eyes is the saddest one;

and of all the roads I ever walked,

this one has brought my heart most pain,

this one I walked to you,

my dearest Ajax, when I heard

your fate, and came to seek its truth . . .

I heard it from a long way off

and groaned beneath a weight of grief,

but, now that I have seen, I want to die.'

But he performs an invaluable service for his dead brother. Menelaos and Agamemnon want to throw Ajax's corpse out to be eaten by the dogs and birds, but Teukros is determined that he shall be honourably buried. He defends the body, until Odysseus steps in and persuades Agamemnon that it is not right to harm 'the bravest man, except Achilles, of all that came to Troy' (1340–41). The play ends with Ajax's body ceremoniously carried out for burial with full honours.

With the two greatest Greek warriors dead, it is Odysseus, with his talent for strategy, who now moves to the forefront of the action. It was largely thanks to his endeavours that Troy was finally taken.

First he captured the Trojan seer Helenos and forced him to prophesy the conditions necessary for the Greeks to take Troy. Helenos revealed that they must have fighting for them both Philoktetes, the possessor of the great bow and inescapable arrows of Herakles, and Neoptolemos, the son of Achilles; and they must capture the Palladion, the ancient image of Athene that was Troy's protective talisman.

Accordingly, Odysseus sailed to Skyros to fetch Neoptolemos from the court of Lykomedes, where he had been brought up. He came willingly to fight with the Greeks at Troy, and Odysseus presented him with the divine armour which had belonged to his dead father, and which had caused so much dissension between himself and Ajax.

Odysseus also sailed to Lemnos, where the wounded Philoktetes had been marooned for the previous ten years. During those years he had lived in a lonely cave, keeping himself alive by shooting wild birds and animals with his great bow, and all that time nursing his hatred for the Greeks – and most of all for Odysseus, who had been the one to suggest that he be left behind. In some versions, Diomedes accompanied Odysseus, though in Sophocles' extant tragedy, *Philoktetes*, his companion is Neoptolemos.

Sophocles depicts Lemnos as completely uninhabited, emphasizing Philoktetes' long isolation. His old wound is still an agony and his hatred undiminished, so not unnaturally he is loath to help the army that abandoned him, but the unscrupulous Odysseus is prepared to go to any lengths of trickery, or even brute force, to carry him off to Troy. At first Neoptolemos too is willing to trick Philoktetes, but then he is swayed by his own basic honesty, and by his respect and compassion for the wounded man, and he promises instead to take him home to Greece. It is only the appearance of Herakles at the end of the play as deus ex machina that puts events back on course. He orders both Neoptolemos and Philoktetes to Troy.

Once there, Philoktetes had his terrible wound cured by Machaon, the healer son of Asklepios, and he was then happy to enter battle. He shot Paris with his great bow, and Menelaos mutilated the corpse, no doubt driven by all the jealousy and rage that had burned in him for ten years, but the Trojans recovered the body and Paris had his burial. With Paris dead, Helen married Deiphobos, another son of Priam.

Now the last major ally came to help the Trojans: Eurypylos, son of Telephos, leading an army from Mysia, where the Greeks had landed when they first came seeking Troy. Eurypylos was another nephew of Priam, for his mother, Astyoche, was Priam's sister. She had until now refused to let her son go to war, but Priam had at last overcome her scruples with the gift of a golden vine, the very one that had been made by Hephaistos, and given by Zeus to Tros, in recompense for the loss of Ganymede. So Eurypylos led his Mysian force to Troy, and there he fought valiantly, killing many Greeks including the healer Machaon and the Boiotian leader Penelaos. Finally he was himself killed by Neoptolemos, whose heroic prowess on the battlefield proved him a worthy successor to his father.

The disheartened Trojans were now once more penned within Troy, and it seemed to the Greeks that the fall of the city could not be far away. The Palladion had still to be captured from Athene's temple, so Odysseus and Diomedes set off to steal it. There are several versions of how they did so: either Odysseus left Diomedes on guard while he went to the temple alone, disguised as a beggar in rags. There he encountered Helen, who recognized him and helped him to steal the sacred statue, and with Diomedes' aid he carried it back to the Greek camp. Or Diomedes stood on Odysseus' shoulders to climb over the city walls, but he then refused to pull up his companion after him and so he alone won the glory of the deed accomplished. Or the two of them went into the city through a sewer and together brought out the Palladion. Whatever the method, the result was the same: Troy's protective talisman was gone, and the city was ready to be taken if only the Greeks could gain entry. It was the ever-ingenious Odysseus who came up with surely the most famous of all wartime stratagems: the Wooden Horse.

THE WOODEN HORSE

From timber on Mount Ida the Greeks built a huge image of a horse and inscribed it with the words: 'For their return home, the Greeks dedicate this thank-offering to Athene.' They then sailed ostentatiously away, leaving the horse outside the gates of Troy, its hollow belly secretly filled with armed warriors under the command of Odysseus (Plate 9). The Trojans dragged the horse inside the city, then feasted joyfully because the Greeks had left, and the long war was over, and Troy was safe. The warriors inside the horse waited for dead of night, then left their hiding place and opened the city gates to their comrades, who had unobtrusively returned. Carnage followed. The Trojans were asleep and unsuspecting when the Greeks attacked them, and were easy prey for men who had fought ten years for this moment. The city, in Greek hands at long last, was savagely sacked. It is ironic that the horse-loving, 'horse-taming' Trojans finally had their defences breached and their city destroyed because of the effigy of a horse.

Greek accounts of the Wooden Horse are surprisingly sparse. Homer mentions it in the *Odyssey* – though not in the *Iliad*, where the man who was credited with the building of it, Epeios, is simply a champion boxer (who prefaces his fight at the funeral games for Patroklos with a familiar kind of boasting: 'I'm the greatest! . . . I tell you this, and I'll do it too: I'll smash his skin open and break his bones, and his friends had better stay around to carry him off after I've murdered him'). It is in the *Odyssey* (8.492–520) that we hear (in brief) the famous story of how the Greeks set fire to their camp and sailed away, while Odysseus and other warriors stayed in the horse. The Trojans dragged it as far as their acropolis, then argued as to whether they should break it open, or throw it down from a high place, or leave it as an offering to placate the gods. The last view prevailed, and by night the Greeks streamed out and the city was sacked.

The story was apparently told in much the same way in the Epic Cycle's *Little Iliad* and *Sack of Troy*. Homer adds another rather odd detail: when the horse was brought into Troy, Helen walked around it, calling to the Greek leaders in perfect imitation of the voices of their wives, and it was only the quick thinking of Odysseus that prevented the men from answering, and the whole plan from coming to nothing (*Odyssey* 4.271–89). It is Menelaos who recounts this tale, explaining that his wife's capricious behaviour was no doubt inspired by some god favourable to the Trojans.

Our most detailed account of the Wooden Horse is given us by the Roman poet Virgil in his *Aeneid* (2.13–267), where Aeneas dramatically describes the sack of Troy. The Greeks sail only as far as Tenedos, but the Trojans fully believe that they have gone home and come out of their city rejoicing. They find the immense wooden horse, 'as big as a mountain', and debate what they should do with it. The priest of Apollo, Laokoon, tries to stop them from dragging it into the city. He realizes that it is some kind of ruse, summing up his suspicions with the famous words '*Timeo Danaos et dona ferentis*', 'I fear the Greeks, even when they bring gifts' (2.49). He casts his great spear into the horse's side to show that it is hollow, and the image booms and echoes.

At that moment the Greek Sinon comes on the scene as part of the Greek plan. He has allowed himself to be captured by the Trojans, and he now wins their confidence by pretending to be a deserter who has good reason to hate his fellow Greeks. He persuades the Trojans that the horse is a genuine offering to Athene, and its huge size is to prevent its being taken into Troy, where it would bring the goddess's favour to the city and make Troy impregnable. The trap is laid and the Trojans fall into it. Their belief in Sinon's words is strengthened even more when they see what happens next to Laokoon and his two sons. He is sacrificing a huge bull to Poseidon, when suddenly:

There came over the calm water from Tenedos two snakes, forging through the sea in great coils and making side by side for the shore. They breasted the waves, their blood-red crests towering high, and the rest of their bodies drove through the water behind, their backs wreathing mighty spirals through the sounding foam of the sea. And now they were on land. Their eyes were blazing and bloodshot, and they hissed as they licked their lips with darting tongues . . . They made straight for Laokoon, and first the snakes twined round the bodies of his two young sons, devouring their poor little limbs. Next, when Laokoon grabbed his sword and hastened to the rescue, they seized him and bound him in their huge and scaly coils, twice round his middle, twice round his throat, their heads and necks towering over him. He struggled frantically to wrench open the knots, his priestly bands drenched with filth and black venom, and his terrible cries rose to the sky, like the bellowing of a wounded bull that flees from the altar, shaking from its neck the axe that has struck awry. (2.203–24)

The Trojans believe that this is Laokoon's punishment for casting his spear at the goddess's offering, so now, full of confidence and rejoicing, they breach their walls and take the horse into the heart of their city. Kassandra warns them that this means disaster, but they ignore her, for she is fated always to be disbelieved. The people of Troy spend their last, doomed day decking the shrines of the gods with garlands of thanksgiving. At night, when they are sleeping soundly and contentedly, Sinon opens the horse to release the warriors within. They kill the guards and throw wide the city gates, letting in the rest of the Greeks who have meanwhile sailed quietly back to Troy. The city is, as always, bloodily sacked.

THE SACK OF TROY

The Greeks massacred the Trojan men, and took the women and children as slaves, and put the city to the torch. The only men left alive were Helenos, who had helped the Greeks with his predictions, the elder Antenor and his sons, because he had saved the lives of Menelaos and Odysseus at the start of the war, and Aeneas, who managed to escape with his old father Anchises and little son Askanios.

There are no full accounts of the sack of Troy in early literature, but here the *Iliad* helps, for although it ends with the burial of Hektor, some time before the fall of the city, it contains several predictions of what horrors will come if Troy is taken. One of these is put into the mouth of old Priam, when he tries to persuade Hektor not to risk his life – and his city – by fighting Achilles, but to come to safety inside the walls (22.56–76):

> 'Come inside the walls, my son, that you may save
> the Trojan men and women, nor give great glory
> to Peleus' son and yourself be robbed of your own life.
> And pity me, helpless, still alive, ill-starred,
> whom the father, Kronos' son, will bring to death
> on the threshold of old age by a grievous fate,
> when I have seen many evils, my sons destroyed
> and my daughters carried off captive, rooms laid waste,
> and little children dashed to the ground in the horror
> that is war, and the wives of my sons dragged off
> by the accursed hands of the Greeks. And myself
> last of all, ravening dogs will tear me at my gateway,
> when some man by thrust or throw of the sharp bronze
> has torn the life from my body – dogs that in my halls
> I reared at my table to guard my doors, maddened now
> will drink my blood and then lie down in my courts.

All is seemly when a young man is slain in battle
and torn with the sharp bronze, and he lies there dead,
and, though dead, everything about him is noble.
But when an old man is killed, and the dogs disfigure
the grey head and the grey beard and the parts
that are private, this, for all sad humanity,
is the fate most pitiful.'

Now, with the Greeks inside Troy, Priam's predictions became reality. He himself took refuge on the altar of Zeus in his courtyard and was butchered there by the young Neoptolemos. In archaic and classical art, where the sack of Troy was a popular subject, Priam's death on the altar becomes the focus of the horrors inflicted on the Trojans by the Greeks. And his death is linked again and again with that of Hektor's son Astyanax, where Neoptolemos attacks the old king while swinging the body of the child like a club – though this is not how the little boy died.

It is Andromache who foretells what the future holds for her little son, as she laments over Hektor's body (24.725–37):

'My husband, you died young and left me a widow
in your house, and the child is only a baby
who was born to you and me, ill-fated. I think
he will never grow up, for before then this city
will be sacked top to bottom, for you, its defender,
are dead, you who protected the city and kept
the women and little children safe from harm,
women who soon will go in the hollow ships,
and I along with them. And you, my child,
must follow me, and there do shameful work,
toiling for a hard master. Or else some Greek
will take you by the arm and hurl you from the tower
to painful death, angry that Hektor once killed
his brother, or his father, or his son.'

Andromache was right, though it was death, not slavery, that came to the little boy: just as she foresaw, he was flung down from the walls of Troy. We know that his killer in the *Little Iliad* was Neoptolemos, and in the *Sack of Troy* Odysseus. Yet these references in the fragments of the Epic Cycle are all too brief, and for a full and moving depiction of the child's death we must turn to Euripides' tragedy *Trojan Women*. Here it is Odysseus who urges that Astyanax must be killed: he cannot be left alive to avenge in years to come his father's death and the destruction of his city. The news that he must die is brought to Andromache, who grieves for her little son's fate (749–60):

> 'Child, you cry. Do you know your death is coming?
> Why do your little hands clutch and cling to my gown,
> like a young bird come to nestle under my wings?
> And Hektor will not come. He will not come,
> great spear in hand, back from the earth to save you,
> nor will his kinsmen, nor all the power of Troy.
> A deathly fall from the walls will break your neck
> and choke your breath, with none to pity you.
> Little one, here in my arms, your mother's darling,
> how sweet the smell of your skin! All for nothing
> this breast nursed you, you in your baby shawls,
> all for nothing now my toil, my weary labour . . .'

She herself can do nothing to protect her son, for she is carried off to be the concubine of Neoptolemos. Astyanax is killed, flung from the walls of Troy, then carried on his father's great shield to his grandmother, Hecuba. She in turn laments his fate, mourning over his broken body (1173–93):

> 'Poor little head, how cruelly your father's walls,
> the towers built by Apollo, have rent the curls
> that once your mother so often tended and kissed,

and now your blood grins out from the broken bones . . .
What could a poet write of you on your grave?
This child the Greeks once killed because they feared him?
Words to bring everlasting shame on Greece.
Now you have lost all that your father had,
but one thing you shall keep, his shield of bronze
in which to sleep . . .'

And Astyanax is dressed and carried out for burial, with Hektor's shield for his coffin.

Polyxena, daughter of Priam and Hecuba, was also killed: the *Kypria* said that she was mortally wounded at the fall of Troy by Diomedes and Odysseus, then buried by Neoptolemos, but the *Sack of Troy* told the more familiar version of her death – that she was sacrificed at Achilles' grave. Neoptolemos – appropriately, as Achilles' son – was her killer.

Her death is poignantly described in Euripides' tragedy *Hecuba*, where the ghost of the dead Achilles has stilled the winds to stop the Greek fleet sailing home, and he himself is demanding the girl's sacrifice. In later times, he was said to have fallen in love with Polyxena while she was still alive – perhaps when he saw her drawing water at the fountain where he ambushed Troilos, or when she came with Priam to ransom Hektor's body. In Euripides, he simply wants his share of the booty. Once Polyxena discovers that her sacrifice is inescapable, she goes to her death willingly and courageously. The herald Talthybios reports her dying words, addressed first to the Greeks and then to Neoptolemos (547–68):

'Listen, you Greeks who sacked my city: I die willingly.
Let no one touch me, for I give my throat with gladness.
Let me go freely to my death, I beg you by the gods,
so I die free: born of royal blood, I shame to be called
a slave among the dead.' The crowd shouted assent,

and Agamemnon told the guards to loose the girl.
Hearing these words of authority, she seized her robe
and tore it open wide from shoulder to navel, showing
her breasts as lovely as a statue's. Then dropping
to her knees upon the earth, she spoke these brave
and pitiful words: 'Look, here, young man, if you
would strike my breast, strike here. But if you want my neck,
here is my throat, here and ready.' Then he, willing
and yet unwilling in pity for the girl, cut her breath-pipe
with the iron sword, and streams of blood flowed down.

Helen too came near to death, but escaped at the last minute. As soon as Menelaos got into Troy, he hurried to the house of Deiphobos, Helen's new husband. In a jealous rage, he murdered him and mutilated his body, then went in search of Helen herself. He was about to kill her too because of her long infidelity, but when he saw the beauty of her naked breasts once more, his drawn sword fell from his hand. Ancient vase-paintings capture this very moment, his sword mid-way to earth. He willingly forgave Helen and took her home again to Sparta.

In Stesichorus's *Sack of Troy* (fr. 201), the Greeks in general had a similar reaction when they came to punish her for causing such a long and bloody war. They were on the point of stoning her to death when they saw her lovely face, and their stones dropped to the ground. Always her beauty had this effect. The old men on the walls of Troy, seeing her approach, had said, 'No one could blame the Trojans and the well-greaved Achaians if, for so long a time, they suffer pain and hardship over a woman like this. She looks terribly like the immortal goddesses' (*Iliad* 3.156–8). And ever since, Helen has been seen as the quintessential symbol of female beauty and sexual attraction, lovely enough to die for. 'Was this the face that launch'd a thousand ships, / And burnt the topless towers of Ilium?' asks Faustus (in Marlowe's

Doctor Faustus); and Shakespeare's Troilus remarks, on hearing the din of battle, 'Helen must needs be fair, / When with your blood you daily paint her thus' (I. i. 89–90).

Andromache, as we have seen, became the concubine of Neoptolemos. Hecuba was awarded as war-prize to Odysseus, the man she hated above all others, though she did not have to endure him long, for she died fairly soon after the fall of Troy (p. 453). Her name, like that of her husband Priam, would become a symbol for someone who suffers the mutability of fortune, as in a well-known verse from the *Carmina Burana*:

> The king sits at the top,
> Let him beware of a fall;
> For beneath the wheel we read
> 'This is Queen Hecuba.'

Hecuba's sorrows are also the subject of the First Player's impassioned speech in *Hamlet*, which provokes Hamlet's haunting retort (II. ii. 552–3):

> What's Hecuba to him or he to Hecuba
> That he should weep for her?

Kassandra was awarded to Agamemnon – but not before she had been raped by the Lesser Ajax. While the Greeks were killing and looting, she took refuge at a statue of Athene, but Ajax dragged her away and raped her, while the statue turned away its eyes in horror. In due course Athene would exact a terrible revenge for this sacrilege, by wrecking the Greek ships on their journey back to Greece in a fearsome storm off Cape Kaphereus. Out of many, only few would return home.

All of the deaths, Greek and Trojan, go back to the elopement of Helen with Paris, and ultimately to the visitation of Zeus to Leda in the form of a swan. This has been a powerful image down the ages, and perhaps it is W. B. Yeats, in his *Leda and*

Kassandra clasps Athene's statue as Ajax comes to rape her.

the Swan, who captures most memorably, in a few words, the
significance of this union between mortal and god:

> A sudden blow: the great wings beating still
> Above the staggering girl, her thighs caressed
> By the dark webs, her nape caught in his bill,
> He holds her helpless breast upon his breast.
>
> How can those terrified vague fingers push
> The feathered glory from her loosening thighs?
> And how can body, laid in that white rush,
> But feel the strange heart beating where it lies?

A shudder in the loins engenders there
The broken wall, the burning roof and tower
And Agamemnon dead.

                     Being so caught up,
So mastered by the brute blood of the air,
Did she put on his knowledge with his power
Before the indifferent beak could let her drop?

The return of the Greeks from Troy

When the Greeks were ready to sail home once more, the goddess Athene stirred up a quarrel between the brothers Menelaos and Agamemnon. Menelaos was all for returning home at once, but Agamemnon wanted to delay until they had placated Athene with splendid sacrifices. 'Poor fool,' comments Homer, 'not realizing that he would not prevail on her, for the mind of the everlasting gods is not quickly changed' (*Odyssey* 3.146–7). The brothers could not agree, nor could their comrades, so Menelaos sailed away with half the fleet, leaving the rest behind with Agamemnon.

Menelaos and those with him stopped off at the island of Tenedos to offer sacrifices for their safe return, and here there was another quarrel, with the result that many ships, including those led by Odysseus, headed back towards Troy for a second attempt at setting sail. The rest carried on. Old Nestor returned safely to Pylos – in the *Odyssey* (Book 3) we see him in his palace once more, entertaining Odysseus' son Telemachos who has come to seek news of his father. Diomedes too returned safely home to Argos, though it was said that he later settled in southern Italy. Menelaos was separated from the others when he stopped to bury his dead steersman, Phrontis, and when he resumed his journey he was struck by a violent storm off Cape Maleia, at the south-eastern tip of the Peloponnese. Many ships were wrecked, and Menelaos himself, with five surviving ships, was driven all the way to Egypt.

Menelaos, and Helen with him, stayed in that region for eight years, gathering many rich treasures, but at last they were ready to return home to Sparta. Now, however, they were becalmed for twenty days on the island of Pharos off the Nile delta. The sea-nymph Eidothea, daughter of Proteus, the Old Man of the Sea, took pity on them, and told Menelaos how to approach her father, who would advise him on how to get home (*Odyssey* 4.400–424):

'When the sun has climbed up to bestride the middle of the sky
the trusty Old Man of the Sea comes out of the water,
under the west wind blowing, with the dark sea rippling over him.
And when he comes out he sleeps, under the hollow caves,
and around him the seals, children of the fair sea's surge,
sleep all together, rising up out of the grey salt water
and shedding the sharp smell of the deep salt sea . . .
First he will go among his seals and count them,
but when he has seen them and finished counting their number
he will lie down in their midst like a shepherd among his sheep.
As soon as you see him asleep, then is the moment
for all your courage and strength: you must hold him there
all the time he frenziedly struggles, trying to escape.
He will try your strength by changing to all kinds of shapes,
all things that move on the earth, and water, and furious fire,
while you must hold him fast and squeeze him the harder.
But then when he questions you, looking the same
as when you saw him sleeping, then you must stay
your strength, hero, and set the Old Man free,
and ask him which of the gods makes life so hard for you,
and how to make your way home over the fishy deeps.'

The next day Eidothea helped Menelaos and three of his companions to lie in wait for Proteus. She hollowed out four beds in the sand for them, then covered them with sealskins, putting ambrosia beneath their noses to counteract the vile stench. In this way they were able to take Proteus by surprise and seize him, just as Eidothea had advised. He changed himself into a great maned lion, a snake, a panther, a massive boar, then running water and a towering tree. But they kept firm hold of him, and at last he yielded and gave Menelaos the advice he needed. Menelaos and Helen finally sailed home again to Sparta.

Mention should be made at this point of a quite different story about Helen and the Trojan War, which also (in the hands of Euripides) involves Proteus – though here he appears as a benevolent king of Egypt, with a palace on Pharos, instead of a seal-herding sea-god. This version of the myth, apparently invented by Stesichorus, made Helen entirely innocent of causing the Trojan War. Stesichorus, so the story goes, was blinded after telling in one of his lyric poems the usual tale of Helen's infidelity and flight. Realizing that Helen's anger was the cause of his blindness, he composed a poem of recantation (a Palinode) beginning, 'That story is not true. You did not sail in the well-benched ships, nor did you come to the citadel of Troy', and claiming that it was merely a phantom resembling Helen who ran off with Paris. As soon as the poem was complete, Stesichorus regained his sight.

Unfortunately only the slightest fragments of this poem are left to us, but we do have an entire play by Euripides on this very theme, his *Helen*. Here the phantom was the work of Hera, angry because she had been passed over in the Judgement of Paris. Paris was completely taken in by the phantom Helen and carried her off to Troy, whereupon the Trojan War took place as usual. Meanwhile the real and virtuous Helen was taken by

Hermes to Egypt, where she was left in the guardianship of the kindly Proteus. Here she lived for the duration of the war, and for ten long years many men died quite needlessly.

When the play opens, the war is over, Proteus is dead, and his son Theoklymenos, the new king, is trying to force Helen to marry him. Menelaos arrives on his journey home from the war, and is understandably bewildered at meeting a second Helen. Eventually matters are straightened out, the phantom disappears, and husband and wife are happily reunited after their long years apart. By some clever plotting they succeed in escaping from the persecutions of the cruel Theoklymenos, and at the end of the play they sail joyfully away together.

But whether Helen did or did not go with Paris to Troy, the end of her story is the same: reunion with Menelaos and return to her home in Sparta. Here we see her in the *Odyssey* (Book 4), every inch the good housewife and hostess when Telemachos comes seeking news of Odysseus. She spins, she eases her guests' sorrows with some wonder-working drugs that she brought from Egypt and now puts into their wine, she entertains them with stories, and she gives Telemachos as a parting gift a beautiful robe for his bride to wear on their wedding-day. She seems full of contentment to be home again, and at her first husband's side once more, and Menelaos seems pleased and proud to have her there.

Perhaps Rupert Brooke's wry and cynical view of Helen's later years might be truer to human reality (*Menelaus and Helen*):

> . . . So far the poet. How should he behold
>   That journey home, the long connubial years?
>   He does not tell you how white Helen bears
> Child on legitimate child, becomes a scold,
> Haggard with virtue. Menelaus bold

Waxed garrulous, and sacked a hundred Troys
   'Twixt noon and supper. And her golden voice
Got shrill as he grew deafer. And both were old.
Often he wonders why on earth he went
   Troyward, or why poor Paris ever came.
Oft she weeps, gummy-eyed and impotent;
   Her dry shanks twitch at Paris' mumbled name.
So Menelaus nagged; and Helen cried;
And Paris slept on by Scamander side.

Realistic too is Thomas Nashe's awareness of mortality and of beauty's brief life in his *In Time of Pestilence*:

Beauty is but a flower
Which wrinkles will devour;
Brightness falls from the air;
Queens have died young and fair;
Dust hath closed Helen's eye.
I am sick, I must die.
   Lord, have mercy on us.

But the ancient Helen is part of the world of myth, and here she was made immortal after her death because she was the daughter of Zeus. Menelaos too was immortalized because he was Zeus's son-in-law. Small wonder that so many suitors had once competed for Helen's hand in marriage, quite apart from her beauty.

Let us return to the wrathful goddess Athene, who punished the Lesser Ajax for his sacrilege at Troy, and his comrades along with him for leaving him unpunished. With the help of Zeus and Poseidon she sent a great storm that wrecked the Greek ships on the rocks of Cape Kaphereus, at the southern tip of the island of Euboia. We have no early full account of the storm, but in Euripides' *Trojan Women*, dramatizing the end of Troy, we have a powerful description of future horrors put into the mouths of Athene and Poseidon.

Zeus has promised Athene a storm, and now she asks the sea-god to play his part too. 'Zeus will send forth rains and endless hail and great, dark storms,' she tells him, 'and he promises me the fire of his thunderbolt to smite the Greek ships and set them ablaze. Then you, for your part, make the Aegean rage with surging waves and whirlpools. Fill the Euboian Gulf with corpses. Then the Greeks may learn henceforth to reverence my altars and respect all other gods.'

'It shall be so,' replies Poseidon. 'I shall stir up the wide Aegean, and the shores of Mykonos, the Delian reefs, Skyros, Lemnos and Cape Kaphereus will all be filled with the bodies of many dead.'

During the god-sent storm, Athene herself hurled a thunderbolt at Ajax's ship and sank it, but Ajax himself swam safely away and hauled himself out on to the Gyraian rock (of uncertain location). Here his own arrogance destroyed him when he uttered one insolent boast too many, as Homer describes (*Odyssey* 4.502–11):

> Ajax would have escaped his doom, though hated
> by Athene, had he not thrown out a reckless,
> boastful word, saying that he had eluded
> the great sea's depths, even against the will
> of the gods, and Poseidon heard him loudly boasting.
> At once in his sturdy hands he seized his trident
> and struck the Gyraian rock and broke it in two.
> Part of it stayed where it was, but a fragment fell
> in the sea, just where Ajax sat when he spoke
> his foolish boast. It carried him down and deep
> in the boundless, surging sea. So Ajax died . . .

It was at Cape Kaphereus too that Nauplios avenged the unjust death of his son Palamedes (p. 323). He rowed out alone to the Cape and there lit beacon fires. In the midst of the fearsome storm, these fires, promising safe harbour, lured many ships to destruction on the cruel rocks. Nauplios himself killed any man who reached shore alive.

Despite the havoc created by the great storm, however, some of the Greeks managed to return home safely. Agamemnon sailed back to Mycenae, though he was murdered on his arrival (p. 447). Old Nestor reports in the *Odyssey* (3.190–92) that Philoktetes had a safe journey, and that Idomeneos, the leader of the Cretan contingent, got back home to Crete (p. 261). Odysseus avoided the storm and arrived home at the end of another ten years and many travels – but these adventures are the subject of our next chapter.

Some Greeks travelled overland and completely avoided the dangers of the sea crossing. The seer Kalchas journeyed with some of his comrades down to the city of Kolophon, and here, having lived safely through ten years of war, he met his fate. It had been predicted that he would die if he ever met a seer better than himself, and here he came across Mopsos, the grandson of the great Theban seer Teiresias. Kalchas challenged Mopsos to say how many figs were growing on a nearby fig tree, and Mopsos gave what turned out to be the right answer. Mopsos in turn challenged Kalchas to say how many piglets a pregnant sow was carrying. He said there were eight, but Mopsos said he was wrong: she was carrying nine, all males, and they would be born at the sixth hour of the following day. It happened exactly as he had said, and Kalchas died of a broken heart.

Achilles' son Neoptolemos also travelled overland, on the advice of his grandmother Thetis, who knew about the coming storm. He took two Trojans with him: Hektor's widow Andromache, his war-prize, and the seer Helenos. In one tradition he settled in Epeiros, and here Andromache bore him a son, Molossos. The people were called Molossians after the boy, and the land was ruled for many generations by Neoptolemos' descendants, one of whom was Olympias, the mother of Alexander the Great.

After Neoptolemos' death (of which there are many variants, though it is generally agreed that he died at Delphi, and by violence), Andromache married Helenos – so two of the defeated Trojans were able to make new lives for themselves in freedom. We see them in Virgil's *Aeneid* (Book 3), when Aeneas visits Epeiros. Here Helenos is now king, and he and Andromache are living in a new city which they have named Pergamon, after Troy. Yet it seems that they cannot recover from the sadness of all that they have lost. For Andromache, it must have been just as Euripides sums up in his extant tragedy named after her: when she is threatened with death, she responds (453–6):

> 'Death is less terrible to me
> than you might think, for I died long ago,
> when my poor city of Troy was sacked,
> when my great Hektor died.'

11

ODYSSEUS AND HIS ODYSSEY

The greatest saga of return from the Trojan War is that of Odysseus, immortalized in the second monumental poem attributed to Homer, the *Odyssey* – so much so that it has given us our own word 'odyssey' for any long and eventful journey.

> Tell me, Muse, of the man of many ways,
> who wandered far after sacking the holy city of Troy.
> Many were the men whose lands he saw, whose minds
> he learned, and many too were the sorrows of his heart
> upon the open sea, striving for his own life
> and the safe return home of his dear comrades.

These are the first words of the *Odyssey*; and just as the very first word of the *Iliad*, 'wrath', pinpoints the main theme that will run through the poem, so the first word in the Greek here – *andra*, 'man' – sums up the *Odyssey*'s focus: Odysseus himself, whose trials and adventures are the subject of the long narrative.

So Odysseus, that 'man of many ways', is probably the best-known character in the whole of ancient literature. We even know from Homer what he looked like. In the *Iliad*, old Priam comments that Odysseus is a head shorter than Agamemnon (who is himself by no means the tallest of the Greeks), but broader in the chest and across the shoulders, and he ranges among his men like a thick-fleeced ram among his flocks (3.191–8). And the Trojan elder Antenor, recalling the time early in the war when Odysseus came to Troy in the hope of recovering Helen by peaceful means, remembers that his looks were not particularly impressive, 'but when he let loose his great voice from his chest, and the words fell like winter snowflakes, then no man alive could rival Odysseus' (3.221–3).

Homer depicts Odysseus as courageous, clever and endlessly resourceful – indeed, his commonest epithets for his hero are *polutlas*, 'much enduring', *polumetis*, 'man of many wiles', and *polumechanos*, 'man of great resource'. All of these qualities would be sorely tested throughout the ten long years it took him to return from Troy to the home he longed for. And even when he at last arrived there, he had to deal with the rapacious Suitors, the young men who had invaded his house during his absence and were wasting his possessions and harassing his wife Penelope. Only then could he reclaim his home and kingdom.

But before we focus in detail on Homer's saga of Odysseus, we should first sketch out the home and family background that lies behind his hero's great odyssey.

ITHACA

Odysseus was born on Ithaca, one of the loveliest of the Greek islands, situated between Kephallenia and the mainland of Akarnania. His father was Laertes, the king of Ithaca. In his youth Laertes had sailed with Jason and the Argonauts, though when we meet him in the *Odyssey* he is a very old man, who long years earlier had given over the rule of the island to his son and gone into retirement.

Odysseus' mother was Antikleia, daughter of the famous thief Autolykos, who lived near Mount Parnassos. Autolykos's especial skill was stealing animals, for he had magic powers to make things vanish, or to change their colour or markings. Many were the flocks and herds that he made his own, changing their appearance so that their real owners had no chance of identifying them. Autolykos finally met his match in Sisyphos, the king of Corinth, who was as great a trickster as he was (p. 112).

Autolykos stole Sisyphos' cattle, transforming them in the usual way so that no one would recognize them, but Sisyphos suspected the truth when he noticed that his herds were gradually diminishing, while those of Autolykos kept increasing. He outwitted the master-thief by fixing lead tablets to his animals' hooves inscribed with the words 'stolen by Autolykos', then all he had to do was follow their tracks and reclaim his beasts. It was said that the two rogues became fast friends. Some writers (not Homer) even said that Sisyphos seduced Autolykos's daughter Antikleia, with the result that he, rather than her husband Laertes, was the father of the wily Odysseus.

It was Autolykos who gave Odysseus his name, choosing it because he himself had been at odds (*odussesthai*) with many people in his life. In his youth, Odysseus visited his grandfather's house and went on a boarhunt with his uncles. He himself killed the boar, but not before he had received a tusk wound in his leg, which left a scar that would be with him for the rest of his life. But for the most part he was brought up on Ithaca. 'A rough place,' he himself said of the island, 'but it breeds good children,' and added that there was no sweeter place on earth (*Odyssey* 9.27–8).

In the fullness of time he became one of the many suitors of Helen, the beautiful daughter of King Tyndareos of Sparta, not because he had any serious intention of marrying her, but because he saw this as an opportunity to win the woman of his choice: Penelope, the daughter of Tyndareos's brother Ikarios. Tyndareos was afraid that violence would break out when one of Helen's suitors was chosen above the rest, so Odysseus advised him to make all the suitors swear an oath, vowing to respect his choice and to defend the marriage against any future threat. They did so willingly, and Tyndareos, grateful for the good advice, interceded with Ikarios on Odysseus' behalf and Penelope became his.

The couple settled on Ithaca and the marriage was a very happy one. They had a son, Telemachos, but while the boy was still only a baby the Trojan War began. Helen ran away to Troy with Paris, and all the rejected suitors were called on to keep their vows and help to recover her, so because of his fateful oath Odysseus was forced to join Agamemnon's army and go to war at Troy. He very unwillingly left his home and dear wife (p. 312), knowing full well from an oracle that he would be away from Ithaca for twenty years, and would return only after much suffering.

He led twelve ships from Ithaca to Troy. And there, as we have seen, he played an important part in the war, not least in conceiving the stratagem of the Wooden Horse, by means of which the Greeks finally entered the Trojan city. After ten years of war, Troy was defeated and Odysseus set sail once more with his twelve ships, heading home to Ithaca.

THE RETURN FROM TROY

In the tenth year of his travels, Odysseus, having lost all his ships, his men and his possessions, was washed up naked on the magical island of Scheria. He was found by the young and beautiful Nausikaa, daughter of the island's king, Alkinoos. She gave him food and clothing, and took him home to her father's palace. Here, in the course of a banquet, Homer has Odysseus himself relate all his perilous adventures during the earlier years of his return home (Books 9–12).

When his narrative opens, he has just left Troy with his twelve ships. A strong wind drives them off-course to south-western Thrace and the land of the Kikonians, who were Trojan allies during the war. Odysseus and his comrades sack their city of Ismaros, killing all the men except for Maron, the priest of Apollo, and capturing their women and possessions. The grateful priest, in return for his life, gives Odysseus many gifts, including twelve jars of strong, honey-sweet wine. This wine will one day save Odysseus from death.

Odysseus urges his men to sail away at once, but they ignore him and linger too long, feasting on their spoils, so that Kikonian reinforcements have time to come from inland. 'They came at early morning, as many as flowers in spring, or leaves,' says Odysseus (9.51–61). 'They fought us in battle there by our swift ships . . . and when the sun passed over to the time when oxen are unyoked, then at last the Kikonians turned back the Greeks and overwhelmed them, and out of each ship six of my strong-greaved comrades were killed.' So already seventy-two of Odysseus' men lie dead.

The rest escape, and despite a storm they sail safely to Cape Maleia, the south-eastern tip of the Peloponnese. Here the North Wind seizes them and drives them off-course for nine days. On the tenth day they arrive at the land of the Lotos-eaters.

THE LOTOS-EATERS

Unlike many of the peoples that Odysseus will encounter, the gentle and inoffensive Lotos-eaters offer no threat of violence. The danger that comes from them is more subtle, for they live on the exotic fruit of the lotos plant, which induces forgetfulness and makes those who eat it lose all desire to return home. Odysseus sends three scouts ashore, and when they too eat of the lotos, they wish only to stay in the land of the Lotos-eaters for ever. Odysseus has to drag them back to the ships by force and tie them down.

The Lotos-eaters live on in the popular imagination as people with a life of indolence and luxury, but this is not directly because of Homer's story, which is short and undramatic, but because of its later elaboration. The first to develop the theme was Tennyson in his seminal poem *The Lotos-eaters*, a little of which is worth quoting here, for it fills out Homer's brief sketch and brings the land of the Lotos-eaters to vivid life. Its sensuous lure is irresistible:

> There is sweet music here that softer falls
> Than petals from blown roses on the grass,
> Or night-dews on still waters between walls
> Of shadowy granite, in a gleaming pass;
> Music that gentlier on the spirit lies,
> Than tired eyelids upon tired eyes;
> Music that brings sweet sleep down from the blissful skies.
> Here are cool mosses deep,
> And thro' the moss the ivies creep,
> And in the stream the long-leaved flowers weep,
> And from the craggy ledge the poppy hangs in sleep.

Nor do Tennyson's seamen resist. The poem ends:

> Surely, surely, slumber is more sweet than toil, the shore
> Than labour in the deep mid-ocean, wind and wave and oar;
> Oh rest ye, brother mariners, we will not wander more.

Homer's mariners, however, sail onwards and come to the land of the barbarous Cyclopes.

THE CYCLOPS POLYPHEMOS

The Cyclopes ('Round-eyed') were a race of giants, each with a single eye in the middle of his forehead. The early Cyclopes, born of Ouranos and Gaia, forged thunderbolts for Zeus and aided the gods in their victorious battle against the Titans. They also built many monumental works for humans, including the Lion Gate at Mycenae and the immense ('Cyclopean') walls of both Mycenae and Tiryns, so huge that it seemed impossible they could have been built by mortal hands. Their forges were thought to be under Mount Etna in Sicily, where their fiery work gave rise to Etna's volcanic activity (p. 96).

Homer's Cyclopes, however, are a race of shepherds, still gigantic, each still with a single eye, but here dwelling in a world of men, on an island that was also later identified with Sicily. They live in mountain caverns and keep flocks, each apart from the others and caring nothing about laws and communal life, or about tilling the soil and growing crops.

Odysseus and twelve of his men go ashore to explore, and they find a cavern full of lambs and kids, milk and cheeses. The men are afraid and urge Odysseus to go back to the ships, but he stays on, hoping that the owner of the cave will return and give him gifts of hospitality. Yet his men are right to be afraid, for the cave belongs to the Cyclops Polyphemos, a murderous savage who delights in feeding on raw human flesh. (Although he will grant Odysseus a gift of a kind: a promise that he will eat him last of all.)

The giant comes home, bringing into the cave all his sheep and goats for milking, and blocking the entrance with a massive boulder. When Odysseus asks him for hospitality, his response is to snatch up two of the men, seizing them in his great hands and dashing their brains out on the ground as if he were killing puppies. Then he tears them limb from limb and eats them for his supper, bones and all. Afterwards he goes to sleep, and Odysseus wonders whether to try killing him with his sword – but this would mean the death of them all, for they would never shift the great rock barricading the cave-entrance. Another plan must be found.

In the morning the Cyclops gobbles up two more men for his breakfast, before going out to pasture his flocks. He carefully blocks the cave-mouth as he leaves, but now Odysseus has a plan. He sharpens an immense wooden stake and hardens its tip in the fire, then hides it ready for evening. Polyphemos comes home as before, bringing all his flocks into the cave. Once again he replaces the boulder, once again he devours two of the men.

Now Odysseus puts his plan into action. He has with him the strong, honey-sweet wine once given him by Maron in the land of the Kikonians, and this he offers to the Cyclops, who gulps it down greedily. He asks Odysseus his name. 'My name is Nobody (*Outis*),' comes the reply.

At last the giant sleeps soundly in a drunken stupor, and Odysseus and his men heat their stake in the fire until it is incandescent, then drive it into the Cyclops' single eye and spin it round and round. 'The blood of his eye spurted around the hot wood,' says Homer (9.388–90). 'The scorch of the burning eyeball singed all his eyebrows and eyelids, and the fire made the roots of his eye crackle.' Blinded and in agony, Polyphemos bellows for help from the other Cyclopes. They all come running from their caves among the mountains, but when he roars that 'Nobody' is trying to kill him, they laugh and go away.

When morning comes, Polyphemos pulls away the great boulder from the entrance and lets out his flocks, carefully feeling their backs as they pass him, to make sure they are carrying no passengers. He does not think to feel beneath them, which is a mistake, for Odysseus and his six surviving men are clinging to the undersides of the sheep as they go out. Now we see for a moment a more sympathetic side to the giant, as he talks to his favourite ram, the largest of the flock and the last to leave (with Odysseus clinging on beneath). 'My dear old ram,' he says (9.447–56), 'why are you the last of the sheep to leave the cave? Never before have you been left behind by the flock, but striding out, far ahead of the rest, you would be the first to pasture on grass and tender flowers, the first at running rivers, the first to come back eagerly to the sheepfold at evening. Now you are last of all. Perhaps you are grieving for your master's eye, which an evil man put out with the help of his wicked companions.'

Once safely back on board ship, Odysseus cannot resist one last display of bravado. As they sail swiftly away, he shouts to

Odysseus escapes from the Cyclops' cave.

the Cyclops, taunting him and telling him his real name. He will pay dearly for this rashness, for Polyphemos calls on his father Poseidon to avenge his hurt, and the god's anger will keep Odysseus away from his home on Ithaca for many long, weary years. He himself, in a later time of tribulation, will look back on his encounter with the Cyclops as his most testing experience, when he says to himself (20.18–21):

> 'Bear up, old heart. You had worse to endure than this,
> the day the overwhelming Cyclops devoured
> your brave companions, but you endured, till cunning
> got you out of the cave, although you expected to die.'

AIOLOS AND THE BAG OF WINDS

Their next port of call is the floating island of Aiolia, surrounded by cliffs of unyielding bronze. The king of the island is Aiolos, who lives a life free from all care with his wife and twelve children, six sons who are married to six daughters. Day after day they feast continually. Zeus has made Aiolos guardian of all the winds in the world, with the power to raise or quell any wind he wishes.

He and his family welcome Odysseus and his men into their palace, and for a month they feast them royally. Then Odysseus feels it is time to leave, so Aiolos helps him by giving him all the boisterous winds sewn up in a leather bag, made from the hide of a nine-year-old ox. He leaves outside only the gentle West Wind to blow them safely back to Ithaca.

All goes well for nine days of sailing, until on the tenth day Ithaca comes into sight. Then, fatally, Odysseus falls asleep from exhaustion. His men open the leather bag, certain that it contains treasure which their leader has no intention of sharing with them, and at once the winds burst out and sweep the ship violently all the way back to Aiolia. Odysseus, despairing, humbly begs Aiolos to help him a second time, but Aiolos brusquely turns him away, thinking it foolhardy to help a man so obviously hated by the gods.

THE LAISTRYGONIANS

For six days they sail on once again, then on the seventh day they come to the land of the Laistrygonians, a race of savage man-eating giants. Unaware of their nature, Odysseus has his men moor their ships in a quiet harbour, walled in by tall cliffs, and sends three scouts to spy out the land. They meet a girl who says she is the daughter of the local king, Antiphates, and she leads them to her father's splendid palace. Inside they find a woman as huge as a mountain peak, who fills them with terror. She calls for her husband Antiphates and he comes at once, then snatches up one of the men and devours him.

The two other scouts escape and flee back to the ships, followed by the whole population – 'thousands of them, not like men, but giants' – who stand on the cliffs and fling massive boulders down to sink the ships below, then spear the men like fish and carry them off for eating. Only Odysseus' ship, moored outside the harbour entrance, escapes. He and his one remaining crew sail sorrowfully onwards.

CIRCE

Exhausted and disheartened by this horrific encounter, they come next to Aiaia, the island of the enchantress Circe, daughter of the Sun-god Helios. When they recover sufficiently to look around them, they find that the only sign of life is a column of smoke rising up from some habitation deep in a forest. Odysseus sends out a scouting party to investigate.

The men come to Circe's secluded home and find huge wolves and lions prowling around it. At first sight these appear to be fearsome animals, but really they are humans who have been transformed by Circe's magic, and they unexpectedly wag their tails and fawn on the strangers. The men can hear Circe singing sweetly inside the house, so they call out to her, and she welcomes them in and gives them wine to drink, flavoured with barley and cheese and honey – but mixed with a magical drug. Soon they are all turned into pigs, with the heads and grunts and bristles of swine, but keeping their human intelligence. Circe drives them into her pig sty and leaves them there, weeping.

Just one man escapes this fate, Eurylochos, the brother-in-law of Odysseus. He had the sense to suspect danger and to wait outside the house, and he now takes the sorry news back to the ship. At once Odysseus sets out to free the rest of his men. On the way he meets the god Hermes in the likeness of a young man, and Hermes supplies him with a marvellous plant called moly, black-rooted and with flowers of milky white, that will make him immune to Circe's spells.

Once again Circe gives her new guest the drugged wine, but this time her intended victim, instead of becoming a pig, rushes at her with a drawn sword as if to kill her. Circe knows that she has been defeated. She guesses that this must be Odysseus, and she suggests that they retire to bed and the pleasures of love. And so they do, once Circe has sworn a solemn oath to do no further harm.

Afterwards, on Odysseus' insistence, she turns all his men back into human beings, as he himself relates (10.388–99):

> Circe walked on out through the hall, staff in hand,
> and opening the doors of the pigsty she drove them out,
> looking like nine-year-old hogs. They stood facing her,
> and she went among them, anointing each of them
> with some other drug. The bristles, grown on them
> from the harmful drug that Circe had supplied,
> fell away from them and they turned once more into men,
> but younger and taller and handsomer than before.
> They recognized me and clasped me by the hand,
> and lovely weeping overtook us all, and the house
> echoed terribly to the sound. Even the goddess had pity.

Odysseus and his men stay with the enchantress for a year, feasting on unlimited food and wine. At the end of that time, urged on by his men, he is ready to be on his way once more, but Circe tells him that first he must go down to Hades, to seek advice about his journey from the shade of the Theban seer Teiresias. This is a supreme test, for only the greatest of heroes, like Herakles, can return alive from the land of the dead.

THE UNDERWORLD

So Odysseus and his men set sail towards the far limits of the world, and following Circe's directions they eventually reach the edge of Hades. There they dig a trench and pour into it libations of milk and honey, wine and water, all sprinkled with white barley. Odysseus summons up the ghosts of the dead by sacrificing a young ram and a black ewe that Circe has given him, and as the blood runs down into the trench, the souls of the dead gather round.

The first to speak is the shade of Elpenor, the youngest member of Odysseus' crew, a man 'not very brave in battle nor quite all there in his mind' (10.552–3). On the hot summer night before Odysseus left Aiaia, Elpenor slept for greater coolness on the roof of Circe's house. In the morning, still groggy from sleep and wine, he blundered off the edge and broke his neck. Now Elpenor begs Odysseus to return to Aiaia and give his body proper burial. 'Burn me with all the armour I have,' he says (11.74–8), 'and heap up a grave-mound for me by the shore of the grey sea, for an unhappy man, so that those to come will know of me. Do this, and set on top of my grave the oar that I used to row with, in the time when I was alive and among my comrades.' Odysseus promises to do as he asks.

Next he speaks to the shade of Teiresias. The seer prophesies his future, saying that Poseidon's anger will give Odysseus a hard journey home, but he will at last arrive, so long as he is careful not to harm the cattle of the Sun-god Helios, pastured on the island of Thrinakia. Teiresias warns him too about the Suitors, who have invaded his palace on Ithaca and are wooing his wife Penelope.

When the seer moves away, many other shades approach Odysseus. He speaks with his mother Antikleia, though he had not known until this moment that she was dead. She explains that she died of grief at his absence (11.202–3): 'It was care and longing for you and your gentleness, glorious Odysseus, that took the sweet life from me.' Three times he tries to take his dead mother in his arms, and three times her shade flutters from his hands like a shadow or a dream, because 'this is the way of mortals, when they die'.

He speaks with many famous women, the wives and mothers of great heroes: with Tyro, Antiope, Alkmene, Epicasta (the mother of Oedipus, later called Jocasta), Leda, Iphimedeia, Phaidra, Prokris, Ariadne and Eriphyle. He speaks with some of the men who were his comrades at Troy: with Agamemnon, who tells of his murder at the hands of his wife Klytaimnestra and her lover Aigisthos, and warns Odysseus to be careful when he too returns home; with Achilles and Patroklos and Antilochos; and with the Great Ajax, who still nurses his anger over the award of Achilles' arms and refuses to reply to his old enemy, stalking away into the darkness in a proud silence.

Odysseus sees Minos, the judge of the dead, and the giant hunter Orion, 'rounding up over the fields of asphodel the same wild beasts that in life he had killed in the lonely mountains' (11.573–4). He sees the tortures of Tityos, Tantalos and Sisyphos, and last of all the shade of the great Herakles. Then finally even he loses his nerve, afraid that some terrible monster may appear, and he leaves Hades and sails back with his men to Aiaia and the land of the living. There he buries Elpenor as he promised, then at dawn he sets off homeward once again, having learnt from Circe the many dangers of the journey ahead.

THE SIRENS

The first danger, Circe explains, will come from singing enchantresses who lure men to their doom (12.39–46):

> 'First you will reach the Sirens who enchant all men,
> whoever comes their way. Anyone coming near,
> not knowing, and hearing the Sirens singing, never
> will he go home to his wife and little children,
> never will they delight in his return, but the Sirens
> enchant him with the sweetness of their singing,
> sitting in their meadow, with all around them
> a great heap of bones from men rotting away
> whose skins wither upon them . . .'

Odysseus, bound to the mast, hears the Sirens' entrancing songs.

Circe advises Odysseus to stop the ears of his men with beeswax so that they can hear nothing. He himself must be bound tightly to the mast and must not be released, however much he begs, until all danger is over. In this way his comrades will row past in safety, while he alone of all men will have the joy of the Sirens' song, yet live. He does exactly as Circe says, and when he hears them singing their mesmerizing songs he does indeed long to be released. His men merely tie him the tighter, and only when they have rowed far away from the Sirens do they set him free.

Homer does not describe the Sirens, and there is nothing to suggest that for him they had anything other than human forms. In later writers they become bird-women, having the faces and voices of women above feathered, winged bodies with birds' feet, and this is how they often appear in vase-paintings. They were usually said to be the daughters of the river-god Acheloos by one of the Muses, Melpomene or Terpsichore (so it is no surprise that they could beguile men with their singing). Later writers also said that the Sirens were fated to die if anyone successfully resisted their song, so after Odysseus heard them and passed by unharmed, they hurled themselves despairingly into the sea and were drowned.

SKYLLA AND CHARYBDIS

Next they have to pass through a narrow sea-channel which offers them the choice of two terrifying evils, the monster Skylla and the whirlpool Charybdis. (And 'to be caught between Skylla and Charybdis' has become proverbial for a situation with two equally dangerous alternatives.) But, thanks to Circe, Odysseus knows which alternative to choose. On one side of the strait is the giant whirlpool Charybdis, which will suck them all down to certain death if they go too near to her. On the other side is the six-headed sea-monster Skylla, whose lair is in a cave, half way up a sheer cliff (12.86–100):

Her voice is no more than a new-born puppy's,
but she herself is an evil monster. No one,
not even a god, could encounter her and be glad
at the sight. She has twelve feet, all waving in the air,
and six long necks with a frightful head on each,
all with three rows of teeth, packed close together
and full of black death. Her lower body is sunk
in a hollow cave, but she holds her heads outside
the terrible pit, and there she fishes, eagerly
peering round from her lookout, for dolphins
or dogfish to catch, or any bigger sea-monster,
so many of which live in the loud-moaning sea.
Never can sailors boast they have passed unharmed
in their ship, for with each of her heads she snatches
one man away from the dark-prowed vessel.

Yet horrific though Skylla is, she will be the lesser of the two evils, since she threatens death to only a few of the crew instead of to all. Armed with this knowledge, Odysseus sails through the strait keeping well away from Charybdis, and planning to fight Skylla off if he can. He stands at the prow, fully armed, gazing up at the high sheer cliff until his eyes grow weary of watching. Suddenly Charybdis goes into horrifying action (12.236–43):

Terrible was the way she sucked down the sea's water,
and when she spewed it up, the whole sea would boil
in turbulence, like a cauldron on a big fire, and high spray
spattered the tops of the rocks on both sides.
But when again she sucked down the sea's salt water,
the turbulence showed all the inside of the sea,
and around it the rock roared terribly, and the ground
showed dark with sand at the ocean bottom,
and pale fear seized upon my comrades.

While everybody on board stares in terrified fascination at the great whirlpool, Skylla acts. She swoops down her six long necks and seizes six of Odysseus' men. Too late, he turns and sees them far out of reach (12.248–59):

> I saw their feet and their hands from below, already
> lifted high above me, and they cried aloud to me,
> calling me by name, the last time they ever did so,
> in the sorrow of their hearts. As a fisherman on a rock,
> using a very long rod, casts down food
> as bait for the little fishes . . . then hauls them up
> and throws them out on land, gasping and struggling,
> so they gasped and struggled as they were hauled
> up the high cliff, and there at her door she ate them
> as they screamed and stretched out their hands to me
> in their terrible death throes. And this indeed
> was the most pitiful thing my eyes ever looked upon
> in all my sufferings sailing the cruel sea.

THE CATTLE OF THE SUN-GOD

They sail onwards, and soon they approach the island of Thrinakia where the cattle of the Sun-god Helios are pastured. Odysseus remembers Teiresias' warning that he must do the cattle no harm, so he is eager to sail on past, but his men, urged on by Eurylochos, persuade him to land, swearing that they will eat nothing but the generous provisions that Circe has given them. Unfortunately they are kept on the island by adverse winds for a whole month, and soon all the food is gone. After this they hunt for fish and game. Finally, when Odysseus is away in another part of the island, Eurylochos persuades his hungry shipmates to kill and eat some of the sacred cattle. When Odysseus returns to the smell of roasting meat, it is too late: the fatal deed is done.

Helios demands that Zeus punish the offenders, even threatening to leave the earth and take his light to the dead men in Hades if no penalty is paid. So when the men put to sea after six days of feasting on the sacred meat, Zeus sends a violent storm against them. The ship breaks up, and only Odysseus, who took no part in the sacrilege, survives to tell the tale: 'My men were thrown into the water, and bobbing like sea-crows were carried away by the waves from around the black ship, and the god took away their homecoming' (12.417–19). Now, of all the men in the twelve ships that left Troy, only Odysseus is left alive.

He lashes together the broken keel and mast of his ship to form a makeshift raft, and perched on this he is driven by the winds all the way back to Skylla and Charybdis. This time he avoids Skylla, but his craft falls prey to Charybdis. She sucks it down deep to the ocean bottom, and Odysseus survives only by clinging to the fig tree that overhangs the whirlpool. When Charybdis eventually spews up the remains of his raft, he escapes by hauling himself on to a spar and paddling away with his hands. He is carried by the sea for nine days until he is washed up on the island of Ogygia, the home of the goddess Kalypso ('Concealer'), daughter of the Titan Atlas.

KALYPSO

Kalypso falls in love with Odysseus and keeps him as her lover for seven years. Their home is a cave in lush and beautiful surroundings (5.63–74):

> Around the cave there grew a flourishing wood,
> poplars and alders and fragrant cypresses.
> Here was the roosting place of long-winged birds,
> owls and falcons and long-beaked sea-crows
> whose daily concerns take them down to the sea.

There around the hollow cave there stretched
a young, luxuriant vine, thick with grapes.
Nearby were four springs, flowing with bright water,
close at their source but running in different directions.
All around grew meadows, soft with violets
and parsley, and even a god who came to that place
would gaze in wonder, his heart delighted within him.

Despite all this verdant beauty, Odysseus, 'sitting weeping on the sea-shore, breaking his heart with tears, lamentations and grief', still yearns all the time to return home to rugged Ithaca. Kalypso even offers to make him immortal and ageless like herself, if only he will stay with her for ever, but Odysseus, despite the delights of the goddess's bed, would rather go home to his mortal and ageing wife Penelope.

At the end of these seven years, Athene intervenes and urges the gods to set Odysseus free. Poseidon is still implacably angry because of Polyphemos's blinding, so she waits for a time when he is far away in Ethiopia, then appeals to Zeus. 'Kalypso keeps the grieving, unhappy man with her,' she explains, 'and she keeps on charming him with soft and flattering words to make him forget Ithaca. But Odysseus, longing to catch sight of even the smoke rising up from his own country, wants only to die' (1.55–9). Zeus sends Hermes to tell Kalypso that she must let Odysseus go. With a heavy heart, the goddess bows to the inevitable. She gives Odysseus tools and materials to build a raft, then dresses him in fine clothing, supplies him with food and water and wine, and sends him on his way with a fair wind.

Homer says no more about Kalypso, left alone on her island paradise. It is Hesiod (*Theogony* 1017–18) who tells us that she had two sons, Nausithoos and Nausinoos, by Odysseus, and Propertius who describes the sad aftermath of her lover's leaving (1.15.9–16):

> She wept to the lonely waves, and many days
> she sat grieving his loss, her hair unkempt,
> and many times cried out to the cruel sea,
> and while she never again would see his face,
> still she grieves, recalling long hours of joy.

NAUSIKAA

For seventeen days Odysseus sails onwards, but on the eighteenth day Poseidon returns from Ethiopia and sees his enemy once more travelling towards home. At once he lets loose a violent storm that breaks up the raft. Odysseus almost drowns, but he is saved by the sea-goddess Leukothea, who in her mortal life was Ino, daughter of Kadmos, the king of Thebes. She gives Odysseus a shawl that ties around his chest and keeps him afloat, and with the aid of this he swims for two days and nights, until at last he reaches land and drags himself ashore at the mouth of a river. After returning his life-preserving shawl to the water, he crawls into a thicket and falls asleep on a bed of leaves. He is on the magical island of Scheria, the land of the Phaiakians.

The first person he sees the next morning is Nausikaa, the young and lovely daughter of Alkinoos and Arete, king and queen of the island. Influenced by Athene in a dream, Nausikaa has come with her maids to the river-mouth to do the family washing. While waiting for the clothes to dry they play ball. Their cries awaken Odysseus and he comes out of the bushes, his nakedness scantily covered by a branch (6.130–39):

> . . . like a mountain lion, trusting in his strength,
> who goes on his way, buffeted by wind and rain,
> his eyes blazing; he goes after cattle or sheep,
> or after wild deer, and hunger drives him on
> into a strong-built sheepfold to try for the flocks;

so Odysseus was ready to meet the lovely-haired girls,
even though naked, for he was in great need.
But to them he seemed fearsome, all encrusted with brine,
and they fled this way and that along the jutting shores.
Only Alkinoos' daughter stood her ground . . .

Homer implies that Odysseus is as terrifying as a lion, and only
Nausikaa is brave enough to face him. There is also a hint of
possible rape in the encounter, for the Greek word translated
as 'meet' is *mixesthai*, which can also mean 'to have sex with',
so this emphasizes her courage even more. Clever Odysseus,
knowing just what the girls are afraid of, stands at a distance
from Nausikaa and reassures her by likening her to Artemis,
the virgin goddess, thus subtly hinting that no thoughts of sex
are in his mind. He goes on to charm her with honeyed words,
and she supplies him with clothes and food and drink, then
takes him back to the city, telling him how to win the help of
her parents.

Alkinoos and Arete live in a rich and splendid palace with
bronze walls, silver pillars and doors of gold. The threshold is
guarded by gold and silver watchdogs, ageless and immortal,
fashioned by Hephaistos. Outside is a magical garden
(7.114–21):

Here trees grow tall and abundant, pears
and pomegranates, trees shining with apples,
and sweet fig trees and flourishing olives.
And the fruit on these never dies or fails,
winter and summer, all the year round,
but always the breath of the west wind
makes some fruit grow, and ripens others.
Pear matures on pear, and apple on apple,
grape too upon grape, and fig upon fig.

Alkinoos and Arete welcome Odysseus to their palace as an honoured guest and promise to convey him home to Ithaca. This will be easy, for the Phaiakians are a seafaring people, with ships that find their own way miraculously over the sea without need of oars or steersmen. They also have a relaxed and luxurious way of life: 'We forever enjoy feasting,' says Alkinoos, 'and the lyre, and dances, and changes of clothing, and our warm baths and beds' (8.248–9). So Odysseus is entertained royally with games and a great feast. There is even a bard, Demodokos, who is blind, just as Homer himself was reputed to be. 'The Muse loved him greatly,' says Homer (8.63–4), 'and she gave him both good and evil. She robbed him of his eyes, but gave him the gift of sweet song.'

Demodokos sings of the Trojan War and the Wooden Horse, and even of the part played by Odysseus himself. Hearing him, Odysseus weeps (8.523–31):

> . . . as a woman weeps,
> embracing the body of her dead husband
> who has fallen before his city and people, trying
> to stave off the pitiless day from city and children;
> she sees him dying and gasping for breath,
> and throwing herself around him she cries
> high and shrill, while the men behind her strike
> at her back and shoulders with their spears
> and force her off into slavery, to have pain and sorrow,
> and her cheeks are racked with the most pitiful grief.

It is now that Odysseus divulges his name and tells the long tale of his wanderings.

Nausikaa has fallen half in love with Odysseus and admits to herself that she would like to marry him. Alkinoos too would be very happy to have him for a son-in-law. Yet just as Odysseus wanted to leave Kalypso, and even refused her offer of immortality, so now again he wishes simply to return home to Ithaca and to his dearly loved wife Penelope. His wish is granted, and he is carried home in one of the Phaiakians' ships, loaded with many rich gifts from the king and queen. He sleeps on the journey, and the sailors deposit him, still sleeping, on his home shore. After twenty long years he is at last in Ithaca once again.

As for the Phaiakians, they have aroused Poseidon's anger by helping Odysseus, and when their ship returns to Scheria, the god turns it to stone and roots it to the bottom of the sea. Recognizing the wrath of the sea-god, they agree never again to escort travellers in their miraculous ships. Odysseus has been their last passenger, and the Phaiakians now disappear for ever from the sight of men.

IN ITHACA ONCE MORE

When Odysseus wakes, he finds himself alone and surrounded by a thick mist. At first he is sure that this cannot be Ithaca and he is close to despair, but his constant ally Athene appears and reassures him. She warns him about the many Suitors who have invaded his home, acting on the assumption that Odysseus is dead. For three years these local nobles have been behaving outrageously, eating and carousing and wasting his house's substance, while doing their utmost to persuade Penelope to marry again. He must avenge these wrongs and reclaim his wife and kingdom, but the Suitors will kill him if they recognize him, so Athene transforms his appearance into that of a decrepit old beggar. Thus disguised, he will be able to go among them until his plans for vengeance are complete.

RECOGNITIONS

On Athene's instructions, Odysseus goes first to the hut of his faithful swineherd Eumaios to seek food and shelter. Eumaios has served Odysseus well, remaining loyal to his interests throughout his long absence and doing his best to keep his pigs out of the hands of the greedy Suitors. Odysseus, who can always conjure up a good story, pretends to be a Cretan who has fought at Troy and so has news of Eumaios's master, and the swineherd welcomes him and entertains this supposed stranger courteously. Later they are joined by Telemachos, who has just returned from seeking news of his father at Pylos and Sparta, and Odysseus has the first sight of his son for twenty years.

Telemachos was an infant when the Trojan War began, so he is now a young man. He has resented the presence of the Suitors in his home, but has not felt himself strong enough to turn them out. This is about to change. When Eumaios goes off on an errand, Odysseus, with the help of Athene, temporarily resumes his true appearance and makes himself known to his son. 'I am your father,' he says, 'and because of me you have been grieving, and suffering great pain, and enduring men's outrages.' Telemachos takes his father in his arms and they both weep for all the lost years since their parting (16.216–19):

> They cried loud and shrill, even more than the outcry
> of birds, eagles or vultures with hooked claws,
> whose children countrymen have taken away
> before they could fly. Such was their pitiful crying.

Father and son together now plot the Suitors' destruction, and from this point onwards Telemachos is all courage and resourcefulness. He will of course keep Odysseus' return a close secret, and by the time Eumaios returns to the hut, the beggar's disguise has been resumed.

The next morning, Odysseus and Eumaios set out for the palace, encountering the goatherd Melanthios on their way. He is a son of the faithful servant Dolios, but he himself treacherously sides with the Suitors, supplying them freely with the best beasts from his flocks for their dinners. Now he is abusive, and he even kicks out at Odysseus as he goes past. The time will come when he will be repaid in full for all his disloyalty – but not just yet.

They come to the palace, and there outside, lying on a dung-heap, is the old hunting dog, Argos ('Swift'), that Odysseus himself once fondly reared. Odysseus knows him at once, and secretly wipes away a tear. Argos too joyfully recognizes his master, even after twenty years' absence. Too weak to get to his feet, he feebly wags his tail in glad greeting, and dies.

Inside the palace the Suitors are feasting as usual on meat from the household's flocks. Odysseus goes among them, begging, and they all give him food except for Antinoos, the ringleader of the Suitors and the most insolent of them all. He hurls a footstool at the 'beggar', then incites the (genuine) beggar Iros to fight him. Iros is 'famous for his ravening stomach and his incessant eating and drinking', and he is quite willing to fight Odysseus, thinking him old and weak.

'How the old varmint runs on when he talks,' he says, 'just like some old oven-woman. I could think up something nasty for him: hit him with both hands, and knock all the teeth out of his jaws on to the ground, as if he was some wild pig eating the crops. Come on, tuck up your clothes, so that everyone can see us do battle' (18.26–31). So Odysseus tucks up his rags, displaying a broad and muscular body. At this Iros completely changes his tune, but Antinoos forces him to fight, and Odysseus fells him with a single bone-crushing blow.

Penelope, prompted by Athene, appears among them and announces her reluctant intention to remarry at last. She reproaches the Suitors for failing to bring her suitable presents, and at once, inflamed with passionate desire for her, they eagerly produce many rich gifts to win her favour. Odysseus is delighted, both with Penelope's long fidelity to him, and with her ability to extract treasures from the Suitors that help to compensate for all their depredations. (Odysseus too has always been ready to acquire gifts in his wanderings wherever he can.)

Telemachos boldly tells the Suitors to spend the night in their own homes, and they obey him, then he and Odysseus prepare for vengeance by stripping the hall of all its armour and weapons and shutting them away in a storeroom. Once Telemachos has retired for the night, Penelope comes down and speaks with the 'beggar'. Of course she does not recognize him as Odysseus, but her heart warms to this stranger and she tells him how for three years she put off the Suitors' demands by pretending to weave her father-in-law's shroud – a trick worthy of *polumetis* Odysseus himself, that 'man of many wiles' (19.139–56):

> 'I set up a great loom in my palace, and began to weave
> a web of threads, long and fine. And I said to them:
> "Young men, my suitors now godlike Odysseus is dead,
> though you are eager to marry me, wait until I finish
> this web, so that my weaving will not be uselessly wasted,
> a shroud for the hero Laertes, for when he is laid low
> and taken by the destructive doom of death . . ."
> So I spoke and their proud hearts obeyed me.
> Then every day I would weave the great web,
> and every night I undid it, lit by torchlight.
> For three years I kept my secret and convinced the Suitors,
> but when the fourth year came . . . then at last
> they came on me and caught me, taking me to task,
> and I was forced against my will to finish it.'

Odysseus tells Penelope that he is the brother of Idomeneos, king of Crete, and that he has once met Odysseus himself. 'He knew how to tell many lies that sounded true,' says Homer (19.204–12):

> and as she listened her tears streamed down
> and her body melted, as the snow itself melts
> on the tops of the mountains, when the East Wind melts it
> after the West Wind has piled it there,
> and as it melts the rivers run full in flood.
> So her lovely cheeks were streaming tears,
> as she wept for her husband, sitting there by her side.

Odysseus is full of pity for her sorrow, but he must not yet make himself known to her, so he tries to reassure her by predicting his own imminent return. Penelope is still full of doubt, but she is comforted by her talk with this likeable stranger, and she calls for the old nurse Eurykleia to wash her guest's feet.

Eurykleia is the chief female servant in the palace, passionately devoted to the family's interests. Now she does as she is bid, and in washing Odysseus' feet she recognizes her master from the old scar on his leg once made by the tusk of a wild boar, when he was out hunting with his uncles on Mount Parnassos (19.467–75):

> The old woman, with the scar in the palms of her hands,
> knew it as she touched it, and she let his foot go.
> His leg fell on the basin, and the bronze vessel rang
> and tipped to one side, and the water spilled on the floor.
> Joy and pain seized her at once, and her eyes
> were filled with tears, and her lusty voice was checked.
> Taking him by his chin, she said to Odysseus: 'Yes,
> dear child, you really are Odysseus, I did not
> know you before, not till I had touched my master.'

She is about to cry aloud the happy news of his return, but Odysseus stops her mouth with his hands, since his life depends on keeping his identity secret for a while longer.

Before she goes to bed, Penelope tells Odysseus of her plan to hold an archery contest for the Suitors, to see which of them can string her husband's great bow and shoot an arrow through a row of twelve double-headed axes. That man, she says, will win her as his wife. Odysseus sees that this would be an ideal situation in which to take vengeance on the Suitors, so he urges her to hold the contest without delay.

VENGEANCE

The next day will be the Suitors' last. They hold another feast, during which the prophet Theoklymenos solemnly warns them of their impending deaths, but they pay no attention and simply mock his words.

After the banquet, Penelope brings out Odysseus' great bow and the twelve axes, and announces the contest. Telemachos fixes the axes into the ground, and the Suitors, one by one, try unsuccessfully to string the bow. Meanwhile Odysseus slips away and finds his two faithful servants, the swineherd Eumaios and the cowherd Philoitios. He makes himself known to them and they greet him with tears of joy, ready and eager to fight alongside their beloved master against the hated Suitors.

Odysseus returns to the hall, where Penelope insists that he be given a try with the bow. Telemachos knows that this will be the start of the fighting, so he wants his mother gone before the bloodshed begins. He orders her back to her room, and there she cries herself to sleep.

Eurykleia bars the doors from the outside, and within the hall Odysseus takes the bow. To the Suitors' amazement he strings it with ease. With his right hand he plucks the bowstring, testing it, and it sings under his hands like the call of a swallow. The Suitors, now terribly alarmed, change colour, and Zeus sends a portent by thundering loudly. Odysseus shoots an arrow through all twelve of the axes, then stripping off his beggar's rags, he leaps on to the threshold of the great hall and turns to face his enemies.

Now at last he can take his revenge for the wrongs they have done him. He begins by shooting Antinoos, the worst of them all (22.8–21):

> He aimed a painful arrow straight at Antinoos,
> who was about to lift a fine two-handled goblet
> made of gold, holding it in his hands to drink
> his wine, with no thought in his heart of death.
> Who would think that one man, alone among
> many men at their feasting, however strong,
> could inflict on him the dark fate of death?
> Odysseus aimed and shot him through the throat,
> and the point of the arrow ran straight through
> his soft neck. He slumped to one side, the cup
> fell from his hand, and a thick jet of mortal blood
> gushed from his nostrils. With a sharp jerk of his foot
> he kicked the table from him, and knocked the food
> to the floor, bread and roast meat all spoiled.

At first the other Suitors are angry, thinking that this shot was an accident, but they soon realize the truth. 'Dogs, you never thought that I'd come home from Troy,' cries Odysseus. 'And now the fetters of death are firmly fastened over you.'

The Suitors are terrified. Eurymachos tries to lay the blame for their past behaviour on the dead Antinoos, hoping for mercy, but when he sees that his words are futile he urges the rest of the Suitors to fight. He draws his sword and leaps at Odysseus with a great shout, but an arrow through the chest makes him the second victim.

The third man to die is Amphinomos. He has been the least obnoxious of the Suitors, liked by Penelope and friendly towards Odysseus, who warned him as clearly as he could that bloodshed was likely and he should leave the house without delay. Amphinomos ignored the warning, and now he is killed by the spear of Telemachos, who then runs to the storeroom to fetch arms and armour while Odysseus picks off more Suitors with his remaining arrows.

Unfortunately Telemachos forgets to lock the storeroom door, and now the treacherous goatherd Melanthios helps the Suitors by bringing them weapons. Eumaios and Philoitios catch him and tie him up, leaving him locked in the storeroom, then return to fight side by side with Odysseus and Telemachos. They are only four against many, but they are helped by Athene, who prevents all the Suitors' spear-casts from striking home. One by one the Suitors are relentlessly killed, and those still alive are terrified (22.298–309):

> Their minds gripped by panic, they stampeded
> about the hall like a herd of cattle, set upon
> and driven crazy by the darting gadfly
> in the spring season when the days grow long.
> The other men were like hook-taloned vultures
> with curved beaks, who come down from the mountains
> and swoop on smaller birds; fearful of the clouds,
> these scatter over the plain, while the vultures
> leap on them and do them to death, and they have
> no defence or escape, and men enjoy the hunt;
> so these men, storming about the house,
> struck down the Suitors, one man after another,
> and terrible cries rose up as their heads were broken,
> and the floor was seething with blood.

At last all the Suitors are dead, apart from the bard Phemios and the herald Medon, both of whom served the others against their will and so are spared. Now Odysseus is once more undisputed king of Ithaca, in a palace piled high with corpses.

He calls in Eurykleia, who on seeing the slaughter begins to raise a great cry of triumph. Odysseus silences her. On his instructions she fetches twelve serving-women who have been disloyally sleeping with the Suitors. One of these is Melantho, the sister of Melanthios and mistress of Eurymachos, who has been particularly insolent towards Odysseus. The women are made to carry the corpses of their dead lovers out into the courtyard, then to clean the blood-spattered hall. When all is done, Telemachos hangs them for their treachery (22.468–73):

> As long-winged thrushes or doves fly into a snare
> set for them in a thicket, trying to get to their nests,
> but a dreadful bed receives them; so the women's heads
> were strung in a row, nooses around their necks, that all
> might die a ghastly death. They kicked with their feet
> for a little while, but not for very long.

Melanthios too is punished for his betrayal: his nose, ears, hands, feet and genitals are cut off and thrown to the dogs, and he is left to die. Finally Odysseus fumigates the house and courtyard with burning sulphur. Now Penelope can be told the joyous news of her husband's return and triumph.

REUNION

Eurykleia excitedly wakes her mistress with the news that Odysseus, the 'stranger', has come home and killed all the Suitors. Cautious Penelope, meeting him once again, appears slow to believe that this can really be her husband, even after he has been bathed and dressed in fine clothing, and Athene has shed beauty over his form. Only when Odysseus describes the unique construction of their marriage-bed, which he himself once built around the bole of an olive tree still rooted in the ground, is she persuaded that this truly is her long-lost husband. She runs to him and takes him in her arms, weeping for joy; and Odysseus

wept, holding his lovely wife whose heart was loyal;
and as when the land appears, a welcome sight,
to men who are swimming, whose well-made ship
Poseidon has wrecked at sea, pounding it with the wind
and the massive waves, and only a few reach the land
by swimming and escape the grey sea, their bodies
caked with salt, and joyfully they set foot on the land,
escaping disaster – so welcome was her husband to her
as she looked at him, and she would not let him go
from the embrace of her white arms.

The simile here (23.232–40) of a shipwrecked sailor is applied to Penelope, but it also describes Odysseus: he was the sailor, shipwrecked by Poseidon, who escaped on to the island of Scheria, caked with salt and joyful at escaping disaster. By making his simile refer to Penelope, who is as joyful as the sailor coming to safety, Homer gently emphasizes the similarity of husband and wife. Theirs is indeed a well-matched marriage. When Odysseus was among the Phaiakians, he said to Nausikaa, 'There is nothing more steadfast or secure than when a man and woman of like mind share a home together' (6.182–4). And Homer, in his depiction of Odysseus and Penelope, makes it clear that they are very much a man and woman of like mind.

After their reunion, husband and wife go to bed together, and Athene lengthens the night for them by holding back Eos, the goddess of Dawn, and her daylight until they have enjoyed each other to the full.

The next day Odysseus goes to find his old father Laertes, and comes upon him wearily toiling in his orchard, dressed in squalid clothes. The old man is overjoyed to have his son with him again and to learn of the Suitors' deaths. But many of the Suitors' relatives are planning a counter-attack, and soon they approach, urged on by Eupeithes, the father of Antinoos.

Laertes, Odysseus and Telemachos go out to meet them, supported by Eumaios, Philoitios, and other faithful servants. Athene breathes great strength into old Laertes, so that he throws the first spear and kills Eupeithes. A pitched battle is about to break out when Athene, shouting out a fearsome cry, separates the warring parties and re-establishes peace between Odysseus and the Ithacans.

This is the end of the *Odyssey*, but we know from Teiresias's prophecies in Hades what is to happen next to Odysseus. He must go on a long journey, carrying with him an oar, until he reaches a place so far inland and a people so unfamiliar with the sea that a wayfarer thinks his oar is a winnowing-fan. There he must plant his oar in the ground and placate Poseidon with a sacrifice. This done, he may return home to Ithaca, where in prosperous old age a gentle death will come to him from the sea.

A different ending was given in a lost epic poem, the *Telegony*, attributed to Eugammon of Kyrene (sixth century BC), according to which a son, Telegonos, had been born to Odysseus and the enchantress Circe. He grew up on Aiaia, but when he became a man he went in search of his father. He landed on Ithaca, and was raiding some cattle when Odysseus came upon him and tried to stop him by force. Neither, of course, recognized the other, and Telegonos wounded Odysseus mortally, striking him with his spear tipped with the deadly sting-ray.

When, with sorrow, he realized his victim's identity, he took his father's corpse, together with Penelope and Telemachos, back to Circe's island of Aiaia. There he married Penelope, and Telemachos married Circe, who made all three of them immortal.

AFTERMATH

Homer's Odysseus is clever, courageous, resourceful and self-possessed, but in later literature his character often changes to one less likeable. In fifth-century tragedy he can be noble and generous, as in Sophocles' *Ajax*, or an unscrupulous cynic, as in his *Philoktetes*, while Euripides gives the Homeric Odysseus a humorous treatment in his *Cyclops*, but makes him callous and cruel in his *Hecuba*. Virgil too depicts him as unscrupulous in his theft of the Palladion and his revenge on Palamedes, and he has often since been seen as an unprincipled rogue, though Shakespeare in his *Troilus and Cressida* reverts to a concept more in tune with Homer's heroic Odysseus.

The focus in later literature is often on an outward-bound Odysseus, ever questing, an insatiable explorer of the unknown world, as in Nikos Kazantzakis's *The Odyssey: a Modern Sequel* (1938). This carries on from where Homer left off, with Odysseus continually travelling in his search for new experiences from Ithaca to Crete and down the length of Africa, to his death in Antarctica. This concept of Odysseus as the perpetual wanderer in search of knowledge begins with Dante, and perhaps is best summed up in one of Tennyson's finest poems, *Ulysses* (the Latin version of Odysseus' name). Here Odysseus is a man who yearns to travel, to explore. 'I cannot rest from travel: I will drink life to the lees,' he says. 'How dull it is to pause, to make an end, / To rust unburnished, not to shine in use!' He and his fellow sailors are now old, and near to death, but even so it is not too late to explore further. The poem ends with Odysseus saying:

> Come, my friends,
> 'Tis not too late to seek a newer world.
> Push off, and sitting well in order smite

The sounding furrows; for my purpose holds
To sail beyond the sunset, and the baths
Of all the western stars, until I die.
It may be that the gulfs will wash us down:
It may be we shall touch the Happy Isles,
And see the great Achilles, whom we knew.
Tho' much is taken, much abides; and tho'
We are not now that strength which in old days
Moved earth and heaven; that which we are, we are;
One equal temper of heroic hearts,
Made weak by time and fate, but strong in will
To strive, to seek, to find, and not to yield.

This has come a long way from Homer's Odysseus, who hates the sea and all the troubles it brings him, and hates the way it keeps him from his home in Ithaca. When, in the *Odyssey*, Kalypso offers him immortality, Odysseus says to her (5.215–20):

'Lady goddess, do not be angry with me. I know all this
for myself, that wise Penelope is never a match for you
in beauty and stature, for she is a mortal, and you are
immortal and ageless. But even so, what I want,
and all my days I long for, is to go back to my house
and to see the day of my homecoming.'

Nevertheless this long journey home, this odyssey of Odysseus, remains in itself inspirational, as for the Greek poet Constantine Cavafy in his poem *Ithaca* (1911).

When you set out for Ithaca, pray that the journey be long, full of adventures, full of things to learn. The Laistrygonians and the Cyclops, angry Poseidon – do not fear them. Such as these you will never find on your way, if you have elevated thoughts, if choice emotions touch your spirit and your flesh. The Laistrygonians and the Cyclops and fierce Poseidon you will not meet, unless you carry them in your heart, unless your heart sets them in your path.

Pray that your journey be long; that there be many summer mornings when with what joy, what delight, you will enter harbours you have never seen before, and stop at Phoenician trading-ports, acquire beautiful merchandise, mother-of-pearl and coral, amber and ebony, and sensuous perfumes of all kinds – as many sensuous perfumes as you can. Visit many Egyptian cities, to learn and learn again from those who know.

Have Ithaca always in your mind. Your destination is to arrive there; but do not hurry your journey at all. Better that it should last for many years, that you cast anchor at the island when you are old, rich with all you have gained on the way, not expecting Ithaca to give you wealth; Ithaca has given you that splendid journey. Without Ithaca you would not have set out. Ithaca has no more to give you now.

And if you find her poor, Ithaca has not cheated you. You have acquired such wisdom, so much experience, that you will have understood what Ithaca means.

12

THE HOUSE OF PELOPS

The legends of the house of Pelops are some of the most violent in the whole of classical myth, with feuds, curses, cannibalism and murder leading to vengeance and bloodshed in generation after generation. They also, as we shall see, proved especially inspirational to the ancient dramatists, providing the plots of many tragedies, several of which we are lucky enough still to possess.

PELOPS

Pelops was the son of Tantalos, who ruled the lands around Mount Sipylos in Lydia. Tantalos was a son of Zeus by a certain Plouto, whose name means 'Wealth' but who is otherwise unknown. Tantalos was proverbial for his own wealth, and was moreover a favourite of the gods, who shared their feasts with him at their tables on Olympos. He abused his privileges and offended them irredeemably, for when Pelops was still a child, Tantalos cut him up and cooked him in a stew, then served it to the gods to test their omniscience. Naturally, being gods, they were not deceived and they refused the food, all except Demeter. She was grieving for her lost daughter Persephone and absentmindedly ate part of Pelops's shoulder, but all was well, for the gods brought the boy back to life and Demeter gave him a new shoulder made of ivory. So beautiful had he now become that Poseidon fell in love with him and carried him off to Olympos, and here he stayed until he became a young man and it was time to return to earth. As for Tantalos, he was made to endure eternal punishment in Hades for his crime (p. 112).

When Pelops began to think of marriage, he chose as his

future wife the beautiful Hippodameia, only daughter of Oinomaos, son of the war-god Ares and king of Pisa in the western
Peloponnesian district of Elis. To win her hand would be a
dangerous enterprise, for Oinomaos had no intention of letting
his daughter marry: either he was in love with her himself, or
an oracle had warned him that he would die by the hand of the
man who married her. Many suitors had wooed her, but not
one of them had returned alive from his wooing, let alone won
the girl of his choice.

It was Oinomaos's practice to challenge each of the suitors
to a chariot race, starting from Pisa and finishing at the altar of
Poseidon in faraway Corinth. The prize for their winning the
race would be the hand of Hippodameia, the price of losing
would be death. The suitor would set out in his chariot, together
with his chosen bride, Oinomaos giving them a start while he
sacrificed a ram to Zeus. Then he too would set out, wearing
full armour and driving a chariot and immortal horses given
him by his father, the war-god Ares. Small wonder that he
always caught up with the pair before they arrived at Corinth,
whereupon he would spear the unhappy suitor between the
shoulder-blades and return home with his daughter.

When Pelops decided to try his skill, Oinomaos had already
triumphantly nailed the heads of many defeated suitors over the
door of his palace: twelve, or thirteen, or sixteen, or eighteen,
according to different sources – certainly quite enough to give
Pelops pause. Yet with no hesitation the young man set out to
his fate. He invoked the help of his old lover Poseidon, and the
god supplied him with a chariot of gold drawn by winged
horses. This is Pindar's version of Pelops's request (*Olympian
Ode* 1.75–88):

'If the dear gifts of Love can recall a favour, Poseidon, then check the
brazen spear of Oinomaos, speed me in the swiftest of chariots to

Elis, and bring me near to power. For thirteen suitors has he killed, putting off his daughter's marriage.

'But great danger does not grip the coward. Since all men must die, why should a man sit in darkness and pursue a futile old age without glory, reft of all blessings? This contest lies before me. May you give me a glad outcome.'

Thus he spoke, and his words were not in vain. The god honoured him with the gift of a golden chariot and tireless winged horses. And he overcame the might of Oinomaos and took the girl as his wife.

Thus in Pindar's version the gifts from the god were sufficient to bring Pelops to victory, to win his bride and kill her wicked father. In the more usual tradition, Pelops won his victory by a trick, though the precise details of the story vary slightly.

Oinomaos had a charioteer called Myrtilos, a son of Hermes, who was (to his own misfortune, as it turned out) open to bribery. Either Pelops bribed him with the promise of a share in the kingdom and a night in Hippodameia's bed, or the girl herself bribed him, promising him a night of passion, because she had fallen in love with Pelops as soon as she saw him. Either way, Myrtilos agreed to betray his master, and he replaced the bronze linchpins in the wheels of Oinomaos's chariot with pins made of wax. The race began as usual and Pelops set off with Hippodameia, but when Oinomaos was in hot pursuit, the wax pins melted. His chariot foundered and he was dragged to his death in the reins. Dying, he cursed his treacherous charioteer, wishing on him death at the hands of the man he had befriended.

This is exactly what happened. Pelops murdered Myrtilos by hurling him from a cliff-top into the sea, either because he wanted to get out of paying the promised reward, or because he found Myrtilos trying to rape Hippodameia. But Pelops was not to be so easily rid of his victim, for with his last breath Myrtilos cursed his murderer, just as he himself had been cursed.

Pelops did his best to nullify any harm that the curse might do. He journeyed to the far ends of the earth and the river of Ocean, where Hephaistos purified him of the murder. He instituted the worship of Hermes, Myrtilos's father, throughout his land. He raised a mound in Myrtilos's honour beside the racetrack at Olympia. (It was later said that the charioteer's ghost, called Taraxippos, 'Horse-frightener', haunted the place. Often at this point during the Olympic Games, horses were thrown into an unaccountable panic – just as Oinomaos's mares had been terrified when his chariot crashed – so that chariots came to grief and their charioteers were injured or killed.) Yet do all that Pelops might, the curse remained. It would be brought to bloody fulfilment among his descendants.

After his marriage, Pelops formally reburied Hippodameia's dead suitors, who had been shovelled into the earth anyhow by Oinomaos, and he raised a monument to honour them, with the expressed intention of pleasing his wife. No doubt he also intended to add to his own honour by announcing to posterity the number and quality of the men defeated by Oinomaos, before the great Pelops came along in his turn and vanquished the evil king.

Certainly the most famous mythical event connected with Pelops was the celebrated chariot race, and both Sophocles and Euripides wrote tragedies (now lost) on the theme, entitled *Oinomaos*. Apollonius (*Argonautica* 1.752–8) chose the final climactic moment of the race as one of the scenes on the splendid cloak, made by Athene, that Jason wore when he went ashore on Lemnos to meet Hypsipyle: Pelops beside Hippodameia in the leading chariot, frenziedly shaking the reins, and Oinomaos close behind, his spear stretched out ready to thrust it into Pelops's back, with just at that very moment the linchpin giving way and the chariot beginning to topple sideways.

Pelops became a tremendously powerful ruler. Not only was he now king of Elis, but he came to rule most of the rest of southern Greece and renamed the entire region the Peloponnese ('Pelops' Island'). Apollodorus (3.12.6) records an unsavoury story in which Arcadia withstood Pelops for a while until he finally won the land by trickery: he pretended friendship for its king, Stymphalos, then killed him and scattered his mangled body over the land. This terrible deed brought the anger of Zeus and a prolonged drought on Greece, until the virtuous Aiakos, king of the island of Aigina, prayed to the god for deliverance, and at last the rain came down.

Zeus must have forgiven Pelops, for he provided him with a magnificent sceptre, made by Hephaistos, as a symbol of his authority, and this was passed from father to son down the generations. Moreover, Pelops was afterwards one of the most renowned of Greek heroes, with a famous shrine at Olympia said to have been established by his even more renowned descendant Herakles.

Pelops and Hippodameia had a large and powerful family, with many connections to other great heroes. Three of their daughters married sons of Perseus, the founder of Mycenae, and thus formed important political alliances: Astydameia and Lysidike married (respectively) Alkaios and Elektryon (all of them becoming the grandparents of Herakles), while Nikippe married Sthenelos (and they would become the parents of Herakles' enemy Eurystheus).

Pelops' and Hippodameia's many sons included Atreus and Thyestes, whose legends will be considered shortly; Pittheus, the wise and just ruler of Troizen, who as we have seen was the grandfather of Theseus; Kopreus, who was the herald of

Eurystheus and thus involved with Herakles; and Alkathoos, a major figure in Megarian legend.

Alkathoos won the throne of Megara by his valour, when the fearsome Lion of Kithairon was ravaging the land. One of the lion's many victims was Euippos, son of the king of Megara, Megareus, who then decreed that whoever killed the beast would win the hand of his daughter, Euaichme, and would succeed to the rule of the kingdom. Alkathoos killed the lion and won both wife and kingship. He built a temple to Apollo and Artemis in gratitude for his achievement, and rebuilt the walls of Megara which had been destroyed by the Cretans in the reign of Nisos. It was said that Apollo himself helped Alkathoos with the work on the walls, and that the god rested his lyre on a certain stone which ever afterwards, if struck with a pebble, reverberated with a sound like a lyre. Pausanias, who records Alkathoos's history (1.41.3–6, 1.42.1–6, 1.43.4–5), saw the stone, and thought it a marvel.

Through his daughter Periboia, who married Telamon, king of Salamis, Alkathoos was grandfather of the Great Ajax, and through his daughter Automedousa, who married Iphikles, he was grandfather of Iolaos, Herakles' charioteer. He also had two sons, Ischepolis and Kallipolis. Ischepolis was killed at the Kalydonian Boarhunt, and it was Kallipolis who was the first to hear the sad news. He ran to tell his father, and found him preparing a fire to sacrifice to Apollo. This seemed inauspicious at such a moment, so Kallipolis flung the logs away. Alkathoos was angry at this apparent impiety, and without waiting to find out the reason for his son's impetuous action, he struck his head with one of the logs, killing him outright. Too late he learnt the truth.

These five, then, are the only sons of Pelops who play any significant part in myth – apart from one other. For Pelops had by a nymph an illegitimate but much-loved son called

Chrysippos, who died young and tragically. There are two quite different versions of his death, and both contain yet another powerful curse.

In one account, he was the victim of a homosexual abduction. Laios, the king of Thebes, was a guest of Pelops and had been teaching Chrysippos the art of chariot-driving. He fell in love with the boy and carried him off to Thebes to make him his catamite. Chrysippos killed himself in shame by falling on his sword, and Pelops laid a curse on Laios that led to his death, since Zeus ordained that as punishment Laios would be killed by his own son – and as we have seen (p. 274), Laios's son Oedipus did indeed kill his father, try as he might to avoid his fate. The first certain appearance of Chrysippos's abduction by Laios was in Euripides' lost tragedy *Chrysippos*.

In another version of Chrysippos's death, he was murdered by his half-brothers Atreus and Thyestes, because even though they were the legitimate heirs of Pelops, they were still afraid that their father, from affection, would bequeath the throne to Chrysippos. When Pelops discovered the murder, he exiled the two killers and proclaimed another powerful and effective curse: that they and their race might die at each other's hands. As we are about to see, this is exactly what happened.

ATREUS AND THYESTES

After the death of Eurystheus, killed while he was persecuting the children of Herakles (p. 225), an oracle proclaimed that the kingship of Mycenae should pass to a son of Pelops. This was the origin of one of the most famous, and most violent, feuds in myth, between the brothers Atreus and Thyestes, and it sowed the seeds of future violence for the next two generations.

In the beginning it revolved around a treacherous wife and a lamb with a golden fleece. Atreus had married Aerope, the daughter of Katreos, king of Crete, and she had borne him two sons, Agamemnon and Menelaos, but she turned out to be an unfaithful wife. She took Thyestes as her lover; and not only that, but she gave him a golden lamb that won him the throne of Mycenae. There are two stories about this lamb, both linking it with the kingship. In one version Hermes provided it, hoping to cause trouble and bloodshed in revenge for the death of his son Myrtilos. The lamb of gold gave its possessor the right to the throne, and at first Atreus owned it and became king. Then Aerope gave it to Thyestes, and he took the throne in his brother's place.

In the second version, it was Artemis who provided the lamb, after Atreus had vowed to sacrifice to her the best animal in his flocks. When he saw the wondrous lamb he ignored his vow, and killed it, and hid its beautiful fleece away in a chest, but Aerope found it and secretly gave it to her lover. Once Thyestes was in possession of the fleece, he declared in public that the throne should belong to whoever owned such a thing. Atreus, of course, agreed, thinking himself the owner – whereupon Thyestes produced the fleece and was made king.

Thyestes' rule, however, was shortlived, for Atreus had the mightiest of champions in the great god Zeus. To demonstrate his approval of Atreus' claim to the throne, Zeus reversed the course of the sun, making it rise in the west and sink in the east, and at this miraculous proof of divine support, Atreus once more became king. He drove Thyestes into exile, and punished his treacherous wife by drowning her.

He later took a hideous revenge on his brother as well. First he summoned him back to Mycenae, pretending that he wanted to be reconciled with him. He then invited him to a feast and served him with a main dish consisting of Thyestes' own sons, killed and cut up and stewed. Thyestes ate heartily, and at the end of the meal he asked for his sons to be brought in. Atreus presented him with their heads and hands and feet, telling him that what he did not see, he already had, and then banished him once more. Some writers, including Sophocles and Seneca, said that it was at this point that the sun reversed its direction, in horror at the appalling feast. Thyestes left, cursing Atreus and all his house and vowing revenge.

He inquired of an oracle how he might get that revenge, and was told to have a child by his own daughter. The outcome, leading eventually to Atreus' death, is related by Hyginus (*Fabula* 88), in what seems to be a composite version based on plots from tragedies. In Sikyon Thyestes came across his daughter, Pelopeia, acting as a priestess in rites to Athene, and when she undressed to wash the blood of sacrifice from her robe, he covered his face and raped her. He ran off, still quite unrecognized by her, but not before she had seized his sword. This she hid away.

Shortly after this, Atreus came to Thesprotia, where he met Pelopeia and decided to make her his wife, believing her to be the daughter of the king, Thesprotos, who said nothing to put him right. So Atreus married his niece, and in due course she gave birth to a baby son – but knowing that the infant was the result of her rape, she cast him out to die. Some shepherds saved him, and gave him to be suckled by a she-goat. When Atreus heard about the baby, he found him and brought him up, believing him to be his own son. He named him Aigisthos because of the goat (*aix, aigos*).

Many years later, Atreus' sons, Agamemnon and Menelaos, came across Thyestes at Delphi and captured him, taking him back with them to Mycenae. Atreus flung his hated brother into prison and told Aigisthos, now grown up, to kill him. Aigisthos was about to run him through with his sword when Thyestes recognized it as his own weapon, lost on the night of the rape, and found out that it had originally come from Pelopeia. He begged to see her, and when she came to his prison he told her the truth about Aigisthos' conception. Appalled to learn of her incest, she seized the sword and killed herself.

Aigisthos was of course unwilling to murder the man who had turned out to be his real father, so he took the bloody sword to Atreus and pretended that he had done so. Atreus, overjoyed at the supposed death of his old enemy, went down to the seashore to offer sacrifices in thanksgiving to the gods. Aigisthos followed, and there killed him.

Thyestes then took the throne once more and banished Agamemnon and Menelaos. Years passed, but as soon as they were old enough they returned to Mycenae to reclaim their father's kingdom, with the armed support of Tyndareos, king of Sparta. They drove Thyestes out, and Aigisthos with him, and Agamemnon became king. The rest of Thyestes' days were unmomentous, spent on the island of Kythera off the south-eastern tip of the Peloponnese. But his old curse on the House of Atreus would lead to yet more violence in the future.

This bloody myth was a powerful source of inspiration for the ancient tragedians. Many plays have been lost, except for fragments, but we know that Sophocles wrote an *Atreus* and a *Thyestes in Sikyon*, plus one (possibly two) *Thyestes* plays, and that Euripides wrote a *Cretan Women* and a *Thyestes*. As for extant tragedies, these often contain substantial references to the myth, as, for instance, Euripides' *Elektra* (699–746), where the chorus sing of Aerope betraying Atreus by giving Thyestes the golden lamb, and of Zeus reversing the course of the sun and the stars in support of Atreus. And we possess Seneca's entire *Thyestes*, where in typical fashion all the horrors of the children's butchery are spelt out (even to a last faint sob issuing from a child's head, as it rolls away from its truncated corpse), and the ghastliness of the hideous banquet is dwelt on to the full.

Yet suggestion can be more effective than grim detail, so

perhaps the most memorable dramatization that we possess is Aeschylus's *Oresteia* trilogy, where Thyestes' curse on the House of Atreus forms a haunting background to the bloody and violent events enacted on and off stage: the murder of Agamemnon by Klytaimnestra with the support of Aigisthos, the murder of Klytaimnestra and Aigisthos by Orestes, and the pursuit of Orestes by the Furies, raging at the murder of his mother. Here is the prophetess Kassandra sensing the unseen but powerful presence of Thyestes' murdered children (*Agamemnon* 1217–22):

> Look, do you see them sitting by the house,
> the young ones, like shapes seen in dreams?
> Children slain by their own kin,
> their hands filled with meat, their own flesh,
> holding out inner parts and vitals,
> a burden most pitiful – food their father tasted.

AGAMEMNON AND MENELAOS

Thyestes' curse had been laid on the whole House of Atreus, but it seems that it did not equally affect Atreus' two sons (who are often jointly known as the Atreidai). Both brothers married daughters of Tyndareos: Agamemnon chose Klytaimnestra and became king of Mycenae, while Menelaos, as we have seen (p. 304), won the beautiful Helen (who was really the daughter of Zeus) and succeeded Tyndareos as king of Sparta. Menelaos certainly had his troubles, which included the loss of Helen to Paris, prince of Troy. Yet all ended well for him, since he regained his wife and lived out his days with her in peace and prosperity. But for Agamemnon it was quite different, and it was in his branch of the family that Thyestes' curse led to recurring bloodshed and vengeance.

Not that this was apparent at first. Klytaimnestra bore

him several children: three daughters, Iphigeneia, Elektra and Chrysothemis, and a son, Orestes. Many years passed peacefully. Then Helen ran off with Paris to Troy and Menelaos turned to his brother for help. A huge force was summoned to fight at Troy, and Agamemnon, as commander-in-chief, marched out from Mycenae, not to return for another ten years.

He had no intimations of future tragedy, not even when he sacrificed his daughter Iphigeneia to raise winds to take his great fleet to Troy (p. 317). His campaign was eventually a success and Troy was captured and sacked. His victory was seen as a tremendous military achievement and he sailed home triumphant.

Iphigeneia's sacrifice, however, had earned him the implacable and enduring hatred of Klytaimnestra, and in one tradition she had an additional reason for resentment. It was sometimes said that her first husband had been Tantalos, a son of Thyestes, until Agamemnon murdered both Tantalos and the son she had borne him, then took Klytaimnestra for himself. In Euripides' *Iphigeneia at Aulis*, before condemning Agamemnon for intending to sacrifice their daughter, she says pitifully (1148-52):

'The first thing I have to reproach you with is that you married me against my will, taking me by force. You killed Tantalos, the husband I had then, and you tore my baby from my breast and dashed him to death on the ground.'

So whether she had one death to avenge, or three, she took Aigisthos as her lover while Agamemnon was away at Troy, and when he returned home, together they murdered him.

Homer's *Odyssey* is the first work to recount his sorry fate. The gods knew that Aigisthos intended to seduce Klytaimnestra and kill Agamemnon on his return home, and they cautioned him on no account to do so. He ignored their warning. He carried off the minstrel who had been left to guard Klytaimnestra and marooned him on a desert island, then set about seducing her. He soon persuaded her to yield to him, then took her into his own house.

Eventually Troy fell and Agamemnon returned to the Argolid. For a whole year a watchman, posted by Aigisthos, had been looking out for his arrival, so when at last he landed, kissing the earth and weeping with joy to be back in his own country, his murderers were ready for him. Aigisthos invited him to a banquet, then set upon him and his followers with a band of twenty armed men, killing him as he feasted 'as a man strikes down an ox at the manger'. We presume that Klytaimnestra had been in hiding, for she had no reason (in her husband's eyes) to be in Aigisthos's house; but as Agamemnon lay dying, she emerged and killed his Trojan captive Kassandra, the daughter of King Priam.

Homer does not mention the sacrifice of Iphigeneia, present in all later accounts, and to him Klytaimnestra's part in the story seems to be one of simple adultery and betrayal, in which she abetted the murder out of loyalty to her lover. It is in fifth-century tragedy, and especially in Aeschylus's *Agamemnon* (the first play in his *Oresteia* trilogy of 458 BC), that her role is developed and she kills out of personal hatred and a fierce desire for revenge. We shall look in greater detail at this Klytaimnestra in our chapter 'Dangerous Women'.

THE REVENGE OF ORESTES

Aigisthos now ruled the kingdom securely for some years, and he and Klytaimnestra had children: a daughter, Erigone, and a son, Aletes. But bloodshed begets bloodshed, and the death of Agamemnon was not forgotten. Orestes had been sent for safety far away from Mycenae, and he grew up with the knowledge that he must one day become his father's avenger. When the right time came, he returned to his homeland and killed his mother and Aigisthos.

His vengeance was viewed rather differently down the centuries. Homer treats it as an act of justice in response to an appalling crime, but by the fifth century BC it was seen as rather more problematic, since it was then said that Orestes was hounded by the Furies of his dead mother in punishment for her shed blood.

According to Homer's *Odyssey*, Orestes returned to Mycenae eight years after Agamemnon's murder. He killed Aigisthos and, it is implied, Klytaimnestra as well, and his vengeance is depicted as an entirely praiseworthy deed for which he won an honoured reputation. The story is used as a moral example for the other characters of the epic: Telemachos is urged to confront and take revenge on the Suitors, just as Orestes did on the evil Aigisthos, and Penelope is depicted as a loyal and virtuous wife,

Orestes, with Chrysothemis next to him, kills Aigisthos.

and contrasted with the treacherous Klytaimnestra. Orestes is seen as a just and avenging hero, and there is no hint of any pursuit by his mother's Furies who later play so important a part in the legend. Agamemnon's murder demanded punishment, and Orestes, as head of the family, would necessarily have been the judge and executioner. No mention is made of Elektra, the sister who would later be reunited joyously with Orestes and support him through the murders.

The first mention of the Furies playing a part in Orestes' revenge is in a fragment of the (mostly lost) *Oresteia* of the lyric poet Stesichorus. After this the legend became very popular during the fifth century, when it was the subject of several extant tragedies. According to these, at the time of Agamemnon's murder the young Orestes was taken for safety to the court of Strophios, the king of Phokis, who was a supporter of Agamemnon. Strophios brought Orestes up along with his own son, Pylades, and the two boys became firm friends. In the vengeance plays, Pylades accompanies Orestes when he secretly returns home to Mycenae, having learnt from Apollo's oracle at Delphi that he must now avenge his father's death.

Here he meets his sister Elektra and they recognize each other with mutual joy. In Aeschylus's *Libation Bearers* (the second play in his *Oresteia* trilogy), this reunion occurs at the tomb of Agamemnon, and brother and sister join in an invocation to their father's ghost, urging him to support the vengeance. The focus of this play is still mainly on Orestes as avenger, and Elektra is not actively involved in the killings. (In later tragedies Elektra's role would be developed further, and we shall look in greater detail at this in the next chapter.)

Orestes gains admittance to the palace by pretending to be a stranger from Phokis, bringing news of Orestes' death, and he kills first Aigisthos, then Klytaimnestra. It is the murder of his mother that, not surprisingly, causes him the greatest anguish.

Klytaimnestra, face to face with her now-recognized son, appeals to him by the bond they shared when he was a baby (896–8): 'Stop, my son! Show pity, child, before this breast, where often you would lay your head in sleep, and with soft gums sucked in the milk that gave you life.'

Orestes falters, appalled at what he is about to do, and turns for advice to Pylades, who (speaking for the first and only time in the play) reminds him of Apollo's instructions and of the sacred nature of his vengeance. His confidence recovered, Orestes leads his mother into the palace and there kills her.

Her terrifying Furies at once begin to hound him, and these form the chorus of the final play in the trilogy, *Eumenides*. Apollo sends Orestes to Athens, where he is tried by a jury of Athenian citizens at the homicide court on the Areopagos, with Apollo acting as his advocate and the Furies as his prosecutors. When the jury's votes turn out to be equal, Athene gives the casting vote in Orestes' favour, on the grounds that a father takes precedence over a mother. (After all, she herself was born from Zeus alone.) Orestes is acquitted, and the Furies are propitiated by a new cult at Athens in which they are honoured as beneficent powers, with the new name of Eumenides ('Kindly Ones'). At last the long cycle of bloodshed is over, and the curse on the House of Atreus comes to an end.

AFTERMATH

Other extant tragedies dramatize later events in the life of Orestes. In Euripides' *Iphigeneia among the Taurians*, Apollo has told Orestes that to gain his final release from the Furies he must fetch to Athens a holy image of Artemis from the land of the barbarian Taurians (the Crimea). He and Pylades are captured on their arrival by the natives and taken, on the orders of the savage king Thoas, to Artemis' temple where they will suffer the fate of all strangers who come to the land: death at the hands of Artemis' priestess. Although they are unaware of it, this is none other than Orestes' long-lost sister Iphigeneia, who did not after all die when Agamemnon tried to sacrifice her, but was carried off by Artemis, and a deer substituted on the altar in her place.

At the last moment brother and sister recognize one another, and now Iphigeneia is filled with joy at the thought of returning home to Greece once more. She tricks the Taurians into standing at a distance while she pretends to wash away in the sea the stain of matricide from her two victims, and to wash the statue of Artemis too, which has been polluted by their presence. Then all three sail swiftly away to safety, taking with them the statue just as Apollo instructed. Athene intervenes to stop the furious king Thoas from pursuing them. Calmed by the goddess, he even wishes them well.

So Iphigeneia returned to Greece, where she became a priestess of Artemis at Brauron. As for Orestes, he married Hermione, the only daughter of Menelaos and Helen, after the death of her first husband Neoptolemos, in this way uniting the two branches of the family tree that sprang from Atreus. Both Orestes and Hermione play a part in Euripides' extant *Andromache*, where Hermione is still married to Neoptolemos, but is very bitter because she is barren. She blames this on spells cast by Andromache, once the wife of Hektor, who is now her husband's concubine, won at Troy, and by whom he has had a son, Molossos.

Aided by her father Menelaos, she tries to have Andromache and Molossos put to death, and almost succeeds – but they are rescued in the nick of time by old Peleus, Neoptolemos' grandfather. Terrified of her husband's anger, Hermione tries time and again to kill herself. 'When she tried to hang herself,' says her old nurse (811–16), 'the servants told to watch her barely managed to stop her, or to snatch a sword she had found and take it away. She is full of remorse, and knows very well that what she did was wrong. I'm just worn out with trying to stop her hanging herself.'

Hermione is hysterical with fear, but then Orestes arrives, whom Menelaos had betrothed to her before the war began, though he later changed his mind and promised her to Neoptolemos if he would help to capture Troy. So now Hermione thankfully escapes her husband's wrath by fleeing with Orestes to Sparta, and there she marries him after Neoptolemos' death (in this play brought about at Delphi by Orestes himself).

Orestes became king of Mycenae, in one version first killing his half-brother Aletes, the son of Aigisthos and Klytaimnestra, who had usurped the throne. He ruled over not only the whole of the Argolid, but Sparta as well after Menelaos died leaving no heir. Hermione bore him a son, Teisamenos, who would succeed Orestes on his death and rule until the Heraklids invaded the Peloponnese and drove him off the throne.

Orestes himself ruled peacefully for many years and at last died in old age, at 70, or even 90 in some accounts, reputedly of a snake-bite. He was buried at Tegea. Centuries later, according to Herodotus (1.67), when the Spartans were trying to capture Tegea, the Delphic Oracle told them that they would be victorious if they brought Orestes' bones back home to Sparta. These, said the oracle obscurely, were at Tegea, at a place where two winds blew under strong constraint, where blow met blow and woe was laid upon woe.

The place turned out to be a blacksmith's forge, the 'winds' being the two pairs of bellows, the 'blows and counterblows' the hammer and anvil, and the 'woe' the beaten iron, because iron is used for weapons and so brings woe to mankind. Buried in the yard of the forge was found a coffin ten feet long, its whole length filled by a huge skeleton. The bones were taken to Sparta, and ever since that day the Spartans had the better of the Tegeans.

13

DANGEROUS WOMEN

Classical myths abound in dangerous women: women who in one way or another bring men to death. Often they are motivated by a passion for revenge and they kill out of rage, or jealousy, or grief. Sometimes the power of their sexuality causes death. Sometimes they kill by accident, out of ignorance or even out of love. But always some extreme emotion drives them on until their victim or victims lie dead. In this chapter we shall be looking in detail at just a few of these dangerous women.

We often get our clearest picture of them from the Athenian tragedies that survive from the fifth century BC. Many hundreds of plays were put on stage in Athens at the festivals of Dionysos, the god of drama, and almost all have been lost. But we still possess thirty-three of them, in many of which we see these women in action – and often very bloody action.

When these plays were staged, tragedy had been in existence for a relatively short while: since about 530, according to the traditional date of its origin. So during the fifth century myths were being dramatized for the very first time, and the plays were turning the characters of mythology for the first time into living, breathing people on stage. Mythical women often become dramatic characters of great power, dominating the action. Often too a tragedy focuses on the woman's predicament more than on the man's, dwelling on the pain of women in extreme situations, and on their reactions to that pain. And this is when these mythical women become dangerous.

So let us begin by considering four particularly dangerous women who kill their victims with their own hands: Klytaimnestra, Hecuba, Medea and Prokne. Their aim is to gain revenge on a man who has wronged them, so instead of sitting passively by on the sidelines, which might have been seen as the typical female role, they step decisively into the male role of action. Yet they cannot easily attack using direct violence, because they are physically weaker than the men they see as their enemies. So they use their own skills – inventiveness, persuasion and deceit – to achieve their aims. And deceit should be viewed in no critical spirit, since deception (*dolos* in the Greek) was seen as a reasonable way to achieve an honourable revenge. We have only to think of the heroic Odysseus of the *Odyssey*, that arch-deceiver, who uses deceit and violence to end up exactly where he belongs, in his wife's bed at home in his own palace. These women too use deceit to achieve revenge on their enemies, and the weapons they choose are taken from within their own domestic sphere of influence.

We should be careful not to judge these women in modern terms. As discussed earlier (p. 19), revenge can be viewed as both honourable and heroic. And as we shall see, these women appear to be justified also by the results of the vengeance which they take so decisively.

KLYTAIMNESTRA

We have seen how the great Agamemnon, king of Mycenae, led out a huge fighting force of Greeks to recover his eloping sister-in-law Helen, and how he sacrificed his daughter Iphigeneia to raise winds to take his fleet to Troy (p. 317). His wife Klytaimnestra never forgave him, and in his absence during the subsequent ten-year-long war she took his enemy Aigisthos as her lover. When Agamemnon at last returned home victorious, together they murdered him.

This story, with its aftermath of revenge killings, was familiar long before the fifth century BC. It occurred first in Homer and was well illustrated in ancient art, but it comes to its most vivid

Klytaimnestra with axe.

life in the tragedies of Aeschylus, Sophocles and Euripides, with the archetypal Klytaimnestra of Aeschylus's *Agamemnon*, the first play in his *Oresteia* trilogy, dominating all others. Before this production, as far as we can tell, Klytaimnestra and Aigisthos had been seen as joint partners-in-crime in Agamemnon's murder, with Aigisthos taking the dominant role – exactly as depicted on a famous Attic vase known as the 'Boston Oresteia Krater', painted about a dozen years before the *Oresteia* was produced. In the centre of the picture is Agamemnon, covered in a filmy robe and staggering backwards. Blood is pouring from his chest. Facing him is Aigisthos, with drawn sword; he has struck once and is about to strike again. Behind Aigisthos is Klytaimnestra, with axe in hand, following on in support.

In Aeschylus, however, the situation is entirely different. His

Klytaimnestra carries out the murder entirely on her own, while Aigisthos' part has dwindled into relative insignificance: he has become a coward, a blustering weakling, who appears onstage only at the end of the play. It is Klytaimnestra, the 'woman with the heart of a man' (10–11), who has nursed her rage and grief down the long years since Iphigeneia's death and now kills Agamemnon with a fierce joy, netting him in a robe while he is unarmed and vulnerable during his bath. Aeschylus has made her a powerful and awe-inspiring figure, one needing the help of no man to kill her treacherous husband.

Standing alone at the doors of her palace, she greets Agamemnon on his return from Troy. She pretends to welcome him home, using words that are a masterpiece of double meaning, and by which he is completely taken in. Even when she makes veiled references to their dead daughter, he fails to see below the surface. Iphigeneia is in her thoughts when she says: 'Our child does not stand here at our side, the child who sealed our pledges, mine and yours, our child who should be here . . .' (877–9). Only at the end of these words does she add their son's name, 'Orestes'. And again: 'For me the gushing fountains of my tears have dried completely up, and left no drop within' (887–8), which Agememnon understands as tears for his absence. But these were tears, wept long since, for Iphigeneia, which are now replaced by hatred for her daughter's killer.

'With such a greeting do I reward him,' she says. 'Let ill-will be absent, for many were the evils that I endured before' (903–5). He thinks she speaks of her loneliness in the long years without him, but once again she is referring to Iphigeneia's murder. And so she is greeting her husband in the way that he deserves – with death.

She lures him indoors to his destruction, persuading him to walk into the palace over the crimson cloths that her servants lay down for him. 'Now, my beloved,' she cries, 'step down from your chariot. Let not your foot, my lord, sacker of Troy, touch the earth. Servants, what are you waiting for? You have been told to strew the ground where he must walk with tapestries. Let there be spread before the house he never expected to see, where Justice leads him in, a crimson path' (905–11). And on Klytaimnestra's command, down flow the tapestries, red as blood, symbol of the blood that Agamemnon shed when he killed Iphigeneia, of all the blood that he shed at Troy, of his own blood about to be shed. Entirely ignorant of the fate his wife plans for him, he walks over the blood-red tapestries into the palace that he believes a safe haven, into Klytaimnestra's power, and to his death.

Quite alone too she kills him, and with him his Trojan concubine, Kassandra. Once Agamemnon is indoors, Klytaimnestra helps him to his bath, then puts him out of action with woven cloths that she throws over him. (A woman's primary domestic role was the weaving of the household fabrics, and fabric in a woman's hand can often become a kind of weapon.) Only then, when he is helpless, does Klytaimnestra attack him, using either an axe or a sword – both weapons are referred to, rather vaguely, in the Greek text, so we may imagine whichever we prefer.

Agamemnon's death cries are heard from inside the palace. Then the doors open to disclose Klytaimnestra standing over the bodies of her victims, her bloody weapon in her hand. Exultant at having at last achieved her revenge, she describes this long-awaited murder (1381–92):

'That he might not escape nor ward away his death, like one who catches fish I cast around him a net with no way out, a vast and deadly wealth of robes. I struck him twice, and with two great cries he buckled at the knees and fell. When he was down I struck a third blow, a thank-offering to Zeus, lord of the Underworld, saviour of corpses. Thus he fell and belched out his life, and as he died he poured forth his blood and spattered me with a dark and crimson rain, and I rejoiced as the sown corn rejoices, drenched with god-given showers when buds break forth in Spring.'

So *Agamemnon* ends with Iphigeneia avenged. In *Libation Bearers*, the second play of Aeschylus's trilogy, Klytaimnestra herself is murdered by her son Orestes in revenge for Agamemnon's death (p. 441). In the third play, *Eumenides*, Orestes is tried for matricide. The jury's votes turn out to be equal, which implies a state of balance and equal justification/condemnation for both his and Klytaimnestra's actions. It is only when Athene gives the casting vote in Orestes' favour, on the grounds that murder of a man is a more serious matter than murder of a woman, that he is acquitted and the cycle of bloodshed comes to an end.

The date of Aeschylus's *Oresteia* was 458 BC, and as far as we can tell this was the first time that this myth had been dramatized, and so the first time also that this avenging Klytaimnestra had, as it were, appeared in the flesh. Certainly, out of all the plays left to us, Aeschylus's Klytaimnestra is the earliest of these dangerous women to dominate the stage, as she steps out and boldly takes action against the man who has wronged her. Since then there have been many such. But when the palace doors open in the *Agamemnon*, and we see her standing over her victims, her bloody weapon in her hand, she is also in a sense standing right at the head of the western tradition of theatre, as the very first woman of her kind.

HECUBA

Klytaimnestra takes a bloody revenge for the death of a child, and so, in Euripides' *Hecuba*, does Hecuba. She was once queen of Troy, the wife of old King Priam, but when the play opens, Troy has fallen to the Greeks, the Trojan men have all been slaughtered, and the Trojan women are being carried off as slaves for the victors. The setting is the Greek encampment on the coast of Thrace, and here Hecuba spends her days lamenting, worn down with grief for the death of her husband, Priam, and for the deaths of her sons, killed in battle.

Yet more grief is still to come for her. Now another death takes place: her daughter Polyxena is sacrificed by the Greeks to appease the soul of the dead Achilles (p. 378). Yet in all this sorrow Hecuba has one solace: she has one son still alive – or so she thinks. At some time during the war she sent her youngest son, Polydoros, to live with Polymestor, the king of Thrace, and now she believes him still safe and well. She is wrong, for Polymestor has betrayed her trust and has murdered the boy for the sake of the gold that he brought with him. Hecuba learns this bitter truth soon after Polyxena's sacrifice, when Polydoros's body is found washed up by the sea.

Now Hecuba is changed from a figure of helpless grief and despair to one of raging, avenging fury. When Polymestor visits the Greek camp, she lures him and his two little sons into her tent with the bait that she knows will be most effective: she promises him more gold. With no hesitation he steps into her trap, and once he is inside the tent, she and her women overcome him by their sheer numbers. As Hecuba herself says: 'Women in a mass are terrible, and with the aid of deception (*dolos*) they are hard to combat' (884). They hold Polymestor down, then take his sword and kill his sons, and they gouge out his eyes with their brooch pins. So for punishment, instead of having a quick and easy death, he is left alive to suffer just what his treachery has cost him.

This is a savage revenge indeed, but Euripides' Hecuba is a true descendant of the Hecuba of Homer some three hundred years earlier. In the *Iliad* (24.212–14), when Achilles has killed her son Hektor, she says: 'I wish I could set my teeth in the middle of his liver and eat it. *That* would be vengeance for what he did to my son.'

After his blinding, Polymestor predicts Hecuba's strange end: that on the ship carrying her to Greece she will be transformed into a bitch with eyes of fire, and will plunge into the sea to her death. The nearby headland will be called 'Bitch's Grave', *kunos sema* (Kynossema, in the Thracian Chersonese), and will act as a landmark for future sailors. It is difficult to interpret this, but we know that fiery eyes were a sign of a supernatural being, and that the Furies (p. 27) were often likened to dogs, hunting down their prey – and certainly Hecuba acted like a Fury in human form, avenging a desperate wrong. This metamorphosis now offers her an escape from the slavery she loathed, and it seems also to grant her a kind of immortality. Kynossema is said still to re-echo with her mournful howling.

MEDEA

Klytaimnestra and Hecuba both avenge the death of a child. In the *Medea* of Euripides, Medea avenges her husband Jason's infidelity when he marries another woman, and she takes the most extreme revenge possible, by killing the children she has borne him.

Jason should have known better than to cross her so blatantly, for he was well aware that he was married to a woman of dangerous power. With her magical skills she had helped him defeat the fire-breathing bulls and win the Golden Fleece (p. 150). After this he carried her off in the *Argo* to be his wife, and she very soon showed herself to be a woman who kills. As they were sailing away, hotly pursued by her father Aietes, she murdered her little brother, Apsyrtos, then dismembered him and scattered his fragmented body over the sea. Aietes, who loved his son, stopped to pick up the sad remains to give them proper burial, and Medea and Jason escaped.

Then when the *Argo* returned to Iolkos, she arranged the death of Jason's enemy, King Pelias. She used her witchcraft to rejuvenate an old ram by cutting it up and boiling it in a cauldron with magic herbs (p. 156). When it jumped out as a lamb, Pelias's daughters were so impressed by Medea's skill that they were persuaded to try the same spell on their ageing father. So Pelias too was killed and chopped up and boiled, but this time Medea left out the appropriate herbs – and that was the end of him. 'And what his daughters received was not even enough to bury,' says Pausanias tersely (8.11.3). Jason and Medea fled from Iolkos and took refuge with Kreon, the king of Corinth.

Corinth is the scene of Euripides' play. Some years have passed and Medea has had two sons by Jason, but, as the Nurse says in the Prologue, 'Now all is hostility, and love has turned sick', because now Jason has deserted Medea and has married the daughter of Kreon, the king. The play centres on Medea's revenge. Savage with jealousy and rage, she at first plans to murder all three of the people who have wronged her – Jason, Kreon and the new bride. But her final revenge is more terrible than this. Certainly she kills Kreon and the new bride, but she also kills the children she has had by Jason, and leaves him alive to suffer forever the dreadful results of having betrayed her.

To achieve her vengeance, she hides her rage and pretends forgiveness for Jason and friendship for his new bride. She will prove her goodwill, she says, by sending beautiful gifts to the girl. Jason is completely deceived by Medea's role of repentant wife. Her weapon is poison: this she spreads on a beautiful coronet and robe (so again a woven fabric comes into play) and sends them to her victim. The girl takes the deadly gifts with delight. Quite unsuspecting, she puts on her new adornments. At first she is entranced by her appearance, but soon the poison turns to flame, and robe and coronet consume her with a fierce fire. 'And the flesh dropped from her bones like resin from a pine torch,' says the servant who reports her death.

Then Kreon, in an agony of grief, takes his daughter's body in his arms, crying, 'I wish I might die with you, child.' And die he does. When he has had his fill of lamentation, he tries to lay her corpse down and stand up, but finds that he is stuck fast to the robe 'as ivy clings to laurel shoots'. In struggling to free himself, he too is killed, the frail flesh ripped from his bones.

Medea does not stop here: she goes on to kill her own two sons as well – and this deliberate murder of the children seems to have been an innovation to the legend made by Euripides himself. In earlier versions too the children died, but for other reasons. In one version, Medea unintentionally killed them while she was trying to make them immortal. In another version, the people of Corinth killed them. In yet another, Kreon's family killed them in revenge after Medea had killed Kreon. But Euripides makes Medea herself choose to murder them as the most potent part of her revenge, because this is the greatest pain that she can possibly inflict on her treacherous husband.

Even though his Medea commits such a horrendous deed, Euripides creates in her a character with whom it is easy to sympathize, a woman very definitely wronged by a selfish, self-satisfied and insensitive Jason. He also puts into her mouth a long and justly famous monologue, in which she agonizes as to her right course of action, and whether she can really bring herself to kill her own sons (1021–80). Her decision sways this way and that.

She begins by lamenting that now she must be parted from her children: she must go into exile, while they, unknowing, are to die. All for nothing she bore them and brought them up, and now she will have no joy of them; she will never see them married, and they will never look after her when she is old or give her burial when she dies. (These are the kind of things so often said by a mother over a dead child.) Her sons smile at her, and 'What shall I do?' she cries. And then (in paraphrase) 'No, I can't do it. Farewell, my plans. Why should I hurt their father by hurting myself twice as much?'

Then she hardens her resolve once again, only to be overcome a second time by love and pity. Finally, despite her anguish, her grim purpose triumphs over her deepest maternal feelings, and the decision is taken for death: 'And yet I have no choice. Now the princess is already dying by her gifts. I *must* kill my sons before my enemies do so. I have to travel the cruellest of roads, and send these children on a crueller road still.'

Yet when the time has come for the boys to die, Medea's last words before she kills them show that, by gaining the ultimate revenge on Jason, she is hurting herself quite as much. They also strangely show the murder to be that of a loving mother. Kreon and the princess are dead, so the children are now certain to die too, since the Corinthians will insist on revenge. Their kindest death will be by the hand of the mother who bore them (1236–50):

'My course of action is clear: to kill my children with all speed and then leave this land; not delay and give my children over to be killed by another and less loving hand. They are bound to die in any case, and since they must, then I shall kill them, I who bore them. Come, my heart, steel yourself. Why do I put off doing the terrible deed that must now be done? Come, wretched hand, take the sword, take it; go forward to the point where life turns into grief. No cowardice, no memories of your children, how dear they were, how your body gave them birth. For this one brief day forget your children – and then mourn them. For even though you kill them, yet they were dear.'

At the end of the play Medea escapes in a chariot drawn by winged serpents, sent to her by her grandfather Helios, the Sun-god, and she is carried off to safety in Athens (where, the later myth tells us, she married King Aigeus). She appears suddenly, high in the air above the stage, on the divine plane where normally only the gods appear. This dragon-chariot was also Euripides' own innovation and must have been a tremendously effective *coup de théâtre*. Vengeance accomplished, at whatever cost to herself, Medea gloats over the broken and grieving Jason down below. 'You don't know yet what grief is,' she says to him, 'wait till you're old.'

Thus Medea ends up in triumph over the man who wronged her, and the arrival of the chariot suggests divine approval for what she has done. Medea has been presented in heroic terms throughout, and she has avenged herself on her enemy, Jason, even at the most extreme cost to herself, the deaths of her own children. So it seems that the Sun-chariot comes as a reward for her heroic revenge; for, in a sense, her self-sacrifice.

But her self has been sacrificed in another sense too, for the Medea who appears high in her chariot seems now to have become something more than human, untouched and untouchable by human hands and by human emotions. Jean Anouilh, in his 1946 version of *Medea*, has Medea commit suicide in the flames of her sons' funeral pyre after she has murdered them. In Euripides too, although Medea stands in triumph on her dragon-chariot, her dehumanization makes the ending a kind of death.

PROKNE

Prokne was the daughter of Pandion, the king of Athens, and was married to Tereus, the king of Thrace. Like Medea, she killed her own son to take vengeance on her husband, and her horrific act was famously dramatized in Sophocles' tragedy *Tereus*. This is now lost, apart from fragments, but we possess an ancient summary of the play, and Ovid gives a moving account of the myth in his *Metamorphoses* (6.424–674) which must owe much to the earlier Greek version, so the story can be easily pieced together.

Prokne and Tereus had a son, Itys. Nevertheless, as the years passed, Prokne grew lonely, so she asked Tereus to go to Athens and fetch her sister, Philomela, to visit her. He did so, but as soon as he saw Philomela's beauty, he was inflamed with lust and planned to make her his own. With no idea of what lay in store for her, she pleaded with her father to be allowed to visit her dear sister, and Pandion agreed.

They set off, and on the journey Tereus raped her. When they arrived in Thrace he imprisoned her, then to stop her telling of what he had done, he cut out her tongue. Leaving her well guarded, he went home to his wife and told her that her sister was dead. Prokne was deeply grieved. Yet tongueless though Philomela might be, this did not stop her from telling her story: like all women she was skilled in the art of weaving, and now she wove a tapestry (fabric again) telling what she had suffered. When at last it was complete, she sent it by a friendly servant to her sister.

Prokne deciphered the harrowing tale and went at once to fetch Philomela, smuggling her back into the palace. Then she set her mind on revenge. She killed her little son Itys – presumably her aim, as with Medea, was to leave her husband to suffer for the rest of his life with no son and no hope, rather than give him a quick death. Then the sisters cut up the little boy's body and cooked his flesh. Prokne served it to Tereus, and he ate, and afterwards, replete, he asked her where Itys was. She told him. At once he leapt up to attack his son's murderers, but at this moment the gods intervened and turned all three of them into birds.

Tereus became a hoopoe (a royal, crested bird), continually uttering the question he had asked his wife just before his metamorphosis, 'Pou?', 'Pou?' ('Where?', 'Where?'). Philomela, having no tongue, became a swallow, who merely twitters inarticulately. Prokne was turned into a nightingale, forever singing her son's name in mourning, '*Itu!*, *Itu!*' (The Roman poets, oddly, reversed the fates of the two women, with Prokne becoming the swallow and Philomela the nightingale. This is the version most often adopted in post-classical treatments, so that 'Philomel' has become a common poetic epithet for the nightingale.)

We cannot say exactly how Sophocles' play presented Prokne, but we know that she and Philomela were the heroine sponsors of the Pandionid tribe, roughly one-tenth of the citizens of Athens. The women were held in high regard throughout the city and were honoured for their resolute reaction to cruelty and oppression, so we must assume that *Tereus* reflected such a spirit. Once again, as with Medea, we may imagine the dramatized Prokne as valiantly destroying the dearest thing she had, her own son, so as to deal her enemy the greatest harm.

Thus, even though Sophocles' *Tereus* has been lost, we can still define the powerful story, which was told and retold by later writers, inspiring creative artists down to this day. And the nightingale still laments – as in the gloriously lyrical words of Swinburne in his *Itylus*, where he speaks of 'The woven web that was plain to follow / The small slain body, the flower-like face', and memorably depicts the nightingale as bird of mourning, calling to her sister:

> Sister, my sister, O fleet sweet swallow,
> Thy way is long to the sun and the south;
> But I, fulfilled of my heart's desire,
> Shedding my song upon height, upon hollow,
> From tawny body and sweet small mouth
> Feed the heart of the night with fire . . .

(how better could one define the nightingale?) and she ends:

. . . The hands that cling and the feet that follow,
The voice of the child's blood crying yet,
Who hath remembered me? Who hath forgotten?
Thou hast forgotten, O summer swallow,
But the world shall end when I forget.

ELEKTRA

Before we move on from the women who kill for revenge, we should include Elektra, the daughter of Agamemnon and Klytaimnestra and the sister of Orestes. Even though she committed no murder herself, she supported her brother and urged him on, when he returned to Mycenae to avenge their father's death. She plays no part in early versions of the myth, and although she is mentioned by the lyric poets, it is in fifth-century tragedy that she comes into her own and plays this central role in Orestes' vengeance.

Her first appearance is in Aeschylus's *Libation Bearers* (458 BC), a play named after the Chorus who come with Elektra to offer libations at the tomb of Agamemnon. Here at the tomb she is reunited with Orestes, and brother and sister together invoke Agamemnon's ghost to support the coming vengeance, but Elektra herself plays no further part in the murders. The focus here is mainly on Orestes, and it is he alone (though supported by the presence of his friend Pylades) who kills first Aigisthos, and then Klytaimnestra (p. 441).

In the *Elektra* of Euripides, Elektra's part in the vengeance has been developed. In this play she has been married off to a poor farmer to ensure that she will bear no son with a claim to the throne, but she is still a virgin, since her husband, respecting her noble birth, has refused to take advantage of her. She is mad for revenge on her father's killers, while Orestes is weak and indecisive, and although he confidently kills Aigisthos, he is altogether unhappy about killing his mother. Elektra is the dominant figure, and it is she who plans how to kill Klytaimnestra, then drives Orestes on to do so, even grasping the sword with him when his own nerve fails at the crucial moment of murder. Afterwards she is as full of remorse as before she was full of desire for revenge.

It is arguably Sophocles' *Elektra* that presents for us the quintessential Elektra. The main focus of the play is Elektra herself, steadfast and enduring, passionately grieving her father's murder and passionately set on revenge. At the time of Agamemnon's death she rescued the young Orestes from the murderers, who would have killed him too if they had had the chance. She sent him to be brought up in safety at the court of Strophios, the king of Phokis. Now when the play opens, many years later, she is longing for him to return, and sings:

'Never shall I cease my dirges and painful laments as long as I look on the bright rays of the stars and on this light of day. No, like the nightingale, slayer of her young, I will cry aloud, for all to hear, sorrows without end before my father's doors. O house of Hades and Persephone, Hermes of the Underworld and hallowed Curse, and Furies, holy daughters of the gods, who look upon all those who die unjustly and those who have their marriage-beds defiled: come, help me, avenge my father's murder and send my brother home.' (103–18)

And again (164–86): 'On and on without end I wait for him, living my sad life forever without a child, without a husband, drowned in tears, bearing this fate in which my sorrow finds no end ... For me the best part of my life has already passed away in hopelessness, and I have no strength left.'

Yet unknown to Elektra, Orestes has already returned, coming back to Mycenae with his friend Pylades, the son of Strophios, and with the old tutor who brought him up.

Obedient to the command of Apollo, he has his plan of vengeance worked out: the old tutor will announce Orestes' death in a chariot race at the Pythian Games, while he himself and Pylades will arrive carrying a funeral urn supposedly containing Orestes' ashes. This will have the dual effect of gaining them entrance to the palace and of lowering Klytaimnestra's guard. (Aigisthos, at this point, is temporarily away from home.)

The plan works perfectly. First the tutor vividly describes Orestes' horrific death, thrown from his chariot and mangled in the traces. Klytaimnestra, after a momentary pang, is overcome with triumphant relief that now her son, whose vengeance she feared, is dead, and she takes the old man into the palace as her honoured guest. Elektra is heartbroken. And who will avenge her father now? She turns to her sister Chrysothemis for help in killing Aigisthos, but Chrysothemis thinks this a crazy plan. Of the two girls, she is the prudent daughter, too fond of the material advantages in being a princess of Mycenae to risk losing them by any display of active hostility. 'I know this much,' she says to Elektra (332–40), 'I too am grieved at our situation, so much so that if I could find the strength I would show them what I think of them. But as it is, it seems best to me to lower my sails in time of trouble ... The right course is not as I say, but as you have chosen. Yet if I am to live in freedom, I must obey our masters in everything.'

So it is no surprise that she denounces Elektra's plan as folly, refusing to dare anything that might put her comfortable life at risk. Elektra now resolves to kill Aigisthos alone and unaided, but it does not come to this. Orestes and Pylades come upon her as they arrive to deliver the funeral urn, and all thoughts of vengeance are flown as she takes the urn in her hands and laments over what she believes to be her dear brother's ashes. Now she wants only to die (1126–70):

'O last memorial of the life of Orestes, the dearest of men to me, how far from the hopes with which I sent you forth do I receive you home! For now you are nothing carried in my hands, but I sent you off from home, child, radiant. I wish that before this I had died, before I stole you with these hands and sent you to a foreign land, saving you from murder, so that on that very day you would have lain there dead, and had your share in our father's grave. But now, far from home, an exile in another land, you died unhappily without your sister near. And I, to my grief, did not wash or dress you with the hands that loved you, nor lift you as was right, a weight of sorrow, from the blazing pyre. No, sadly you had your rites from alien hands, and so are come to us, a little weight inside a little urn.

'All sorrow now for my care of you long ago, gone for nothing; I gave it you often with labour of love. For you were never more dear to your mother than you were to me, and I was your nurse, and not the servants, and always you called me sister. Now with your death, in a single day all this is ended; like a hurricane you have gone and swept it all away. Our father is gone; I am dead because of you; you yourself are dead and gone. Our enemies are mocking us, and our mother, who is no mother, is mad with joy – she of whom you often sent me secret messages, that you would come yourself as an avenger. But this our evil fortune, yours and mine, has torn away, and sent you on to me as you are now, no more the form I loved, but dust and empty shadow.

'What sorrow! O body pitiable! You who were sent, to my grief, on a dreadful journey, my dear love, how you have ended me! Yes, ended me, dearest brother! Therefore receive me to this little room of yours, nothing to nothing, that with you below I may live for all the time to come. For when you were on earth I shared all with you equally, so now I long to die and share your grave. For I see that the dead no longer suffer pain.'

Orestes has taken Elektra, clad in rough clothes, for a servant, and it is only when he hears these words of love and grief that he realizes this must be the beloved sister who brought him up. He gently makes himself known to her, and Elektra's move from despair to joy, when at last she believes that the man standing beside her is in fact the living Orestes himself, gives us one of the most moving recognition scenes in extant Greek tragedy.

Orestes goes into the palace to kill Klytaimnestra, while Elektra stands at the doors to keep watch for Aigisthos. At the first death-cry of her mother she shouts: 'Strike, if you have the strength, a second blow.' Orestes strikes again, and Klytaimnestra gives a last cry. There is no time to linger over her death, for now Elektra sees Aigisthos approaching. She tricks him into believing that Orestes, his enemy, is indeed dead, and that his corpse is within the palace. 'Can I see the body with my own eyes?' asks Aigisthos.

'Indeed you can,' replies Elektra, 'though I don't envy you the sight.'

At the command of Aigisthos, the doors are opened and Orestes and Pylades bring out the covered body of Klytaimnestra. 'Zeus,' cries Aigisthos piously (and truthfully), 'what I see here must be someone brought down by the gods' displeasure.'

'Take the coverings off the face,' he commands; and then, eager to share this triumphant moment with his wife: 'Call Klytaimnestra!'

'No need,' says Orestes. 'She's nearby.'

And then (in what has been called 'the most glorious moment of pure theatre in all Greek tragedy') Aigisthos lifts the covers and recognizes the body beneath. He starts back in horror, realizing what fate now awaits him. Orestes drives him indoors to meet his death, and the play ends with the Chorus rejoicing that Elektra has come, at long last and after much suffering, to freedom and fulfilment.

Elektra, like Antigone, is one of the great female figures of

Greek myth and Greek tragedy. She has been an inspiration to a great many later artists – perhaps most notably to Richard Strauss in his opera *Elektra*, which has as its libretto a play by Hugo von Hofmannsthal, based on Sophocles' *Elektra*. Sophocles' play ends with Elektra's joy as she is reunited with her dear brother and triumphs over her enemies. Hofmannsthal develops that joy, so that Elektra, uplifted by victory, dances in triumph until she collapses and dies. (An aftermath to vengeance very different from the mythical one, where Elektra married Pylades and had two sons by him, Medon and Strophios.)

Moreover modern psychology has given the name 'Elektra complex' to a girl's fixation on her father and jealousy of her mother, the counterpart of Freud's Oedipus complex. There is even a hint of the Elektra complex in ancient tragedy for, in Euripides' *Elektra*, Klytaimnestra says to Elektra (1102–4): 'My child, love for your father is in your nature. This happens sometimes. Some children belong to their fathers, while others love their mothers more.'

Other things apart from revenge can be dangerous. There is also, for instance, the power of sex: sex in its many aspects can be a killer. The most obvious example from mythology is **Helen** – wife of Menelaos, king of Sparta – who was not only the most beautiful woman who ever lived, but also the archetypal sexually dangerous woman. Helen's beauty brought death to thousands of men, after Aphrodite offered her love as a bribe to Paris when he judged the beauty contest between the three squabbling goddesses (p. 309). Helen's love seemed to him more desirable than all the imperial power offered by Hera, or the military victories offered by Athene, so he chose Aphrodite as the loveliest of the three, then claimed his prize, carrying Helen off to Troy. Menelaos wanted her back, so he and his brother

Agamemnon sailed out with a huge fighting force of about 100,000 Greeks to recapture her. The resulting war lasted ten long years, and many Greeks and Trojans died because of Helen.

Homer is indulgent towards Helen in the *Iliad*, where even as the long war drags on, the Trojan elders on the walls of Troy say of her: 'No one could blame the Trojans and well-greaved Achaians if, for so long a time, they suffer pain and hardship over a woman like this. She looks terribly like the immortal goddesses (3.156–8).' Later writers were not so kind, and she was often bitterly blamed for setting the Trojan War in motion by her infidelity and for causing the deaths of so many men. Hostility to Helen thus runs through much of what we have left of fifth-century tragedy, such as Aeschylus's *Agamemnon*, where the chorus sing of Helen stepping lightly through the gates of Troy, bringing to the Trojans her dowry, death (403–8). When they welcomed her as Paris's bride, they little realized that they were bringing into their midst a lion cub, sweet and loving at first, who as time passed would reveal its true nature and repay those who cherished it with blood and death (717–49). Helen, says Aeschylus, was suitably named, for '*hel*' in Greek means 'destroyer', and Helen did indeed bring death and destruction to men, to ships, to cities (681–98).

At the other extreme from Helen are the women who rejected sex, like the virgin huntress **Atalanta**. Her father abandoned her in the wilds when she was born because he wanted only male children, and she survived only because a she-bear heard her crying and suckled her until some hunters found her. They adopted her and brought her up, and when she grew to womanhood she too became an expert hunter and was interested only in manly pursuits. She took part in the Kalydonian Boarhunt, where she shot the boar and drew first blood (p. 179), and she famously wrestled against Peleus, and won, at the funeral games of Pelias, king of Iolkos. She had no desire for marriage: many men wished to wed her, but she would have none of it. Confident in the speed of her feet, she swore that she would never marry unless her husband could first beat her in a foot race. Suitors might run against her, but only on the understanding that if they lost, they would die.

In spite of this threatening fate, many men were moved by her beauty to risk their lives. And they were given every chance: they had a head start and ran naked, while Atalanta ran fully clothed and armed. But always she caught up with them before they reached the finishing line and speared them as they ran. Thus many men died for love – until one final suitor tried his luck. This was Hippomenes (sometimes called Melanion), who unlike Atalanta's other suitors had the wit to invoke Aphrodite's aid on his behalf. The goddess gave him three golden apples, so he began his contest with his would-be bride, armed with the means of her defeat. Three times he threw down an apple as they raced, and three times she lost precious ground as she ran aside to pick it up. The third time Aphrodite intervened to make the golden apple heavier, and with a final burst of speed the joyful Hippomenes passed the winning post.

And so he married his love, who in the end seems to have happily given up her freedom. The story goes that one day the couple, overcome by passion, made love in a sacred precinct, and because of this sacrilege were transformed into lions (some said into the lions that drew the goddess Kybele's chariot). So we may assume that Atalanta had at last found joy in sex after rejecting it for so long.

In contrast to this, the **Amazons** (no chapter on 'dangerous women' can ignore these female warriors) shunned as far as possible the entire male sex, and for life. Their home was rather vaguely located to the east or north-east of Greece, at the outer reaches of the known world, and there they lived resolutely

An Amazon attacking from horseback.

apart from men. They looked on sex simply as a means of procreation, so they would copulate occasionally with males from neighbouring tribes, but naturally they reared only the female infants born to them.

The Amazons' name was thought to mean 'breastless' (*maza*, 'breast'), and was said to derive from their custom of amputating the right breast to facilitate their use of weapons during battle (the left breast was needed to suckle their daughters). But there is no trace of this physical singularity in ancient art, where Amazons are a popular subject from the seventh century BC onwards, both in vase-painting and sculpture, and are often depicted with their (intact) right breast exposed. They are usually shown in full combat, fighting with spears and bows, and sometimes axes. Several of the great heroes – Herakles, Bellero-phon, Theseus – were thought to have battled successfully against the massed tribes of Amazons, and the conflicts between these warrior-women and victorious Greeks were generally seen as symbolizing the triumph of Greek civilization over the forces of barbarism.

Finally, there are several Greek myths, similar to the biblical tale of Potiphar's wife, that tell the story of an older, married woman who sets out to seduce a young and unmarried man. When he rejects her, which he always does, she wants revenge, so she accuses him to her husband of rape, or attempted rape. The husband tries to kill the young man (and usually fails) and the woman comes to a bad end.

For instance **Stheneboia**, the wife of Proitos, king of Tiryns, tried to seduce the young hero Bellerophon (p. 176). When he rejected her, she accused him to her husband, and Proitos sent him off to his father-in-law Iobates, king of Lycia, with a sealed message demanding death. Iobates set Bellerophon fearful tasks to accomplish, which should have killed him – but he completed them all triumphantly, and Iobates rewarded him with lands and riches and the hand of his own daughter in marriage. Bellerophon then went back to Tiryns to take vengeance on Stheneboia for her lies. He persuaded her to mount the winged horse Pegasos with him, then flew out high over the sea and flung her down to her death.

A similar story is told of **Astydameia**, the wife of Akastos, king of Iolkos. Her victim was the hero Peleus (who later mar-ried the sea-goddess Thetis and became father of the great Achilles). When Akastos heard the false tale of attempted rape, he was unwilling to kill Peleus directly, so he took him hunting on Mount Pelion, that haunt of wild Centaurs, and during the night, while Peleus was asleep, he stole his sword and hid it in a pile of cow dung. He then left him on the mountain, alone and defenceless, hoping that either wild beasts or the ferocious Centaurs would kill him.

His hope was almost fulfilled, for the Centaurs gathered to attack Peleus, but just in time the wise and kind Centaur Cheiron appeared and gave him back his sword. So Peleus escaped, and in due course he returned to Iolkos with an armed force to take his revenge. He sacked the city, then killed Astydameia, cut her in two, and marched his army into Iolkos between the severed halves of her corpse.

PHAIDRA

The same type of story was told of Phaidra, wife of the great Theseus, king of Athens. Phaidra was just such a shameless woman as Stheneboia and Astydameia, and when she fell in love with her stepson Hippolytos she tried – and failed – to seduce him. Wanting revenge for her rejection, she lied to Theseus that Hippolytos had tried to rape her, and Theseus cursed his son and called on his father Poseidon to kill him. The god sent a huge bull from the sea, which stampeded Hippolytos's terrified horses. His chariot crashed and he was dragged to his death, tangled in the reins. (According to one interpretation, his name means 'torn apart by horses'.) Phaidra, her treachery exposed, committed suicide.

This story was the theme of Euripides' lost tragedy *Hippolytos*, his first version of the legend for the stage. We have only fragments of this play left, but he also wrote a second *Hippolytos* which we possess in its entirety, and this became the basis for Racine's great tragedy *Phèdre* and many later adaptations. In this second version, the presentation of Phaidra is rather different. Yes, she is in love with Hippolytos, but quite against her will: the love has been forced on her by Aphrodite, who is angry because of the chaste Hippolytos's neglect of her and his exclusive worship of the virgin huntress Artemis.

Aphrodite herself explains this at the beginning of the play and outlines her plan for the young man's destruction. Theseus will curse his son, and Hippolytos will be killed. 'And Phaidra, although she will keep her honour, yet she will die,' adds the goddess (47–50). 'For I do not care for her suffering as much as having my enemies pay a penalty that satisfies me.'

Phaidra's reaction to feeling what she knows is a truly shameful love is entirely virtuous (392–401):

'When love wounded me, I tried to find the best way of bearing it. I began by keeping quiet and concealing this disease ... Secondly I determined to bear the madness decently and conquer it with self-discipline. And third, when I was failing to master desire by these means, I decided to die.'

And so she has been starving herself, preferring death to the dishonour of yielding to her passion. Unfortunately she is not allowed to waste away in silence, because her nurse worms out of her the secret of her obvious illness and is fatally swift to interfere. She tries to convince Phaidra to give in to all-powerful Love (443–50):

'The tide of Aphrodite in full flood cannot be borne. To the man who yields to her, she comes gently, but she seizes the man who is proud and arrogant, I tell you, and then she tortures him. Aphrodite roams through the air and is in the swell of the sea. Everything is generated from her, for she is the one who sows the seed of desire, from which all of us on earth are born.'

'What you need,' declares the nurse roundly, 'is not fine speaking, but the man', and she goes indoors to approach Hippolytos on her mistress's behalf, despite Phaidra's pleas that she do nothing of the kind.

Hippolytos is appalled. Phaidra, listening at the door, hears his horrified reaction as he curses and abuses the nurse, calling her 'whore's matchmaker' and 'betrayer of her master's bed', following this with bitter condemnation of the entire female sex. 'Zeus,' he begins (616–27),

'why did you create and put on earth with men so vile and worthless a thing as woman? If you wanted to propagate the human race, you didn't have to do it through women. Better that men should buy children from you, paying at your temples in gold or iron or bronze, each man what he could afford. Then they could live in freedom in their own homes, without women. Women are a great curse to men.'

Now that her shameful secret is out, Phaidra resolves there and then that the only thing left to her is to die. She hangs herself from the rafters. But to defend her children against a disgrace which they do not deserve, she leaves a suicide note for Theseus, accusing Hippolytos of rape.

Theseus returns home to find his wife dead and his son, supposedly, the cause of it – and Hippolytos is honourable enough to keep his stepmother's secret, so he says nothing to excuse himself. As in the usual story, Theseus curses him and Poseidon sends the bull from the sea. In the final scene, Hippolytos is carried onstage in his death agonies, and father and son are reconciled after Artemis tells them the truth of Aphrodite's machinations and of Phaidra's innocence.

Yet this Phaidra, for all her virtue, has been in effect just as deadly as her earlier counterpart, the shameless would-be seducer. And from Hippolytos's fate we conclude that, just as unrestrained yielding to the sexual impulse, as in the case of Helen, can bring death in its wake, so can the complete rejection of sexual love. We deny Aphrodite and all she stands for at our cost.

AGAUE

We can say the same about the god Dionysos, as evidenced by Euripides' tragedy *Bakchai*, named after the followers of the god who form the Chorus of the play. The drama centres on the tragic fate of Pentheus, the young king of Thebes, though it can be argued that his mother Agaue, our final 'dangerous woman', suffers a fate more tragic still.

As we have seen, Medea and Prokne killed their own children to gain revenge on the men who had wronged them. Agaue too kills her own son, but unwittingly, believing him to be a mountain lion, then still in a state of delusion she carries his severed head home in triumph, thinking it a splendid trophy of the hunt. In one of the most painful and moving scenes in the whole of Greek tragedy, she is brought to recognize what she carries so proudly as the head of her son, and to realize too her own part in his destruction.

The play opens with Dionysos himself coming to Thebes in the disguise of one of his own priests. He is in a sense coming home, for he is the son of Zeus and Semele, the daughter of Kadmos, the old king of Thebes (p. 103). Semele is long since dead, burnt up by Zeus's lightning bolt, and her sisters Agaue, Ino and Autonoe have always refused to believe that she was ever united with the great god. In their opinion, she was seduced by some mortal man, then lied that her lover was Zeus to cover the shame of her pregnancy. Dionysos has now punished them by driving them mad, along with all the other women of Thebes, and they are living up on Mount Kithairon as maenads, worshipping this new god with impassioned zeal.

Young Pentheus returns home and tries to remedy this critical situation. He imprisons the stranger, this dangerous 'priest', and even when he sees that Dionysos easily escapes from his prison, and hears that the women on the mountain are performing miraculous feats in the god's name, he refuses to countenance Dionysos's divinity. Finally the god drives him mad too, and dresses him in women's clothes, and takes him up Kithairon to spy on the women there.

We learn the tragic outcome from a messenger, one of the palace servants who accompanied Pentheus and the god on their journey. When they came to the glen where the maenads were, Dionysos, with miraculous power, pulled down the topmost branch of a towering pine-tree and seated Pentheus on it, then let the tree slip upright once again, carrying Pentheus with it. Then the god cried aloud to the women: 'I bring you the one who mocked you, and me, and my holy rites. Now punish him.' This, in the servant's words, is how they did so (1084–1142):

'The high air fell still. The wooded glade held its leaves in stillness, and you could not hear the cry of any beast. The women, not having heard the words clearly, stood up and gazed around. Again the god commanded them, and when the daughters of Kadmos recognized the clear summons of Dionysos, they darted off with the speed of doves, and all the maenads after them. Through the torrent-filled valley and over the broken rocks they leapt, frenzied by the breath of the god.

When they saw my master seated high in the pine-tree, at first they climbed the cliff which towered opposite, and violently hurled rocks at him or flung fir branches like javelins. Others aimed with the thyrsos through the high air at Pentheus, their wretched target, but all to no avail, for the poor boy was out of reach of their striving, sitting there helpless.

At last they ripped down branches of oak, and using these as crowbars tried to tear up the tree's roots. When all their struggles met with failure, Agaue cried out, "Come, Maenads, stand in a circle around the tree and take hold of it, so that we catch this climbing beast and stop him revealing the god's secret dances."

Countless hands gripped the pine and ripped it from the earth. Pentheus, torn from his lofty seat and hurled to the ground, came falling down from on high with one unceasing scream, for he knew what terrible end was near. His mother first, as priestess, led the rite of death and fell on him. He tore the headband from his hair, that wretched Agaue might recognize him and not kill him, and "Mother," he cried, touching her cheek, "Look, it is I, your son Pentheus, whom you bore in the house of Echion. Have mercy, mother. I have been wrong, but do not kill your own son."

But she was foaming at the mouth and rolling wild eyes, completely out of her mind and possessed by Dionysos, so his words had no effect. Grasping Pentheus' left hand, she set her foot against his ribs and tore the poor boy's arm out of his shoulder, not by her own strength, but because the god made it easy. Ino was working at his other side, rending his flesh, and now Autonoe and the whole horde of maenads went at it. They all cried out together, Pentheus shrieking as long as life was in him and the women howling in triumph. One of them carried off an arm, another a foot with its boot still on. His ribs were stripped clean, and each one of them with bloody hands was playing ball with Pentheus' flesh.

His body lies scattered under harsh rocks or in the deep foliage of the woods, no easy task to find. His poor head has been taken by his mother and fixed to the end of her thyrsos, and she is carrying it over Kithairon, thinking it the head of a mountain lion.'

In due course Agaue comes on stage with her trophy, exulting in her triumph. 'Where is my son Pentheus?' she cries. 'Let him set a strong ladder against the house and nail up this lion's head which I have hunted and brought home.'

Her old father, Kadmos, who has lovingly gathered up the broken pieces of his grandson's body scattered through the glens of Kithairon, now painfully sets about bringing her confused mind back to reality. He begins gently. 'Look up at the sky,' he says. 'Does it seem the same to you, or has it changed?'

'It's brighter than before,' she replies, 'and more translucent.'

'And this disturbance of your mind, is it still there?'

'I don't know what you mean, but somehow my mind is surer, and changed from what it was before.'

'So will you listen and answer clearly?' he asks.

'Yes, father, for I have forgotten what we said before.'

Now he continues with questions that have simple answers. 'To whose house did you go when you were married?'

'You gave me to Echion, one of the Sown Men, they say.'

'And who was the child born to your husband?'

'Pentheus, from my union with his father.'

Finally Kadmos brings her close to the tragic truth. 'Yes, and whose head are you holding in your arms?'

'A lion's,' she replies with certainty. And then doubt creeps in: 'At least, that is what the women who hunted it said.'

'Look properly at it,' says Kadmos. 'Looking is no great task.'

And Agaue looks, and screams in horror. 'What am I looking at? What am I carrying?'

'Look again closely and see more clearly,' says Kadmos.

She does so. 'Surely it doesn't look like a lion's head?' he says.

'No,' she cries out in grief. 'I'm holding the head of Pentheus.' But worse is to come. 'Who killed him?' she asks, and she has to hear the dreadful answer: 'It was you who killed him, you and your sisters.'

A modern poet, Patrick Hunt, captures this most pitiful aspect of Pentheus' death, that of a mother killing the child that she herself has borne (*Kithairon*):

> Pruning wild limbs on Kithairon
> is no impediment to a vine god,
> dismemberment to him is temporary

like the faith of mortals.
Here on this mountain
some see his beard in the clouds
or his thigh knotted in a root.

But in the eyes of Pentheus
pruning was in troubled wood,
powerless to take root again
or stitch torn flax together,
since his sad mother has both
knit and unknit the cloth of him.
Is it wind you hear howling on Kithairon?

14

AENEAS AND THE DESTINY OF ROME

I sing of arms and the man, who was made an exile by fate, and was the first to come from the land of Troy to Italy and the shores of Lavinium. He suffered many hardships on both land and sea by the power of the gods above, all through the implacable anger of cruel Juno, and great too were his sufferings in war, before he could found a city and bring his gods into Latium. This was the origin of the Latin race, the fathers of Alba and the high walls of Rome.

Thus begins Virgil's twelve-book epic, the *Aeneid* (first century BC), from which the story of Aeneas, the legendary founder of the Roman race and the national hero of Rome, is best known. His story begins, however, in early Greek myth, where he was the son of Aphrodite and the Trojan prince Anchises, conceived after the goddess was forced by Zeus to fall irresistibly in love with a mortal (p. 73). She gave birth to her son (Aineias in Greek) on Mount Ida and left him there to be brought up by the nymphs. When he was five years old, she delivered him to his father's care.

Anchises was a descendant of Tros through his son Assarakos, whose brother Ilos founded Troy (p. 297). Aeneas was thus a member of the junior branch of the Trojan royal house. In due course he married Creusa (Greek, Kreousa), a daughter of King Priam, and the couple had a son, Ascanius (Askanios).

During the war, Aeneas led the Dardanian contingent of Trojan allies. We see him in action in Homer's *Iliad*, where in prowess he is second only to the Trojan leader, Hektor, fighting bravely and effectively in defence of Troy. He is blessed with divine support, for during a duel with the Greek hero Diomedes (p. 331) both Aphrodite and Apollo intervene to keep him safe. He even fights the great Achilles (20.75–350) and almost loses his life, but here it is Poseidon – usually a supporter of the Greeks – who comes to his aid and magically transports him far away to the edge of battle. The sea-god explains his unexpected action to the other immortals by saying that Aeneas is destined to survive the war, and that he and his descendants will rule over Trojans.

The legend of Aeneas's escape from Troy developed soon after Homer. Vase-paintings from the sixth century BC show Aeneas leaving his ruined city, accompanied by his little son Ascanius and carrying his father Anchises, now very old, on his back. The story of his voyage to Italy was well established by the third century, and when Pyrrhos led the Italian Greeks against Rome in 280 BC, he saw himself as a descendant of Achilles making war on a colony of Troy. Long before Virgil's time, Aeneas was acknowledged as the man who led the remnants of the Trojans from Troy, and became the ancestor of a line of kings who ruled for generations in the city of Alba Longa. From his stock came Rhea Silvia, the mother by Mars of Romulus, the founder of Rome. But it was Virgil who created the canonical story of Aeneas and his Trojan followers, of their long wanderings after leaving Troy, and of the bitter war they fought against the peoples of Latium on their arrival in Italy.

Although the *Aeneid* is set largely in pre-Roman Italy and continually looks ahead to the world of Rome (traditionally said to have been founded in 753 BC), its events take place in the same legendary time as Homer's *Odyssey*. Odysseus is still on Kalypso's island, and will be there for some years yet, when Aeneas reaches his destination in Italy. Virgil portrays his hero as dutiful (*pius*), compassionate and courageous, an admirable leader and a devoted father and son. His unfolding of Aeneas's story begins with the appearance of the Wooden Horse, which brings about the fall of Troy, and ends with Aeneas's victory over the Latins, which will make possible the foundation of a new 'Troy' in Italy.

THE ESCAPE FROM TROY

While Troy is being laid low by fire and violence, Aeneas fights desperately alongside a small band of Trojan followers and becomes a horrified witness of all the bloody carnage taking place. Worst of all is the butchery committed by Achilles' son Neoptolemos, who kills Priam's son Polites in front of his parents' eyes, then drags Priam through pools of his son's blood to slaughter him on his own altar.

Aeneas also sees Helen hiding in the palace, afraid of vengeance from the Greeks. He is ready to kill her for causing this disastrous war, but his mother Venus (Aphrodite) intervenes and urges him to go at once and save his family. He returns home, resolved to take them out of Troy to safety. At first old Anchises refuses to leave, but he changes his mind when the gods send three signs: Ascanius's head is lit with divine flame, Jupiter (Zeus) rolls a peal of thunder, and a star falls from the sky, trailing a path of light. These are enough to convince the old man and he hesitates no longer.

Taking with him his household gods, the Penates, Aeneas carries Anchises on his back and leads Ascanius by the hand. Creusa follows behind, but on the way through the burning city she is somehow separated from the others and disappears. Aeneas rushes back to search for her, only to see her ghost rise before him. She reassures him that the gods wish him to leave Troy without her and found a new kingdom far away. Three times in his sorrow he tries to clasp her in his arms, but three times her phantom escapes him, as weightless as the winds, and fades away. Grieved by this cruel blow, he returns to the rest of his family and leads them out of Troy.

Aeneas, carrying Anchises, escapes from Troy.

THE VOYAGE TO LATIUM

On the coast beneath Mount Ida, Aeneas musters a band of followers and builds a fleet from mountain pines. At last they set sail with twenty ships, having no sure idea where they will find a new home. First they land in Thrace, hoping to found a city there, but they inadvertently disturb the grave of Polydoros, a son of Priam, who was treacherously murdered by Polymestor

(p. 452). From below the earth comes a voice from Polydoros's corpse, telling Aeneas of his sad fate and warning him to leave such a cruel land. Aeneas and his men perform the funeral rites that will give peace to the murdered boy's spirit, then depart.

Next they land on the island of Delos, where they find a welcome from Anios, king of the island and priest of Apollo. Here they learn from Apollo's oracle that they will find a home in the land from which the Trojans originated. 'Seek out your ancient mother,' instructs Apollo, 'for there the house of Aeneas, and his sons' sons, and their sons who come after them will rule over all the world' (3.96–8). Anchises is sure that this refers to Crete, the home of their ancestor Teukros, so they voyage onwards. When they reach the island they begin to build a city, but a plague afflicts them, and Aeneas is told in a vision by the Penates that this interpretation of the oracle is wrong: the god was really pointing them towards Italy, the home of their ancestor Dardanos.

They set sail once again. Thrown off course by a storm, they land on the Strophades Islands. Here the monstrous Harpies attack them, screeching as they swoop down and snatch up their food (3.214–18):

No monster is more repellent, no pestilence from the waters of Styx or stroke of divine wrath more savage. They are birds with the faces of girls and filth oozing from their bellies; their hands are hooked claws and their faces always pale with hunger.

The Trojans fight them off and they fly away, all but their leader, Kelaino. She lingers long enough to utter a solemn and discouraging prophecy that comes from Jupiter: they will found a city only after they have been driven by deadly famine to eat their own tables.

They land next in Epeiros, which they find is ruled by a fellow-Trojan, the seer Helenos, now married to Hektor's widow Andromache. They have named their city Pergamon after their dearly loved Troy, though Andromache still weeps for her lost city and husband and son, especially when she sees young Ascanius, who is the age that her own Astyanax would have been, had he lived. Helenos, with his seer's vision, offers advice about the dangers and difficulties of the journey to Italy and foretells a prosperous outcome. He predicts that the place for Aeneas's new city will be where he finds a white sow lying with her thirty white piglets.

They sail on to Sicily. Thanks to Helenos's warning, they avoid the dangers once posed to Odysseus by the monster Skylla and the whirlpool Charybdis (p. 405), although they see in the distance the terrible Cyclops Polyphemos, now blind, who caused Odysseus and his men (p. 395) so much affliction (3.658–65):

He was a terrible monster, huge and hideous, blind in his one eye and using the trunk of a pine to guide his hand and steady his steps. His woolly sheep were with him, and these were his only pleasure, the only consolation in his pain. He waded out into the sea until he reached deep water, then groaning and grinding his teeth he washed the blood still trickling from his gouged-out eye. He walked on into mid-ocean, but still the waves did not wet his towering thighs.

Terrified, they make their escape as quickly as possible, and looking back they see the shore thronged with a multitude of Cyclopes, standing in silent menace, their heads towering to heaven and all glaring out of their single eyes.

The Trojans put in at Sicily's port of Drepanum, but here Aeneas has to suffer another cruel loss, for his father Anchises dies. They bury the old man and consecrate an altar of mourning. 'I rescued him from so many dangers,' says Aeneas sadly (3.711), 'and all in vain.'

On leaving Sicily they head for Italy, but now the goddess

Juno intervenes. Always implacably hostile to the Trojans because of the slight to her beauty in the Judgement of Paris (p. 309), she now intends to foil their plans to found a new Troy. She commands the guardian of the winds, Aiolos, to send a storm that will wreck their fleet. Aiolos lives in Aiolia (1.52–9):

where the storm clouds have their home, a place teeming with furious winds from the south. Here Aiolos is king, and in a vast cavern he controls the brawling winds and the roaring storms, keeping them curbed and fettered in their prison. Resentfully they rage from door to door in the mountainside, protesting loudly, while Aiolos sits in his high citadel, sceptre in hand, taming their arrogance and controlling their fury. But for him, they would snatch up the land, the sea, the very depths of the sky, and sweep them all through space.

Aiolos obeys Juno's command to whip up winds that will overwhelm Aeneas's ships (1.81–91):

He struck the butt of his spear against the side of the hollow mountain and the winds came streaming out, rushing through the opening he had made, and blew a hurricane over all the earth. They swept down on the sea at once, the east wind, and the south wind, and the stormy wind from Africa, stirring it up from its bottom-most depths and rolling great waves to the shores. Now men were shouting and ropes shrieking. All at once clouds snatched from the Trojans' eyes the sky and the light of day, and black night brooded over the ocean. Thunder rolled in the heavens, lightning flashed through the air again and again, and wherever the Trojans looked, death stared them in the face.

The ships are scattered over the face of the waters and Aeneas despairs, even wishing that he had died at Troy, 'where fierce Hektor lies, dead by Achilles' sword, where great Sarpedon lies, where Simoeis caught up so many shields and helmets and

bodies of brave men, and rolled them down in his current'
(1.99–101). But all ends well, for Neptune (Poseidon) intervenes, angry that his authority over the sea has been usurped,
and calms the storm. Aeneas and his men come safely to Libya.

They are welcomed by Dido, the queen and founder of
Carthage. She had been a Phoenician princess, daughter of the
king of Tyre and happily married to the wealthy Sychaeus, but
her wicked brother Pygmalion murdered her husband out of
greed for his riches. Dido escaped from Tyre with her sister
Anna and a band of followers and fled to Libya. Here she
founded her new city. When Aeneas arrives, Carthage is a hive
of activity, with new and splendid buildings everywhere under
construction.

Dido gives a banquet in the Trojans' honour, and while they
are feasting, Venus sends Cupid to inflame her heart with desire
for Aeneas. She hears him tell of the fall of Troy and of all his
subsequent adventures, and by the end of his moving narrative
she has fallen deeply in love with him. She is torn between the
memory of her dear husband and this new and overwhelming
emotion, but her sister Anna encourages her to put the past
behind her and to give in to her passion. She wanders all over
the city, aflame with love – and Virgil likens her to a deer, shot
by a shepherd in the woods, that runs away far over the wooded
slopes of Mount Dikte, while all the time, lodged in her side, is
the arrow that will bring her to death.

While out hunting, Dido and Aeneas take shelter in a cave
during a violent storm and here they consummate their love.
'And that day was the beginning of her death,' says Virgil
(4.169–70), 'and the beginning of all her sufferings' – though
at first it is all pleasure, for now Dido and Aeneas think only of
each other, and time slips away as they enjoy their new life
together. At last Jupiter sends down Mercury (Hermes) to
remind Aeneas of his destiny and urge him to sail for Italy.

Against his will, and despite all Dido's pleas and reproaches, he dutifully prepares to depart, obedient to the call of fate.

Anna unknowingly helps the inconsolable Dido to prepare for death. They have a pyre built, piled high with all possessions reminiscent of Aeneas, supposedly so that Dido may destroy everything that reminds her of her lost lover. But when in the first light of dawn she sees the Trojan fleet moving out to sea, she climbs on to the top of the pyre, and there on the bed on which she so often lay in love with Aeneas, she kills herself with his sword. It is a slow and difficult death, and Juno has to send Iris, the goddess of the rainbow, to free her struggling spirit. 'And Iris flies down on her saffron wings, bathed in dew and spreading all her colours over the sky opposite the sun' (4.700–702). She cuts a lock of Dido's hair as an offering for Dis (Hades) and at once all warmth leaves her tortured body as her spirit passes into the winds.

Aeneas's abandonment of his love, in response to the call of duty and the divinely directed destiny of Rome, would no doubt have been understood and appreciated by a Roman audience. But there is equally no doubt that it is the tragic love and death of Dido which has become the best-remembered part of the *Aeneid*, and the most inspirational to later artists of all kinds.

As the Trojans sail into the distance, they see Carthage glowing from the flames of Dido's funeral pyre, and although they know nothing yet of her death, their hearts are filled with a dark foreboding. A storm drives them back again to Sicily. A whole year has passed since they buried Anchises there, and now they hold funeral games in his honour, with a boat race, a foot race, and boxing and archery contests. The Trojan women, weary of wandering and goaded by Juno, set fire to some of the ships in the hope of staying in this friendly land, so Aeneas allows the oldest and frailest of his followers to stay behind in the newly founded city of Acesta (later Segesta), named after his host, Acestes. He sets out once more with the others, hoping at last to reach Italy.

Venus too is eager for her son's dangerous journey to be over, so she pleads with Neptune for the ships to have a safe crossing. The sea-god promises that they will indeed arrive safely in Italy with only one man lost, one life given for many. That man turns out to be the helmsman Palinurus. Somnus (Sleep) comes down to him while he is steering the ship through a clear night and puts him to sleep at the helm. He falls headlong overboard, taking with him the tiller and part of the stern, and as he falls he wakes, and calls again and again to his comrades, but they too are asleep and no one hears him. Only later in the night does Aeneas realize that his helmsman is missing. He takes control of the ship himself, grieving for his lost friend. 'You trusted too much in a clear sky and a calm sea, Palinurus,' he says, 'and now your body must lie naked on an unknown shore' (5.870–71).

At last they land at Cumae in Italy, the home of the Sibyl, a famous clairvoyant and priestess of Apollo. Aeneas consults her, begging to be allowed to go down to the Underworld to meet his father once again. Orpheus has travelled there, and Theseus and mighty Herakles, so why not now Aeneas?

'The descent to the Underworld is easy,' replies the Sibyl (6.127–9). 'The door of black Dis lies open night and day. But to retrace your steps and escape back to the upper air, that is the challenge, that is the labour.' Yet she recognizes Aeneas's determination, so she tells him what must first be done: he must pluck a golden bough as an offering for Proserpina (Persephone), and he must bury a dead comrade, of whom at this moment he is unaware.

Aeneas talks long with his loyal friend and henchman Achates, wondering who this dead man might be, but the question is soon solved. They walk to the shore and there, above the tide line, they find the body of Misenus. He had been a comrade of Hektor in the Trojan War, a courageous warrior and a fine trumpeter, who excelled at stirring the troops with his music and firing them up for battle. After Troy fell he accompanied Aeneas on his journey to Italy. Then one day, while blowing into a sea shell until the waves echoed with the sound, he became so carried away by his skill that he challenged the gods to play as well as he did. The sea-god Triton heard and jealously killed his rival, catching him up and drowning him in the surf among the rocks.

Now the Trojans mourn for their dead comrade, then give him a funeral with full honours, burying his bones on the headland that to this day bears his name. They pile a huge grave-mound over him, and set on it the oars he used to row with and the trumpet he once blew.

Led by two doves sent by Venus, Aeneas finds the magical golden bough growing in a sacred grove. He plucks it, and now, with his tasks completed, he returns to the Sibyl ready for his journey to the Underworld. They pass through her cave and make the fearful descent. On the shore of the river Styx they see the restless souls of the unburied dead, who must wait a hundred years before they are allowed to cross to Hades. Among them is the lost helmsman Palinurus. He tells Aeneas his sad story, of how he survived in the sea for three days, only to be killed by ruffians when he was washed up on the Italian coast. He begs to be taken across the Styx so that his soul may be at peace. This the Sibyl cannot allow, but she foretells that his bones will be laid to rest by the inhabitants of the place where he was killed, and that the locality (still called Cape Palinurus) will bear his name for all time to come. Palinurus is comforted, and he rejoices at the thought of the land that will be named after him.

At the sight of the golden bough, the dread ferryman Charon

willingly carries Aeneas and the Sibyl across the Styx in his boat, even though the large and sturdy body of Aeneas is almost too heavy for the frail craft, accustomed only to carrying spirits. They come to the monstrous guard-dog Kerberos, lying in his cave, and the Sibyl throws him a drugged honey-cake (hence the expression 'a sop for Cerberus'). 'He opened wide his three throats, each of them mad with hunger, and gulped the food down. Then his massive back relaxed and he sprawled all his length across the floor of the cave' (6.421–3). Now they can gain entry to the land of the dead.

Passing countless sorrowing souls whose death was unhappy, Aeneas sees Dido among those who died of love, the wound in her breast still fresh. He sheds tears for her fate and swears to her that he left Carthage against his will, but in hatred and bitterness she moves away, without a look, without a word, into the shadows. There she rejoins her first husband, Sychaeus, who responds to her grief with comfort and love.

Among the many souls of valiant warriors, Aeneas sees his kinsman Deiphobos and learns of his hideous death at the fall of Troy, torn and mutilated by the Greeks. The Sibyl warns that time is passing, so they move on and come to a fork in the road. On the right is the road to Elysium, the home of the blessed, and on the left the road to Tartaros, the place of the damned, where evildoers are punished after death. These can be heard groaning and shrieking horribly as the Furies flog and torture them.

Aeneas and the Sibyl take the right-hand fork and soon they come to the threshold of Elysion. They place the golden bough as an offering for Proserpina, then enter this happy land where the good souls live in blissful ease. They find Anchises, who weeps for joy because his son has come to him. Three times Aeneas tries to take his dead father in his arms, but three times the shade melts in his hands, as light as the winds, as fleeting as a dream. Anchises predicts for him the future glories of Rome and shows him the souls of some of the great Romans to be born in the years to come.

Comforted and encouraged, Aeneas returns to the upper world and sails onwards with his followers towards their destined home. They come near to the island of Circe (p. 400), which resounds with growling and roaring and howling from all the penned beasts – lions and boars and bears and wolves – who once were men. Neptune fills the Trojans' sails with favouring winds to keep them from putting in at that deadly shore.

They land at last in Latium, and there on the banks of the river Tiber they eat a scant meal. So hungry are they that they also eat the thin, wheaten bread which they are using as platters. 'Look,' jokes Ascanius, 'We are even eating our tables!' So the prediction of the Harpy Kelaino has now been fulfilled. Jupiter thunders three times and spreads in the heavens a burning cloud, confirming that they have at last found their new home. The next day they begin to build their first settlement, surrounding their camp by the shore with ditches and a stockade and rampart.

WAR IN LATIUM

The king of Latium is Latinus, son of the pastoral god Faunus (Pan) and the water-nymph Marica, and great-grandson of Saturn (Kronos). Latinus is by this time an old man, having reigned over his land for many peaceful years. His only child by his wife Amata is a daughter, Lavinia, who is now of an age to marry. She has many suitors, the favourite being Turnus, prince of the Rutulians. The queen, Amata, longs above all things to see him married to her daughter, but the prophetic oracle of Faunus has predicted that Lavinia must marry someone from overseas and not a native Italian.

When Latinus hears of Aeneas's arrival, he is very willing to accept him as a son-in-law and to welcome the Trojans as peaceful settlers in his land. The hostile Juno, however, will not allow this to come about easily, so she sends the Fury Alekto to stir up violent animosity to the Trojans in both Amata and Turnus.

Hostilities are triggered between Latins and Trojans when Ascanius wounds a pet stag belonging to Silvia, the royal herdsman's daughter, and these soon develop into full-scale war. Latinus is powerless to prevent it, though he himself keeps apart from the fighting, but Turnus, thanks to Alekto, is only too happy to join battle with the foreigners.

Many allies flock to support him. Mezentius, an exiled Etruscan king, comes with his son Lausus and a thousand men. Caeculus, the founder of Praeneste, leads an army of peasants, most of them armed with slings and small missiles of lead. Aventinus, a son of Herakles, brings many heavily armed troops, and he flaunts his parentage by displaying on his shield the Hydra, fringed with a hundred snakes, and by wearing a lion-skin with its scalp serving as a helmet, just as his father wore the pelt of the Nemean Lion. Camilla, the warrior maiden of the Volsci, rides like an Amazon at the head of her cavalry, a band of selected warrior-women aglitter with bronze. These and many others arrive to join Turnus, until the entire plain beyond the Trojan camp is crowded with his allies.

At the sight of them all, Aeneas is anxious and disheartened, but he has a dream in which he is encouraged by the god of the river Tiber. In the morning he finds, just as the god promised, the white sow prophesied by Helenos lying on the river-bank with her thirty piglets, a sign that on this spot Ascanius will found a city thirty years later, and will call it Alba Longa ('Long White') after the sow. On the god's instructions, Aeneas rows up the Tiber to Pallanteum, a city on a hill that will later be the

Palatine Hill of Rome, and asks its king, the Arcadian Evander, to be his ally. Evander welcomes him, and although he himself is too old to fight, he entrusts his beloved son Pallas to Aeneas and provides a large contingent of cavalry for his war with the Latins.

Nor is this Aeneas's only support. Tarchon, the king of Etruria, becomes his ally out of hatred for the exiled Mezentius and supplies thousands of Etruscan troops, together with a fleet of ships to transport them. And Venus has new and splendid armour made for her son by Vulcan (Hephaistos), just as he once made armour at Thetis's request for Achilles. Aeneas's huge and ornate shield has on its surface countless intricately worked scenes, just like that of Achilles, but in his case they depict famous events from later Roman history, with in the middle the future Emperor Augustus, Virgil's patron, defeating Antony and Cleopatra at the battle of Actium (31 BC).

While Aeneas is away gathering his allies, Turnus and his army advance on the Trojan camp. The Trojans, obedient to Aeneas's earlier instructions, stay resolutely behind their fortifications and Turnus is frustrated of the battle he so ardently desires. He prowls around the walls, searching in vain for an access to the camp – just like a wolf outside a pen full of sheep, says Virgil, one who goes round at dead of night, growling at the gaps in the fence, while the lambs keep on bleating, but he cannot reach them; yet he keeps on through the wind and the rain, driven by hunger and beside himself with rage. Just so does Turnus blaze with anger as he wonders how to get into the camp, or how to get the Trojans to come out on to the plain.

He decides to set fire to the Trojan fleet. Yet here too he is frustrated, for these are ships built from the pines of Mount Ida, sacred to the Phrygian goddess Kybele. Now that Aeneas has reached his new home and has no more need of them, she turns the ships into sea-nymphs and they swim far away. The Rutulians settle down to besiege the Trojan camp instead.

During the night, while the enemy are sleeping, two Trojans, Nisus and Euryalus, attempt to get through their lines to go and summon Aeneas. The two are constant companions, Euryalus young and beautiful, Nisus the older man. Always they go into battle together, side by side, and each is devoted to the other. In the foot race at the funeral games for Anchises, when Nisus fell, he made sure that Euryalus won the race by bringing down his chief competitor.

Now Nisus leads out Euryalus in the hope of glory, but this time the outcome is tragic. They move among the sleeping enemy, slaughtering them as they go. Unfortunately Euryalus cannot resist gathering up various pieces of booty, including a shining helmet with gorgeous plumes. He puts it on, and when a detachment of enemy cavalry approaches, their attention is caught by the glittering metal, reflecting the light of the moon in the dim shadows. The two Trojans flee into a rough wood, and while Nisus escapes through to the other side, Euryalus is weighed down by his booty and in his fright loses his way. The enemy troop captures him. Nisus rushes back to save him, but too late, and has to watch him brutally killed by the cavalry leader, Volcens (9.433–7):

Euryalus rolled writhing in death, and the blood flowed over his lovely limbs, his neck drooped and his head sank on his shoulders, like a scarlet flower wilting and dying when cut by the plough, or like poppies that droop their heads on tired necks when rain weighs them down . . .

Nisus fights his way through the massed enemy, indifferent to countless wounds, until he is face to face with Volcens. Then he kills him – even as he himself dies, throwing himself down on the body of his beloved friend and joining him in death.

The next day the Latin army mounts an attack against the walls and towers of the Trojan camp, while Aeneas's men strive to defend them. Many of both sides die, until the ditches around the camp run red with blood. When at last Aeneas sails in with Pallas and his reinforcements, they too are attacked and there is more bitter fighting. Young Pallas urges his men into the thick of the battle, killing as he goes. He slaughters many fine warriors before he himself is killed by Turnus, who takes his sword-belt and wears it as a battle spoil.

Aeneas is full of grief for his young ally and storms through the enemy ranks, seeking revenge. He calls out for Turnus, but Juno has created a phantom Aeneas and has lured the Rutulian leader away from the battlefield to safety. Aeneas, unable to find the prey he seeks, kills every man who crosses his path, dealing out death all over the plain like a raging torrent of water or a black tornado.

He encounters Mezentius, the exiled Etruscan king, who holds his ground in front of him, huge in his massive armour, hoping to kill his Trojan enemy and win a fine trophy for his son, Lausus. Each hurls his spear, but only Mezentius is wounded. He falls back, defenceless. Before Aeneas can reach him to strike a deadlier blow, Lausus leaps forward to defend the father he loves. Reluctantly, while admiring the boy's courage and pitying the futility of it, Aeneas kills him.

Now it is the wounded Mezentius who seeks revenge. He orders his horse to be brought: Rhaebus, his pride and joy, who has been his faithful companion through all his many campaigns. Now either they will avenge the death of Lausus and carry off the head of his killer, or they will die together in the attempt. They gallop in a circle around Aeneas, and Mezentius hurls three spears, all of them in vain. Then Aeneas throws his own spear and hits Rhaebus full in the forehead. The horse rears, thrashing the air with his hooves and throwing his rider, then falls, pinning Mezentius to the ground. Aeneas can now kill him at leisure, and Mezentius dies with courage, asking only that he be buried together with his dear son.

Both sides agree a truce for twelve days in which to bury their dead. The city of the Latins resounds with cries of mourning, and Latinus himself, losing heart, summons his council and suggests that they offer peace to the Trojans. Turnus disagrees and is all for war, and the question is still being debated when a messenger rushes in panic into the palace, mistakenly claiming that Aeneas and his troops are about to attack. Turnus, seizing the moment, at once calls his men to arms and they all pour out on to the plain.

In the battle that follows, Turnus's Volscian ally Camilla comes into her own. Diana (Artemis) is watching from afar, for she has loved Camilla since she was a baby. At that time her father Metabus was driven from his throne, and he fled into exile with his infant daughter in his arms, hotly pursued by his enemies. When he found his way blocked by the flooded river Amasenus, he swiftly lashed the baby to his spear, dedicated her to Diana, then flung her over the torrent to safety before swimming across himself, just in time to escape his pursuers. He brought up his daughter on the lonely mountains, feeding her on milk from wild mares, dressing her in a tiger-skin, and teaching her to hunt and fight. She grew up a favourite with Diana, chaste and courageous, and so fleet of foot that she could run over the standing corn without crushing it, or over the surface of the sea without wetting her feet.

Now in battle she leads out her cavalry troop of warrior-women, all riding like Amazons with one breast exposed, armed with spears, and bows and arrows, and double axes. She kills many of the enemy before she herself is brought down by the Etruscan Arruns, a spear lodged in her naked breast. At once Arruns flees, more terrified than anyone when he sees what he has done. He is like a wolf who has killed a shepherd or a great bull, says Virgil, then flees to the woods in fear, his quivering tail tucked under his belly for comfort. And Arruns is right to be afraid, for Diana has sent down the nymph Opis to avenge any harm to her favourite, and now Opis draws her lethal bow and shoots him dead.

The Latins are routed as the Trojans carry all before them, and the next day Turnus resolves to spare his men by meeting Aeneas in single combat to settle the issue. Latinus and Amata do all they can to dissuade him, but he is determined (12.4–9):

Just like a lion on the African plains, who moves into battle only when he is badly wounded in the chest by hunters, and then rejoices in it, and tossing the thick mane on his neck he breaks off undaunted the shaft planted in him by some ruffian, and opens his bloody mouth and roars – just so did hot violence rise in Turnus.

But before the duel can take place, the Latins are incited to fight again by Turnus's sister Juturna, a water-nymph who has been given immortality by Jupiter in return for her favours. The two armies join battle. Aeneas is wounded by an arrow, but he is quickly healed by Venus and strides onwards, looking for Turnus. Juturna does her best to save her brother, disguising herself as his charioteer Metiscus and driving him all around the plain, but always out of Aeneas's range.

Aeneas attacks the Latins' city with fire, and when the queen, Amata, sees it she thinks that Turnus must be dead. Deranged with grief and guilt, she hangs herself. Lamentations ring through the palace and spread through all the city. A horseman gallops to take the desperate news to Turnus, and he, hearing the clamour and seeing fire billowing to the sky, rushes to confront Aeneas. At last the decisive duel can take place.

The two heroes meet and exchange blow upon blow – like two enemy bulls, says Virgil, who charge against each other, gouging with their horns till their necks and shoulders run with blood and the woodland echoes with their bellowing, while the herdsmen and the rest of the cattle stand back in terror, and the heifers low quietly together as they wait to see who will become leader of the herd.

Juturna helps Turnus by returning to him his lost sword, made by Vulcan. Then Jupiter sends down a Fury to confront her as an omen of death, and when she sees it she recognizes that she can do nothing more, and Turnus must be left to his fate. Lamenting his now certain death and her own immortality, she plunges back into the depths of her river.

Turnus heaves up a huge boulder and flings it at Aeneas, but it does not even reach its target. He falters, afraid, and now Aeneas hurls his deadly spear and wounds Turnus in the thigh. He goes down, acknowledging that he is the loser, and begging that he may be restored to his aged father Daunus and to his own people. Aeneas is about to spare his life when he sees that he is wearing Pallas's sword-belt as a battle spoil. 'Are you to escape me now, wearing spoils stripped from one I loved?' cries Aeneas (12.947–9). 'It is Pallas who with this blow makes sacrifice, Pallas who takes his vengeance for your crime.' And overcome with a mighty rage, he plunges his sword full into Turnus's heart, slaying him pitilessly.

The *Aeneid* ends with the death of Turnus, but we know that Aeneas now made peace with the Latins and married Lavinia, founding the city of Lavinium in her name and ruling over a union of Latins and Trojans (now all called Latins). Lavinia bore him a son, Silvius, after his death. Aeneas was rewarded with immortality.

15

THE FOUNDATION OF ROME

Thirty years after the settlement of Lavinium, Aeneas's son Ascanius founded Alba Longa at the place where Aeneas had seen the white sow lying with her thirty piglets. After Ascanius's death, twelve hereditary kings ruled the city, beginning with Silvius and ending with Proca. It is with the two sons of Proca, Numitor and Amulius, that events begin to move towards the foundation of Rome, the traditional date of which was said to be 753 BC. Livy's history (Book 1) has become the canonical version.

ROMULUS AND REMUS

Numitor succeeded to the throne of Alba Longa on the death of Proca, but his younger brother Amulius deposed him and murdered his sons. Not only that, he forced Numitor's only daughter, Rhea Silvia, to become a Vestal Virgin so that no other male heir could be born. He reckoned without the gods, however, for the war-god Mars lay with the girl and she bore him twin sons, Romulus and Remus.

Amulius flung Rhea Silvia into prison and ordered the babies to be thrown into the river Tiber – but again he took no account of the gods. Mars was looking after his own, and the basket in which his sons lay floated safely to the shore and ran aground under a fig tree, later known as the Ficus Ruminalis and re-garded as sacred. Here a she-wolf, coming down from the hills, heard the infants' cries and suckled them, and a woodpecker fed them scraps of food. Both creatures were sacred to Mars.

The royal shepherd, Faustulus, happened to be passing by, and he saw the she-wolf tenderly licking the babies as if they were her own young. Guessing the boys' royal parentage, he took them home, and he and his wife Acca Larentia adopted them and brought them up as their own. Because *lupa* can mean both 'she-wolf' and 'prostitute', some writers rationalized the boys' legend by claiming that Acca Larentia herself had saved their lives by suckling them.

The she-wolf suckles Romulus and Remus.

The boys grew into fine, strong young men who often led a gang of young shepherds on daring exploits. They not only hunted wild beasts, but attacked brigands and shared out their stolen spoils. The brigands resented this, and one day they captured Remus in an ambush and handed him over to Numitor to be punished. Numitor suspected that he and his brother might be his lost grandsons, and Faustulus confirmed his suspicions. Romulus and Remus, with the help of their loyal gang of young men, attacked the palace and killed the usurper Amulius. Numitor seized the citadel and once more became king.

The brothers now decided to found a city of their own. They chose a site not far from Alba Longa, and near the Tiber where they had been cast out to drown. But now they quarrelled as to who should give the city its name and become its king, and since they could not tell which twin was the elder, they left it to the gods to send a sign. Remus took up his position on the Aventine Hill and Romulus on the Palatine, both of them watching out for birds that would tell them the divine will. Remus first saw six vultures, then Romulus saw twelve. Each of them was named king by his own followers, Remus because he saw the birds first, Romulus because he saw more birds. In the brawl that followed, Remus was slain. In another version of his death, Remus mocked his brother and leapt over the partly built city walls, acting like an enemy instead of a friend who enters by the gates. Romulus lost his temper and killed him, declaring, 'So perish anyone else who shall leap over my walls.' Now Romulus was left alone to found the city, which he called Rome after himself.

The city flourished. Men flocked to live there, many of them outlaws and fugitives to whom Romulus gave willing sanctuary, since they made Rome the stronger – but of course the city also needed women. Unfortunately the Romans were both feared and despised by their neighbours, so any plea for marriage with the local women was scornfully rejected. Romulus overcame this problem by holding a great festival and inviting the neighbours and their families. The Sabines in particular came en masse. In the midst of the festivities, the Romans drove off the unarmed men and carried away their daughters (the 'Rape of the Sabine Women'). At first the girls were terrified, but Romulus reassured them that they would be properly married, and their captors wooed them with words of passionate love, so they were soon happily won over to their new situation.

But their fathers and brothers were not at all happy and

rallied to win them back by force. Various small raids against Rome were unsuccessful, but finally the Sabines made a major attack under their king, Titus Tatius. They took the Roman citadel through the treachery of the commander's daughter, Tarpeia, who was happy to be bribed to let the army inside the fortress by night. She asked for her reward to be what the soldiers wore on their left arms, expecting golden armlets, but instead they repaid her treachery by crushing her to death beneath their shields. Tarpeia was said to have given her name to the Tarpeian Rock, the precipice on the Capitoline hill at Rome from which murderers and traitors were later flung to their deaths.

Now fierce fighting broke out between Sabines and Romans, but the Sabine Women saved the day. They ran out into the thick of the battle, begging their husbands and fathers not to make them widows and orphans by killing each other (Plate 7), so the Romans and Sabines made peace. They agreed to merge their two peoples into one, with Rome as their capital and Romulus and Titus Tatius their joint rulers. Some years later, Titus Tatius was killed in a quarrel with the people of Lavinium and Romulus once again became Rome's sole king.

He ruled for almost forty years, during which time Rome grew and prospered. At the end of his life he left the earth in a mysterious fashion. He was holding a muster of troops in the meadows that would one day be the Campus Martius (Field of Mars) when a storm blew up. Thunder rolled, and he was enveloped in a cloud so thick that he disappeared from view. When the cloud dispersed, he had vanished. The senators who had been nearest him declared that he had been caught up into heaven, and the soldiers, who loved Romulus, hailed him as a god. He was thereafter worshipped as the god Quirinus.

According to Livy (1.16), there was a rumour that Romulus had been murdered and torn to pieces by the senators, envious of his power. This suspicion was put to rest when a certain Iulius Proculus reported that Romulus himself had appeared before him at dawn, saying: 'Go, and tell the Romans the will of the gods that my Rome shall be the capital of the world. Let them cultivate the arts of war, and let them know and teach their descendants that no human strength can resist Roman arms.'

LATER KINGS OF ROME

After Romulus's death, a further six kings ruled at Rome before the monarchy came to an end. Their stories are part myth and part history. The first of these, and thus the second king of Rome, was a Sabine, **Numa Pompilius** (715–673 BC), who was famous for his wisdom and piety. His was a long reign of peace, in which he established most of the Roman religious system and made all kinds of cultural reforms, inspired, or so he claimed, by his divine consort, the water-nymph Egeria, who lived in a grove near the Capena Gate.

He was succeeded by the warrior king **Tullus Hostilius** (673–642 BC), who was as fond of fighting as his predecessor was of peace. During a war between Rome and Alba Longa, he agreed with the Alban king that to spare bloodshed the matter should be settled by a battle of champions, fought between two sets of triplets, the three Horatii (Romans) and the three Curiatii (Albans). On the appointed day the six champions met and all three Curiatii were wounded, but then first one Horatius, and then a second, was killed. The last Horatius ran away and the three Albans pursued him, though at different speeds, and as each of them caught up with him separately, he turned and killed them one by one. He then marched back to Rome in triumph, carrying the cloaks of the Curiatii as his spoils.

He was met by his sister, who had been betrothed to one of the Curiatii, and when she recognized the cloak that she herself had woven for her lover, she shrieked out in anguish. Horatius stabbed her to the heart, crying, 'So perish all Roman women who mourn an enemy.' He was tried before the king for taking the law into his own hands and was found guilty, but on appeal he was acquitted because of his heroism in saving Rome.

After the Alban defeat, Tullus forced the Alban people to live in Rome and he destroyed Alba itself. Not content with this, he declared war on the Sabines, over whom he won a notable victory. He died while he was trying to propitiate Jupiter using a ritual taken from Numa's books, but he got the procedure wrong and was consumed by lightning.

The fourth king of Rome was **Ancus Marcius** (642–617 BC), the grandson of Numa on his mother's side, and like Numa himself a king of peace, a culture-hero and originator of customs. He is credited with the construction of the first bridge – a wooden one – across the River Tiber.

The fifth king was an immigrant from Etruria, **Tarquinius Priscus** (616–579 BC), who was married to an Etruscan woman named Tanaquil. Having made himself indispensable to Ancus Marcius, he took the throne even though Ancus had sons, but they were always deeply resentful of Tarquin's preferment, and finally had him assassinated.

He was succeeded by his son-in-law **Servius Tullius** (578–535 BC). Servius had been born in the royal palace, possibly as the son of a slave, but when Tanaquil saw flames playing around the infant's head without harming him, she and Tarquin recognized this as a clear sign of divine approval. They brought up the boy as their own son and married him to their daughter. When Tarquin was assassinated, Tanaquil helped Servius establish himself in power. His rivals fled the country.

Servius was another excellent king who did a great deal of good for Rome, but his end was unhappy. He had two daughters named Tullia, whom he had married to the two sons of Tarquin.

The younger Tullia, who was ambitious, was married to the mild Arruns, but she contrived his murder, and that of her gentler sister; then she married the other son, Lucius Tarquinius, later called Superbus, who was quite as ambitious as she was. They had Servius assassinated, and Tullia even drove her carriage over her father's body as it lay bleeding in the street.

Tarquinius Superbus ('the Proud') succeeded Servius as the seventh and last king of Rome (534–510 BC). He denied the dead king burial and killed his supporters, then ruled Rome as a despot. Tradition has it that the Sibyl of Cumae, who had escorted Aeneas to the Underworld, offered nine books of oracular utterances to Tarquin, asking a huge price for their purchase. When he refused, she burnt three books and offered him the remainder for the same sum. Again he refused, so she burnt three more, and finally sold the last three to him for the price that she had asked for the full nine. These books were identified with collections of oracles that in historical times were carefully preserved in the Roman temple of Capitoline Jupiter for consultation in national emergencies. They were burnt in a temple fire in 83 BC.

The Sibyl herself had an unhappy end. Apollo had once desired her and had promised her any gift she might choose if she would take him as a lover. She asked for as many years of life as there were grains of dust in a pile of floor-sweepings, which numbered a thousand, but just like the goddess Eos before her when she won immortality for her lover Tithonos, the Sibyl forgot to ask for perpetual youth. As the centuries passed she slowly shrivelled up. Petronius's Trimalchio (*Satyrica* 48) saw her in her cave at Cumae, hanging in a bottle, and when some children asked her what she wanted, she replied, 'I want to die.' In the second century AD, Pausanias (10.12.8) saw in a temple of Apollo at Cumae a small stone urn said to contain her bones.

Tarquin's was a reign of terror, which came to an end – as did the monarchy – when his son Sextus raped a virtuous Roman lady named Lucretia. One night, while the Roman forces were besieging Ardea, Tarquin's sons were drinking with their kinsman Collatinus and they fell to arguing about which of them had the best wife. Collatinus suggested that they settle the question by riding back to Rome unannounced and finding out what the women were doing in their husbands' absence.

It turned out that all the women were at lavish parties with their friends, except for Collatinus's wife, Lucretia. She was sitting quietly at home among her slave-women and working at her weaving, so he won the argument. But Sextus had been aroused by Lucretia's beauty and virtue, and a few days later he returned to the house, where he was welcomed as a guest. During the night he went with drawn sword to Lucretia's bedroom and declared his desire for her. He pleaded with her, and mixed threats with his pleas, but she refused to yield to him. Finally he threatened her with disgrace, saying that he would kill her, and a slave as well, then leave the slave's naked body next to hers so that it looked as if she had been caught in adultery. At this, Lucretia gave in. But the next morning she told her husband and father what had happened, making them promise to avenge her, and then plunged a dagger into her heart.

As a result of this crime, the Roman nobles rose against the king. Tarquin, together with his family, was driven out of Rome. He went to Etruria and took refuge with Lars Porsenna, the king of Clusium, who undertook to restore him to his throne. Porsenna and his Etruscan army marched on Rome, aiming to invade over the wooden bridge across the Tiber, the Pons Sublicius. Seeing them approaching, the Roman guards began to flee, but Horatius, called Cocles ('One-eyed'), urged his comrades to hew the bridge down, while he held off the enemy single-handed. Two others, Spurius Larcius and Titus Herminius, helped him to keep the Etruscans at bay until the bridge was about to fall, then he sent them back to safety while he stood alone. Still he held the enemy off, until suddenly the bridge crashed down and his escape was cut off.

With a prayer to the god of the Tiber, Horatius leapt into the river in full armour and swam across under a hail of missiles. He had saved Rome, and the Romans rewarded him by setting up a statue in his honour, and by giving him as much land as he could plough round in a single day. Tarquin never regained the throne, and Rome now became a republic (traditionally in 509 BC). The stories of the Roman leaders who followed the seven kings belong more to the realm of history than to that of myth.

METAMORPHOSES

Many myths contain tales of metamorphoses – the transformations of bodies into different shapes by the power of the gods. In ancient literature, the greatest treasure house of these is Ovid's *Metamorphoses*, a fifteen-book epic relating a rich assortment of some 250 stories, each of which contains a transformation of some kind, and all cleverly woven into one vast and elaborate tapestry. In the later Middle Ages and the Renaissance, Ovid was one of the best known and most widely read of classical authors, and his *Metamorphoses* in particular has proved an inexhaustible source of inspiration to poets, painters and sculptors alike.

Many stories of metamorphosis have already been included in earlier chapters of this book. This chapter comprises a personal selection of those remaining tales which seem to me the most resonant and memorable. They are largely based on Ovid's narrative, though not entirely so, for almost all of them have their origin in the Greek myths, even though they may find their most powerful expression in Ovid. For consistency the Greek names for the gods are kept throughout.

PHAITHON

Let us begin with the myth of Phaithon, which includes two popular types of transformations, into tree and into bird. The story had a vigorous early life in Greek literature, but only fragments of this remain, and it is Ovid who gives us our first detailed version of Phaithon's sad fate (*Metamorphoses* 1.750–2.380).

Phaithon was the son of the Sun-god Helios and the Oceanid

Klymene, wife of the Ethiopian king Merops. He grew up in the home of Merops, but he wanted to be reassured that Helios was his true father, so Klymene sent him to the Sun's magnificent palace in the furthest East, at the gates of dawn. Here Helios confirmed that Phaithon was indeed his son and promised to prove it by granting him any gift he might desire.

Phaithon asked to drive his father's sun-chariot across the sky for just one day. The god knew that the feat would be beyond the boy's powers and begged him to change his mind, to choose another boon, but Phaithon was adamant. All he wanted was to drive the chariot and horses of the Sun. He ignored all his father's pleas, and now there was no time for more: the sky was reddening with the coming dawn and the chariot must set off on its day's journey. Helios was forced to stand by his promise.

With many anxious instructions from his father, Phaithon leapt into the chariot and joyfully caught hold of the reins. The four horses hurled themselves upwards into the air, and all too soon they raced out of control, dragging the chariot and the terrified boy completely off course, soaring up close to the stars and setting them smoking. When Phaithon looked down from the heights of heaven and saw the tiny earth so far below, he wished that he had never learned who his father was – too late he wanted only to be Merops' son.

They hurtled down too near the earth and set it all on fire. Rivers dried up and the seas contracted. Scorched by the intense heat, the skins of the Ethiopians were burnt black and North Africa was turned into a desert. At last Zeus intervened to save the world from complete destruction. He hurled a thunderbolt to strike Phaithon from his chariot, and the boy plunged down towards the earth like a falling star. His blazing corpse dropped into the river Eridanos and was quenched.

The Italian nymphs buried Phaithon's body, and his grieving

mother Klymene searched the earth until she found his tomb. His sisters, the Heliades, came here too, and they wept so long and so unceasingly on the banks of the Eridanos that they were turned into poplar trees, and their tears into amber. In Aeschylus's lost tragedy *The Heliades*, Phaithon's sisters made up the Chorus, and it seems from the remaining fragments that here his request to drive the sun-chariot was refused by his father, and that the Heliades secretly yoked it for him. In this version, then, they had even more reason to mourn when their brother met so terrible a death. To commemorate his sad fate, Phaithon was immortalized in the stars as the constellation Auriga, the Charioteer. The river Eridanos too became a constellation, stretching far through the sky to the west of Orion.

The story of Phaithon is not quite over, for another mourner came to the place of his death: Kyknos, a relative of the dead boy and king of the Ligurians in Italy. He had loved Phaithon dearly, and now he grieved for him unceasingly, wandering the river-banks and singing of his loss, until the gods took pity on him and turned him into a swan. While he lived, remembering Zeus's thunderbolt, he shunned the dangerous skies and chose as his element water, haunting lakes and rivers and marshes in his fear and hatred of fire. When at last he grew old and it was time for him to die, he left the earth and became the constellation Cygnus, singing as he flew towards the stars. Swans have ever afterwards sung songs, 'swan songs', when they are about to die.

HELIOS, LEUKOTHOE AND KLYTIE

The Sun-god had other earthly loves apart from Phaithon's mother Klymene. When Aphrodite wanted to punish him for telling tales of her affair with Ares (p. 69), she made Helios fall helplessly in love with a mortal woman, Leukothoe, daughter of the Persian king Orchamos (*Metamorphoses* 4.169–270).

Burning with passion, Helios gained entrance to Leukothoe's room by disguising himself as her mother, Eurynome, but once he was alone with the girl he returned to his true form. She was overcome by the god's magnificence and accepted his embraces without a murmur.

This affair caused bitter jealousy in an old flame of the Sun-god, Klytie, who still loved him and wanted him for herself. She spread abroad the story of Leukothoe's seduction until it came to Orchamos's ears. He was too angry to listen to his daughter's excuses and he buried her alive, deep in the ground. She died, crushed by the weight of earth above her, and although Helios uncovered her, and tried his utmost to warm her cold body back to life with his rays, he tried in vain. Stricken with grief, he transformed her into the tree that gives frankincense.

Klytie too suffered, for Helios now felt only hatred for his one-time love and would have nothing to do with her. She wasted away in sorrow, sitting alone on the ground and every day turning her face to the Sun-god as he passed across the sky. When she died, she became the heliotrope, whose flower turns to follow the course of the sun from morning to evening.

NARCISSUS

Another flower-transformation – perhaps the most famous of them all – was that of Narcissus, the beautiful son of the river-god Kephissos and a nymph, Liriope (*Metamorphoses* 3.341–510). When Narcissus was still a baby, Liriope asked the blind Theban seer Teiresias, who was then little known, whether her son would live to a ripe old age. 'Yes,' he replied, 'so long as he never comes to know himself.' At the time no one understood what this prophecy meant, but when years later it was shown by events to be true, Teiresias became famous and his reputation thereafter was assured.

By the time Narcissus reached his sixteenth year, he was so

The beautiful Narcissus, lost in admiration of himself.

beautiful that many fell in love with him, youths and girls alike, but his heart was cold and proud and he scorned them all. One of these lovers was Echo, a nymph who loved to talk, but could only repeat words spoken by someone else. This was an affliction bestowed on her by Hera, who had often tried to catch Zeus making love to the nymphs on the mountainside, but had been detained by Echo with an endless flow of chatter while the nymphs had a chance to escape. When Hera realized what Echo was doing, she turned on her in a rage and took from her the ability to say anything of her own volition: she could now only repeat the last words spoken by others.

Echo fell in love with Narcissus the moment she saw him, but he spurned her contemptuously, as he had spurned all the others who loved him. In her sorrow she wasted away until only her plaintive voice was left. Since then, she has never been seen in the woods or on the mountains, though she can be heard there by anyone. Finally one of the many rejected suitors of Narcissus prayed that the youth himself might suffer unrequited love, just as he had made others suffer, and Nemesis heard, and granted his prayer.

In the woods there was a clear pool, with shining, silvery waters, where shepherds never came, nor goats, nor cattle. Its smooth surface stayed undisturbed, and around it grew a grassy sward, always fresh and green. Sheltering trees encircled it and kept it cool, even in the fiercest sun. Here Narcissus came, hot and tired from hunting, and lay down to drink. When he saw his beautiful reflection in the still surface of the pool, he fell in love with himself. Spellbound, he stayed stretched on the grass, gazing at his own image, and as day followed day he fell more deeply in love with what so many others had loved so hopelessly. Again and again he leaned down to clasp the longed-for image in his arms, but always it eluded him.

He stayed there, caring nothing for food and drink, and as time passed he slowly wasted away. Echo, even though angry at his treatment of her, still grieved for him. When he sighed, 'Alas', so did she. When he cried aloud for the love he loved in vain, she echoed, 'In vain.' And when he murmured his last farewell, 'Farewell,' she replied. Worn out by his hopeless love, he laid down his weary head on the grass by the pool, and died.

Even in the Underworld he kept looking at his reflection in the waters of the river Styx. On earth the wood nymphs all mourned for him and Echo re-echoed their laments. They prepared for his funeral, but his body could nowhere be found. In its place grew a flower with a circle of white petals around a yellow centre.

The traveller Pausanias adds a postscript to the story (9.31.7–9). He saw the pool of Narcissus on Mount Helikon, but declared the tale that he fell in love with himself to be complete nonsense. He preferred a rationalized version of the myth: that Narcissus had been in love with his twin sister who looked exactly like himself and, after she died, he found consolation in looking into the pool at the reflection of himself that was just like his lost love.

DAIDALION – NYKTIMENE – THE PIERIDES – AISAKOS

Several mortals were transformed into birds, and in their new forms retained the traits they had once displayed in their human lives. **Daidalion,** for instance, the son of Phosphoros, the Morning Star, was a fierce and war-loving man. He had a beautiful daughter, Chione (*Metamorphoses* 11.291–345), who at fourteen was so lovely that she had countless suitors. Even the gods Apollo and Hermes desired her when they chanced to see her one day. Hermes put her magically to sleep there and then and took his pleasure of her at once, while Apollo deferred his enjoyment of her love until the night, then came to her after dark disguised as an old woman. In the fullness of time she bore twin sons, each taking after the god who had fathered him: Autolykos became an expert thief like the crafty Hermes, and Philammon an accomplished musician like Apollo.

Unfortunately Chione allowed the divine favour she had enjoyed to go to her head. She foolishly boasted that she was more beautiful than Artemis, and at this the angry goddess bent back her bow and shot her dead. Daidalion was so grieved by his daughter's death that he ran to the summit of Mount Parnassos and flung himself from a towering rock, but Apollo took pity on him and bore him up. The god changed him into a hawk, a bird with the same fierce and courageous nature as the man, and he lived on, still suffering, and by preying on other birds caused others to suffer too.

Nyktimene was the daughter of Epopeus, king of the island of Lesbos (*Metamorphoses* 2.589–95). When her father had sex with her, she fled in shame to the woods, hiding herself away, until at last Athene took pity on her and turned her into a night-bird (*nykt-*, night), the owl, so that she could hide her guilt in darkness. This is why owls still shun the daylight and live their lives by night, and if they ever come out by day they are mobbed by all the other birds.

The Pierides (*Metamorphoses* 5.294–678) were the nine daughters of Pieros, a king of Pella in Macedonia who had given his name to Pieria, the region north of Mount Olympos where the nine Muses were born (and were also sometimes known as 'Pierides' because of their place of birth). Pieros's daughters were so proud of their expertise at singing – unduly so, as it happened – that they challenged the Muses to a singing contest. The Muses agreed, so the local nymphs were chosen as judges and the contest took place.

With one accord the nymphs agreed that the Muses were the winners, but the girls resented their defeat. They went on hurling abuse at their victors until the Muses punished them by turning them into magpies. Even now, as birds, they retain their old style of speech, which is why magpies are garrulous creatures and chatter long and harshly.

Aisakos (*Metamorphoses* 11.751–95) was the son of Priam, king of Troy, but he himself hated cities and preferred to live in remote country places. He was in love with a nymph, Hesperia, daughter of the river-god Kebren, and he often pursued her through the woods, though she always escaped him. One day he found her sitting in the sun on the banks of her father's river and drying her flowing hair. At the sight of him she fled away as usual, and as usual he chased after her. But this time, as she ran through the woods, she was bitten on the foot by a venomous snake and died. Overcome with remorse, Aisakos flung himself from a high cliff into the sea, but the sea-goddess Tethys pitied him and would not let him die: she caught him as he fell and turned him into a water-bird, a diver. Forced to live against his will, he now spent all his days flying up and dashing himself down into the waves, forever seeking the death he longed for.

Yet perhaps the most moving of all these bird-transformations related by Ovid is the myth of Keux and Alkyone, a tale of faithful wedded love and one of his poem's highlights.

KEUX AND ALKYONE

Keux, like Daidalion, was a son of Phosphoros, the Morning Star, and he was married to Alkyone, a daughter of Aiolos, lord of the winds (*Metamorphoses* 11.410–748). The couple loved each other devotedly. One day, distraught at the death of his brother, Keux decided that he must go to consult an oracle and he made preparations for sailing. Alkyone had a vivid premonition of disaster and begged him not to leave her: she feared the sea and the savagery of storms, and was quite sure that if Keux sailed away, he would never return. Nevertheless, Keux was determined on his voyage, and he did his best to soothe his wife's fears, promising to come home again within two months.

He set off, but Alkyone was right to be afraid, for the ship had sailed only halfway to its destination when it foundered during a violent storm and Keux was drowned. Alkyone, knowing nothing of this, sacrificed every day to Hera, praying for her husband's safety, until the goddess took pity on her ignorance and hope, and sent the dream-god Morpheus to her during the night. As Alkyone slept, he came to her in the guise of Keux himself, pale as death, his clothing gone, his hair and beard sodden with seawater, and he told her of the shipwreck and of her husband's death by drowning.

Overcome with grief, Alkyone awoke and rushed to the seashore, and there she knew her dream was true when she saw Keux's body washed towards her. In her sorrow she tried to drown herself too, but the gods took pity on her and transformed them both into halcyons, kingfishers, that they might still live together and love one another. Every winter they mated, and the gods calmed the sea for fourteen days, the Halcyon Days, while Alkyone floated peacefully on the waters, brooding over her nest and hatching her eggs.

ARACHNE

Arachne (*Metamorphoses* 6.5–145) was another mortal who retained her human traits after metamorphosis. She was a young Lydian woman of humble origin, the daughter of Idmon of Kolophon, but her unparalleled skill at weaving made her famous throughout Lydia, and even the nymphs flocked from the countryside around, just for the pleasure of watching her at work. At last she grew so proud of her skill that she said she would challenge Athene, the goddess of crafts herself, to a weaving contest.

When Athene heard of it, she came to Arachne disguised as an old woman and warned her to beg the goddess's pardon for her folly. The girl rudely scorned her advice. Even when Athene resumed her own shape, Arachne was unafraid and persisted in her foolhardy challenge. She knew how good she was.

The contest began. Athene wove a tapestry depicting her contest with Poseidon for the patronship of her city, Athens, while all the other gods looked on. In the corners of her design she wove four smaller scenes, all showing the punishment of presumptuous mortals who had dared to set themselves against the gods, and she bordered her work with woven branches of her own tree, the olive. Arachne in her turn depicted the multitude of disguises assumed by the gods in their many and various love affairs: Zeus as a bull with Europa, a swan with Leda, a shower of gold with Danae, Poseidon as a horse with Demeter, a bird with the Gorgon Medusa, and so on. Around this array of divine deceptions she wove a border of flowers and twining ivy.

Every stitch of Arachne's work was perfect. Athene ripped it to rags in fury, then attacked the girl with her shuttle until she could bear no more, but put a noose around her neck and hanged herself. Yet as she dangled there, Athene took pity on her: she lifted her up and changed her into a spider, who could carry on weaving in peace and with all her old skill. To this day her descendants still weave their webs.

KALLISTO AND ARKAS

Not all girls liked to spend their time indoors, working on traditional domestic tasks. Kallisto ('Most Beautiful') was a huntress in the mountains of Arcadia (*Metamorphoses* 2.409–531), a favourite companion of the goddess Artemis and vowed to chastity. 'But a favourite is never a favourite for long,' says Ovid cynically (2.416). One day the ever-amorous Zeus spotted the nymph as she was resting in the woods, hot and tired from the hunt, and at once he saw his chance. He came to her disguised as Artemis, and Kallisto in her ignorance welcomed him warmly. He kissed her, and by now was close enough to clasp her to him and overpower her. Even though she fought against him with all her might, he raped her and left her pregnant.

Nine months passed. Finally one hot day came when Artemis led her companions into a shady grove to bathe in a cool stream. They quickly undressed – all but Kallisto, who delayed and made excuses, until at last her friends stripped the clothes from her by force. Now her secret was out, and the goddess in fury banished her from their company.

Kallisto gave birth to a son, Arkas, and this made Hera so angry and jealous that she punished the innocent girl cruelly. She caught her by the hair and flung her to the ground (2.477–85):

And when the girl stretched out her arms to beg for mercy, they began to bristle with thick black hairs, and her hands curved round, tipped with crooked claws, and turned into feet. Her face, which once Zeus had admired, was deformed by wide gaping jaws. And lest she might win sympathy with her prayers and pleas, her powers of speech were taken from her, and only an angry threatening growl, terrifying to hear, came harshly from her throat. She was now a bear, but still her mind remained as it was . . .

For fifteen years Kallisto lived in the wilds, afraid of humans and wild beasts alike, often running for her life and always grieving her sad fate. Meanwhile Arkas grew up, knowing nothing of his mother, but with a passion for hunting, just as she had once had. One day he came face to face with her in the woods. She seemed to recognize him, but he shrank back in fear from this bear who gazed at him so fixedly. Eagerly she tried to approach him, but he was sure that the great beast was about to attack. He drew back his spear to thrust and kill.

Then at last, after long years, Zeus took pity on Kallisto and stayed her son's hand. He caught up mother and son in a whirlwind and carried them into the sky, where he immortalized them among the stars. Kallisto became the constellation Arktos, the Great Bear (Ursa Major), and Arkas became the brilliant star Arktouros (Arcturus), 'Bear-guardian', forever following his mother through the night sky. Now Hera was even angrier than before, and she begged the sea-gods Ocean and Tethys never to allow her rival's constellation to sink for rest into the waters of Ocean that surrounded the earth. This is why the Great Bear never sets, but revolves eternally around the Pole Star, high in the heavens.

This was a popular myth (understandably so) and other versions vary its details. Sometimes Kallisto was turned into a bear by Artemis, angry that her companion had broken her vow of chastity, sometimes by Zeus himself, to try and hide his infidelity from Hera – as always, in vain. Sometimes Kallisto was hunted and killed by Artemis. Sometimes in her bear-form she wandered unknowingly into a forbidden sanctuary of Zeus, or was chased into it by Arkas, and because such a violation was punishable by death, mother and son were once again rescued by Zeus and transported to the heavens. Yet the essence of the story remains the same: Kallisto was raped by Zeus; she bore a son and was parted from him; she was turned into a bear and as a bear was hunted and killed, or almost killed; and at the end of her misery she was rewarded with immortality in the stars.

ARETHUSA

Arethusa too was a nymph who loved hunting (*Metamorphoses* 5.487–641). She took delight in roaming the forests of Elis in the Peloponnese and had no desire for the pleasures of love. One hot day, exhausted, she came to the river Alpheios, cool and clear and quiet, and it was so tempting that she stripped off her clothes and hung them on a willow, then plunged naked into the waters. As she swam, she suddenly sensed the river-god near her, so she leapt back out on to the bank in fear. She fled from his embrace, naked, for her clothes were on the opposite bank, and the god chased eagerly after her. They ran over plains and mountains, over rocks and crags, until Arethusa felt that she could run no further and called to Artemis for help. The goddess heard, and hid the nymph in a cloud of thick mist, but still the river-god persisted in his pursuit, circling the mist and watching it closely, for he knew that his quarry was inside.

Then suddenly she was turned into a stream flowing down the hillside. She might have escaped, but Alpheios recognized the waters as the nymph he desired, so he assumed his watery form and mingled his current with hers. Now Artemis helped Arethusa again: she split open the earth, so that the nymph could travel across the sea to Sicily. There, on the island of Ortygia at the entrance to the bay of Syracuse, she became the sacred spring called Arethusa.

But Alpheios did not give up his love. It was said in ancient times that the river flowed beneath the sea all the way to Ortygia, and there mingled his waters with those of the spring. The geographer Strabo (6.2.4) expresses a natural disbelief in the possibility of this phenomenon occurring. Nevertheless he reports the claim that a cup, thrown into the Alpheios in the Peloponnese, reappeared in the spring of Arethusa on Ortygia, and also that the waters there in Sicily were discoloured as a result of the sacrifices of oxen at Olympia, past which the Alpheios flows.

DAPHNE

Daphne too was a nymph devoted to chastity, and she too suffered a transformation aimed at protecting her virtue (Plate 2), though a more solid one than that of Arethusa (*Metamorphoses* 1.452–567).

The god Apollo was an unerring archer whose special weapon was the bow, and he once very unwisely belittled Eros's prowess at archery. The Love-god took his revenge by inflicting on Apollo the pains of an unrequited passion: he flew to the summit of Mount Parnassos and from there shot forth two of his powerful arrows. The first, sharp and golden, the kind that kindles love, pierced Apollo to the very marrow of his bones and he fell violently in love with the nymph Daphne, daughter of the river-god Peneios. The second arrow, blunt and tipped with lead, the kind that repels love, pierced Daphne herself. She now cared nothing for men, nothing for marriage, even though she had many suitors because of her beauty. All she wanted was to remain a virgin for the rest of her days.

So when Apollo pursued her, she ran from him, swifter than the wind's breath. The god, inspired by love, ran faster still, and was just about to catch hold of her when they drew near the banks of her father's river. Daphne, in desperation, prayed to her father for help, and the river-god acted at once (1.548–67):

Her prayer was scarcely ended when her limbs grew numb and heavy, her soft breasts were covered in delicate bark, her hair became leaves, her arms branches, and her swift feet were rooted into the ground, while her head became a tree-top. Nothing of her was left, except her grace, her shining.

Apollo loved her, even as a tree. He put his hand where he had hoped and felt her heart still beating under the new bark. Embracing the branches as though they were still limbs he kissed the wood, but even as wood she shrank from his kisses. Then the god said: 'Since you can never be my bride, my tree at least you shall be. The laurel will henceforth adorn my hair, my lyre, my quiver . . . and just as my head is always young and my hair never shorn, so may you also wear for ever the crowning glory of leaves that never fade or fall.' The laurel bowed her new-made branches and seemed to nod her leafy head in consent.

A laurel crown became the prize for the victor at the Pythian Games in honour of Apollo, and has been a symbol of victory ever since.

HERMAPHRODITOS

Not all nymphs were devoted to chastity and fled from male pursuit: sometimes they took the sexual initiative. Salmakis was one such (*Metamorphoses* 4.285–388).

Hermaphroditos was the son of Hermes and Aphrodite, and named after both of them. He was brought up by nymphs in the caves of Mount Ida, but as soon as he was fifteen he set out to see the world, visiting many remote places for the sheer joy of travelling. He went even as far as Lycia, and then on to Caria – and here one fateful day he came to a pool, crystal-clear, and ringed with fresh grass. This was the home of the water-nymph Salmakis. She liked to spend her time, not in hunting with fleet-footed Artemis and her companions, but in bathing her body in the lovely pool, and combing out her long hair, and lying on the soft grass.

She was gathering flowers when Hermaphroditos approached, and as soon as she saw the beautiful boy she knew she had to have him. She suggested that they make love there and then, but he, knowing nothing yet of sex, simply blushed in bewilderment. When she slid her arms around his neck and tried to kiss him, he brusquely repulsed her.

She pretended to go away, but hid behind a bush and watched as he stripped to swim in her pool. As soon as she saw him in the water, she flung aside her garments and plunged in after him, then clung to him passionately, twining herself around him like ivy around tree trunks. He resisted her, struggling violently against her embraces, but all to no avail, for just as she prayed to the gods that they might be united for ever, the two bodies melted into one flesh. It was now neither male nor female, but a single body with female breasts and proportions, and both male and female genitals.

When Hermaphroditos felt the sudden weakness in his limbs

and saw that he was now but half a man, he too uttered a prayer (in a more feminine voice than before). He asked his divine parents to ensure that any other man who bathed in the pool should become similarly weak and effeminate – and this prayer too was granted.

The geographer Strabo reports (14.2.16) that even in his time the pool was said to have this same power.

IPHIS

Another myth that told of a sex change was that of Iphis, born to humble parents, Ligdos and Telethousa, near Knossos in Crete (*Metamorphoses* 9.666–797). Ligdos had the means to support only one child and he wanted a son, so when Telethousa was about to give birth for the first time, he warned her that if the baby was a girl, it could not be allowed to live. Both of them wept at the thought, but Ligdos was adamant that this was how it must be

In due course a girl was born, but Telethousa, inspired by the goddess Isis in a dream, pretended that she was a boy. No one doubted her word, so the baby was named Iphis, a name common to both boys and girls, and for thirteen years the fond mother kept her secret and brought up her daughter as a son.

At the end of that time, Ligdos betrothed his supposed son to Ianthe, the most beautiful girl in the area, and the two of them fell in love. Ianthe, who of course knew nothing of Telethousa's deception, longed for their marriage with unalloyed pleasure, but poor Iphis was torn apart with what she felt to be her unnatural love for a member of her own sex. Telethousa too was in a frenzy of anxiety, and kept finding pretexts to postpone the wedding ceremony. At last she had used up all the excuses she could find and it could be put off no longer. In desperation she appealed to Isis for help once again.

The goddess, taking pity on her, turned her daughter into a boy, and the now joyful Iphis married his own Ianthe.

VERTUMNUS AND POMONA

A different Iphis was the subject of a story told by Vertumnus, the Roman god of orchards and the changing seasons, in the hope of winning the woman he adored (*Metamorphoses* 14.623–771).

Pomona was a wood-nymph who loved the countryside. Best of all she loved fruit trees, and she spent all her days happily tending her fertile orchards, with no desire for a mate. Of her many suitors, Vertumnus loved her the most, but he was no luckier than the rest. He could change his shape at will, and by disguising himself as a harvester, an ox-herd, a fisherman and suchlike, found many ways of approaching his love and gazing at her beauty. Not once did he catch her fancy.

Finally he changed himself into an old woman. Leaning on a stick, he entered Pomona's gardens and admired her beautiful fruit. Then he pleaded his own cause by praising the splendid qualities of Vertumnus and the ardour of his love. To soften Pomona's heart, he told the story of Anaxarete and Iphis.

Anaxarete was a Cypriot princess who was loved by Iphis, a man of humble birth. He worshipped her from afar, sending messages to her through her servants and hanging garlands wet with tears on her doorposts, but the object of his love was a cruel and arrogant girl, and she responded to all his overtures by mocking him callously. At last Iphis could bear no more, and he hanged himself from the lintel of her door. On the day of his funeral procession, Anaxarete climbed to the top of the house to look down on the street from her windows. As soon as she saw Iphis, dead of love for her and lying on his bier, the life left her body and she was turned to stone, to match the hardness of her heart.

Vertumnus finished his story, then changed back into his own shape. So handsome was he that Pomona, entranced by his beauty, at last loved him with a passion to match his own.

PICUS AND CANENS

Picus too was a Roman divinity: as well as being the son of Saturn and an early king of Latium, he was in his origins a god of the wild countryside. He took the form of a woodpecker, the sacred bird of Mars, and as such was thought to have prophetic powers.

When Picus was approaching twenty, he was so handsome and brave that he had attracted all the wood-nymphs and water-nymphs from the countryside around, but he himself loved one nymph only: Canens ('Singing'), daughter of the god Janus (*Metamorphoses* 14.310–434). Canens was very lovely, but her voice was lovelier still, so beautiful that her singing could move rocks and trees, soothe wild beasts, and stay the rivers in their courses. She too had many suitors, but of them all she chose Picus and became his bride.

One day Picus left her singing in their house and went off with his friends to hunt wild boar in the woods. Mounted on his spirited horse and wearing a fine purple cloak, fastened with a brooch of gold, he made a splendid sight. Certainly the enchantress Circe thought so when she saw him passing by. The herbs she had been gathering fell from her hands, as she was struck through with a fierce desire for him. As soon as she could collect her thoughts, she created a phantom boar that ran in front of the young king and led him far into the forest until he was quite lost. There she appeared before him and begged time and again for his love, but all in vain, for he refused to be untrue to his beloved Canens. The rejected sorceress turned him into a woodpecker: his feathers had a purple hue, the colour of his cloak, and his brooch became part of his plumage, encircling his neck with a ring of gold. His hunting companions searched for him everywhere, but found only Circe – who turned them all into wild beasts of many kinds.

Canens watched and waited in vain for her dear husband, then went anxiously in search of him. For six days and six nights she roamed the countryside without food or sleep, and at last, worn out with grief and wandering, she lay down by the river Tiber. Here she stayed, weeping and singing her sorrow, until at last her body was dissolved by sadness and she vanished into thin air.

PHILEMON AND BAUCIS

Philemon and Baucis (*Metamorphoses* 8.618–724) were aged Phrygian peasants who, like Picus and Canens, loved each other devotedly, but unlike the young couple they were lucky enough to have many happy years together, living in a humble cottage on the side of a mountain. They had always been poor, and their home was roofed with reeds and thatch and was scantily furnished, but here they had lived contentedly ever since they were married.

There came a time when Zeus and Hermes, disguised as mortals, were travelling through Phrygia seeking for a place to rest. They were turned away from a thousand homes, but at last they came to the cottage of Philemon and Baucis, who welcomed them warmly and prepared a meal for them of good but simple fare. As the dinner went on, the old couple noticed with amazement, mingled with fear, that the wine jug kept refilling itself of its own accord. At the sight of this miracle they realized that they had been entertaining gods unaware, and they made ready to kill their one and only goose in honour of their divine visitors.

But age had made them slow and the goose was nimble. It eluded them, and before they could catch it, the gods told them to let it live, then to follow them up the mountainside. The old people struggled upwards, leaning on their sticks, and when they were very nearly at the top, they turned and looked down on the countryside below. They saw a land now drowned in water, sent by the gods to punish all the inhospitable mortals, and with only their own cottage still above the surface. As they gazed in astonishment, the little building was turned into a gleaming temple, with columns and floor of marble and roof of gold. The gods offered to grant the old couple any boon they chose, and they asked that they might serve in the temple as priest and priestess for the rest of their lives, and that when the time came for death, they might die at the very same instant and so not suffer the grief of parting.

And thus it came about. They looked after the temple for as long as they lived, and one day, when they were very old, in the moment of their dying they were turned into trees, an oak and a linden, growing side by side.

Dryope

Not all transformations into trees were as peaceful and pleasant as this. Dryope was the daughter of Eurytos, king of Oichalia (*Metamorphoses* 9.327–93), and of all the women in Oichalia she was the loveliest, so beautiful that Apollo desired her. He raped her and left her pregnant, but she kept this a secret and soon afterwards married the mortal Andraimon. In due course she gave birth to Apollo's son, Amphissos.

One day, when Amphissos was not yet a year old, Dryope was wandering near a lake with her baby in her arms when she saw a lotus tree covered with bright red blossoms. She picked some of the flowers for the infant to play with, but unfortunately this tree was no normal tree: it had once been a nymph, Lotis, whose transformation had saved her from rape as she was fleeing from the rampant Priapos. Now the tree's branches trembled and its plucked blossoms began to bleed. Dryope was terrified and tried to run away, but found that her own feet were rooted to the ground and that she too was slowly becoming a lotus tree. She had just time to make her farewells, and to beg her husband to look after their little son, before the creeping bark spread and shrouded her.

MYRRHA

Myrrha too was turned into a tree, though in her case it was in answer to her own prayers (*Metamorphoses* 10.298–514). Her father was Kinyras, the king of Cyprus, and Myrrha had the misfortune to fall in love with him. She had a throng of eligible suitors who came from far and wide to court her, but she could love none of them and desired only her father. Animals mated freely with each other regardless of ties of blood, she reasoned to herself, so why not humans? And yet she was ashamed of her incestuous love, knowing it to be wrong, and time and again she prayed in vain that it be taken from her.

At last one night came when she was in such despair, seeing no end to her torment, that she decided to hang herself. Her faithful nurse caught her in the act of doing so. The old woman would not rest until she had wrung the cause of her misery from her; then, wishing only to ease her mistress's pain, she brought father and daughter together. She persuaded Kinyras to sleep with Myrrha by telling him that a beautiful young girl was in love with him and longed to share his bed – so he made love to her, not knowing in the darkness that this was his own daughter. For many nights she came to him in the dark, but at last he wanted to see the face of the girl he had slept with so often. He brought in a lamp, and when he saw his bedmate he was filled with anger too great for words. He took his sword to her, but she escaped from him and fled far away from the palace.

Myrrha was pregnant, and for nine months she wandered

through the world in sorrow. At last, sick of life and yet afraid of death, she prayed to the gods to save her from both life and death by changing her into something other than she was. Even as she spoke they transformed her into a myrrh tree, and the drops of myrrh that fell from her trunk were her tears as she wept for her sad fate. The goddess of childbirth brought forth her baby from the tree-trunk, and the nymphs laid him on the soft grass and bathed him in his mother's tears. He was named Adonis, and he too would live to suffer from a tragic love affair – but that will be the subject of another section (p. 542).

Byblis and Kaunos

Another incestuous love with a tragic outcome was that of Byblis for her twin brother Kaunos (*Metamorphoses* 9.450–665). They were the children of Miletos, a son of Apollo and king of the city that bears his name, and of Kyanea, a nymph who was a daughter of the river-god Maeander. Brother and sister grew up happily together, and for a long time Byblis believed that the love she felt for Kaunos was simply family affection. Gradually she realized that it was more than this when each night brought her ecstatic dreams of their shared passion.

Eventually she wrote a letter telling Kaunos of her desire for him, but her confession won her only a fierce rejection. Still she persisted, approaching him face to face to try and seduce him and laying herself open to constant rebuffs. Eventually Kaunos felt himself forced to leave Miletos for ever and went to southern Caria, where he founded the city named after him.

Grief and longing drove Byblis quite out of her mind. She too left her country and roamed over many lands, seeking her brother unavailingly. At last, too tired to go further, she lay on the ground despairing, and wept so unceasingly that she was consumed by her own tears, and was changed into a spring of water that would never run dry.

PYGMALION AND GALATEA

Pygmalion too suffered a kind of incestuous love, though the outcome here was a happy one (*Metamorphoses* 10.243–97). He was a sculptor, living on Cyprus, and a confirmed bachelor disenchanted with the whole female sex – so much so that he had given up all hope of finding a living woman worthy of his love. Meanwhile, with marvellous artistry, he carved an ivory statue lovelier than any woman ever born. So beautiful was this perfect figure that he fell passionately in love with his own creation. Often he would kiss her and imagine that she kissed him back. He embraced her, and talked to her, and brought her the kinds of little presents that girls enjoy: bright shells and stones, flowers, beads and amber. He dressed her in women's robes and adorned her with jewellery, then stripped them off her and laid her on his couch, on pillows of the softest feathers, calling her his bedfellow.

The time came for the festival of Aphrodite to be held, and after he had made his offering to the goddess, he prayed that he might find a wife just like his ivory maiden. But Aphrodite knew what wish was really in his heart, and when he returned home and kissed his statue, she came to life in his arms. Opening her eyes for the first time, she saw the light of day and her lover together. She became his bride and bore him a daughter, Paphos, after whom the city of Paphos, the chief centre of Aphrodite's worship on Cyprus, was named.

Ovid gives no name to Pygmalion's ivory maiden, and she was called Galatea only in post-classical times.

POLYPHEMOS, AKIS AND GALATEA

Another Galatea was a sea-nymph for whom the Cyclops Poly-phemos had an unrequited passion (*Metamorphoses* 13.738–897). We are familiar with the brutal savagery of the Cyclops from his encounter with Odysseus in Homer's *Odyssey* (p. 396), and this unexpected courtship shows a softer side to the old monster.

Polyphemos was so on fire with love for Galatea that he neglected his flocks and even forgot his bloodthirsty love of killing. Instead he spent his time on his appearance, combing his bristling hair with a rake, trimming his shaggy beard with a scythe, and inspecting his unprepossessing looks reflected in the water. It was all pointless, for Galatea loathed the Cyclops quite as much as she loved the handsome Akis, the young son of Faunus and the river-nymph Symaithis.

As she lay in her lover's arms, she listened to the song the giant sang to tempt her to him, sitting on a mountainside and accompanying himself on a set of pan-pipes made from a hun-dred reeds. He had caves, he told her, cool in summer and warm in winter. He offered her all the wealth of nature – apples, strawberries, grapes, cherries, plums, chestnuts – as well as the richness of his vast flocks. Pets he could give her too, and not just the usual ones like deer or hares or doves, but a pair of bear cubs that he had been keeping just for her. And his looks need be no deterrent, for he was *big*, and surely a body all covered in a fleece of bristling hair was becoming in a man. True, he had only one eye, but that one eye was as huge as a shield.

So he sang, but to his frustration his efforts brought no response. Furious now as a bull that has lost its cow, Poly-phemos strode through the island – and there he came upon Galatea lying in Akis's arms, oblivious to everything but love.

Overcome by rage, he hove up a huge chunk of the mountainside and flung it at them. Galatea escaped to the sea, but her poor lover was completely crushed beneath the rock. She did for him the only thing she could, and changed him into a river that would ever afterwards bear his name.

SKYLLA AND GLAUKOS

Skylla too is a fearsome Homeric monster, lying in her cave half-way up a cliff and fishing for sailors with her six frightful heads (p. 405). Yet she was not always like this: she was once a beautiful girl (*Metamorphoses* 13.730–14.74). She rejected her many suitors, preferring to spend her time with the sea-nymphs, and she even spurned the sea-god Glaukos (p. 144) when he tried to win her love. Nevertheless he would not give up hope, and he went to the enchantress Circe to ask for a love-potion. Unfortunately Circe fell in love with Glaukos and wanted him for herself, but he refused all her pleas, telling her that he could think of no one but Skylla while she lived.

The jealous enchantress was furious that a mere girl was preferred to herself, and since she could not harm the divine Glaukos, and would not have wished to do so, she poisoned the pool in which Skylla liked to bathe, pouring in magical drugs and uttering mysterious spells. When next Skylla slipped into the water, six ferocious dogs grew in place of her lower limbs and became the terrifying heads which thereafter preyed on her victims. In later times she was changed into a rock, and as such is still a terror to sailors.

MIDAS

To end on a light-hearted note, we have the story of Midas, king of Phrygia (*Metamorphoses* 11.85–193). When the god Dionysos was passing through Phrygia with his retinue of maenads and satyrs, some peasants captured a fat old man,

well fuddled with wine, and took him to their king. Midas
at once recognized him as Silenos, the oldest and wisest of
Dionysos' revelling companions. Midas honoured the old
man, entertaining him richly for ten days, and on the eleventh
day he took him back to his god. Dionysos in gratitude granted
Midas one wish, and Midas – who was not the most far-
seeing of mortals – asked that all he touched might turn into
gold.

Silenos is brought before an ass-eared King Midas.

His wish was granted, and he went away rejoicing, finding
that everything he touched – twigs, stones, earth, ears of corn,
apples – did indeed become gold. But very soon he regretted his
choice. Even his food and drink changed into inedible metal
and he could do nothing to ease his hunger and thirst. At last
he begged Dionysos to take away his ill-chosen gift, and the
god told him to wash in the river Paktolos, near Sardis. Midas

did so, and washed off his wondrous 'golden touch' into the river, which has ever afterwards had golden sand.

After this Midas had no desire for riches and lived a rural life, worshipping Pan, the god of the wild countryside, but he was still no wiser than before. One day Apollo and Pan held a musical contest, with the mountain-god Tmolos as judge. Tmolos pronounced Apollo the winner, and everyone who had been listening, the nymphs and even Pan himself, agreed – all except Midas, who foolishly intervened, saying that the mountain-god's decision was unjust. The furious Apollo transformed the ears that had obviously misheard so grievously into asses' ears, long, twitching, and covered with grey and bristling hair.

Midas was mortified. He tried to hide these shameful ears under a handsome turban, but one person in the world was bound to find out his humiliating secret: his barber saw the ears when he cut the king's hair. The barber longed to pass on this fascinating piece of news, but dared not, for after all this was the king; yet neither could he stay absolutely silent. So he dug a hole deep in the ground and whispered into it what he had seen. He filled up the hole and went quietly away. But a thick bed of reeds grew there and gave away the buried secret, for every time a breeze rustled them they whispered the truth to the whole world, 'King Midas has ass's ears; King Midas has ass's ears.'

MYTHS OF LOVE AND DEATH

The earlier chapters of this book have contained countless myths telling of war, violence, monster slayings, revenge, and suchlike, so let us end in unashamedly romantic fashion with some inspirational stories of love – and of what so often accompanies love in such myths: death. Though in our final story, it is (appropriately) Death who is defeated, his dominion broken, while love lives on.

Hero and Leander

Hero and Leander were lovers who lived on opposite sides of the narrow Hellespont (Dardanelles). Hero was a priestess of Aphrodite at Sestos, and each night she would light a lamp in the window of the tower in which she lived, to guide Leander as he swam across to her from Abydos. He stayed with her until daybreak and then swam home again. In this way they met and made love through many summer nights.

Winter came, with its stormy weather, and still Hero lit the lamp, and still Leander braved the treacherous seas. Then one night, during a violent storm, Hero failed to notice that the lamp had been blown out by the wind. Without his signal light, Leander lost his way among the dark and heaving waves and was drowned. The next morning Hero looked down and saw his body washed up on the shore. In her grief she flung herself from the tower, falling to her death beside her lover.

The story of this tragic love affair probably originated in an Alexandrian poem, but in extant literature we come across it first in Virgil (*Georgics* 3.258–63) and Ovid (*Heroides* 18 and 19). Its fullest treatment is in the poem *Hero and Leander* by

Musaeus, probably of the late fifth or early sixth century AD. It has inspired many other poets since. Shakespeare gives the story a humorous twist in his *As You Like It*, where Rosalind uses it to demonstrate that no one ever dies for love (IV. i. 88–95):

Leander, he would have liv'd many a fair year though Hero had turn'd nun, if it had not been for a hot midsummer night; for (good youth) he went but forth to wash him in the Hellespont, and being taken with the cramp, was drown'd; and the foolish chroniclers of that age found it was 'Hero of Sestos'. But these are all lies. Men have died from time to time, and worms have eaten them, but not for love.

Lord Byron was moved to try and repeat Leander's achievement, and in May 1810 (not, we note, at the most testing time of year) he himself swam from Sestos to Abydos and reported the result (*Written after Swimming from Sestos to Abydos*):

> If, in the month of dark December,
>   Leander, who was nightly wont
> (What maid will not the tale remember?)
>   To cross thy stream, broad Hellespont!
> If, when the wintry tempest roar'd,
>   He sped to Hero, nothing loth,
> And thus of old thy current pour'd
>   Fair Venus! how I pity both!
>
> For *me*, degenerate modern wretch,
>   Though in the genial month of May,
> My dripping limbs I faintly stretch,
>   And think I've done a feat today.
>   . . .
> 'Twere hard to say who fared the best:
>   Sad mortals! thus the Gods still plague you!
> He lost his labour, I my jest;
>   For he was drowned, and I've the ague.

We turn to A. E. Housman to restore us to romantic mood. He characteristically saw Hero and Leander's love as symbolizing the transient nature of happiness ('Tarry, delight, so seldom met', from *More Poems*):

> By Sestos town, in Hero's tower,
> On Hero's heart Leander lies;
> The signal torch has burned its hour
> And sputters as it dies.
>
> Beneath him, in the nighted firth,
> Between two continents complain
> The seas he swam from earth to earth
> And he must swim again.

PYRAMUS AND THISBE

Pyramus and Thisbe lived next door to one another in Babylon. They became friends, and when they grew up they fell in love. Their parents refused to let them marry or even to meet, but luckily they found a chink in the wall between the two adjoining houses, and through this they would spend hours whispering their love. When they had to say goodnight, they each kissed the wall between them since they could not kiss each other.

Longing to be truly together, they arranged to steal away at dead of night and meet in the countryside at a local landmark, the tomb of Ninus, in the shade of a mulberry tree hung thick with snowy fruits. When the time came, Thisbe, with her face veiled, arrived first and sat down beneath the appointed tree, but she was startled away by a lioness who approached, fresh from her kill, to drink at a nearby spring. The frightened girl ran away into a cave that was close by, but as she ran she dropped her veil. When the lioness was returning to the woods, she found the garment and tore it to pieces in her bloodied jaws.

A little later, Pyramus arrived. He saw the footprints of the lioness and, worse still, the torn veil all stained with fresh blood. Recognizing the garment, and full of remorse for causing, as he thought, Thisbe's death, he killed himself with his sword in the shade of the tree where they had planned to meet. Now Thisbe returned and despairingly found her beloved's body. She joined him in death, stabbing herself with the same sword still warm from his own mortal wound. When their parents found their corpses, they were moved too late by the young couple's love for one another and buried their ashes in a single urn. The snowy fruit of the mulberry tree was coloured by all the spilt blood, and has ever since been a dark red.

The myth of these star-crossed lovers was immortalized by Ovid (*Metamorphoses* 4.55–166) and was inevitably inspirational to later poets, such as Chaucer, who tells the story in *The Legende of Goode Women*, and – perhaps most famously – Shakespeare. He turns it into the 'most Lamentable Comedy and most Cruel Death of Pyramus and Thisbe' played by Bottom the weaver and his friends in *A Midsummer Night's Dream* (where the lovers meet at 'Ninny's tomb'). Here is Thisbe discovering the dead Pyramus (V. i. 332):

> Asleep, my love?
>> What, dead, my dove?
> O Pyramus, arise!
>> Speak, speak! Quite dumb?
>> Dead, dead! A tomb
> Must cover thy sweet eyes.
>> These lily lips,
>> This cherry nose,
> These yellow cowslip cheeks,
>> Are gone, are gone;
>> Lovers, make moan!
> His eyes were green as leeks.

O Sisters Three,

Come, come to me,

With hands as pale as milk;

Lay them in gore,

Since you have shore

With shears his thread of silk.

Tongue, not a word.

Come, trusty sword;

Come, blade, my breast imbrue:

[*Stabs herself.*

And farewell, friends;

Thus Thisby ends:

Adieu, adieu, adieu.

[*Dies.*

PROKRIS AND KEPHALOS

Pyramus. Not Shafalus to Procrus was so true.
Thisbe. As Shafalus to Procrus, I to you.

This is how Bottom and Flute garble the names of Kephalos and Prokris in *A Midsummer Night's Dream*. Once again it is Ovid who gives us the most familiar version of the couple's ultimately tragic love (*Metamorphoses* 7.672–862).

Kephalos was the grandson of the Thessalian king Aiolos and was happily married to Prokris, a daughter of Erechtheus, the king of Athens. It was in the second month of his marriage that Eos, goddess of Dawn, fell in love with Kephalos. She was always of an amorous disposition, ready to seize any particularly handsome young man she noticed, and now she carried Kephalos off for her own delight, though much against his will. She soon tired of him, for she grew so annoyed by all his talk of his young bride, and the ties of matrimony, and his marriage vows, that she wanted only to be rid of him, so she sent him home again. Unfortunately she was vengeful enough to inspire Kephalos with the idea of disguising himself and testing Prokris's fidelity, and she even helped him by altering his appearance.

Kephalos arrived back in Athens so thoroughly disguised that no one could recognize him. He made his way to his own home, and there he made advances to Prokris, offering countless gifts to win her over to him. For a long time she stayed resolutely faithful, firmly rejecting all his lures, but when he finally promised her a vast fortune in return for a night in her bed, she hesitated. At this Kephalos revealed his true identity and accused her of infidelity.

Overwhelmed by shame, and hating all men because of her husband's deceitful trick, Prokris ran away and lived in the mountains. There she devoted herself to hunting as a follower of the virgin goddess Artemis. Yet now that he had lost her, Kephalos loved her more than ever, so he found her and begged her to forgive him, confessing (quite rightly) that he had been totally in the wrong. Eventually she accepted his apology. Reunited once more, they returned home and spent some years together in great happiness.

Prokris, however, had not come empty-handed from the mountains: she brought home two gifts given her by Artemis, a hound called Lailaps that could not fail to catch its prey, and a javelin that could not miss its mark. She gave both gifts to Kephalos. He used the hound to get rid of the Teumessian Vixen, a fierce fox, fated never to be caught, that was preying cruelly on the people of Thebes (p. 186). So the infallible hound served a good purpose. But the unerring javelin eventually brought only tragedy in its wake.

Every morning Kephalos went hunting, always quite alone, since his javelin was all that he needed to kill as many animals as he chose. When he had hunted enough and was hot and tired, he would lie in the shade and call on a cool breeze, *Aura*, to come and soothe him. One day some passer-by overheard him and misunderstood, thinking that Aura must be a nymph with whom he was in love. At once this busybody hurried to Prokris to report his infidelity.

In her unhappiness, and hoping still that it was all a mistake, she followed her husband the next morning when he went off to hunt. He made his kill, then as usual lay down and called on *Aura* to come and soothe him. Prokris, overhearing, moaned in sorrow, and Kephalos, thinking that some wild creature was hiding in the bushes, threw his javelin towards the sound. Prokris cried out in pain as it found its mark, and he recognized the voice of his dear wife, and ran to her. She died in his arms.

Apollodorus (3.15.1) interestingly draws a quite different picture of Prokris in which she is an utterly faithless wife, and this probably reflects a tradition much earlier than Ovid's adaptation. He says that she went to bed with a certain Pteleon when he bribed her with a golden crown. Kephalos discovered her infidelity, so she ran away to King Minos of Crete, who tried to seduce her. His wife Pasiphae, however, was angry because of his general promiscuity, and had drugged him in such a way that whenever he had intercourse with a woman, he ejaculated snakes and scorpions, and she died.

Prokris wanted to possess the inescapable hound and the unerring javelin that Minos had promised her in return for her favours (in this version, they had once been given to Europa by Zeus and then passed down to Minos), so she in her turn drugged him to prevent any harm coming to her, then went to bed with him. She took her payment, the hound and javelin, and went home, where she and Kephalos were reconciled. The couple went hunting together and Prokris was killed, though her death here was the result of a simple hunting accident. It is hardly surprising that it was Ovid's romantic story, rather than this, which captured the imagination of later artists and became the standard version of the myth.

APHRODITE AND ADONIS

We have seen how Myrrha made love with her own father, Kinyras, and gave birth to the baby Adonis (p. 528), but that is far from being the end of the story. Once again Apollodorus' version is rather different from that of Ovid. According to Apollodorus (3.14.4) the baby was so beautiful that Aphrodite wanted him for herself, so she secretly hid him in a chest and entrusted him to Persephone, queen of the Underworld, to keep for her. But Persephone too loved him and she refused to give him back. The two goddesses took their dispute to Zeus, who decreed that Adonis should spend a third of the year with each of them and have the remaining third for himself. He always chose to live his own third of the year with Aphrodite, and the months that he spent in her arms became the living, burgeoning time of spring and summer. His disappearance from the earth marked the harvesting of the crops, and his time in the arms of Persephone was the dead, winter period when seed lay dormant below the earth.

In Ovid's version of the story (*Metamorphoses* 10.519–739), Aphrodite fell in love with Adonis only when he grew to be a beautiful young man. She became his constant companion, and because like most young men he was a passionate huntsman, she too learnt to enjoy hunting, roaming woods and mountains with her skirts kilted up to her knees, just like Artemis, and shouting encouragement to the hounds. She was careful to pursue only creatures safe to hunt, like hares or deer, and she warned Adonis against the dangerous beasts – wild boars and wolves and lions and bears – who were always ready to turn and attack their hunters.

Unfortunately his natural courage made him pay too little

heed to her advice. One day he roused a wild boar from its lair and wounded it in the side with his spear. (It was sometimes said that the boar was Aphrodite's husband Hephaistos or her lover Ares in disguise, jealous because of her affair with Adonis.) The boar easily dislodged the weapon, then rushed after Adonis as he was making for safety and slashed him deep in the groin with its tusk. Aphrodite heard from afar the groans of the dying boy and hurried to him, but too late. She did what little she could: she decreed that his death would in the future be lamented every year, and she made the dark red anemone spring from his blood as an everlasting token of her grief. It was elsewhere said that Adonis's death was also the origin of the red rose, for as Aphrodite rushed to her dying love she pricked her foot on a white rose. Stained with her blood, it was ever afterwards red, and thus it naturally became a symbol of passionate love.

Shakespeare's *Venus and Adonis*, probably his first published work (1593), is based on Ovid's account of Adonis's death, with once again the anemone springing up from his blood. Venus plucks the flower and addresses it as she puts it in her bosom:

> 'Here was thy father's bed, here in my breast;
> Thou art the next of blood, and 'tis thy right.
> Lo, in this hollow cradle take thy rest;
> My throbbing heart shall rock thee day and night;
> There shall not be one minute in an hour
> Wherein I will not kiss my sweet love's flow'r.'

PARIS AND OINONE

The tale of Paris's love affair with the beautiful Helen, she of 'the face that launched a thousand ships' and brought all Troy to destruction, is told and retold throughout ancient literature.

Yet Paris had another, earlier love: the nymph Oinone, daughter of the river-god Kebren, and this story is seldom mentioned. Apollodorus, as so often, is helpful in sketching out the bare details (3.12.6).

Paris married Oinone while he was still a herdsman on Mount Ida and lived with her happily. Then one fateful day he was called by Zeus to judge the beauty contest between the three goddesses, Hera, Athene and Aphrodite. When he chose Aphrodite as the loveliest and awarded her the prize of the golden apple, he won for himself the promised love of the most beautiful woman in the world, Helen of Sparta (p. 309). Oinone, however, was skilled in the art of prophecy, and she knew just what disasters would follow if Paris sailed to Greece to fetch Helen. She warned her husband as eloquently as she knew how, but he ignored all her good advice and made ready to leave. Finding that she could not influence him, and knowing what lay in store, she told him to come to her if he were ever wounded, because she alone could heal him.

Paris travelled to Greece and carried Helen off to Troy, and the Greeks sailed out in force to fetch her back: the Trojan War had begun, and Paris thought no more of Oinone. But in the tenth year of the war, soon after he had killed the mighty Achilles, he himself was mortally wounded by an arrow from Philoktetes' great bow. Then he remembered Oinone's words and asked to be carried to Mount Ida. She was still angry at his desertion of her and refused to help him, so he was carried back to Troy. Too late she changed her mind, remorsefully hurrying to Troy with her healing drugs, but she found Paris dead. She hanged herself from grief.

Oinone's rejection of the wounded Paris is narrated in great detail by Quintus of Smyrna in his late epic *Sequel to Homer* (10.262–489). 'I wish I had in me a lion's heart and strength, to devour your flesh and then to lap your blood, for all the pain your folly has brought on me,' Oinone cries (315–27). 'Where is Aphrodite now? ... Just leave my house and go to your Helen, for *her* to heal you of your grievous pain.'

Paris dies on Mount Ida, and all the shepherds mourn, and all the nymphs too, remembering him as a little boy growing up on the mountain, and even the glens of Ida mourn. So, of course, does Oinone when she learns of Paris's death. She rushes down the slopes of Ida, 'just as a mountain heifer, stung in her heart with passion, speeds with flying feet to meet her mate' (441–3), and she flings herself on to Paris's funeral pyre, joining him in death.

Many later poets took up the story, the best remembered work probably being Tennyson's *Oenone* (the Latinized version of Oinone's name). Here is Oinone waiting for Paris, not yet knowing that he has been chosen to award the golden apple to the loveliest of the three goddesses. He brings the apple to show Oinone just before the fatal contest, on the day that will change everything for her for ever:

> 'O mother Ida, many fountain'd Ida,
> Dear mother Ida, harken ere I die.
> I waited underneath the dawning hills,
> Aloft the mountain lawn was dewy-dark,
> And dewy-dark aloft the mountain pine:
> Beautiful Paris, evil-hearted Paris,
> Leading a jet-black goat white-horn'd, white-hooved,
> Came up from reedy Simois all alone.
>
> 'O mother Ida, harken ere I die.
> Far-off the torrent call'd me from the cleft:
> Far up the solitary morning smote
> The streaks of virgin snow. With down-dropt eyes
> I sat alone: white-breasted like a star
> Fronting the dawn he moved; a leopard skin

Droop'd from his shoulder, but his sunny hair
Cluster'd about his temples like a God's:
And his cheek brighten'd as the foam-bow brightens
When the wind blows the foam, and all my heart
Went forth to embrace him coming ere he came.

'Dear mother Ida, harken ere I die.
He smiled, and opening out his milk-white palm
Disclosed a fruit of pure Hesperian gold,
That smelt ambrosially . . .'

PSYCHE AND CUPID

Psyche ('Soul') was the mortal lover of Cupid (Eros), god of love (Plate 5). Her story was first and most famously told by Apuleius in the second century AD in *The Golden Ass* (4.28–6.26) and has all the characteristics of a fairy-tale. In later times it came to be seen as an allegory of the soul's difficult journey through life towards a mystic union with the divine after death.

Once upon a time there lived a king and queen who had three daughters, all of them very beautiful, but the youngest girl, Psyche, was quite breathtakingly lovely. The fame of her beauty spread until people came from far and wide just to gaze on her, and all were so overwhelmed by her loveliness that they paid her the divine honours which they should have been offering to Venus (Aphrodite). The goddess naturally grew very angry and wanted to avenge this insult. She told her son Cupid to visit Psyche and inflame her with a dishonourable passion for some completely worthless man, but Cupid disobeyed his mother, for when he saw the girl's great beauty he fell in love with her himself.

Psyche's two elder sisters had been married to foreign kings from distant cities, but she herself remained unmarried – nor indeed had she any suitors, for she was so amazingly beautiful that all men adored her from afar and never dared to approach her. At last her father went to Apollo's oracle at Miletos and asked where he could find a husband for this youngest daughter of his. The reply, influenced by Cupid, said that Psyche must prepare to marry an evil spirit, feared even by the gods, who would come to fetch her as she stood on a lonely mountain-top.

With great sorrow the king and queen obeyed the oracle's instructions. Psyche's bridal day arrived, and she was accompanied to a craggy hill-top and left there, alone and afraid. Yet her fears were needless, for Zephyros, the gentle West Wind, lifted her up and wafted her softly down into a flowery valley, and there she found in the middle of a nearby wood a fairy-tale palace, full of unbelievable treasures. Here she was waited upon by unseen hands, until night came and it was time for bed. In the darkness Cupid came to her and made her his wife, and she lay in delight with this unseen, unknown husband. He left her just before dawn. And so the days and nights passed for her: lonely days with only invisible servants for company, and love-filled nights with Cupid coming after dark and always vanishing before the morning light.

Psyche found that she was missing her family, so at last she persuaded Cupid to allow her sisters to visit her. He warned her urgently that they were likely to bring her great unhappiness, and that she must pay no attention if they tried to make her find out what he looked like. If she ever saw his face, he would leave her for ever. She promised that she would do just as he wanted, and on the sisters' first visit, after they had been carried down from the high crag by Zephyros, she kept her word. At the end of their visit, Zephyros carried them back up the mountain and they returned home.

Unfortunately both sisters had been struck with a violent jealousy because of Psyche's good fortune and they agreed to do all they could to ruin her. They visited her again, and then again, with the West Wind delivering them and carrying them away as before, and they wormed their way so far into Psyche's confidence that at last she confessed she had no idea what her husband looked like. They terrified her by saying that she must be married to a fearful monster, who would end up by devouring both her and the baby that she was now carrying. She had best kill him before she herself was killed.

So that night poor, credulous Psyche waited until Cupid was asleep after their love-making, then she lit a lamp and approached him, armed with a sharp carving knife. At once she recognized with awe the beautiful Love-god. She saw his bow and arrows lying at the foot of the bed, and in curiosity she drew one of the arrows out of its quiver. The sharp tip pricked her thumb enough to draw blood, and now she was even more in love with her husband than before, quite overcome with wonder and desire. Just then a drop of scalding oil, spurting from the lamp, fell on to Cupid's shoulder and he was startled awake. He leapt up in pain, and when he saw that his wife had broken her promise, he spread his wings and flew away from her, just as he had said he would.

Psyche, in despair, searched everywhere for him, but in vain. On her travels she came at different times to the cities where her sisters lived and sadly told them exactly what had happened. Each sister in turn, burning with desire to have for herself Cupid's love – and Cupid's palace – hurried to the crag from which Zephyros had always wafted them down. They each leapt confidently into the air, but this time no West Wind came for them, and each in turn was dashed to pieces on the rocks below. The birds and beasts feasted on their remains.

Psyche carried on wandering through country after country, searching for her lost Cupid. She prayed for help at the temples of Ceres (Demeter) and Juno (Hera), but neither goddess was willing to help her for fear of offending Venus, who by now had heard that her son had been Psyche's lover. At last Psyche plucked up the courage to come to the palace of Venus herself. The goddess, furious that her son had not only failed to punish Psyche but had even made her pregnant, treated her cruelly and gave her formidable tasks to perform.

The first task was to sort out a vast heap of mixed grains into their separate kinds by nightfall. Psyche had no idea where to begin, but a passing ant saw her plight and sympathetically scurried to round up every other ant in the district to help. They worked furiously and the job was soon done.

The next morning, Venus told Psyche to fetch a hank of golden wool from a flock of murderous sheep. Once again the poor girl felt quite hopeless, but this time a kindly green reed whispered advice to her as the breeze blew over it. It told her to wait until the sheep were asleep in the heat of the afternoon, then to gather up the loose wisps of wool clinging to the nearby briar bushes. Psyche did so and carried a whole lapful of the golden wool to Venus, but still the goddess was not satisfied.

The third task was harder still: Psyche had to fetch a jar full of ice-cold water from the river Styx, where it cascaded out from halfway up a steep precipice, near the summit of a high mountain. When she arrived there, she found the outlet guarded by fierce, ever-watchful dragons, and she knew she could never complete her task and escape them alive. At that moment Jupiter's eagle flew by. He owed a debt of gratitude to Cupid, so he snatched Psyche's jar and filled it for her, and she delightedly carried it back to Venus.

The furious goddess set her one final, fatal task: she must go down to the land of the dead and fetch a day's supply of Proserpina's store of beauty. Realizing that she was being sent to her death, Psyche climbed to the top of a high tower, intending to throw herself down and die there and then. But the tower spoke to her, explaining how she might carry out Venus's command and still live.

Psyche did exactly as the tower said. She entered the Underworld by way of Tainaron in the Peloponnese, carrying two coins and two pieces of barley bread soaked in honey water. She paid Charon one coin to be ferried across the river, and she threw one of her bread sops to Kerberos to gain entry to the dark palace of Hades, all the while avoiding the various snares that Venus had set along her journey. When she reached Proserpina (Persephone), who offered her a chair and a magnificent meal, she was careful to sit on the ground and to eat only a crust of common bread. The goddess gave her what she came for in a sealed box, then she returned to the land of the living, appeasing Kerberos with her second sop and paying Charon with her second coin.

She came thankfully back to the daylight, but disobeyed one last instruction that the tower had given her: that on no account must she open the box. She allowed her curiosity to get the better of her and lifted the lid, intending to use a little of the beauty within on herself, so as to win back Cupid's love. Out stole a fatal sleep and overpowered her, and she fell to the ground as if she were dead.

Cupid, however, had been desperately missing his lost love, and he now flew to her aid and brushed the cloud of sleep away from her. She sprang up to deliver the box to Venus, while Cupid went to plead his love with Jupiter (Zeus). The great god gave divine consent to his marriage with Psyche, and appeased Venus by making Psyche immortal so that the match was no disgrace. All the gods held a great wedding breakfast to celebrate the union, and in the fullness of time Psyche's baby was born, a daughter called Voluptas (Pleasure).

ORPHEUS AND EURYDICE

Orpheus, a son of one of the Muses, was the supreme singer and musician of Greek myth, so skilled that he entranced the whole of nature with his song, taming savage beasts and moving even rocks and trees. As Shakespeare would put it (*Two Gentlemen of Verona* III. ii. 78–81):

> For Orpheus' lute was strung with poets' sinews,
> Whose golden touch could soften steel and stones,
> Make tigers tame, and huge leviathans
> Forsake unsounded deeps to dance on sands.

The story of Orpheus descending to the Underworld to fetch his beloved wife Eurydice back from the dead is one of the best known of all myths, becoming an endless source of inspiration to post-classical artists of all kinds. The legend was an early one, for Euripides refers to it in his *Alkestis* of 438 BC, a play which also tells of a wife returning from the dead (see below); but it is only in the Roman poets that the story of Orpheus' descent is first told in detail. We find a full and moving version in Ovid (*Metamorphoses* 10.1–85, 11.1–66).

Soon after Orpheus married the nymph Eurydice, she died of a snake-bite, and he so mourned her loss that he was even willing to brave the journey down to Hades to try and regain her, hoping to rouse the sympathy of the shades and so win for her a reprieve from death. He passed through the entrance to the Underworld at Tainaron, then courageously made the long and lonely descent. He sang for Charon, the ferryman, and for the watchdog Kerberos, and both were so charmed by his music that they allowed him to enter. When he reached the abode of Hades and Persephone, he sang again, pleading for his wife who had been cut off before her prime, and with his song he entranced the entire world of the dead. All the shades listened

Hermes claims Eurydice, as she and Orpheus say farewell.

and wept. Tantalos forgot his hunger and thirst, and the wheel of Ixion stayed motionless. The vultures stopped tearing at Tityos's liver. The daughters of Danaos held their pitchers still, and Sisyphos sat idle on his great rock. Then, for the first time, the cheeks of the Furies were wet with tears. Most important

of all, Hades and Persephone could not bear to refuse Orpheus'
pleas and said that he might take his Eurydice back to earth.
Their only conditions were that he must lead the way on the
journey out, and that he must not look back at her until they
had both regained the light of the sun.

It may well be that in the early, lost version of the myth
Orpheus succeeded in winning back his wife, but this is not so
in the familiar, later version. The two of them set off, with
Eurydice following her husband, and Orpheus was just reaching
the end of the long ascent when, eager to see his wife and afraid
that her strength might be failing, he looked back. At once she
slipped away into the darkness, dying for the second time.

Orpheus tried to follow her, but this time Charon firmly
refused to take him over the Styx, so he had no chance of
gaining a second entry to Hades. Eventually he returned to
Thrace and wandered through the land, mourning inconsolably
and singing of his loss, and refusing to look at any other woman.
His end was a violent one, for Thracian women tore him to
pieces, resentful because he had scorned them.

The birds and the beasts, and even the rocks and the trees,
wept for Orpheus. His limbs were scattered in different places,
and his head was thrown into the river Hebros where it floated,
still singing, down the stream and into the sea. It was carried
southwards to Lesbos and buried there by the people of the
island, who were thereafter rewarded with an especial skill in
music and poetry (and in particular the great poets Sappho,
Alcaeus and Arion).

The Muses gathered up the scattered fragments of Orpheus'
body and buried them in Pieria, where he was born. Here over
his grave the nightingale was said to sing more sweetly than
anywhere else in Greece. Pausanias (9.30.4) tells us that there
was a famous statue of Orpheus on Mount Helikon, home of
the Muses, where he was surrounded by animals of stone and

bronze, all entranced by his singing. Zeus immortalized his music by setting his lyre among the stars as the constellation Lyra.

As for Orpheus himself, his shade passed once more to Hades, where at last he could clasp Eurydice in his eager arms. Now he was able to walk with her and gaze his fill, and never again need he fear to lose her by an incautious glance.

ALKESTIS AND ADMETOS

In the myths as in life, love, however strong, is all too often cut short by death, so let us end with a myth where the opposite happens, and it is love, not death, that triumphs.

Admetos was the king of Pherai in Thessaly and a favourite of Apollo. The god had once been forced by Zeus to serve a mortal for a year as a punishment for killing the Cyclopes, and because Admetos had so great a reputation for justice and hospitality, it was to his home that Apollo chose to come. There he served as a herdsman, and Admetos treated him so well that the god made all his cows bear twins. He also helped Admetos to win the hand of his chosen bride, Alkestis, the beautiful daughter of Pelias, king of Iolkos. She had so many suitors that her father set an apparently impossible test to decide between them, saying that he would give her to whoever could yoke a lion and a boar to a chariot. Apollo tamed the beasts and harnessed them, and Admetos drove the chariot to Pelias. Alkestis became his.

At their marriage, Admetos forgot to sacrifice to Artemis and the angry goddess filled the bridal chamber with snakes. Apollo once again intervened to help, advising Admetos to appease Artemis with sacrifices. This he did, and all was well. Then the god won an even greater boon for his friend from the Fates. He made them drunk, then persuaded them to agree that when Admetos arrived at his fated day of death, he might still live on, so long as he could find someone willing to die in his place.

Admetos felt sure that one of his parents would be only too happy to sacrifice themselves for their own son. After all, they must love him, and they were now old, with most of their lives behind them. Why should not one of them at least be willing to go down to the dead as his substitute? They soon put him right, for they had no intention of leaving the sweetness of life before they had to, and in the end it was his wife Alkestis who agreed to make the supreme sacrifice and die for him. The outcome is movingly dramatized in Euripides' *Alkestis*, his first surviving play (438 BC), and here, when Admetos upbraids his father Pheres for his selfishness in being unwilling to die, Pheres indignantly gives his reasons (690–704):

'Don't you die on my behalf, and I won't die on yours! You love to look on the daylight. Don't you think your father does too? As I see it, we shall be dead for a long time, while life is short and very sweet. You, with no shame at all, have taken pains enough to avoid dying ... So should you be abusing any relative of yours who does not wish to die, when you are a coward yourself? Hold your tongue! Remember that if you love life, so do all men.'

The play opens when Alkestis and Admetos have been happily married for several years, with children born to them, but now at last the fated day of death has arrived. Thanatos, the implacable god of death, comes to take Alkestis to the Underworld. Even as Admetos, with a complete change of heart, begs her not to leave him, she dies. Now he must come to terms with his loss. Yet this seems impossible, for he finds that, with Alkestis dead, he no longer wants the life that she has won for him. Now at last it is clear that his avoidance of death, through her loving self-sacrifice, has condemned him to a life of permanent mourning, a kind of living death (935–49):

'I think my wife's fate is happier than my own, even though it may not seem so. No pain will ever touch her now, and she has ended life's many troubles with glory. But I, who have escaped my fate and ought not to be alive, shall now live out my life in sorrow. Now I understand . . . Whenever I come indoors, the loneliness will drive me out again when I see my wife's bed, and the chair in which she used to sit, now empty, the floor in every room unswept, the children clinging round my knees and crying for their mother, the servants lamenting the beloved mistress they have lost.'

The situation is saved by the great hero Herakles. He visits Pherai on his way to catch the man-eating mares of Diomedes, and Admetos, still hospitable even in his deepest grief, takes him in without telling him that Alkestis is dead, pretending that the signs of mourning in the house are for a woman of no importance.

Herakles happily accepts the hospitality offered him, and in his usual fashion: he cheerfully eats and drinks to excess – to the outrage of one of the servants, who tells him the truth about Admetos's loss. Herakles sobers up at once, and plans how best to help the friend who has welcomed him while ignoring his own sorrow: he will risk his life by contending with Death himself (837–49):

'Come, my heart that has endured so much, and come, my hand: now show what kind of son Tirynthian Alkmene, daughter of Elektryon, once bore to Zeus. For now I must save this woman lately dead, now I must bring Alkestis home again and serve Admetos out of gratitude. I shall go and keep watch for the black-robed lord of the dead, for Death himself, and I think I shall find him near his victim's tomb, drinking the blood of offerings. And if I rush from my place of ambush and grasp him tight, throwing my arms around him, there is no man shall free him from that rib-crushing grip until he yields the woman to me.'

Herakles adds that, if need be, he will even go down to Hades itself to fetch Alkestis back to the land of the living, but it does not come to this. He wrestles with Thanatos by Alkestis's tomb until Death gives up his victim, then he brings Alkestis home again. Husband and wife are miraculously reunited, and Admetos is only too happy to accept ordinary mortal existence once more.

SELECT BIBLIOGRAPHY

Anderson, G., *Fairytale in the Ancient World* (London and New York, 2000)

Anderson, M. J., *The Fall of Troy in Early Greek Poetry and Art* (Oxford, 1997)

Boardman, John, *The Archaeology of Nostalgia: How the Greeks Re-created Their Mythical Past* (London, 2002)

Bremmer, J. N. (ed.), *Interpretations of Greek Mythology* (London, 1987)

Bremmer, J. N. and Horsfall, N. M., *Roman Myth and Mythography*, *BICS* Suppl. 52 (London, 1987)

Burkert, W., *Structure and History in Greek Mythology and Ritual* (Berkeley, 1979)

Buxton, Richard, *Imaginary Greece: The Contexts of Mythology* (Cambridge, 1994)

Buxton, Richard (ed.), *From Myth to Reason? Studies in the Development of Greek Thought* (Oxford, 1999)

Buxton, Richard, *The Complete World of Greek Mythology* (London, 2004)

Calasso, Roberto, *The Marriage of Cadmus and Harmony* (London, 1993)

Carpenter, T. H., *Art and Myth in Ancient Greece* (London, 1991)

Condos, T., *Star Myths of the Greeks and Romans: A Sourcebook* (Grand Rapids, Mich., 1997)

Csapo, Eric, *Theories of Mythology* (Oxford, 2005)

Davies, J. K. and Foxhall, L. (eds), *The Trojan War: Its Historicity and Context* (Bristol, 1984)

Doherty, Lillian E., *Gender and the Interpretation of Classical Myth* (London, 2001)

Dowden, Ken, *The Uses of Greek Mythology* (London, 1992)

Easterling, P. E. and Muir, J. V. (eds), *Greek Religion and Society* (Cambridge, 1985)

Edmunds, L., *Approaches to Greek Myth* (Baltimore and London, 1990)

Edwards, R. B., *Kadmos the Phoenician: A Study in Greek Legends and the Mycenean Age* (Amsterdam, 1979)

Feeney, Denis, *Literature and Religion at Rome: Cultures, Contexts and Beliefs* (Cambridge, 1998)

Forbes-Irving, P., *Metamorphosis in Greek Myth* (Oxford, 1990)

Frazer, J. G. (ed.), *Apollodorus: The Library* (2 vols, Loeb Classical Library, Harvard and London, 1921)

Gantz, Timothy, *Early Greek Myth: A Guide to Literary and Artistic Sources* (Baltimore and London, 1993)

Grant, Michael, *Myths of the Greeks and Romans* (New York and London, 1962)

Grant, Michael, *Roman Myths* (London, 1971)

Hard, Robin, *The Routledge Handbook of Greek Mythology* (London, 2004)

Henle, Jane, *Greek Myths: A Vase Painter's Notebook* (Indiana, 1973)

Herington, J., *Poetry into Drama* (Berkeley, 1985)

Jacobs, M., *Mythological Painting* (Oxford, 1979)

Johansen, K. Friis, *The Iliad in Early Greek Art* (Copenhagen, 1967)

Kirk, G. S., *Myth: Its Meaning and Function in Ancient and Other Cultures* (Cambridge, 1970)

Kirk, G. S., *The Nature of Greek Myths* (Harmondsworth, 1974)

Lefkowitz, Mary R., *Women in Greek Myth* (London, 1986)

Lefkowitz, Mary R., *Greek Gods, Human Lives: What We Can Learn from Myths* (New Haven and London, 2003)

Lexicon Iconographicum Mythologiae Classicae (18 vols, Zürich and Munich, 1981–97)

Lloyd, A. B. (ed.), *What is a God? Studies in the Nature of Greek Divinity* (London, 1997)

Lloyd-Jones, H., *The Justice of Zeus* (Berkeley, 1971)

March, Jennifer R., *The Creative Poet*, *BICS* Suppl. 49 (London, 1987)

March, Jenny, *Cassell Dictionary of Classical Mythology* (London, 1998)

Mayerson, Philip, *Classical Mythology in Literature, Art and Music* (New York, 1971)

Miles, G. (ed.), *Classical Mythology in English Literature: A Critical Anthology* (London and New York, 1999)

Morales, Helen, *Classical Mythology: A Very Short Introduction* (Oxford, 2007)

Morford, Mark P. O. and Lenardon, Robert J., *A Companion to Classical Mythology* (New York, 1997)

Morford, Mark P. O. and Lenardon, Robert J., *Classical Mythology* (New York, 1999)

Murgatroyd, Paul, *Mythical Monsters in Classical Literature* (London, 2007)

Nilsson, M. P., *The Mycenean Origin of Greek Mythology* (Berkeley, 1932)

Olalla, Pedro, *Mythological Atlas of Greece* (Athens, 2002)

Price, Simon and Kearns, Emily (eds), *Classical Myth and Religion* (Oxford, 2003)

Reid, J. D., *The Oxford Guide to Classical Mythology in the Arts, 1300–1990s* (2 vols, New York and Oxford, 1993)

Reinhold, M., *Past and Present: The Continuity of Classical Myths* (Toronto, 1972)

Schefold, K., *Myth and Legend in Early Greek Art* (London, 1966)

Schefold, K., *Gods and Heroes in Late Archaic Greek Art* (London, 1992)

Shapiro, H. A., *Myth into Art: Poet and Painter in Classical Greece* (London, 1994)

Simpson, Michael, *Gods and Heroes of the Greeks: The Library of Apollodorus* (Massachusetts, 1976)

Taplin, Oliver, *Greek Fire* (London, 1989)

Trzaskoma, Stephen M., Smith, R. Scott, and Brunet, Stephen (eds), *Anthology of Classical Myth: Primary Sources in Translation* (Indianopolis and Cambridge, 2004)

Vernant, J.-P., *Myth and Society in Ancient Greece* (Brighton, 1980)

Vernant, J.-P., *Myth and Thought in Ancient Greece* (London, 1983)

Vernant, J.-P. and Vidal-Naquet, P., *Tragedy and Myth in Ancient Greece* (New York, 1981)

Veyne, P., *Did the Greeks Believe in their Myths?* (Chicago and London, 1986)

Vickers, Brian, *Towards Greek Tragedy* (London and New York, 1973)

West, M. L., *The Hesiodic Catalogue of Women: Its Nature, Structure and Origins* (Oxford, 1985)

West, M. L., *The East Face of Helicon: West Asiatic Elements in Greek Poetry and Myth* (Oxford, 1997)

Winkler, M. M., *Classical Myth and Culture in the Cinema* (Oxford, 2001)

Wiseman, T. P., *Clio's Cosmetics* (Leicester, 1979)

Wiseman, T. P., *The Myths of Rome* (Exeter, 2004)

Wood, Michael, *In Search of the Trojan War* (London, 1985)

Woodford, Susan, *The Trojan War in Ancient Art* (London, 1993)

Woodford, Susan, *Images of Myths in Classical Antiquity* (Cambridge, 2003)

INDEX

Page numbers in **bold** refer to main discussions in the text.
Page numbers in *italics* refer to illustrations.

PENGUIN REFERENCE LIBRARY

THE PENGUIN DICTIONARY OF CLASSICAL MYTHOLOGY

EDITED BY PIERRE GRIMAL

'An essential source' *Library Journal*

Who bore children by a bear and was transformed into a bird as punishment? Why exactly did Zeus turn his lover into a cow? Classical myth is a vibrant and entertaining world, and Pierre Grimal's seminal text *The Penguin Dictionary of Classical Mythology* is indisputably the finest guide available. Meticulously researched and thoroughly cross-referenced, the text is accessible and informative, sweeping in its breadth and comprehensive in its detail. You will find the no less than *four* versions of the beautiful *Helen*'s birth, as well as lengthy explanations of all the major figures and events – from *Odysseus* to *Heracles* to *Troy* to the *Jason* and the *Argonauts*.

- Discusses all the heroes and heroines of Homer, Sophocles, Aeschylus and Euripides (amongst many others), from *Venus* to *Pandora* via *Apollo* and *Aphrodite*

- Demonstrates how and where classical mythology has resurfaced and influenced the works of later painters and writers, from Freud to James Joyce

- Includes comprehensive cross-referencing and genealogical tables to show the complex links between different characters and myths

ONLY PENGUIN GIVES YOU MORE

PENGUIN HISTORY

ALEXANDER THE GREAT
ROBIN LANE FOX

'So enjoyable and well-written ... Fox's book became my main guide through Alexander's amazing story' Oliver Stone

Tough, resolute, fearless, Alexander was a born warrior and ruler of passionate ambition who understood the intense adventure of conquest and of the unknown. When he died in 323 BC aged thirty-two, his vast empire comprised more than two million square miles, spanning from Greece to India. His achievements were unparalleled – he had excelled as leader to his men, founded eighteen new cities and stamped the face of Greek culture on the ancient East. The myth he created is as potent today as it was in the ancient world.

Robin Lane Fox's superb account searches through the mass of conflicting evidence and legend to focus on Alexander as a man of his own time. Combining historical scholarship and acute psychological insight, it brings this colossal figure vividly to life.

'I do not know which to admire most, his vast erudition or his imaginative grasp of so remote and complicated a period and such a complex personality' *Sunday Times*

'A magnificent, compelling epic ... He has honoured him splendidly' *Sunday Telegraph*

'An achievement of Alexandrian proportions' *New Statesman*

PENGUIN HISTORY

PAGANS AND CHRISTIANS
IN THE MEDITERRANEAN WORLD FROM THE SECOND CENTURY AD
TO THE CONVERSION OF CONSTANTINE
ROBIN LANE FOX

'This brilliant book is a wholly unexpected and central contribution to its subject. What is more it is readable and rereadable, even gripping' Peter Levi, *Spectator*

How did Christianity compare and compete with the cults of the pagan gods in the Roman Empire? This scholarly work from award-winning historian, Robin Lane Fox, places Christians and pagans side by side in the context of civil life and contrasts their religious experiences, visions, cults and oracles. Leading up to the time of the first Christian emperor, Constantine, the book aims to enlarge and confirm the value of contemporary evidence, some of which has only recently been discovered.

'A massive and humane study. On my shelf it will rest with pride between Edward Gibbon and Peter Brown' Charles Thomas, *Daily Telegraph*

'Here is richness indeed …on the one hand a magisterial analysis and reconstruction of an apparently remote and alien society, on the other a detailed study of the single most significant process in our history and still the most important determinant of our present attitudes and beliefs'
Donald Earl, *The Times*

'This book is important indeed' Henry Chadwick, *Financial Times*

Penguin History

THE CLASSICAL WORLD
ROBIN LANE FOX

The classical civilizations of Greece and Rome dominated the world some forty lifetimes before our own, and they continue to intrigue, inspire and enlighten us. From Greece in the eighth century BC to Rome at the time of Julius Caesar and Augustus in the first century BC, their art and architecture, drama and epics, philosophy and politics have been the foundation of much of what we value today. Their heroes, from Achilles to Alexander, are still powerfully evoked in our modern culture, films and writing.

The Classical World brilliantly describes the vast sweep of history in which these two great civilizations ruled – from the epic poems of Homer and the beginning of literacy through the foundation of Athenian democracy and the turbulent empire-building of Alexander the Great to the establishment of the Roman Republic, the rise of Christianity, and the challenges this new faith faced in the Roman imperial age.

For those who are new to this enthralling subject and for the many who continue to share his fascination with classical Greece and Rome, Robin Lane Fox's account is a wonderfully exciting historical tour of two of the greatest empires the world has ever seen.

Praise for Robin Lane Fox

Pagans and Christians

'Brilliant…it is readable and rereadable, even gripping' *Spectator*

'This open-hearted and learned book is one that any scholar of the ancient world and of early Christianity would be proud to have written… Lane Fox has opened his pages to let in an entirely new world' *The New York Review of Books*

'Here is richness indeed… a magisterial analysis' *The Times*

PENGUIN HISTORY

A HISTORY OF HISTORIES
JOHN BURROW

This unprecedented book, by one of Britain's leading intellectual historians, describes the intellectual impact that the study of the past has had in the western world over the past 2,500 years. It brings to life the work of historians from the Greeks to the present, including Livy, Tacitus, Bede, Froissart, Clarendon, Gibbon, Macaulay, Michelet, Prescott and Parkman, explaining their distinctive qualities and allowing the modern reader to appreciate and enjoy them. It sets out to be not the history of an academic discipline, but a history of choice: the choice of pasts, and the ways they have been demarcated, investigated, presented and even sometimes learned from as they have changed according to political, religious, cultural and patriotic circumstances.

Burrow argues that looking at the history of history is one of the most interesting ways we can try to understand the past. Nothing on the scale of or with the ambition of his book has yet been attempted in English.

'A triumphant success. The result is a highly enjoyable book, based on a vast amount of reading, written with attractive simplicity, brimming with acute observations, and often very witty. Anyone who wants to know what historical writing has contributed to our culture should start here' Keith Thomas, *Guardian*

'This book is magnificent: a daunting combination of vast range, profound learning and high literary art. In 500 superbly crafted pages (miraculously succinct for the task in hand), Burrow's chapters treat almost every important historian of the last two-and-a-half thousand years' John Adamson, *Sunday Telegraph*

PENGUIN REFERENCE

THE LORE OF THE LAND
WESTWOOD AND SIMPSON

Where can you find the 'Devil's footprints'?

What happened at the 'hangman's stone'?

Did Sweeney Todd, the demon barber of Fleet Street, really exist?

Where was King Arthur laid to rest?

Bringing together tales of hauntings, highwaymen, family curses and lovers' leaps, this magnificent guide will take you on a magical journey through England's legendary past.

'A real treasury' Philip Pullman

'A treasure-house of extraordinary tales, rooted in the wildly various and haunted landscapes of England' *Sunday Times*

'A fascinating county-by county guidebook to headless horsemen, bottomless pools, immured adulteresses and talking animals' *London Review of Books*

'Wonderful . . . Contains almost every myth, legend and ghost story ever told in England' Simon Hoggart, *Guardian*

PENGUIN NATURAL HISTORY

HATFIELD'S HERBAL
GABRIELLE HATFIELD

From ivy-wreathed buildings to the dandelions growing through the cracks between paving stones, we are surrounded by a wealth of native plants.

In the past they were a hugely valued resource: magical, mystical and medical. When Charles I visited Staffordshire his chamberlain wrote to the local sheriff asking him to ensure that no fern should be burnt or cut during the king's visit, so that the weather would be fine. Puppies were once fed daisy flowers in milk to keep them small while children wore daisy chains to protect against fairy kidnapping.

Packed with stories and memorable information, this book is the highly personal, very readable result of a lifetime spent researching folk cures and the science behind them. Outlining the history and uses of over 150 British plants, *Hatfield's Herbal* offers a fascinating history of what life was once like, a beautifully illustrated, evocative guide to our native plants and a passionate argument for why we should better appreciate the riches we already have.

'Hatfield, a contemporary botanist and plant historian, covers remedies from agrimony to yew and the history of their use' *Sunday Times*, Books of the Year

Penguin Travel/Architecture

ENGLAND'S THOUSAND BEST HOUSES
SIMON JENKINS

'The perfect guide to England's best houses' *Country Life*

'Buy, beg, borrow or steal a copy to keep in the car' *Daily Mail*

'This wonderful book will be in everyone's car pocket for decades …
It makes me want to take a year off … and plunge off into what Jenkins has
memorably described as "the theatre of our shared memory"'
Adam Nicolson, *Evening Standard*

England's houses are a treasure trove of riches and a unique, living record of
the nation's history. Simon Jenkins's lavishly illustrated guide selects the finest
homes throughout the land, from Cornwall to Cumbria, in a glorious
celebration of English life.

• Ranges from famous stately homes and palaces to humble cottages and huts

• Organized county-by-county for easy use

• Features a star ratings system for each house

• Highlights the very best 100 of all the properties in the country

'A heritage enthusiast's *Ode To Joy* … Any passably cultured inhabitant of the
British Isles should ask for, say, three or four copies of this book'
Max Hastings, *Sunday Telegraph*

'This is the perfect book to have beside your bed or on the back seat of your car
… Jenkins's zeal is infectious. He quite rightly sees England's greatest houses as
collectively nothing less than a wonder of the world' Geordie Greig,
Literary Review

'A great book … a feast, enlivened by the sort of tasty snippets that only a
master journalist can produce' Hugh Massingberd, *Daily Telegraph*

He just wanted a decent book to read ...

Not too much to ask, is it? It was in 1935 when Allen Lane, Managing Director of Bodley Head Publishers, stood on a platform at Exeter railway station looking for something good to read on his journey back to London. His choice was limited to popular magazines and poor-quality paperbacks – the same choice faced every day by the vast majority of readers, few of whom could afford hardbacks. Lane's disappointment and subsequent anger at the range of books generally available led him to found a company – and change the world.

'We believed in the existence in this country of a vast reading public for intelligent books at a low price, and staked everything on it'
Sir Allen Lane, 1902–1970, founder of Penguin Books

The quality paperback had arrived – and not just in bookshops. Lane was adamant that his Penguins should appear in chain stores and tobacconists, and should cost no more than a packet of cigarettes.

Reading habits (and cigarette prices) have changed since 1935, but Penguin still believes in publishing the best books for everybody to enjoy. We still believe that good design costs no more than bad design, and we still believe that quality books published passionately and responsibly make the world a better place.

So wherever you see the little bird – whether it's on a piece of prize-winning literary fiction or a celebrity autobiography, political tour de force or historical masterpiece, a serial-killer thriller, reference book, world classic or a piece of pure escapism – you can bet that it represents the very best that the genre has to offer.

Whatever you like to read – trust Penguin.

read more
www.penguin.co.uk